An
Autobiography of

URBAN RESEARCH INSTITUTE, INC.
Chicago, IL

BLACK CHICAGO

Dempsey J. Travis

Copyright© 1981 by Urban Research Institute, Inc.
840 East 87th Street, Chicago, Illinois 60619
All rights reserved
Printed in the United States of America
First Edition

ISBN: 0-941484-00-9 (case)
ISBN: 0-941484-01-7 (paperback)
Library of Congress Catalogue Card Number: 81-53024

Some of the material in this book appeared in Dollars & Sense Magazine in a different form.

Grateful acknowledgement is accorded to Mr. Ripley B. Mead, Jr. who made a gift of the photographs appearing in "Voices From the Past and The Present" to the author.

All cartoons by Mr. Buck Brown appeared originally in articles by Dempsey J. Travis written for Dollars & Sense Magazine.

PHOTO CREDITS
Chicago Historical Society: Part I, p.38; p.82; p.102; p.118; p.150
The Negro In Chicago (1922 edition): Part I, pp. 21-24

First Printing, November 1981
Second Printing, April 1982

My wife, Moselynne, to whom I have dedicated this book, has been both patient and supportive in my writing efforts. In addition to reading and criticizing my drafts, she has permitted the author to clutter one room of the house with over 1,500 books and several thousand news clippings. I have promised her that I will straighten the library as soon as I have finished this project. Hah! that's the same thing I said after the last project.

CONTENTS

Illustrations/viii
Foreword/x
Acknowledgements/xii
Prologue — Before My Time/xvii ·

PART ONE: BEATING THE ODDS

Chapter 1.   BEGINNINGS/1
Chapter 2.   THE EARLY 1900's: TIME OF CHANGE/13
Chapter 3.   RACIAL STRIFE: I NEVER LEARNED TO SWIM/19
Chapter 4.   HARD TIMES/27
Chapter 5.   IF BAD DREAMS WERE MONEY, BLACKS WOULD BE RICH/35
Chapter 6.   LISTENING BACK/41
Chapter 7.   HOOVER'S DEPRESSION AND GRANDMA'S SESSION/47
Chapter 8.   CHANGING TIDES: BOYHOOD TO MANHOOD/59
Chapter 9.   DUSABLE HIGH, CLASS OF '39/69
Chapter 10. MY STREET OF BROKEN DREAMS/83
Chapter 11. WORLD WAR II/93
Chapter 12. CAMP SHENANGO/103
Chapter 13. FACING FACTS/119
Chapter 14. DON'T STOP ME NOW/127
Chapter 15. CIVIL RIGHTS STRUGGLE—NORTHERN STYLE/135
Chapter 16. FRONT LINES/143
Chapter 17. RAISING THE "COTTON CURTAIN"/153
Chapter 18. THE CONTRACT BUYERS LEAGUE/165
Chapter 19. READING THE OBITS/173

PART TWO: VOICES FROM THE PAST
AND THE PRESENT

Alice Blair: *Educator*/184
Alvin J. Boutte: *Banker*/191
Johnny Brown: *Corporate President*/197
William Y. Browne: *Realtor*/202
Earl B. Dickerson: *Attorney (retired)*/207
Alfreda M. Barnett Duster: *Social Worker (retired)*/211
Lovelyn J. Evans: *Personnel Director (retired)*/216
Paul King: *Building Contractor*/221
Jewel Lafontant: *Attorney*/228
Louis Quarles Lawson: *Banker*/236
Robert Lucas: *Community Activist*/243
Ripley B. Mead, Sr.: *Real Estate Broker (deceased)*/256
Renault Robinson: *Political Activist*/259
Reggie Theus: *Professional Athlete*/273
Thomas N. Todd: *Attorney*/277
Donald C. Walker: *Publisher*/293

PART THREE: PICTURES FROM CHICAGO ALBUMS
OF THE PAST, /300

The period 1850 to 1915 _____

A Selective List of Interviews Conducted by Dempsey J. Travis
Between June 10, 1969 and July 30, 1981 / 325
Notes and Documentation/326
Index/355

viii

PHOTOGRAPHS

PAGE

Pullman Company Instruction Manual xviii
Richard B. Harrison.. 12
Ida B. Wells 14
Black Strikebreakers, 1904 17
Louis Travis 30
Mittie Travis 31
Willard Elementary School-Grade 7B 48
Ralph Crawford 49
Scottsboro Boys 51
Travis' Maternal Grandmother & Daughters 62
Black Coalminers 67
A Youthful "Jack" Travis at the piano 75
Du Sable High School Classmates 76
The Regal Theatre 77
Savoy Ballroom Diploma 81
A. Philip Randolph 89
Earl B. Dickerson 89
Willa Brown & Lola Jones 89
Pearl Harbor 92
Fort Custer 98
Marva Louis 115
Zinkey Cohen 116
47th & South Parkway 117
The Pershing Hotel 121
Moselynne Travis 126
Cicero Riot .... 130 & 133
Mittie Travis with Congressmen Gus Savage
and Harold Washington 134
Frank London Brown 139
Dearborn Real Estate Board 139
Dempsey J. Travis and Charles W. White 142
Dempsey J. Travis, Al Raby & Dr. King 143
Freedom Now 147
Dempsey J. Travis with Sammy Davis, Jr. &
Daddy-O Daylie 150
Dempsey J. Travis, Earl B. Dickerson and
Cora Carroll 151
Dempsey J. Travis and Dr. M. L. King, Jr. 151
Dempsey J. Travis with Dr. King and
Fred Shuttleworth 152
Dempsey J. Travis and Robert C. Weaver 155
Dempsey J. Travis and Robert Kennedy 155
United Mortgage Bankers of America 156
Diahann Carroll 161
Dempsey J. Travis and Otto Kerner 162
Dempsey J. Travis and Hubert H. Humphrey 162
Dempsey J. Travis and George Romney 163
The Chicago Riot, 1968 164
Contract Buyers League 171
Mr. and Mrs. Dempsey J. Travis and

Vice President Nelson A. Rockefeller 175
Presidential Task Force on Urban Renewal 176
Black Caucus Joint Session 176
Lake Grove Village Ground Breaking 177
Dempsey J. Travis with Jimmy Carter......................... 178
Dempsey J. Travis and Roy Wilkins........................... 181

CHARTS
Free Negro Property owners In Chicago, 1850-1860 6-7
Negro Property Owners In Chicago, 1870...................... 8
Distribution of Blacks by Wards: 1870-1900 11

MAPS
DuSable's House, 1779 3

FOREWORD By St. Clair Drake

I became an ardent admirer of the author of this important contribution to black autobiographical writing during the Seventies as I read his occasional articles in *The Black Scholar*. I was especially impressed by a frank but forward-looking discussion in the February, 1974 issue, "Can Black Builders and Bankers Survive?" Here was an "insider" talking without condescension to a public not familiar with the intricacies of high finance and making complex matters plain while stating a strong case for sympathy and understanding of industries that are often "scapegoated." At the same time he was telling his colleagues what they needed to do if they wanted the confidence and support of the black masses. The article taught me things about money and about black institutions seeking to control and channel some of it, both for private profit and social development, that I should have learned when Cayton and I were revising *Black Metropolis* in 1970 and didn't. Of the 52 Contributing and Advisory Editors of this "Journal of Black Studies and Research", Dempsey Travis has the distinction of being the only business man among them. That, in itself, makes him unique, a banker with serious scholarly interests and a flair for lucid communication. Everything he writes has relevance and is marked by clarity.

I had known of the author as a man of great talent and outstanding promise long before I began to read the *Black Scholar* articles, however, because he is a graduate of Roosevelt University of Chicago, an institution where I taught sociology and anthropology for over two decades. I knew he had gone on to Northwestern for graduate work and had then become greatly concerned with the problem of trying to make adequate housing available for black people in Chicago, in any area they wanted to live in, at prices that were not exorbitant. Before "Black Power" became a slogan he was seeking ways to achieve some of it, was succeeding, and teaching others. I have tried to follow the careers of Roosevelt graduates who were making substantial contributions to black liberation and to the solution of economic, political, educational, and cultural problems throughout The Black World. They scatter across a wide spectrum from left to right. Some years ago, alumnus James Forman of SNCC fame wrote an autobiography, *The Making of Black Revolutionaries*. Now Dempsey Travis presents us with a book that might well have as a subtitle, "The Making of a Progressive Black Banker." I consider it a privilege to have the opportunity of writing a foreword to it. If we are to "overcome" we need entrepreneurial skill of a high order combined with honesty and social concern within specific personalities as well as militant protest leadership—and every conceivable kind of professional, semi-professional, and artisan competence, too. I have always been influenced by a scriptural quotation my preacher-father liked to use "Wisdom is justified of all her children." Hopefully, this book will make the author a role model for some young people seeking their place in the ongoing struggle for a piece of the action in this complex American milieu, and who will take to heart the quotation from Paul Robeson he uses to make his social commitment clear.

The making of this book was, for its author, a labor of love, inspired by his warm family relations, a host of loyal friendships, and his commitment to the welfare of black people of every clime and condition. The many hours of reading, interviewing, sifting and sorting of data, reflection and writing, that went into this chronicle of his own life in relation to the black community's life, are a testimony to unusual dedication and discipline. Always busy, as he was, with the affairs of Travis Realty Company, as well as the United Mortgage Bankers of America, Dempsey Travis managed to conserve enough time to design and complete this work whose *"Notes and Documentation"* and list of *"Voices From the Past and Present"* reveal the full dimensions of the task. He was determined to pay tribute to unsung pioneers and quiet heroes in black families and institutions, distinguished leaders and role models, some now passed away, and others still bearing the burden and the heat of the day. And he has not forgotten the few rare individuals of the other race who gave encouragement and support to black people, especially a former teacher, Mary Herrick. He can say proudly, "mission accomplished."

The author gives us a guided tour of Black Chicago through time and constantly expanding space, calling our attention to landmarks, human and physical; reminding us of crucial historical turning points; introducing us to makers of history, living and dead, letting them tell us their stories in their own words. His synthesis of data in the prologue, *"Before My Time"* is a fascinating presentation distilled from a mass of historical detail that it evokes the spirit of a past that should not be forgotten.

Dempsey Travis has intuitively mastered a technique of research and presentation that I had to be trained in by anthropologists at the University of Chicago, what we call "participant-observation." He has lived a full, creative, useful life, with his eyes wide open, his ears attuned, and ever-ready to listen as well as to ask questions. Acting constantly, but observing all the while, thinking all the while, reacting sensitively all the while. And then, withdrawing occasionally to think about it and write about it. Now he has shared some of that life with us, thereby enriching ours. We appreciate his decision to share what he has found out about our world with us.

St. Clair Drake
Palo Alto, California
August 27, 1981

Dr. Drake is Professor Emeritus, Department of Anthropology, Stanford University and former Chairman of the Program in African and Afro-American Studies; author (with Horace Cayton) of *Black Metropolis: A Study of Negro Life in a Northern City* (1945, revised 1962, 1970) and *Race Relations in a Time of Rapid Social Change.*

ACKNOWLEDGEMENTS

I despair of calling the role of all the persons who assisted and encouraged me through every stage of the manuscript for this book, but I am confident that I shall be forgiven if I name only those whom I pressed hardest to be critical of my work. My mother, Mrs. Mittie Travis, who is 84 years old, was a major contributor to my writing this book. She was the fountainhead for all of the early family history. Her life long habit of saving family pictures (over 2,000) and letters enabled me to document what would have otherwise been naked oral history. Much of the dialogue in the beginning Chapters of this book is a by-product of her excellent memory.

The late Lois Dubin was one of my most avid readers and a very constructive critic. Ripley Binga Mead Jr., cousin of the late Jesse Binga, the pioneering banker, was a constant resource in that he made aged members of his family available to me to discuss old Chicago as it was for Blacks before the turn of the century. In addition, Mr. Mead gifted me with hundreds of unpublished photographs of old Chicagoans; some have been used in this work with proper credits. I am also deeply indebted to Anthony Overton, III, grandson of Anthony Overton, the banker, industrialist, insurance pioneer, and Spingard Medal winner. The use of the Overton files and papers was an invaluable ingredient in my research. Attorney Oscar Hill, another Overton grandson, was very helpful in arranging several interviews with his late father, Richard Hill, the President of the Douglas National Bank. In subsequent interviews with Oscar Hill, I was able to gain a great deal of insight into the elder Overton. Attorney Hill and Overton resided in the same house for over thirty years.

Dr. Donald Joyce and his staff at the Carter G. Woodson Public Library literally opened the doors for me to Chicago's historical past through the use of their excellent Vivian Harsh Afro-American collection. A special appreciation to Archie Motley of the Chicago Historical Society for the use of the Claude A. Barnett files. Innumerable thanks are due Mary F. Grady, Regional Coordinator of Community Services, United States Department of Commerce, Bureau of the Census. Thanks, too, to Nina Tabb, Vice President of Dollars & Sense Magazine, for making their historical library available to me.

My high school civic's teacher, Mary J. Herrick, who is a young 84 year old, gave me a great deal of encouragement and advice. In addition, she presented me with an invaluable series of DuSable High School senior class books dating from the first class that graduated in 1936 through 1976. The series was used extensively in the writing of this book. She also made me the recipient of a box filled with more than 300 personal letters to her from DuSable G. I.'s who were serving all over the globe during World War II. Several of the letters were used in that chapter of the book concentrating upon the war years.

Letters in support of my writing efforts from both Dr. Sterling Stuckey, Professor of History, Northwestern University, and Dr. William M. Tuttle, Jr., Professor of History at the University of Kansas, gave me the necessary buoyancy to stay afloat in Chicago literary waters.

I owe more than I can say to Donald C. Walker, Editor and Publisher of the Dollars and Sense Magazine who published in his distinguished periodical many of the articles which proved to be the genesis of this book.

Thanks to my administrative assistant, Robert Warner, Jr., for his unlimited patience in deciphering and making sense of my script. I also owe a special thanks to my senior researcher, Ruby Davis, for doubling in brass at a critical hour and transcribing in long hand the last eight taped interviews for this book. I was also very fortunate to have been encouraged, some years ago, by Barbara Reynolds, Vice President and Editorial Director of *Dollars & Sense Magazine;* Joy Darrow, Managing Editor of the *Chicago Daily Defender,* and Louis Martin, former President of the *Chicago Daily Defender,* to exercise what they perceived as writing talents. My only hope is that I lived up to their expectations.

Chicago, Illinois
November 11, 1981
D.J.T.

There can be no greater tragedy than to forget one's origin and finish despised and hated by the people among whom one grew up. To have that happen would be the sort of thing to make me rise from my grave.

Paul Robeson, 1938

"Man, I'm sorry, but I just remembered — you s'posed to have BLUE sheets!"

PROLOGUE

Before My Time

He was 18 years old, a tall, broad-shouldered young man with a habitual half smile. The brightness of his eyes and the slightly defiant tilt to his black derby hat were the only signs he gave that he was embarking on the biggest adventure of his life.

Louis Travis was traveling from Georgia via Memphis, Tennessee, to Chicago. He would not be going back.

It was June 1, 1900, and Louis was only vaguely aware that he was participating in the beginning of the greatest mass migration in American history, as Blacks fled the South to seek jobs and self-respect in the cities of the North. Some 1.5 million Blacks have made the same journey to Chicago in the 80 years since Louis Travis' journey.

Louis' two older brothers had gone before him. From one of them he had had word that there was a job for him as a strikebreaker, working construction at the Mandel Brothers' department store in the Loop. More and more Chicago companies were beginning to bring in Blacks as strikebreakers. For their part, Blacks, like the Travis brothers, accepted the work because, since they were barred from most unions, it was the only opportunity they had for a better life.

This was the very first time the young man in the faded green boxback suit had ever ridden a train. It turned out to be a bad trip.

The train's swaying motion as it rushed and clattered over the Tennessee farmland combined with the heat and Louis' excitement and produced a predictable result: he got sick. He started vomiting within a half hour after the train pulled out of the Memphis station.

The elderly black car porter became alarmed and went to get a white doctor from the train's Pullman section. The doctor took Louis' temperature and then pressed both sides of his stomach firmly with his huge hands while the young man stared at him gravely. He peered into his eyes and mouth and then handed him two giant yellow pills.

"This boy will be all right if he can lie down and get some sleep," the doctor said, turning to the porter.

The porter scratched his head. It wasn't going to be that simple. The only place for a colored person to lie down was in the aisle of the Jim Crow coach, but the "colored section" was so tightly packed that that was out of the question.

The porter finally went to ask "George," the Pullman porter, if Louis could sleep in his berth in the small smoking room of the white folks' Pullman coach. "George" wasn't really his name, of course: it was really a slave tag that indicated he was the "boy" of his employer, in this case George Mortimer Pullman. "George" was reluctant to give up his bed, but the older man was firm.

So Louis Travis spent a night of unheard-of comfort and privilege in the Pullman porter's bed. And he wasn't so sick that he didn't use that occasion to learn about another face of Jim Crow.

Jim Crow laws dictated what washrooms and drinking fountains Blacks were supposed to use, but he never suspected that there was a mandatory requirement by the Pullman Company for black porters to sleep under old blankets and faded sheets that had been dyed blue in order to avoid integrating the colored linen with that was to be used for "white bodies only."

At daybreak the next morning, Louis arose and found "George" busy making up the berths of the early risers who had already gone to breakfast. Louis thanked "George" for the use of his bed. "Why is your bedding blue and the white peoples' white?" he asked. "George" raised his head with a startled expression on his face as he pulled a used white sheet from a lower berth. The porter than rotated his head up and down the aisle to see if there was anyone within a earshot. He decided there was no one listening.

"Boy! Are you some kind of a fool trying to get me fired?" he said. While Louis stood there open-mouthed and wide-eyed, "George's" eyes softened. He laid the sheet in a crumpled heap on the berth. "Boy! Follow me. I am going to show you something." The young man followed "George" to the front of the Pullman car, where he opened a small overhead locker that was stuffed with papers and pamplets. "George" again pivoted his head to make sure no one was watching. Then he showed Louis the following instructions:

PORTER'S BERTH, BLANKET, ETC. The porter, when off duty, should occupy berth in smoking room. In exceptional cases, when smoking room is occupied by passengers to a very late hour, the conductor may assign the porter to an upper end berth, but in no instance should the porter occupy a berth in section over lady passenger.

The blanket provided for the porter is intended for his exclusive use, and passengers' blankets must not at any time be used by him.

The porter will use only the comb and hair brush provided for his use, and under no circumstances use those furnished for passengers.

Louis Travis later learned that the president of the Pullman Company that published the "for white bodies only" linen instructions was Robert Todd Lincoln, the son of the martyred President Abraham Lincoln, the Union savior. The 12th Street Station where Travis began his urban odyssey was the same Chicago train station to which President Lincoln's body had been transported before being placed aboard Pullman's "Pioneer" coach for the final journey to Springfield.

On the morning of June 2, 1900, Louis Travis was watching the hot, white steam gush from the black steam pipes of the engine of the New Orleans and Vestibule Limited as he clutched his few belongings and prepared to enter the city he had been dreaming of after months of planning.

Looking north from the 12th Street Station, he got a breathtaking view of row after row of three-story mansions, with hundreds of windows sparkling in the morning sun. The tallest building in the city was the 17-story Auditorium Hotel, presently the home of Roosevelt University.

But he was not heading north. Instead, he walked west to catch the southbound State Street cable car. As he walked, he began to notice the foul odor that was rolling in on a northeast wind from the Union Stockyards, about five and three-quarters miles southwest of the train terminal.

That was the direction Louis was heading: down to the "Black Belt" of Chicago, at 3715 Butterfield (Federal) Streets.

But even as he noted the growing pervasiveness of the stockyards odor and the increasingly squalid appearance of the housing as the cable car headed south, he could feel his face breaking into a smile. It was a bright sunny day, and he was young. If he had met up with a shameful crust of impersonal discrimination on his trip to the North, he had also discovered friendship and concern. He had found some strengths in himself as well. And he had folks waiting for him at the end of the journey.

Whatever challenges and opportunities Chicago had in store for the black man, Louis Travis was going to participate in them. It was his city now.

Part One:

BEATING THE ODDS

Chicago 1900

Chapter 1

BEGINNINGS

When my father, Louis Travis, arrived in Chicago in 1900, he found a city that had little experience with racial animosity. With only a small black population, Chicago was still fairly open in its dealings with Blacks. All that, though, was beginning to change as the importation of Southern Blacks into the city accelerated. Where Blacks and Caucasians had been able to live and work together in relative harmony, white folks would begin to perceive Blacks as a threat, and housing segregation by race and class would become rigid and cruel as the numbers increased.

In 1900, Blacks lived in all thirty-five wards of the city. Their numbers were large enough to constitute a community in eight wards.

The Travis family lived in the south section of the Fourth Ward. Its unsightly houses, dirty alleys and pitted and littered streets emphasized a general shabbiness. A snowfall was the only cosmetic that ever alleviated this drabness.

Well-to-do and highly-educated black people shared this environment with poorer folks. Attorney John G. Jones, the nephew of the late tailor, John Jones, lived next door to my family at 3717 Butterfield (Federal) Street. and conducted his law practice from room number four at 194 South Clark Street. The Autumn Club, the "in" place for the literary and social set, met each month at 3623 Butterfield Street.

For myself, class mixing would later have great benefits because it would expose me to an educational and economic dimension that would lead to a higher intellectual life in the middle of a physically depressing environment. But my maternal grandmother had already long understood that such a thing was possible. She used to tell her children, "You can learn something on the hottest day in the cotton field if you open your mind, eyes and ears."

My father had been in Chicago less than two months when he attended the first Bible class held at Rev. Reverdy C. Ransom's newly opened Institutional Church and Social Settlement House at 3825 South Dearborn Street. It was July 24, 1900. The large brick building had been known as the Railroad Chapel when the area was occupied by white Irish Catholics who came into Chicago as railroad employees.

The settlement house could seat more than 1,200 in its main auditorium. It also had eight community rooms, a dining room, a kitchen and a gymnasium. The well-equipped gym in the basement offered the first structured, racially integrated physical education programs in Chicago outside of the public school system. The settlement house got encouragement and support from Jane Addams of Hull House, the Rev. Graham Taylor of Chicago Commons, and Mary McDowell of the University of Chicago Settlement. The community rooms were used daily to study social literature and remedies for ethnic problems. In other rooms of the building young boys between eight and seventeen were being taught to read. Black and white working mothers were permitted to leave their young children in the daycare center for five cents a day.

Institutional House was an American prototype for the NAACP, the Urban League, and the Colored YMCA and YWCA. Dr. W.E.B. DuBois wrote that Bishop Reverdy C. Ransom's speech in 1906 at the second meeting of the Niagara Movement at Harpers Ferry did more to inspire the eventual founding of the National Association for the Advancement of Colored People than any other single event.

My father was one of twenty-two young men in the Institute's Bible class. Among the others in attendance were Oscar DePriest and Louis B. Anderson, who later distinguished themselves in Chicago politics——DePriest, as Illinois' first black Congressman, and Anderson as a Chicago alderman. The teacher of the Bible class was Mose Hardwick, a 65-year-old ex-slave.

Hardwick was familiar with all of the books of the Bible and was a self-taught authority on the history of black people in Chicago. He was a tall, friendly man with the physique of a prize fighter and the strong features of a W.E.B. DuBois.

My father asked Hardwick to help him learn more about the city. Hardwick asked my father to visit him and his family in their home at 2949 South Dearborn Street. Prior to moving there, they lived at 211 Third Street in downtown Chicago. Their present home was just a couple of doors north of Bethel A.M.E. Church, where Rev. Ransom was pastor from 1896 to 1900. Hardwick invited several other young men from the Church, who were also newcomers to Chicago.

Hardwick's introductory lesson on Chicago was very graphic and one my father never forgot. I haven't either.

From maps on easels he had placed along the south wall of his very small parlor, he pointed out the Chicago River and Lake Michigan and a small house on the north bank of the Chicago River labeled "DuSable House, 1779" and "Kinzie House, 1804". "Jean Baptiste Point DuSable exercised the first ownership of real estate within the present limits of the City of Chicago," Hardwick said. "His claim to ownership was based not on federal tenure or purchase from the lord of the manor or holder of eminent domain, but by allodial tenure, that is, by right of the plow."

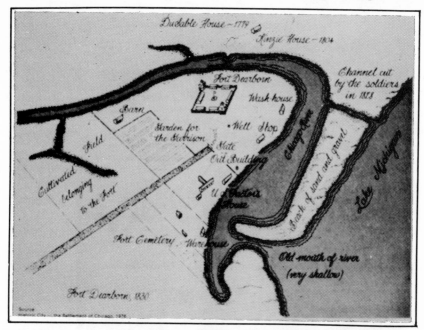

A 1779 British Army report described DuSable as a "tall, handsome, muscular built frontiersman who displayed great talents as a barterer. He was either a black freedman or a fugitive slave from Kentucky. He was intelligent, well educated, genteel mannered (his home was filled with fine, imported furnishings and paintings) and sufficiently American to have been arrested by the British. DuSable was married to a Potawatomi Indian named Catherine, and they had two children."

In 1800, DuSable sold his Chicago real estate and personal property to a white Frenchman named Jean La Lime of St. Joseph for 6,000 livres. Items in the sale were a wooden house, which measured forty by twenty-two feet, one horsemill, one pair of millstones, one bakehouse, a smokehouse, a dairy, a workshop, two barns, a large number of tools, household goods, furniture, thirty head of cattle, two spring calves, thirty-eight hogs, two mules, and forty-four hens. DuSable's house and chattel is prima-facie evidence that he was not simply a trader passing through the night; he was Chicago's founder in that he was its first landed proprietor. La Lime subsequently sold the DuSable House to John Kinzie in 1804. Kinzie, the first white American to establish a domicile in Chicago, fled the city in 1812 after stabbing Jean La Lime to death.

DuSable moved to East Peoria, Illinois, with a group of Potawatomi Indians and died sometime later at the home of an old friend, Glamorgan, who lived in St. Charles, Missouri, according to Hardwick.

Hardwick next directed his students' attention to a second easel, where he had placed a map that was dated 1830 and highlighted the south bank of the Chicago River. There, he pointed out a garrison called Fort Dearborn. Other subjects identified in the general vicinity of the Fort were a wash-house, well shop, barn, garden for the garrison, and a little further south, near the mouth of the river, was a U.S. Factors House. The third map in the room, dated 1840, outlined Chicago's new city limits which extended south to 22nd Street, west to Ashland Ave-

This gentleman of white pigmentation was identified as an Octoroon in the 1850, 1860, and 1870 census, as noted at the bottom of each chart on the following pages, because of the fact that he was 12.5%
black. The descendants of this gentleman still reside
in the black community and are known to the author.

The above photograph of this distinguished black person is typical of an individual who was classified as African—100% pure black as a result of his pigmentation. Such persons are identified in the 1850, 1860 and 1870 census as noted at the bottom of each chart on the following pages.

Free Negro Property Owners In Chicago - 1850

Ward	Name	Age	Property Location	Old Occupation	New Occupation	Value of Real Estate
2	James B. Bower	33	Dennis Lardon's	Hairdresser	Laborer	$ 1,600.00
2	John Jones	34	Lake Street House	Tailor	Same	1,500.00
2	Maria Smith	39	39th & Buffalo Street	not known	not known	1,000.00
3	A. J. Hall	28	North Wells Street near Harrison	Barber	Same	400.00
3	W. Wynder	30	183 West Monroe Street	Cooper	Cook	500.00
4	C. C. Hansen	39	250 West Madison St.	Barber	Same	3,000.00
9	Henry Knight	30	126 Dearborn Street	Livery stable owner	Same	10,000.00

Note: Included among colored property owners were persons of
the following pigmentation:
African - 100% pure black
Mulatto - 50% black
Quadroon - 25% black
Octoroon - 12.5% black
Total number of property owners = 7

Source: 1850 U. S. Census Report, and City of
Chicago Directory, 1850
Graphics: Urban Research Institute

Free Negro Property Owners In Chicago - 1860

Ward	Name	Age	Property Location	Old Occupation	New Occupation	Value of Real Estate
1-3	Bonaparte Morgan	36	326 West Clark Street	Grocer	Same	$ 225.00
	Eliza Nox	42	Not Available	Washer Woman	Same	500.00
	Willis Revels	25	9 Buffalo Street	Minister	Same	4,000.00
	James M. Smith	56	161 Jackson	Blacksmith	Same	600.00
	Maria Smith	36	39 Buffalo Street	Washer Woman	Same	2,500.00
	William Smith	50	Edina Pl. South of 12th	Cook	Same	15,000.00
	Edmund Walker	24	224 Buffalo Street	Porter	Same	100.00
	Martha West	25	43 Buffalo Street	Washer Woman	Cook	1,000.00
	Edward Whipple	38	232 Buffalo Street	Waiter	Janitor	250.00
	Thomas Wilson	32	122 Griswald	Waiter	Cook	100.00
	Issac Smith	23	Des Plaines	White Washer	Same	5,000.00
4	Charles Condell	27	162 Wells	Barber	Same	800.00
	Olivere Henson	42	252 Madison	Saloon Keeper	Confectionary	1,500.00
	Henry Taylor	24	253 Buffalo Street	Laborer	Same	2,000.00
5	Joseph Gomer	26	48 Michigan Avenue	Porter	Waiter	500.00
1-3	Issac Ackerson	40	76 Buffalo Street	Omnibus Driver	Baggage Driver	2,500.00
	Joseph Adams	41	137 Buffalo Street	Porter	Sleeping Car Waiter	500.00
	George Alexander	25	168½ Edina Place	Janitor	Laborer	1,000.00
	James Blanks	47	129 Buffalo Street	Janitor	Porter	8,000.00
	William Bailey	32	239 Wells Street	Waiter	Same	800.00
	T. L. Bigelow	67	62 West Harrison	Carpenter	Ship Carpenter	15,000.00
	Henry Bradford	50	139 Buffalo Street	Barber	Same	8,000.00
	Mary Dailey	21	247 Buffalo Street	Washer Woman	Washer Woman	5,000.00
	Louis Douse	30	7 Buffalo Street	Clerk	White Washer	1,000.00
	Jared Gray	48	77½ Clark Street	Wig Maker	Same	1,000.00
	William Harris	34	Richmond House	Waiter	Same	600.00
	Joseph Hadley	26	Not Available	Janitor	Same	800.0
	Carter Jackson	28	218 West Madison Street	Laborer	Porter	100.00
	Lewis Johnson	48	391 Clark Street	Barber	Same	300.00
	William Johnson	19	DuPage County	Waiter	Hairdresser	300.00
	John Jones	44	218 Edina Place	Tailor	Same	17,000.00
	Abraham Logan	50	166 Union	Porter	Same	1,200.00
8-10	John Johnson	42	367 Wells	Whitewasher	Same	$ 1,200.00
	Robert Nelson	32	204 Eric	Whitewasher	Same	11,000.00
	Alfred Richardson	52	180 Maxwell	Laborer	Blacksmith	2,000.00

Note: Included among colored property owners were persons of the following pigmentation:

African - 100% pure black — Mulatto - 50% black

Quadroon - 25% black — Octoroon - 12.5% black

Total number of property owners = 35

Source: 1860 U. S. Census Report, and City of Chicago Directory, 1860

Graphics: Urban Research Institute

Negro Property Owners In Chicago - 1870

Ward	Name	Age	Property Location	Old Occupation	New Occupation	Value of Real Estate
1	Robert Chatman	22	365 Wells	Porter	Waiter	$ 700.00
	F. B. Grinton	26	24 West Madison	Mailer	Barber	500.00
	Robert Grow	68	44 South Peoria	Janitor	Same	400.00
	John Holmes	40	209 Market	Whitewasher	Same	3,000.00
	Thomas Moore	21	291 Des Plaines	Janitor	Same	1,500.00
	John Smith	36	Adams near Quincy	Restaurateur	Same	100.00
	Charles A. Spruce	32	733 West Lake Street	Janitor	Gardner	300.00
	Stephen Stamps	42	183 Monroe	Saloon Keeper	Same	20,000.00
	Oliver Wenson	60	263 Clark Street	Caterer	Same	10,000.00
	Albert Whiting	26	200 4th Avenue	Mailer	Same	500.00
	Andrew Winslow	25	158 4th Avenue	Porter	Same	500.00
2	George Alexander	40	Loomis Street	Porter	Janitor	6,000.00
	James Blanks	58	89 4th Avenue	Janitor	Same	7,000.00
	Henry Bradford	59	139 4th Avenue	Saloon Keeper	Confection-er	8,000.00
	Allen Dorsey	50	20th & Steward	Laborer	Same	2,000.00
	Oliver J. Jacobs	35	88 4th Avenue	Carpenter	Restaura-teur	10,000.00
	John Jones	54	218 Edina Place	Tailor	Same	100,000.00
2	John Nelson	40	453 South Clinton	Saloon Keeper	Coachman	$ 1,300.00
	Charles Payne	40	835 Clark Street	Porter	Railroad Conductor	1,000.00
	William Randall	51	112 4th Avenue	Cook	Same	1,000.00
	David West	57	43 Buffalo Street	Cook	Same	1,000.00
3	William Alexander	46	212 4th Avenue	Teamster	Drayman	5,000.00
	Charles Anderson	40	331 State Street	Church Sexton	Same	700.00
	John Davis	50	365 Wells	Banker	Teamster	20,000.00
	Dempsey Grant	38	375 Clark Street	Janitor	Porter	4,000.00
	Edward Hawkins	44	Not Available	Porter	Same	4,000.00
	John Henry	43	Not Available	Butcher	Waiter	1,500.00
	Eisse Casher	38	Not Available	House Keeper	Same	50,000.00
	Adelaida Jackson	49	72 Quincy	House Keeper	Same	2,000.00
	John Johnson	42	229 4th Avenue	Laborer	White Washer	4,000.00
	Philip Miles	57	14 Taylor Street	Teamster	Same	4,000.00
	Clara Pane	24	80 Sherman	House Keeper	Same	3,000.00
	Henry Moore	46	196 4th Avenue	Laborer	Porter	3,000.00
3	John Thompson	40	326 South Clark Street	Butcher	Drayman	$ 4,000.00
4	Andrew Adams	24	Not Available	Bell Boy	Same	4,000.00
	Frank Boone	68	365 State Street	Teamster	Room Tender	1,000.00
	George W. Browne	35	129 4th Avenue	Carpenter/ Builder	Same	7,000.00
	William Johnson	33	Not Available	Post Office Clerk	Same	1,200.00
	John Young	30	363 Clark Street	Mailer/Cook	Same	5,400.00

Note: Included among colored property owners were persons of the following pigmentation:

African - 100% pure black — Mulatto - 50% black
Quadroon - 25% black — Octoroon - 12.5% black
Total number of property owners = 39

Source: 1870 U. S. Census Report, and City of Chicago Directory, 1870

Graphics: Urban Research Institute

nue, and north to North Avenue.

The total population of the city in 1840 was 4,417, of which 53 were Blacks, a decrease of 24 from the 77 Blacks included in the 1837 census. The 1837 count has been interpreted by some historians to mean that the count may have included fugitive slaves awaiting passage for an underground railroad that would be destined to a safe haven in Canada.

Hardwick emphasized that Chicago was the western center of the abolition movement and one of the most important stations of the underground railroad. Abolition activities were boldly described in ads appearing in Chicago-based abolitionist newspapers such as the *Western Citizen* and the *Western Herald.*

Only one of the seventy-seven Blacks in Chicago at the time it was incorporated in 1837 appeared to be an owner of real property. However, the local census of 1844 reflected 155 free Blacks in Chicago, which included five black real estate owners. Their properties were all located in the original 1st and 2nd Wards of the city in downtown Chicago on the following streets: Lake, Madison, Fifth Avenue (Wells), and two parcels on the corner of Clark and Harrison Streets and at Buffalo (Federal) and Harrison Streets.

Black realty ownership increased from five to ten parcels between 1844 and 1847. The additional five properties were also located in the original 1st and 2nd Wards. The fugitive slave law of 1850 compelled many Chicago Blacks to flee to Canada and dispose of their property at great sacrifice. The result was a net reduction in black property owners from ten in 1847 to seven in 1850, as revealed in the census of that year.

The 1850 census showed that John Jones, a black tailor, was the owner of property that had a value of $1,500. This was a significant economic achievement.

Jones had arrived in Chicago five years earlier from Greene County, North Carolina, via Memphis, Tennessee, and Alton, Illinois, with his wife and the total sum of $3.50. After pinching every penny of that $3.50 to furnish his house, he had to pawn his watch to purchase two heating stoves, one for his house and the other for his tiny tailor's shop. His rented one-room cottage was located on the northeast corner of Madison Street and Fifth Avenue (Wells.)

Jones' original tailor shop was six and a half by thirty feet and was located at what will be the Clark Street entrance to the new State of Illinois Building, scheduled to be completed in 1983. For groceries he was extended $2 in credit by a black man named O.C. Hanson.

Jones became the undisputed business and civil rights leader for Blacks in Illinois. As the leading black abolitionist in the state, he met and corresponded with John Brown and Frederick Douglass as well as Joseph Medill, editor of the *Chicago Tribune,* and Republican leaders such as Governor Richard Yates and Cook County Senator Francis Eastman. John Jones understood that freedom for wealthy and influential Blacks was impossible without recognition of equality for all Blacks. Ensconced in the surroundings of his merchant tailoring business for the Chicago elite, he was quoted in the Friday, January 2, 1874, edition of the *Chicago Tribune:* "We must have our civil rights; they must not be withheld from us any longer; they are essential to our complete freedom."

Jones' life-long battle for civil rights enabled him to become the first Black to hold an elective office in Cook County and in the State of Illinois. Jones became a Cook County commissioner in 1871. Jones used a smooth rhetoric, black ink and green bucks in a continuing battle against Illinois' Black Laws. His victorious struggle made him the first effective black civil rights and business leader in the history of the state.

The "Black Laws" deprived black people of the right to testify in courts or to purchase property; moreover, Blacks were taxed for public schools they could not use. A constitutional revision in 1847 prohibited free Blacks from settling in Illinois and also prevented slave owners from bringing them into the state in order to free them.

The "Black Laws" were repealed on February 7, 1865, a political victory which can be attributed to John Jones' leadership. It had a heartening effect on black migrants coming into Illinois.

Before the Great Chicago Fire of 1871, Jones' real estate improvements were valued at $100,000. Included in his real estate holdings was the northeast corner of Madison and Dearborn Streets, commonly known as 119 Dearborn Street.

John Jones' contribution to the black community and to the city certainly merits the placing of his name on a school or public building. This honor had not been bestowed upon him as of 1981, 102 years after his demise, though there is a common impression that Jones Commerical High School is named for him. In fact, the school was named after a William Jones, who served as president of the Board of Education from April 11, 1840, to April 26, 1843, and again from April 26, 1851, to April 10, 1852. In 1857, William Jones established a fund of $1,000 for Jones students who could not afford the cost of textbooks. These were the first free textbooks in the Chicago public schools.

The day after John Jones' death in 1879, the *Chicago Tribune* reported that he had been the most prominent black citizen of the city. No single Black to this date has been endowed with the overall power displayed by John Jones during his thirty-four years in Chicago. Jones' business was continued until 1906 by his son-in-law, Lloyd G. Wheeler, (first Black to pass the Illinois Bar and the grandfather of Lloyd G. Wheeler, III, the current president of the Supreme Liberty Life Insurance Company.)

There is no reliable data on black property owners between 1854 and 1860. However, the 1860 census reveals that there were thirty-five black property owners in Chicago. The values of these properties ranged from $100 to $17,000. The John Jones real estate fortune escalated in the ten years between 1850 to 1860 from $1,500 to $17,000, compared to the more normal increase, for example, in the real estate investments of Maria Smith, a washerwoman, whose holdings rose only 150 per cent from $1,000 in 1850 to $2,500 in 1860. Jones' real estate holdings were valued at $100,000 in 1870 .

The Great Fire of 1871 stopped at Harrison Street, and only a small percentage of the black community was burned. However, another fire in 1874 started at 449 South Clark Street on the afternoon of July 14th continued to burn in a northeasterly direction for twenty-four hours. The fire covered forty-seven acres. Eight hundred and twelve buildings were gutted at an estimated loss of $2,850,000.

The burned area included 85 per cent of the black-owned property in the city.

The fire was the second major setback in realty ownership for Chicago Blacks in less than twenty-five years, the first being the exodus caused by the Fugitive Slave Law of 1850.

The 1874 fire burned down and closed an era of black realty owner-ship in the area now known as the South Loop (Dearborn Park). The movement south of 16th Street into the 2nd, 3rd, and 4th Wards is re-flected in the distribution of Blacks by wards in 1880, 1890, and 1900. (The ward boundaries were the same in 1870, 1880, 1890 and 1900.)

Data on black housing for the sixteen years after the fire of 1874 are missing, but the 1890 census showed an increase of 208 colored owners of area real estate from 39 in 1870 to 247 in 1890.

Louis Travis' history lesson introduced him to a city that had offered a mixed reception to Blacks. On the one hand, it had had a strong Abo-litionist tradition; on the other, Blacks were hardly welcomed into full participation in the city's economic life. Nevertheless, there were signs of encouragement and movement. John Jones' political success as a Cook County Commissioner in 1871 created an acceptance for Blacks in politi-cs somewhat akin to the climate generated by Jackie Robinson's base-ball success in 1947. The first black police officer was appointed in 1872, and, later in the same year, a nine-man black fire company was commis-sioned by Mayor Joseph Medill. In 1876, John W. E. Thomas, a lawyer whose office was located at 181 Third Avenue, became the first Black to be elected to the Illinois House of Representatives.

Another young lawyer, Ferdinand L. Barnett, founded the *Chicago Conservator,* Chicago's first black newspaper, in 1878.

These were the beginnings. The frontier still had openings.

DISTRIBUTION OF BLACKS BY WARDS: 1870-1900

Ward	1870	1880	1890	1900
1	319	761	3381	1528
2	1180	2309	2744	4762
3	1437	416	2997	7618
4	96	384	722	3370
5	100	66	401	339
6	12	43	33	83
7	11	13	3	18
8	14	38	4	2
9	23	222	16	4
10	122	120	73	168
11	42	87	222	410
12	51	144	335	396
13	54	427	695	1250
14	120	5	41	21
15	20	13	49	45
16	10	9	14	6
17	7	13	51	288
18	2	89	610	483
19			98	114
20			38	111
21			38	104
22			88	286
23			149	267
24			306	550
25			18	180
26			41	79
27			88	79
28			53	120
29			36	868
30			479	3246
31			422	596
32			218	1439
33			19	166
34			207	1176
35			0	88

One of the most prominent black stage actors of his period, Richard B. Harrison played the role of "De Lawd" 1,658 times in one of the greatest achievements of the American theatre, "Green Pastures." A young Travis witnessed Harrison's body in state after his death on March 14, 1935, in Harrison's home at 60th and Indiana.

Chapter 2

THE EARLY 1900'S:
TIME OF CHANGE

Chicago's social patterns began to change under the impact of growing immigration of Southern Blacks. While Black Chicagoans of an earlier generation can still recall a relatively easy, hostility-free mixing of the races in early Chicago, accelerated black recruitment quickly changed all that.

The housing community had not been organized like the trade unions to exclude the black workers by ritual or constitution, and consequently Blacks had been able to live in just about any area of the city. For example, the Joseph Millers, who were the parents of Lovelyn Evans, lived at 4015-4017 Broadway for years, operating a large warehouse business at that address, the Millers Buena Park Fireproof Warehouse and Moving Company. Joseph Miller employed a crew of thirty workmen composed of Swedes, Poles, Blacks and Germans. Oneida Daniels Woodard and her parents lived at 315 Webster Avenue in the Lincoln Park area from 1908 to 1918. At the south end of town, on 72nd and Vincennes, lived the Oscar Freeman family, who shared a three-flat walk-up with white families without conflict.

Although black people in 1900 represented only 1.9 per cent or 30,150 out of a city population of 1,698,575, the competition for urban space and jobs with Whites, especially recent European immigrants, quickly became a threatening problem.

It was during this time that the managements of many businesses in Chicago began to recognize that hiring Southern Blacks could be a strategic move in their conflict with the unions. Blacks represented an almost inexhaustible supply of cheap labor. Other groups, like Polish immigrants, had been exploited in the same way, of course, but the hostility of white labor unions toward Blacks offered employers the added attraction of deflecting some of the animosity away from themselves.

Louis Travis' youngest brother, Joseph, was recruited in Atlanta by a stockyards headhunter and shipped to Chicago by train with several hundred other young Blacks to break the stockyards strike of 1904. Uncle Joe and hundreds of other strike-breakers were smuggled into the stockyards the evening of the same day that the regular white employees laid down their tools and walked out.

The press constantly spotlighted the activities of black strikebreakers, intensifying racial animosity. In fact, it was considered a plus for corporate-labor relations to ship Blacks back South on special trains after a strike was broken. A sad irony of the American labor movement is that the racism of the labor organizations allowed management to keep black and white workers separated and mutually hostile, weakening the power of the unions and prolonging the struggle for improved working conditions and higher wages for all workers.

Living far south or north in the city was not convenient for the Blacks who were recruited to Chicago to work in the stockyards or factories located south of the Loop. Proximity to the job was important because of travel time on both the cable cars and streetcars. The new influx of Blacks in search of housing west of State Street forced the early black settlers to seek better accommodations east of State.

Ida B. Wells, the civil rights fighter from Tennessee, was one of many Blacks attracted to Chicago during the 1893 World's Fair who decided to make the city by the lake their home.

A white Unitarian minister, Mrs. Celia Parke Wooley, tried unsuccessfully to rent a house on Wabash Avenue for an interracial community center. She then purchased a house at 3032 South Wabash Avenue in 1903. Ida B. Wells had outlined a proposal for such a center four months earlier at a meeting held at Hull House. Within eight months after the center's opening, the first black family moved into the 3100 block on Wabash. Between 1904 and 1912 the black population on Wabash Avenue between 31st and 39th increased from .05 in 1904 to 100 per cent in 1912. Between 39th and 47th on Wabash the black population was approximately 50 per cent by 1917.

The block-by-block racial transition was costly to both the white seller and the black buyer. The loss to sellers could vary from $50,000 to $350,000 per block depending upon the price and quality of the average house or apartment building in the block. On the other hand, the real estate speculator who urged the seller to move out and packaged the Blacks who moved in realized as a profit the seller's loss plus an override of 10 to 50 per cent, subject to market demands.

As a very young man in 1915, William Y. Browne, currently president of Riley-Browne Real Estate Company, observed brightly-colored handbills being passed out by employees of the Frederick H. Bartlett and Company of 69 West Washington Street. The handbills carried a propaganda message advising Whites to sell because a black invasion of the neighborhood was imminent. Hitler's Goebbels could not have prepared the troops better. The appearance of the first Blacks in an all-white block triggered a response that caused the Whites to treat them as invading enemy aliens.

Such a reception was received by the family of "de Lawd," better known as Richard B. Harrison, who played "The Lord" in "Green Pastures" on Broadway. The Harrison family became the first visible black buyer of real estate in the all-white section of Grand Boulevard (King Drive) when they purchased 3624 Grand Boulevard in March, 1918. Blacks had lived on South Park Avenue in the 3400 block prior to moving to the 3600 block on Grand in 1919. After two bombings in May, 1919, the Harrisons moved out in mid-June.

The three-story, fourteen-room, four-bath mansion was purchased for $8,000 by Attorney Ferdinand L. Barnett and Ida B. Wells Barnett, the parents of Alfreda Duster. The Barnetts were the first black family in the 3200 block on Rhodes, where Mrs. Duster was born in 1904. However, by 1917, Rhodes was 75 per cent black between 31st and 39th Streets. According to Mrs. Duster, the family lived at 3234 South Rhodes for over fifteen years without any major incidents.

In 1919, Blacks flanked Grand Boulevard on the west on Calumet between 31st and 39th and Vernon on the east. Both areas were about 85 per cent black. Whites violently resisted surrendering Grand Boulevard; it represented a prominence and golden era they did not want to forget. Gone were the days when Grand Boulevard would be the thoroughfare for the thousands of expensive carriages that augustly transported the rich and super-rich to the racetrack south of Washington Park, an eighty-acre plot located between South Park and Cottage Grove Avenue from 61st to 63rd Street. Washington Park Racetrack was moved to its present location in Homewood in 1908. This affected the South Side commercially; however, the area had already begun to decline at the close of the 1893 World's Fair.

After war was declared in 1917, the influx of Southern Blacks to Chicago was overwhelming—to the point that Blacks constituted 20 per cent of the workers in the meat-packing industry in 1918, compared to 3 per cent in 1909.

Many black professionals and business pioneers living in the South watched their clients board the Jim Crow cars of the New Orleans and Vestibule Limited heading north and then decided themselves to get on board the train going to Abe Lincoln's city on the lake.

The founders and officers of Supreme Life Insurance Company, the largest black-owned insurance company in the North today, all came out of the South: Frank L. Gillespie, founder, born in Osceola, Arkansas, in 1876; Harry Herbert Pace, president, born in Covington, Georgia, January 6, 1884; Truman Kella Gibson, Sr., treasurer, born in Macon, Georgia, August, 1882; W. Ellis Stewart, secretary, born in Columbus, Indiana, 1892; Dr. M. O. Bousfield, vice president and medical director, born in Tipton, Missouri, August 22, 1885. (Blacks were treated with the same Jim Crow attitude and restrictions in Columbus, Indiana, as they were in Columbus, Georgia.) Robert S. Abbott, who founded the *Chicago Defender* in 1905, was born in St. Simon Island, Georgia, in 1870 and migrated to Chicago in 1896. Anthony Overton, founder of the Victory Life Insurance Company, the Douglas National Bank, Overton-Hygienic Products Company, the *Chicago Bee* newspaper, and the *Half-Century* magazine, was born a slave in Monroe, Louisiana, in 1864, and moved to Chicago in 1911. In 1919, he was a millionaire.

The trains could not bring Blacks to the North fast enough to fill the job vacancies left by more than 350,000 Illinois men who had either enlisted or been drafted into the 1917-18 European conflict.

Many of the newcomers felt that they knew Chicago through the wide circulation of Abbott's *Chicago Defender* in the South. What also helped was their acquaintance with the Sears Roebuck and Montgomery Ward catalogues, which tended to minimize the difference between rural and urban dress.

By 1918, the mass debarkation of Blacks in Chicago had burst all the prescribed black housing belts. Friction was developing with the competition for the right to lay down one's body in the squalor of fourth-rate dwellings. On a single day, in July, 1918, the Chicago Urban League received 664 applications for only fifty-five available dwellings.

Blacks participated in the American armed forces in World War I in the larges numbers since the Civil War, the war against slavery, in hope that the new war to save democracy would advance the struggle for equality and justice at home. But, of course, there were two separate American armies until President Truman started desegregating the Armed Forces in 1945. A new integration policy was not adopted by the Army until 1949; similar policies were subsequently adopted by the Navy and Air Force.

Black soldiers returning in early 1919 were overwhelmed with an outburst of gratitude and affection from both black and white Chicagoans. However, after a very brief feast on the affection of all Chicago, they soon discovered that there were no jobs for yesterday's black heroes except a few low-paying menial ones.

But Chicago never had a serious love affair with the returning "Black Devils" of the 370th Infantry—formerly the Eighth Illinois National Guard.

A family friend, Mae Robinson, who lives in the Rosenwald apartments near 46th and Michigan Boulevard, remembers that in 1919 when
she was a student at the Haven Elementary School (15th and Wabash)
"the school permitted only the black children" to attend the "Black
Devils" celebration at the spacious Coliseum on Wabash. In contrast, in
1919, the entire school was dismissed when the white soldiers returned.

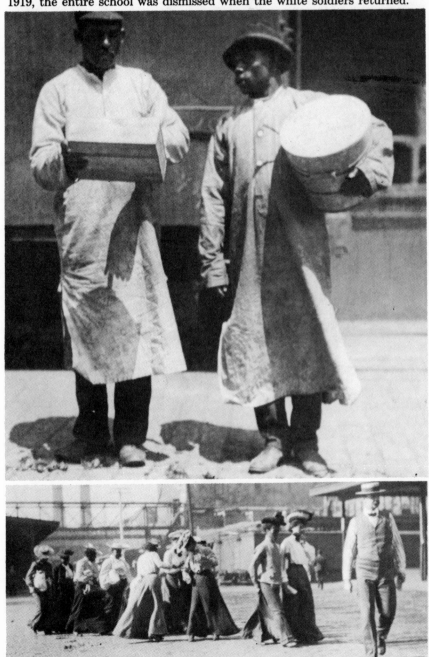

Black men and women strike breakers in 1904
walking through the stockyards.

Oscar Freeman, 80

Anna Mary Grinnell, 94

Earl B. Dickerson, 86

Lovelyn J. Evans, 82

Alfreda M. Barnett Duster, 73

William Y. Browne, around 74

By Buck Brown

CARICATURES DRAWN IN 1977

Elmore Baker, 92

Chapter 3

RACIAL STRIFE: I NEVER LEARNED TO SWIM

My father, dreaming of better days in Chicago, had a rude awakening on June 5, 1900, when he reported for work as a strikebreaking construction laborer at Mandel Brothers Department Store at 1 North State Street (now Wieboldt's).

Louis Travis' oldest brother, Otis, had been working as a strike-breaker since February, but he had failed to warn Louis of the danger that surrounded the job. Uncle Otis had already learned to accept strikebreaking as a way of life for black workers. His first job in Chicago had been as a scab at the stockyards in 1894. White meatpackers had struck in sympathy with the American Railway Union in dispute with Robert Todd Lincoln's Pullman Co. The black stockyards strikebreakers had participated from two motives: they needed the jobs, and it offered an opportunity to protest the anti-black clause in the American Railway Union Constitution.

My father, however, like many of the Southern immigrants, had a lot to learn about the harsh realities of life in a Northern city. That first day, Louis Travis wandered off the job site without protection—without realizing he needed protection. He walked up State Street to do a little sightseeing, casually inspecting the tall buildings of the Loop.

He had reached State and Lake when he ran into some union men. They quickly recognized that he was a strikebreaker because of his construction clothes. Gathering in front of him in a tight, angry little knot, they yelled at him: "Scabbing coon!" they shouted, shaking their fists.

As my father used to tell the story, he wheeled around immediately and headed south on State Street at a steady trot that quickly turned into a full gallop as the Whites pursued him, shouting. His fleet-footedness, and a friendly cop, saved him after a sweaty sprint back to the construction site at State and Madison.

Though my father usually told the story as if it had been a huge joke on him, the very real pain and fear of such an experience always came through. Resentment between union members and black strikebreakers had escalated to the point that union members publicly burned Blacks in effigy.

In spite of all this, my father and his two brothers decided not to go back South because Chicago offered them more freedom and opportunity. It was true that both trained and untrained Blacks found their freedoms restricted in the North, but they preferred the Northern situation to the Southern suffocation born of the fear with which they had grown up.

My father and his brothers were laborers, and, like many Blacks, they took great pride in doing their jobs well. They stayed and later became part of a cadre of the best workers in the packing houses.

Just before the United States entered the war in 1917, my mother, Mittie, was invited to Chicago to visit her middle sister, Claudie. She immediately became fascinated with the people and the bright lights of Chicago's 31st and 35th Streets and South State Street, the focus of social activity for the black community. In her hometown of Birmingham, Alabama, she had never seen such glitter.

Besides, during this visit Mittie had met Louis Travis, a dude with a fondness for black women and black derby hats. She married him within five months of her arrival and never went back South except for brief family visits and funerals.

My folks lived first in a frame shanty at 3715 Butterfield (now Federal Street), with wooden sidewalks and on a street laid with wooden blocks. During the war, however, the Urban League helped them move to a stone-front house at 3514 Calumet Avenue, with concrete sidewalks and a street paved with asphalt. They had been there for only a few months when the Armistice was signed on November 11, 1918.

But Louis and Mittie Travis were carrying out their lives against a background of impending violence. The return of thousands of robust, healthy ex-servicemen arriving in Chicago to look for work—and their failure to find it—built up to the violent summer of 1919. My mother became pregnant with me in May, 1919, and the nine months that she carried me were among the most violent periods of racial confrontation in the history of Chicago.

In May, a neighbor's home on the next street was fire-bombed. This bombing of the Richard B. Harrison home at 3624 South Grand Boulevard (now Martin Luther King Drive) was just one of a series of violent acts directed at black-occupied homes. Black and white realtors' offices and homes were also hit if it became known that the Whites had sold or leased to Blacks outside of the "Black Belt." The expansion of the "Black Belt" in Chicago could be measured by the bombings: between July 1, 1917, and March 1, 1921, bombings occured on an average of once every twenty days.

And on July 27, 1919, Chicago ignited into one of this country's bloodiest race riots.

Blacks and whites leaving 29th street beach after the drowning of Eugene Williams sparking the beginning of the Chicago race riot.

(Above) Young Black man being chased by mob of whites; (below) cornered, the victim is stoned to death.

Blacks under protection of police and militia buying provisions brought into their neighborhood in wagons.

Blacks being escorted by police to safety from the neighborhood of 48th and Wentworth Avenue.

Black family leaving their wrecked home under police protection.

My first cousin, Joe Crawford, now age 72, was living with his parents and two brothers in a racially-integrated, three-apartment building at 5915 South Wentworth Avenue, adjacent to the Englewood elevated tracks, when the race riot broke out. On July 28th, the second night of the riot, a white woman who lived on the second floor in the same building told my Aunt Claudie that she had heard that a group of teenagers had planned to give the entire Crawford family a public flogging if they did not move out of the neighborhood.

An hour had not passed before there was knocking and loud angry voices at both the front and rear doors of the Crawford's first floor apartment.

"Niggers, come out and get your ass whipped or stay in there and be barbecued," were the words Joe Crawford heard, loud and clear. Cousin Joe, his two brothers, Ralph, and Cornelius, along with my Uncle Bee and Aunt Claudie, slipped single-file through a small bathroom window directly under the "El" tracks. The giant iron legs of the "El" provided perfect cover for them to move in a squatting position down the alley until they reached LaSalle Street. There they saw a dim light from a cracked back door about fifteen feet away and a black woman beckoning for the five of them to come in. The stranger who offered the Crawford family a haven was Mrs. Ruth Embry. They were fed and bedded down in her home for the next forty-eight hours.

The heavy rain on the fourth night of the riot provided cover for them to make a three-and-a-half-mile trot to my parents' home, which was in the heart of the "Black Belt" at 3514 South Calumet Avenue.

Frank Alexander, now turned 80, a former Pullman porter, was living between Wabash and State on 36th Street during the riot. Because of his light complexion and straight black hair, friends advised him to stay off the streets for his own safety. Wisely, he followed that advice.

William Y. Browne, now owner of Riley-Browne Realty Company at 63rd and Langley, lived at 6530 South St. Lawrence during the riot and remembered that Woodlawn area Blacks were heavily armed. They were ready to meet a rumored threat of an invasion by Whites. At least eight Blacks were injured at the street car transfer corner on 63rd Street and Cottage Grove Avenue.

In the aftermath of the riot, the national office of the NAACP cooperated with the Chicago branch in offering counsel and legal assistance to all the riot defendants. Members of the Cook County Bar Association, an organization of black lawyers, tried some of the cases that resulted in complete acquittal. In the end, sixteen black and eight white persons were tried for murder and manslaughter. Three Blacks and two Whites were convicted.

Thus the first score of years of the twentieth century ended on a sour note for Chicago's Blacks. The next decade held an economic depression for Blacks and reinforcement of racial hatred evident in the resurgence of the Ku Klux Klan, whose membership swelled to four million by 1924. The Klan in 1925 was permitted to march 40,000 strong down Pennsylvania Avenue in their white-sheet regalia past our nation's Capitol. Many non-sheet-wearing Whites supported the Klan ideology because Whites were beginning to feel the economic pressures of black competition for living space and jobs in urban areas.

It started when a gang of Whites hurled rocks at a black teenager named Eugene Williams at a beach on Lake Michigan near 29th Street. Williams was hit in the head and drowned.

The tragedy forever affected my parents' attitude toward Lake Michigan. Mom is now 84 years old and has never put even a toe into Lake Michigan's water. My father never wore a swimming suit after that bloody Sunday. Blacks continued to barely tread water.

I was never permitted to learn to swim. For six years, we lived within two blocks of the lake, but that did not change their attitude. To Dad and Mama, the blue lake always had a tinge of red from the blood of that young black boy.

The clouds of racial hatred that had hovered over Chicago for months thickened on that July day, looming lower and darker to the west of Wentworth, the boundary of the "Black Belt," as the racial temperature continued to rise. The murder of Williams was the culmination of the racial inequities and humiliations heaped upon black soldiers who returned to find that the democracy they had fought for in Europe still did not exist for Blacks at home. They had been drawn up sharply by the competition for poor but expensive housing, frequently punctuated by bombings; by educational material for children that included sickeningly offensive images of 20th Century Uncle Toms, Topsys and Little Black Sambos, purveyed by a school system that failed to educate; and by gang attacks by Back of the Yards hoodlums that resulted in the murder of two Blacks five weeks before the riot.

Though racial violence had flared briefly in the city before, the race riot of 1919 was too hot and intense to be extinguished quickly. It took military assistance as well as a thunderstorm and heavy rain that started Wednesday night and lasted through Thursday, July 31, to bring the conflict under control. But by that time 38 men and boys, including twenty-three Blacks, had been killed. At least 537 people were injured, 342 of them Blacks. Anna Mary Grinnell, now 96 years old, described an incident in which four of the Whites killed in the riot had participated.

Mrs. Grinnell and her husband ran a bakery at 3308 South State Street, living in an apartment on the second floor with their eighteen-month-old daughter. They spent most of Monday night, July 28, lying on the floor of their apartment to avoid bullets fired by Whites from the windows of automobiles racing up and down State Street at high speeds. Through the night, groups of Whites in auto caravans kept shooting wildly from both sides of the cars, using rifles and handguns in rapid fire.

One car with four occupants passed 33rd and State. But by this time Blacks had set up army-like barricades to defend their community with sniper fire. All four Whites in the car died from gunshot wounds before the car reached 35th Street.

The Grinnells spent the anxious hours trying to figure out a way to get their child to safety. Blacks were unable to travel north of 16th Street to get to the Loop train stations. The white man who delivered flour for their bakery offered to take Mrs. Grinnell and the child to the depot, but he couldn't come south of 16th Street for fear of Blacks. So Mr. Grinnell tried to make arrangements to get his wife and child to 16th Street, where the friendly flour man could meet them and escort them through to take a train for Ohio. But before the arrangements could be made, the riot ended.

Chapter 4

HARD TIMES

Chicago's black population reached 109,594 in 1920, and an estimated 20 per cent of the Blacks were unemployed. Although they were indigent, most would not accept free transportation to the South, where there was a critical shortage of sharecroppers. They preferred to sleep in the cold halls and doorways of Chicago when they could not get accommodations at the police stations.

Fortunately, my father retained his job in the stockyards during those hard times, and that is where he was when mother gave birth to me at noon February 25, 1920, in St. Luke's Hospital at 14th and Michigan.

My earliest accident happened at Riverview Amusement Park on the Northwest Side of Chicago when I was about three and one-half years old. I fell from a beautiful, hand-carved merry-go-round horse, then rolled off and under the revolving platform. I was rescued by the brakeman-operator and an hysterical mother. I remember vividly on another visit to Riverview that we witnessed a game called "Dunk the Darky in the Water." Black men sat on a seat above a pool of water with their heads stuck through a hole in a white canvass. For a dime, a customer could buy three balls. If the player successfully hit the "darky" on the head, he would fall into the water. This generated a great deal of laughter that was repugnant to me even at age five. The game was still being played when I was drafted into the Army in World War II in 1942.

In May, 1925, we moved to 3609 South Cottage Grove Avenue, the first black family to move into the building. The white boys in the building tried to scare me by making sounds like an alley cat: "meow...meow....hiss....hiss." They were older boys who, with their green and gray eyes, looked to me quite a bit like mean old alley cats, sitting there at the top of the stairs. It was my first real contact with white folks.

The integration experience did not last more than a year, before the last white family moved out. Within that same period of time, the whole block turned black with the exception of a white boy named Wayne, whose folks operated a Singer Sewer Machine repair shop on the ground floor at 3615 Cottage Grove. We were playmates at a time when black and white children in the city rarely played together. Wayne's family stayed for three years after the neighborhood changed. He and I stayed in touch with each other until he was killed in the Normandy beach landing in World War II.

As an only child, I always slept by myself, except when my Cousin Frank came over for a visit. Frank was the son of Mama's younger sister, Willie, who came to Chicago from the South in 1918. Sleeping alone was not a problem until we moved to 3609 South Cottage Grove Avenue, only two blocks from Lake Michigan. Some nights I heard spooky and eerie sounds that made me shiver and put my head under the blanket, hoping not to be discovered by whatever was making the noise. This spooky situation lasted for several weeks before my father took my fright seriously enough to explain that the noise was from fog horns on the large ore ships sailing in the fog near shore off 36th Street. He assured me that it was not a ghost from the funeral parlor down the street.

The silent movies of this period were filled with plots about ghosts and trap doors. I remember seeing "Uncle Tom's Cabin," in which Uncle Tom actually came back as a ghost after he was killed. We saw these movies at theatres such as the Lyceum at 38th and Cottage Grove, the Pickford near 35th and Michigan, and the State Theatre at 35th and State, all of which had predominantly black audiences.

The pictures had subtitles and were shown with the accompaniment of a live piano player playing mood music, ranging from a progression of minor chords sounding like spooky footsteps to the rhythmic beats and scales of galloping horses.

Nineteen hundred and twenty five was an eventful year for me. It was the year that I decided to become a businessman. I was five. This decision was triggered by a big green Buick with side-mount tires driven by a black man who owned four or five adjoining storefronts across the street from us at 3606 to 3616 South Cottage Grove. Sometimes this man brought a little boy along with a tricycle. He would lift the tricycle out of the back seat of the green Buick, and the little boy would ride up and down the street in front of the stores. I wished the man with the big green Buick were my father; I wanted to ride a shiny new tricycle.

The man was Charles Murray, who had developed a hair pomade. Murray was successful. Nearly every man I knew, except Uncle Otis, who wore his hair natural, used Murray's Pomade. Murray's Pomade and Overton Products were to the 1920's what Fashion Fair and Ultra Sheen are to the 1980's. I did not know if my father would ever own a big green Buick, but I knew that I would someday use Murray's Pomade, which I did when I finally had some hair. I tried to look like the picture on the orange can of Murray's.

I finally met the boy with the tricycle ten years later in a freshmen Spanish class at DuSable High School. Charles Murray, Jr. and I became good friends and saw each other regularly until he married and dropped out of school to pursue a career as a wrestler. After the death of Murray, Sr., Mrs. Murray sold the Murray label to a white firm in Detroit.

A few weeks after I first saw Murray and the tricycle, a man opened a barbershop in the store at 3613 Cottage Grove. I asked him if he needed a young barber. "No," he said, "but I need someone to pass out my business cards." He agreed to pay me fifty cents, and I started work immediately.

I was not satisified with simply passing out the cards on one side of the street; I had to cover both sides. Running across the street, I noticed a big red streetcar headed straight at me. I dodged the streetcar just in time—just in time to be hit by a Model T Ford coming up on the right side parallel with the streetcar. When I woke up, I was in Provident Hospital at 36th and Dearborn. My mother and a doctor dressed in white were standing at the foot of the bed.

My mother was wringing her hands and asking, "Is he going to be all right?"

"He doesn't seem to be too badly injured," the doctor said. "All he seems to have is a fractured left leg."

Mom began to smile a little. But she didn't seem convinced until she leaned over the bed and tickled my right foot. I giggled. She smiled at the doctor and said, "Yes, he's going to be all right."

My first job ended at age five with my employer's bringing me a hand basket full of apples and oranges and an extra dollar for service beyond the call of duty.

My next venture came just three weeks before Thanksgiving in 1925 as a result of an ad in the funny paper. The ad offered a toy train in exchange for the sale of 200 miniature, pencil-sized, multicolored bottles of perfume. Each color represented a different fragrance. My mother mailed the newspaper coupon, and I received the shipment on December 1. My thought was to sell the perfume fast enough to get the train for Christmas. Again, I did not succeed. Everybody I attempted to sell sniffed the bottle of perfume and frowned. However, for reasons I did not understand at the time, some people gave me ten cents and told me to keep the perfume.

Santa Claus did not leave a train for me, but he did leave a player piano for the family. The piano had two functions: you could play it manually like an ordinary instrument, or you could put a roll on it and by a see-saw pumping of the feet, watch the keyboard move rapidly with the sounds of Jelly Roll Morton, Scott Joplin, and many popular tunes of the day. My father had learned to play the piano skillfully without the ability to read music. But he was determined that I was going to be a music-reading piano player.

I took my first lesson from Elmer Simpson in January, 1926. I wanted to learn to play like my father, but I found learning to play very hard work requiring a lot of discipline. By late spring, my music teacher had me ready to appear in a children's program at West Point Baptist Church, a black church still located on the northwest corner of 36th Street and Cottage Grove Avenue. This piano debut started me on a music career that did not end until I was 26 years old. The self-discipline I acquired in the many hours required to learn a single number on my instrument made it easier for me to go from music to hard academic studies at age 27.

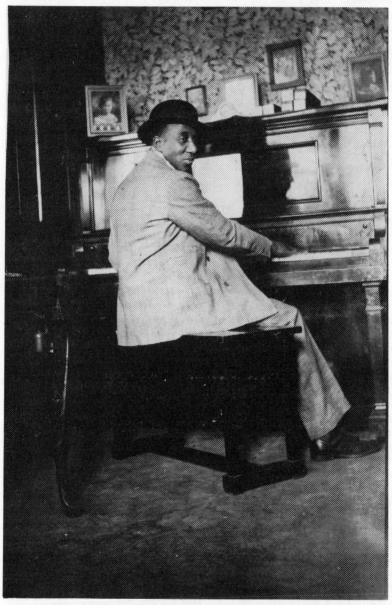

Louis Travis, father of Dempsey J. Travis, at the piano in their home at 3609 South Cottage Grove Avenue in January, 1926.

This photograph of Mrs. Mittie Travis, mother of
Dempsey J. Travis, was taken on the front porch of
Mrs. Travis' mother's home in Birmingham, Ala-
bama, one year before she came to Chicago in 1916.

I studied music under a series of teachers for twelve years. Three of my teachers were Blacks, and two were German (whether German Jewish or otherwise German, I didn't know—we Blacks were not aware of any difference). From both black and white teachers, I learned sonatas of Mozart, the preludes and nocturnes of Chopin, and other standard pieces by European composers. My instructors taught me very little American music and no black music. Although my interest was always in jazz, my teachers said I had the touch, talent and flair of a concert pianist. But I couldn't see such a career, largely because I knew no Blacks who made a living playing concert piano, except some who played in the black churches.

My initial formal education started in a private kindergarten where I was considered a very bright child. My parents were proud of my progress. They always had me counting to 100 or saying the alphabet and reciting simple poems and rhymes for their friends. I was pleased with myself and with school. Then suddenly my whole world changed.

My father became ill, and my mother could no longer afford the tuition, so I went to a public school, Doolittle School, just east of Cottage Grove at 35th Street. My teacher was a white lady named Mrs. Green. For reasons unknown to me now or then, I did not like Mrs. Green, and she returned the emotion. I found the teacher and the school so distasteful that I was playing hookey after my third day.

To me it seemed that I walked around for months, although I'm sure that it was only a few days of kicking cans and other stuff in the alleys while my parents thought I was in school.

Sitting on a stoop one rainy morning, I was picked up by a truant officer who took me back to Doolittle. I was glad that I had been caught and happier still when Mrs. Green refused to accept me back in her class and had me transferred to another teacher. I had no problem with the new teacher, but neither can I remember her name. No problems and no names is a posture I maintained for the next eleven years that I was in public school, with the exception of two elementary teachers and two high school teachers, who I thought made a contribution to my education.

When my parents learned of my hookey-playing, they both beat my behind and grounded me from all activities, including the Saturday afternoon movie matinee for one month. From that point through college, I never missed a full day in school. Of course, occasionally I cut classes to catch famous bands like Duke Ellington's and Jimmy Lunceford's when they came through Chicago during my high school days. But I was never excessively absent.

"Black boys are not admitted here" is the greeting my cousin Frank and I received when we attempted to buy two tickets at the Oakland Square Theatre at 39th and Drexel Boulevard in 1928. We wanted to see Douglas Fairbanks in "The Three Musketeers" but the ticket seller told us that if we did not move from in front of the theater, she would have that big burly usher at the door "kick our nigger behinds." We turned and saw the blonde, blue-eyed, burly usher glaring at us. We ran.

Holy Angels Catholic Church around the corner on Oakwood Boulevard treated Blacks better. Well, at the time it seemed mighty nice that we were allowed to sit in a section reserved for Blacks, the six back pews on the right side. The Oakland Square Theater folded long ago, but Holy Angels remains an influential community institution under the leadership of a black pastor, Father George Clements.

In 1929, at age nine, I became a *Chicago Defender* paper boy. I still remember vividly the first issue that I sold with its red headline over the picture of a black man hanging from a tree. I sold my twenty-five copies of that issue in less than an hour and realized a dollar profit. Ordinarily it would take three or four hours to hustle that many papers on Saturday. In those days, the headlines were always red in the *Defender*, but not always as dramatic. My *Defender* business continued to prosper right up until "Black Thursday," October 24, 1929, the day the stock market failed. Before the year's end my customers were more concerned about feeding their stomachs than feeding their minds.

The Depression hit everybody, including my Uncle Otis. Up until the Depression I remember Uncle Otis as a high-spirited person who occasionally gave me a nickel for an ice cream cone or a dime to see the Saturday afternoon matinee. During the good days he would bring his pretty girlfriends around to see my parents. My mother always hoped he would marry the one named Mildred. Even though I was a child she appeared to me to be both attractive and sophisticated. As a matter of fact, I still think of her as the model for Duke Ellington's "Sophisticated Lady." I missed seeing her almost as much as my uncle must have after he lost his job, his savings and his spirit.

Uncle Otis was laid off his job on December 22, 1929. He had always been thrifty and had saved his money in the Binga State Bank, the financial rock of the black community, located one door north of the northwest corner of 35th and State. The family never knew exactly how much money Otis had saved, but he managed to live comfortably without apparent worry until July 31, 1930. On that day, the examiners closed the doors of the Binga bank. Thrifty Uncle Otis became destitute with the turn of the examiner's key in the front door of the bank.

Otis Travis died in 1933, broke and broken-hearted, without having recovered one penny of his savings. Many savers suffered such losses in those days before deposits were insured by the Federal Deposit Insurance Corporation.

Hard times, indeed.

"Young Dempsey was successful as a newsboy."

Chicago's Roaring '20's

Chapter 5

IF BAD DREAMS WERE MONEY, BLACKS WOULD BE RICH

The 1920's roared like an economic lion for white folks, but they bare-ly meowed for Blacks.

Chicago's black population increased from 44,000 in 1910 to 109,000 in 1920, an increase from two to four per cent. By 1950 the total had in-creased to 492,000, or 14 per cent of the total population.

The city's geographical limits within which most Blacks would be housed was established by 1920. The growth pattern would be continu-ous and not leap-frog. The exceptions, to name a few, were Lillydale, Morgan Park and Robbins. Some of the old settlers, in an effort to es-cape from the influx of Southern migrants, relocated in areas that were a long ride away via the interurban street car. Morgan Park attracted middle-middle-income Blacks, that is, middle-middle on the scale of black employment opportunities—clerks, Pullman porters, dining car waiters and semi-skilled laborers. Lillydale and Robbins attracted lower-middle class Blacks in search of space to rear large families. Both Rob-bins and Lillydale have dramatically improved the quality of their hous-ing stock within the past twenty years.

The industrial depression that embraced the city during the last six months of 1920 caused the lay-off of some 20,000 Blacks, many of whom drifted to pool halls, police stations and doorways for shelter. On the shore of Lake Michigan north of 31st Street, the homeless sought shelter in a "Village of the Deserted" in make-shift shanties made of rocks, newspapers and other junk.

The economic depression, however, did not relieve the housing crisis for the employed Black, who was still forced to pay extremely high rent for furnished or unfurnished quarters. At the same time it was estimated that 25 per cent of the units in north Kenwood were vacant.

In 1921, Whites began to demand both apartments and houses in the Kenwood-Hyde Park area, suddenly a highly desirable area. The Hyde Park Owners Association launched a campaign to move out the 1,000 black families who were living between 39th and 55th Streets between Lake Michigan and Cottage Grove Avenue. They tried to move them back into the old, defined "Black Belt" north of 39th Street. But they learned that many had paid cash money for their property, some of it realized from the sale of their homes in the South, and there was no legal way to move them out. In this instance, violence was not used. The Blacks had landed. The beachhead had been established.

But Blacks' penetration of the southeast area was still painfully slow, because the Whites' defenses were many, including neighborhood associations and individual opposition, restrictive covenants and local political actions to restrict Blacks to certain areas.

Waking up a Black in Chicago was always a continuation of the previous night's bad dream. If bad dreams were money, all blacks folks would be rich.

An attempt to capitalize on bad dreams created a dream book industry that is still not well known outside the black community. There were more than twenty dream books or policy games. The most popular during the '20's and '30's were "The Three Witches," "The Gypsy Witch," "The Japanese Fate," "Aunt Della's" and "Aunt Sally's." These books were best sellers whose popularity was exceeded only by the Bible in the black community. Dream books translated the meaning of a dream into policy numbers, which were usually a combination of three numbers. For example, a dream of Death Row translated into 9-9-29, and the name "Henry" translated into 27-31-33.

The black millionaires of the 1930's were the policy kings such as "Big Jim" Martin of the West Side and on the South Side was "Giver Dam" Jones and his brother Teennan, and Illy Kelly with his brothers, Walter and Ross. Pop Lewis was a cultured college-trained gentleman, who ran the Monte Carlo Wheel and owned the Vincennes Hotel at 36th and Vincennes, with its 200 rooms, ballroom, and banquet halls featuring full orchestras.

There were other successful operators but none compared with another set of Jones brothers—Eddie, George and McKissick. Their headquarters at 4724 Michigan employed as many as 250 people, a number which does not include several hundred working their stations and runners. At the height of the Jones brothers' career they grossed $25,000 per day. An efficiency expert once said that the Jones' wheels operated like clockwork, as efficient and as well run as many of the marble-lined banks and brokerage houses on LaSalle Street, and many times more profitable. In addition to a villa in Paris, a summer home in Peoria and a villa in Mexico City on Compe 73, they owned four hotels, the Vienna Bathhouse, the Grove, the Garfield and the Alpha. They were the first Blacks to own a piece of real estate at 47th and King Drive. They opened their Ben Franklin Store at 436-44 East 47th Street in 1937 which was considered such a major achievement that thousands of people filled the street, and celebrities such as Joe Louis and Bill (Bojangles) Robinson appeared.

One of the most prominent lawyers in the city dubbed the opening of the store "a milestone in the progress of our business." The Franklin Store property was the first to be owned by a Black in the heart of the business district on 47th Street. According to the late Dr. Bishop Smith, a Black could not rent a ground floor store between Forrestville and Prairie on 47th Street for any retail purpose. The only exceptions were barber shops, beauty shops, taverns, and the Morris Eat Shop, which was located at 410 East 47th Street.

A nickel bet on the right combination of numbers could make a player a five dollar winner. Five dollars represented two days' pay for me at the Quality Laundry in the summer of 1939. Policy was and still is the poor man's sweepstakes. Some people played seven or eight different combinations of numbers a day, because they had bad dreams in multiples.

Not everyone turned to dream books to find the meaning of their bad dreams. My Uncle Otis sought a solution for the bleakness of black life in the Marcus Garvey Movement in the early 1920's. The name of Marcus Garvey was always spoken with reverence in our home.

Uncle Otis had described Garvey, that twentieth-century dreamer, as an "unsynthetic" black man. He was short, with a slightly rotund trunk under an average-sized neck and shoulders, which supported a large head. Garvey's speeches on black nationhood stirred his audiences into a fever of excitement, his colorful style leaning heavily on rhetorical questions.

"Where is the black man's government?" he would ask. "Where is his president, his country, and his ambassadors, his army, his navy, and his men of big affairs? I could not find them, and I declared, 'I will help make them!'" Such a speech always had his audience foot-stamping, shouting and clapping.

Garveyism generated more serious street talk than any other subject along "The Stroll," which was State Street between 31st and 39th Streets, in the '20's. Robert S. Abbott, founder of the *Chicago Defender,* could be found holding court on the corner of 35th and State with a big cigar in his mouth, discussing the similarity of the Garvey scheme with that of "Chief Sam," who, earlier in the century, flim-flammed some black people with a scheme to establish a black kingdom in Africa. Like Garvey, "Chief Sam" had purchased some second-hand boats for a black exodus to the homeland.

Another heavy topic on "The Stroll" might be Jack Johnson, the "Great Black Hope" and first black heavyweight champion of the world. The last three of Johnson's four marriages were to white women and were eagerly discussed in the black community.

Johnson's victories in the ring were interpreted by Blacks and Whites as a "Black Manifesto" against white supremacy. With each blow, Jack Arthur Johnson was laying to rest the 19th Century myth of the white superman. The reaction to Johnson's championship victory over Tommy Burns on December 26, 1908, in Sidney, New South Wales, was pandemonium. Black jubilation was met with white mob violence and police suppression after the defeat of the "White Hope" Jim Jeffries on July 4, 1910. There were disturbances in many cities, and victory celebrations turned into brick and bottle-throwing riots by Whites.

Johnson was finally stopped by a conviction under the Mann Act, passed in June, 1919, after a press blitz on Johnson's activities with white women. This "white slave traffic" act was sponsored by James

Robert Mann, Congressman from Illinois. It prohibited transportation of women across state lines for immoral purposes.

Johnson was convicted under this act for associating with his favorite lady of the evening, Belle Schreiber, who was the star Daughter of Joy at Chicago's Everleigh Club, located in the red light district at 2131-33 South Dearborn Street. Johnson allegedly sent money to Belle in Pittsburgh so that she could come to Chicago for a specific and immoral purpose. The Ku Klux Klan mentality of many Americans dictated that the black hero must be punished for this act, though there is no record of any white convictions for similar transportation of black women from the South to the North.

Johnson's conviction was reversed on appeal, but he had gone into hiding and remained a fugitive until he gave himself up to the U.S. government in Mexico. He served a year and a day in a federal penitentiary at Leavenworth, Kansas. As a result, Blacks were "white-lined" out of the contest for the heavyweight championship for two decades after Johnson's reign.

The "Champ" Jack Johnson, first black heavyweight boxing king in Joliet, Illinois, in 1921.

Thirty fifth and State Street was home to thousands of Black Chicagoans who sought breathing space outside of their cubicle rooms and kitchenettes. People walked, talked, laughed and gestured around the intersection all night long. The attaction was the theatres, nightclubs and lively businesses of the area.

This intersection spawned a lively round of interests. There are many examples. The business empire of Anthony Overton was led by his cosmetics company. In his "fleet" of businesses he had the Victory Life Insurance Company, "Half Century" magazine, the "Bee" newspaper, and his Douglas National Bank, all located on the east side of State Street at 36th.

On the northwest corner at 35th Street was Jesse Binga's office building, known as the Binga Arcade. Next door, to the north, was the Binga State Bank.

Jesse Binga had been a railroad porter. In 1908 he founded a private bank. He married the sister of "Mushmouth" Johnson, who ran a lucrative gambling business, and much of the Johnson foundation went into Binga's bank. In 1920, Binga's bank became a state bank.

Binga built the Binga Arcade in 1929. It was a five-story building of imposing design, with office space and a dance hall on the roof. Binga had been warned that such a building at such a location would not prove a really practical investment, but the building represented a dream. In 1929, when the Depression started, Binga was riding high—he had become chairman of a new and thriving insurance company, and his bank had nearly $1.5 million in deposits.

But on July 31, 1930, Binga's bank was shut down by the state examiner. Banks were closing across the country, and controversy surrounded Binga's various real estate deals. Depositors started a run on the bank, and that was the end of it. Eventually Binga served time in jail for embezzlement.

Binga remained a figure of controversy to Black Chicago. Some said he was simply a crook. Others said he was merely a creative businessman who ended up taking too many risks, and that without the Depression he might have continued as black Chicago's foremost businessman. Other said he was a victim of circumstances brought down by the white system, and that his mistake had been in overextending the bank by making too many first mortgages to Blacks desperate to buy homes.

At 37th and State stood the first and largest black-built high-rise office building, developed by the black fraternal organization, the Knights of Pythias. This structure was converted to residential use during World War II, and its shell remained standing until 1980.

State Street was both Wall Street and Broadway to the black community in the '20's. The white lights of South State went on after the red lights of New Orleans' Storeyville section went out in November, 1917, when New Orleans' mayor, on order of the Secretary of the Navy, closed down the houses of prostitution. That produced instant depression among the jazz men who had played those houses and the honky-tonks of Storeyville. Many of those talented musicians, along with their jazz-loving fans, rode the rails north to Chicago.

That shift from New Orleans to Chicago made State Street, and its cross streets at 31st and 35th, the jazz mecca of America. The Royal Garden, the Sunset Cafe, the Pekin, the Dreamland, Elite #1, Elite #2, the Entertainers Club, and the Plantation on 35th Street, where King

Oliver, the great New Orleans' trumpeter, played nightly, were centers of entertainment for black and white Chicagoans. Jack Johnson's Cafe de Champion at 42 West 31st Street was a forerunner in entertainment for "black and tan" audiences in Chicago.

Other New Orleans' jazzmen who kept the South Side jumping were Louis Armstrong, Freddy Keppard, Johnny and Baby Dodds, Sidney Bechet, Perez St. Cyr, and Jelly Roll Morton, who was the most popular underworld pianist around.

Underworld characters, jazz, prostitution, alcohol and dope moved through the residential sections of the black community the way the Illinois Central Railroad ran through the little towns and cities between Chicago and New Orleans. Vice first surrounded and then infiltrated the "Black Belt." It was all but impossible for black families to escape the stench of corruption and immorality, because it operated under a protective political umbrella. Blacks were powerless to stamp out the vice and powerless to flee from it, since they could not freely move about the city in search of more wholesome neighborhoods.

But, of course, all Blacks did not regret the introduction of vice into the black community. It offered color in a drab existence and money in a time of restricted opportunity. Black jazz musicians could not have exploited their talents without the permissive sponsorship of the vice operations.

The comfortable identification that Cab Calloway, the entertainer, had with vice in Chicago is described in his autobiography, *Of Minnie the Moocher and Me.* He tells about his first wife, Betty, a tall, light-skinned beauty who earned $50 a day and gave him more than $200 a week.:

> "On July 26, 1928, we were married. By that time we had moved out of the Joneses' house to live with a woman named Mae Singleton in another house on the Southside. Mae had one fine house, and she did a beautiful business. She had two or three prostitutes living in there. You might think it would bother me to be living in a house run by a madam, but it didn't. It was a damned comfortable life."

But it was hell for those Blacks who were trying to build a strong, moral family. A further extension of the vice virus could be found in the typical jazz club environment on the South Side in the '20's and '30's as Earl "Father" Hines, the famous pianist, described it in his autobiography, *World of Earl Hines:*

> "The club where I was working brought in, as I said, a lot of underworld people, and among them many pimps. They used to hang out there until their girls finished working at two or three o'clock in the morning. Then they would bring them there to thrash out whatever went on during the day. The big-time pimps had Packards and Pierce-Arrows, and I often wished I could get a car like they had. They were dressed up at all times . . ."

The infectious environments described by both Calloway and Hines are models that laid the groundwork for the moral and social disorganization of the urban black community.

Chapter 6

LISTENING BACK

In 1931, Uncle Otis was still unemployed, and Uncle Joe and my father had been cut from six ten-hour days a week to three eight-hour days. And in January, the Willard Elementary School, where I was enrolled, went on a double shift that cut my school day almost in half.

Fortunately for me, the lost classroom hours were recovered at home in a totally different educational environment. Those harsh realities of the '30's had an unexpected benefit—they allowed me to listen to my uncle and my father discuss the issues of the day and the personalities of Black Chicago. Those discussions shaped my views as a young black man.

My home study took place at least three afternoons a week when I came home to find my father and his brothers sitting around the dining room table, sometimes sipping home brew, talking about the good old days—what they called "the silk shirt days"—when the overtime pay of the better days of the '20's had given them some economic freedom. They let me sit on the floor and listen to their discussions, which ranged from Abyssinia to Zanzibar. I was only barred when they started talking about women, since at the age of ten, I was judged too young to fully participate.

My mother seldom took part in these skull sessions, but when she talked, she made it clear she had her own views. I remember once, when I was five years old, some older white boys in the building we had integrated at 36th Street and Cottage Grove Avenue called me a "black son of a bitch." They said it in such an ugly, frightening tone that I ran to my mother and repeated the phrase. She only smiled.

"Have you ever seen black velvet?" she said. She took a velvet jacket out of a drawer and showed it to me.

I touched it. "Yes. It's soft and pretty."

She put her arms around me. "This is the best and most expensive material in the world," she said.

"Is it?"

"You're my black velvet," she said. For me, that simple exchange provided a structure for the resolution of most of the future problems I was going to have about my color. If I had gone to my father or his brother Joe that day, however, I know they would have advised me to "punch the honkies in the mouth."

Dad and his younger brother were tough, no-nonsense, strike-breaking laborers. They fought any black or white man who crossed them. Uncle Otis, on the other hand, was gentle and philosophical. Their differences kept their talks spirited. I found it especially exciting when they talked about such heroes as Jack Johnson, the heavyweight champion, Marcus Garvey, Booker T. Washington or W.E.B. DuBois.

Uncle Joe, who was the family playboy, opened the Johnson argument one night with a smile. "Any black man who achieves the world's heavyweight championship deserves the best that womanhood can offer."

That got a sardonic grin from my mother: "Does that mean the best white prostitute?"

"I didn't say anything about pay-for-play girls," Uncle Joe said.

Uncle Otis tried to lift the discussion to a higher level. "Jack Johnson's contribution to vertical black pride should not be diminished by his taste in horizontal relaxation," he said.

My father agreed: "That's right. Jack's victories have lifted more bent backs and bowed heads than any other event since the Emancipation Proclamation."

But Mama wasn't having any of that. She glared around the table at the men: "Name one instance when Jack Johnson took a public position on behalf of colored people."

There was a long silence.

"I'm going to bed," Dad said finally. And that was the end of that discussion.

Mom had little sympathy with black males' need for symbolic props to their masculinity in a society that offered them little else. Nor did she understand the argument that Johnson took no public positions for black people because Whites kept him off balance outside the ring.

But Mama had another go at it at a subsequent session. It came about at the end of a talk about the Garvey movement.

"We don't have a black army, navy, or such," my father said, rubbing his chin and referring to Marcus Garvey's favorite challenge to Blacks. "The Garvey movement has failed."

"No! Garvey did not fail," Uncle Otis said, speaking with a special deliberateness. "He gave colored Americans a pride that never surfaced before on any continent. He's laid a foundation on which all the colored people of the world could coalesce."

Dad dismissed the argument with a gesture of his big, calloused fist: "How do you bring people together on a sinking ship? Didn't the black-owned Black Star Line fail?"

"Yes," Otis admitted, looking straight into Dad's eyes. "It was an economic failure, even though Whites occupied most of the important administrative and operational posts. There weren't any trained Blacks with experience in the steamship business. But it was a psychological success."

Dad snorted.

"Yes, it was," Otis said. "That venture, like the other Garvey enterprises, created a spirit that has yet to be parallelled in any other black movement."

Dad was silent.

"Louis, you must have felt that spirit the last time we heard Garvey speak at the Eighth Regiment Armory at 35th and Giles," Otis said. "Chicago may have had only 9,000 contributing members in the Universal Negro Improvement Association, but more than six million people worldwide were committed at the peak of Garvey's influence. Any movement that can attract that much attention is never a failure."

That was when my mother, who had been sitting silently in the doorway between the kitchen and the dining room, made her move. She coughed as if to clear her voice.

"Garvey was a sensible and sensitive man," she said placatingly. And then she produced a book, as if she had been already prepared for this discussion. "I want to read you this poem 'The Black Woman,' because it reflects his inner soul on Negro purity and beauty."

She made sure she had their attention, and then she read out in a clear voice:

"Black queen of beauty, thou hast given color to the world!
Among other women thou art royal and the fairest!
Like the brightest jewels in the regal diadem,
Shin'st thou, Goddess of Africa, nature's purest emblem.

"Black men worship at thy virginal shrine of purest love,
Because in thine eyes are virtues steady and holy mark,
As we see no other, clothed in silk or fine linen,
From ancient Venus, the Goddess, to mythical Helen."

My mother rose from the chair after reading the poem, walked over to my father and placed her right hand on the back of his neck. She looked with airy confidence at the other two men.

"How did you Jack Johnson fans like that message?" she said.

Dad's face lit up with a broad smile. Uncle Joe scratched his head. End of that discussion.

I saw a graphic illustration of the wide-open nature of vice in 1926, when I was six years old and living at 3609 South Cottage Grove Avenue. I often saw black and white women stopping men on the street. At that time, I thought they were lost and were asking for directions. But it seemed strange that the man would follow the woman into a nearby alley or hallway. One day some older boys curiously followed the "lost" lady and her new "friend" into a hallway and were immediately chased out as the woman cursed them for harassing her "client."

At dinner that evening, I described my itinerary to Uncle Otis and Dad. Both laughed noisily, nearly choking on their food. Later that night, after I had gone to bed, I could hear them discussing the "lost" lady through a crack in my bedroom door.

"You know, that boy wouldn't have seen anything like that episode of our red light district if the law hadn't closed all the whorehouses down. I think it's a damn shame they turned all those whores loose in our neighborhood," my father said.

Uncle Joe responded with a Chicago history lesson: "Colored folks have always lived on the edge of this city's vice district," he said. "That's just the way it's always been. And now that they're closed, we are the vice."

"Listen, you know the district would still be open if some rich white merchant's kid hadn't been killed in a whorehouse," Uncle Otis put in. "The bitches would still be legal, licensed, and confined to their houses between 18th and 22nd Streets." Some 260 houses of prostitution had been in operation between 18th and 22nd Streets, from Wabash on the east to Wentworth on the west, in the area called the Levee.

There was silence as the men considered this. Then Uncle Joe spoke.

"My old lady's sister lost her job as a maid there and she hasn't had a regular job since." Over 2,000 black women had worked as maids or personal servants in those houses. Like Amy Lou, Uncle Joe's friend's sister, they made good money, because in addition to their wages, they got healthy tips from the wealthy patrons.

Dad agreed that these facts were well known in the black community. "And Frank Brown says when he was tending bar at the Everleigh Club, they had a $15,000 gold-plated piano that was made to order. And they had three eight-piece orchestras that played alternately dusk to dawn, seven nights a week."

By this time I was so interested in the wider implications of the discussion that my "lost" lady had evoked that I got up and cracked my bedroom door open a little wider. Uncle Otis was sitting with his back to the dining room window, and I could look directly into his face across Dad's shoulder. Otis was rubbing his hands and looking quizzically at Dad and Uncle Joe.

"Do you think a block club protest would get rid of the street-walkers?" he said. But his expression changed and he answered his own question before the others could speak.

"No! There's too much money in it. The papers say the graft from prostitution is more than $15 million a year. And Mayor Big Bill Thompon, the black folks' favorite Republican, died leaving over $2 million in currency."

Dad shook his head. "Clam it, Otis! Booker T. Washington said black people have to wipe out vice in their own communities."

"How can we do that when the white man pays the fiddler and calls the tune?" Otis said. "It's like attacking elephants with bean guns."

"My boy deserves a better environment. I'm going to move," my father said glumly.

"Move where?" Otis jeered. "You can't escape the whores. The landlords will make room for them as long as they pay double rent. You haven't got the money. You haven't got the political power to fight it."

He watched my father's face as his words sank in.

"And you can't move away from it," he said. "Face it. You're black."

I watched them sitting there in the long silence that followed. Then I got up and quietly tiptoed back to my bed.

The Travis family moved to 4826 South Evans in 1930. The above photograph was taken in their backyard picturing young Travis and his dog, Prince. The family was only at the new address a short time before Dempsey discovered that another "lost lady" was operating out of 4824 South Evans—the house just north of the fence in the picture.

(bottom left) This 1932 photograph was taken of Travis' cousin Lucille, his mother, and himself in Lincoln Park.

(bottom right) 10 year old Dempsey is pictures here with a buddy sitting on the rocks in 1930 at 36th and the Lake.

Life with Grandma in the troubled '30s.

Chapter 7

HOOVER'S DEPRESSION AND GRANDMA'S SESSION

In 1930, President Herbert Hoover promised two chickens in every pot and a car in every garage. Black Americans hardly noticed. They knew the promise wasn't for them.

Almost half of Chicago's black families (the black population was 233,903) were receiving some form of public welfare that year. Without aid, they could not have afforded the 10 cents for a quart of milk, 29 cents for a dozen eggs, 5 cents for a 20 ounce loaf of bread or 7 cents for transportation across town to try to find a job.

The search for work sent 200,000 boys, girls, men and women criss-crossing the country as stowaways on freight trains. The railroad detectives ignored their human freight since there were not enough jails to accommodate the ride-stealing, light-traveling "Hoover Hobos" moving from city to city, town to town, looking for the prosperity their president had promised was just around the corner.

Several members of my family joined the wandering freight riders. Both Uncle Glenn, my mother's step-brother, and cousin Ralph, my Aunt Claudie's oldest son, had become experts at hopping freights.

Uncle Glenn showed up at our back door suddenly one summer afternoon after having paid a very high price for a freight ride: six months earlier he had lost both legs up to the knee riding the rails. But this had not stopped him from freight-hopping. He could still get around almost as quickly as a normal man, wearing special inverted shoes strapped to his knees. He would use his strong arms to hoist his body into the railroad car. He left Chicago as suddenly as he came one morning, heading for the freight yard. We never saw or heard from him again.

Cousin Ralph was the globe-trotter in the family. He told us he had ridden freight trains through forty-two of the forty-eight states. A gregarious, loud-laughing, fun-loving individual, Ralph had a capacity for deep scholarship in many subjects, ranging from the Bible to Buddhism, and he was the first member of our family to attend college. He studied at Oakwood Junior College, a Seventh-Day Adventist school in Huntsville, Alabama, and during his frequent visits with us, he introduced me to the thoughts of such men as Dr. W.E.B. DuBois, Booker T. Washington and George Washington Carver. Then again, on several occasions he took me to see a burlesque show at the Rialto Theater on State Street, just north of Van Buren. That was cousin Ralph, a man who enjoyed all seasons. When I was 11, he took my mother and me to see a Paul Robeson concert and introduced us to the great singer after the recital.

This photograph of Travis' grade 7B class at the Willard Elementary School was taken in 1932. Dempsey Travis is pictured in the top row, second from the right. Also pictured are the late Jessie Miller, famous band leader and trumpet player (top row, 1st from the left), and Robert Anderson, gospel pianist and singer (top row, 3rd from the right).

Even more exciting was the first time Ralph took me to Washington Park to hear the "Reds" give a lecture on the bourgeois injustices of tenant evictions. The joint efforts of Blacks and Whites to resettle evicted families was the first integrated action I had ever witnessed in which the races acted as equals. Not surprisingly, during this period I thought that any white person seen associating with a Black was a Communist.

Ralph was a wrestler, and he was always challenging me or my father when he was in town. He was a feisty man and a fervent believer in Adventistism. In fact, this led to his death years later. He was preaching in a bus station in Kansas City when some policemen tried to get him to stop. He refused to leave the station, and he was shot to death.

With all of its sorrow, the Depression brought some free excitement for kids called "Put the furniture back in." Every day someone was evicted on our block for non-payment of rent. Before the bailiffs had put the last piece of furniture on the street, someone would contact the Communist Red Squad that met in Washington Park. The Squad would send a group of men to put the furniture back into the apartment. On other occasions they would arrive just as the furniture was to be removed by the bailiffs and would advise the tenants to sit on the furniture to prevent its removal. The seated tenant was soon joined by neighbors and the squad who would lead in the first chorus of an old spiritual, "I shall not, I shall not be moved," the theme song of the resistence in the 1930's.

The Communists held mass meetings daily in Washington Park. There was usually one very large crowd listening to a prominent guest speaker, and at the same time there were dozens of smaller groups listening to lesser known personalities. Cousin Ralph told Dad and his brothers after returning from the park one evening that they could get a liberal education in Washington Park by simply moving from one bench speaker to another.

"What subjects were you educated in today?" Dad asked.

"The Scottsboro Boys," Ralph said.

"Who was the speaker?" Uncle Otis.

"Some white New York lawyer who was at the nine boys' first trial in Scottsboro, Alabama."

"Weren't they arrested on a freight train in Paint Rock, Alabama?" Uncle Otis asked.

"Yep! But they shipped the niggers by open truck to Scottsboro, the Jackson County seat, because they didn't have a cage big enough for them in Paint Rock," Ralph said.

Cousin Ralph spent the rest of the evening relating what the New York lawyer had said to the big crowd in the park. According to him, the nine black boys were arrested for fighting seven white hobos who had been trying to force them to jump from a moving freight train. Instead, the black boys beat and kicked all of the white hobos off the train except one. They spared the last white hobo because the train had picked up too much speed for them to put him off without causing him serious injury or possibly death. The bruised and infuriated white boys hitch-hiked ahead to Scottsboro, where they pressed charges with the sheriff against the Blacks for beating the hell out of them. Deputy Sheriff Charlie Latham put together a posse to capture the Blacks on the freight train. They were arrested at the next scheduled stop, which was Paint Rock. To everyone's surprise, in addition to the nine Blacks and one white boy on the train, two young white female hobos, wearing men's caps and overalls, were also aboard.

Ralph Crawford

Only twenty minutes had passed after the arrest had been made when the younger girl, who identified herself as Ruby Bates of Huntsville, had accused the nine Blacks of raping both her and her girlfriend, Victoria Price. The nine boys were arrested on March 25, 1931. They went to trial on April 6, 1931, and three days later, April 9, 1931, eight of the nine were sentenced to die. Roy Wright, who had barely reached his thirteenth birthday, was sentenced to life in prison.

A death silence fell over the dining room. Everyone at the table was stunned at the severity of Judge Hawkins' sentence and the swiftness of the trial. It seemed like an hour of silence passed before Uncle Joe asked Ralph, "How did the Washington Park crowd react to this?"

"Shock," Ralph answered. "Just plain shock!"

Uncle Otis cut in, "Those boys were lucky they weren't arrested in my home state of Georgia; there they might have been given an instant trial. I understand the lynching quota for niggers in Georgia was something like eleven a year compared to an average of six in Alabama between 1882 and 1927. Alabama was about 40% less."[4]

Ralph gave a grim chuckle. "You fellows have been away from the South so long that you have forgotten 'Uncle Charlie's first commandment, haven't you?' " he said. "The first commandment is, 'Don't ogle or touch "Charlie's" ladies unless you have already made your peace with God.' "

Uncle Joe, jumping from his seat, shouted, "Damn, man! How can any civilized court sentence eight teen-aged boys to die on the word of two white prostitutes?"

"Easy," Ralph said. "Black men in the white man's scheme of things are a sub-class. Keeping this premise in mind, then you will understand the white man's rage when he discovers that his woman has been violated by a lower order of being."

Uncle Joe smiled. A cynical, streetwise Chicagoan now, with a streak of the playboy in him, he was often amused at Ralph's fervor in explaining just how White America worked. "Aren't you drawing some pretty broad conclusions from one incident?" he said.

Ralph stared at him seriously. "The real issue is not the violation of the white woman, but a systematized program devised by the white man to detour the sub-class from economic and political parity for another two hundred years."

Uncle Joe smiled again. "Those are some pretty strong words, Ralph."

Ralph was scowling now. "The Anglo judicial system condones black genocide by refusing to deal with Black-on-Black killing or crime seriously. The legal and social institutions do not see the individual black man as a personality, but as a blur of an impersonal mass. Therefore, many Blacks have been brainwashed into accepting this indistinctiveness and have adopted a self-defeating 'Nigger ain't nothing' attitude response to his social and legal individual invisibility.

"In the absence of individual distinctiveness, Blacks have taken on a group guilt complex exhibited by such remarks as 'We tore up the neighborhoods,' or 'Why don't we learn how to act,' and 'Why can't we behave like white folks,' or the acceptance of the white man's highest commendation: 'You are not like the others.' "

Everybody let his words hang in the air while they studied each others' faces. Then Dad said "Ralph, you didn't finish telling us what happened to the Scottsboro Boys. Did they try to escape?"

"You have got to be kidding," Ralph said.

"The NAACP ain't going to let those black boys burn," Dad said.

"They will if they don't dismiss those white New York lawyers hired by the International Labor Defense. Everybody knows the ILD is a Communist group. As a matter of fact, Walter White, the Executive Secretary of the NAACP, said, 'The prejudice against Communism and Blacks combined guaranteed the Scottsboro Boys going to the electric chair,' " Ralph said.

The ILD attorney, Walter Pullock, defending the Scottsboro boys,

The Scottsboro Boys

(top) The Scottsboro Boys shortly after their arrest; (below) pictured with their ILD attorney Walter Pullack in 1932. Pullack successfully took the case of the young men to the Supreme Court where they were guaranteed new trials. It was a clear matter of the rights of the boys having been violated.

took the case to the Supreme Court. On November 7, 1932, the Scottsboro Boys were guaranteed new trials based on the landmark decision in Powell v. Alabama. The decision of the lower court was reversed on the grounds that their rights under the Fourteenth Amendment had been violated and that they had not received adequate counsel at Scottsboro. On April 7, 1933, Ruby Bates took the witness stand and denied she or Victoria Price was raped. On October 25,1976, Governor George Wallace approved the pardon of Clarence Norris, the only survivor of the Scottsboro Boys.

But the Communists never managed to make a dent in Blacks' loyalty to the party of Abraham Lincoln. In the presidential election of 1932, most stayed with the Republicans in spite of disillusionment with Herbert Hoover and his promises of prosperity just around the corner.

The Roosevelt era began just four months prior to the opening of the Century of Progress on Chicago's lakefront. The white newspapers were saying eagerly that the fair would attract enough visitors to restore the prosperity the city had known in the '20's. But Black Chicago was less optimistic.

The World's Fair of 1933 found the Chicago Urban League with a full-time staff of one. That was the Executive Secretary, A. L. Foster, who tried to get both white collar and menial jobs for the Blacks at the World Fair. But the placement of menial jobs was given to a white employment agency. According to Willie Randall, the orchestra leader, the only black professionals working on the fair grounds were musicians, members of the Freddie Williams Orchestra, playing at the Jensen Pavilion.

The Chicago World Fair of 1933 and '34 was commercially successful. Nearly 28 million people went through its turnstiles.

One person attracted to Chicago by the Fair was my maternal grandmother, Winnie Strickland Simms.

Grandma arrived by train from Birmingham, Alabama, on May 30, 1933, two days after the fair opened its doors. For Grandma's announced four-week visit, she brought with her two large trunks, three tightly-packed carpet bag suitcases, three Bibles, and a three-volume set of "Patriarchs and Prophets," a five-volume set of "The Greatest Controversy," a three-volume set of "The Desire of Ages," four "Christ in Song" books, and my Aunt Della's thirteen-year old-son, Joseph Strickland. Grandma was a vociferous believer in the Seventh Day Adventist faith.

I was 12 that year and I couldn't take my eyes off Grandma and all that baggage. When I raised my eyes to her face they were caught by a cold school-teacher-like stare. She reached out and gave me a quick pat on the back, but her eyes kept staring into mine.

Grandma's voice was soft but stern; she seldom smiled. Prior to her marriage to Grandpa, she was a rural schoolteacher. My mother was convinced that Grandma was smarter and better educated than any of her six daughters, although she was born a slave in 1860 on a Georgia plantation owned by a white Seventh Day Adventist family.

Adventistism wrapped itself around Grandma early in her life and she, in turn, brought that truth to her children and grandchildren with such conviction and force that almost all of my relatives are practicing Seventh Day Adventists.

I will never forget the commanding tone of Grandma's voice on that first Friday when she reminded my father, who was not an Adventist, that all cooking for Saturday's meals would be prepared on Friday, before sundown, because at sundown on Friday we opened the Sabbath, which meant much singing, prayer and scripture reading. Adventists kept the Sabbath on Saturday instead of Sunday.

That first Friday evening, Grandma handed me one of her "Christ in Song" books and said, "Junior! I want you to open the Sabbath by playing and singing 'Don't Forget the Sabbath' on page 653."

I sheepishly began to sing out of key in a high-pitched voice: "Don't forget the Sabbath the Lord our God hath blessed, of all the week the brightest, of all the week the best; it brings repose from labor, it tells of Joy devine, its beams of light descending, with heavenly beauty shine. Welcome, welcome, ever welcome, blessed Sabbath day."

My grandmother and the group joined me in singing the second and third verses. Grandma seemed pleased with both my piano playing and singing and requested in a cheerful voice that I play and sing the following hymns: "Another Six Days Work is Done," "Blessed Be the Tie That Binds," and "Rock of Ages, Cleft for Me." I had never tried to perform church songs before, or any song without practice, but I was pleased to find myself playing them easily.

That particular Friday marked the beginning of my 106-week engagement as the family musical director for opening and closing the Sabbath. The closing of the Sabbath ritual took place on Saturday afternoon at home, after church, and commenced just before sundown. Grandma used the sunset table published in the "Morning Watch" to determine the exact time the sun would go down.

Grandma was so bent on our being prepared for the second coming of the Lord that she kept my cousin, Joseph Strickland, and me in some form of religious services five days a week. Mondays, we had prayer meetings at home; Wednesday evenings, we would go to prayer meetings at church; Friday evenings, we held an opening of the Sabbath Ritual. We attended both Sabbath School and church on Saturday; and on Saturday evenings we held a closing of the Sabbath service; and then there was a Sunday evening service, which we always attended. Sunday evening at the Shiloh Seventh Day Adventist Church (which was located on the northeast corner of 46th Street and St. Lawrence Avenue and is currently located at 7000 South Michigan Avenue) was the closest thing to a movie I would experience for the next two years, since we often had as guest speaker a traveling Elder of the Church. Some were great orators. Often they would present slide shows. Those evenings offered entertainment plus news about the outside world.

Also forbidden was the adornment of one's body with cosmetics and worldly dress styles. Grandma was so modest in her clothing selections that she literally followed the dictates of Disciple Timothy: "In like manner also, that women adorn themselves in modest apparel, with shamefacedness and sobriety; not with braided hair, or gold, or pearls, or costly array." (Tim. 2:9) Grandma was careful not to wear any powder or jewelry and restricted the color of her dress and outer coats to two colors, black and blue.

Adventistism not only dictates the type of dress you wear, but it also restricts the food that dresses the lining of your stomach. (A recent medical survey indicated that Adventists as a group enjoy the best health and the longest life span as a result of their dietary habits.) As a true believer of the Adventist faith, Grandma never prepared or ate pork or fish with shells. The only fish that we ate had fins and scales in keeping with the 11th chapter of Leviticus in the Bible.

"And the Lord spake unto Moses and to Aaron, saying unto them.(Lev. 11:1)

"Speak unto the children of Israel, saying these are the beast which ye shall eat among all the beasts that are on the earth. (Lev. 11:2)

"Whatsoever parteth the hoof, and is clovenfooted, and cheweth the cud, among the beast, that shall ye eat. (Lev. 11:3)

"And the swine, though he divide the hoof, and be clovenfooted, yet he cheweth not the cud; he is unclean to you.(Lev. ll:7)

"Of their flesh shall ye not eat, and their carcass shall ye not touch; they are unclean to you. (Lev. 11:8)

"These shall ye eat of all that are in the waters: Whatsoever hath fins and scales in the waters, in the seas, and in the rivers, them shall ye eat. (Lev. 11:9)

"Whatsoever hath no fins nor scales in the waters, that shall be in the waters, that shall be an abomination unto you." (Lev. 11:12)

To add a variety to our daily diet, Grandma would prepare complete vegetarian meals at least three days a week. Her recipes were famous among friends and family. I enjoyed vegetarian meals (such as the recipes which are included at the end of this chapter), but before we could get to the food, we had to show her clean hands, a clean face and orderly clothes. Then we had to quote a different Bible verse and its biblical source at every meal for thirty consecutive days. My love for Grandma's food and after-dinner stories inspired me to memorize one hundred and eighty verses within a sixty-day period.

Grandma would always tell one or two stories about the olden days after dinner. One evening she talked about the eating, cooking and working habits of the slaves on the plantation where she was born. Her slavemaster, being a Seventh Day Adventist, made them follow the eating doctrine of the Seventh Day Adventist Church and keep the Sabbath on Saturday. The slaves on the next cotton farm kept Sunday and ate swine.

"Grandma, why did those slaves eat pigs?" Cousin Joe asked.

Grandma replied, "Slaves did not really eat the pig, but they ate the hog leftovers, such as the jowls, or chitterlings and the fat of the back. The slavemasters' primary use for chitterlings, the small intestines of the pig, was to obtain the intestinal grease by boiling the intestines, to be used for soapmaking. The rubbery remains of the gut were the leftovers. They were given to the slaves and they creatively turned them into a delicacy."

"Grandma, what's the good part of the pig?"

"There is no good part. However, the slavemaster ate the muscle cuts of the pig, such as pork chops and pork roast. The price that many of the slavemasters paid for eating low on the hog was a painful and crippling leg and arm disease known as trichinosis. You get trichinosis from eating half-cooked pork. Chitterlings were boiled to a rubbery substance before the slave received them, so few field slaves suffered the disease. Lots of house slaves were afflicted with trichinosis because they ate in the kitchen of their masters the same meals their masters were eating in the dining room."

"What kind of bread did the slaves eat?" Cousin Lucille asked. "Did they eat biscuits?"

Grandma smiled and said, "White folks didn't eat many biscuits because white flour was scarce. The slaves ate hoecake, a corn meal mixed with water and baked on the blade of a field hand's hoe over an open fire. Remember, children, most slaves didn't have pots and pans."

"Grandma, did you ever see a slavemaster beat a field hand for not working?" Junior asked.

"It's past your bedtime," Grandma said. "Good night and don't forget to say your prayers."

We didn't.

Travis (on the left) with his first cousin Joseph Strickland in 1933.

Mock Chicken on Toast

1 c. diced chicken
  style soybean meat
  alternative
1 c. water
1 c green peas
1 medium chopped
  onion
2 green onions,
  chopped
2 T. margarine

1/2 cup tomatoes,
  diced
1/4 t. paprika
1/3 c. chopped
  celery
1 1/2 c. eva-
  porated milk
1 t. seasoning
  salt
1 c. water
1/2 c. grated
  cheese

Soak chicken-style soybean preparation in one cup water for two hours, then drain. Saute onion and celery in margarine; add drained chicken-style soybean meat substitute. Let cook for 10 minutes. Add peas, cornstarch, milk, water, cheese, and seasoning. Simmer for 20 minutes. Serve over toast and top with tomatoes. Yield: 4 servings.

Vegetarian Meat Loaf

4 c. VegeBurger
  (a meat substi-
  tute)
2 eggs
2 t. cornstarch
1 large onion,
  chopped
1/3 c. milk
1/4 c. chopped
  bell pepper

2 cloves garlic
1 T. oil
1 t. sage
1 t. seasoning
  salt

Mix in a bowl all the ingredients; put into a loaf pan and bake for 1 1/2 hours at 300°.

Vegetarian Roast

1 1/2 cans (medium-sized)
  VegeBurger
1 c. pecans
1/2 green pepper
3 medium sized onions
3 or 4 pods garlic
1/2 t. soy sauce
1/4 c. thyme
1 t. leaf sage

1 t. Bakon Yeast
1 egg, slightly
  beaten
1 t. salt
3/4 c. Accent
3 bay leaves
2 t. margarine
1 t. Vegex

Grind first five ingredients through the food chopper twice, saving the liquid that may come from chopper. Add remaining ingredients and mix thoroughly. Put in oiled loaf pan, placing three bay leaves across the top. To the liquid add enough water to make 1 cup. Add 2 tablespoons margarine and 1 teaspoon Vegex. Heat liquid. Pour heated liquid over loaf and bake 1 1/2 hours at 325°F. Serve warm or cold, sliced.

The following recipes were referred to in this chapter:

Mock Chicken A La King
Over Hominy Spoon Bread

1/4 cup margarine	1 4-oz. can mushroom
3 1/2 T. flour	pieces
1 1/2 cups milk	1/2 cup ripe olives,
1/2 t. salt	minced
1 t. paprika	Dash of Accent
1/4 cup slivered	Leftover Choplets,
pimentos	Stakelets, or Vete-
	meat pieces

Melt margarine in saucepan. Stir in flour, mixing smooth. Add milk gradually, stirring constantly until thickened. Add salt, paprika, pimentos, mushroom pieces, olives, Accent, and leftover protein food. Heat well. (Accent is listed because it is at least close to Grandma's collection of seasonings.)

Hominy Spoon Bread

1 1-lb can hominy	1 cup milk
1/4 cup margarine	1 t. salt
3/4 cup hominy	1 T. sugar
liquor	1 cup evapor-
2 eggs, beaten	ated milk

Drain hominy. Add enough undiluted evaporated milk to make 1 cup. Into a saucepan put hominy, milk mixture, salt and sugar. Heat, but do not boil. Add margarine, stirring until melted. Cool slightly. Combine well-beaten eggs and the one cup of milk. Add hominy mixture. Mix well and pour into well-greased baking dish. Bake in oven (300° F.) 1 hour. Top should be nicely browned. Over each portion serve Mock Chicken a la King.

Wham and Rice Steaks

2 cups cooked rice	3 eggs
1/3 cup chopped	1 t. vegetarian
celery	beef-style seasoning
2 T. bell pepper	2 T. soy sauce
1/2 cup green onions	2 T. flour
2 cloves garlic	
1 cup chopped Wham	

Mix in a bowl the cooked rice, chopped onions, celery, bell pepper, garlic, Wham, eggs, seasoning, soy sauce, and flour. Fry in skillet, using two tablespoons of oil. Makes 12 large steaks.

This recipe is simple to prepare and the eggs are a good source of protein. Some may wonder what Wham is. This is a product made from Soybeans.

Chapter 8

CHANGING TIDES: BOYHOOD TO MANHOOD

I was awakened before daybreak on May 4, 1935, by my mother's shrieking: "Junior! Junior! Your father' is sick. We have to rush him to the Cook County Hospital."

The fear in my mother's voice frightened me almost as much as my concern about the seriousness of my father's illness. I knew that Dad would only go to the County Hospital as a last resort because he had always talked about the discrimination and graft demanded by the white nurses and interns and the fatal "black bottle" for those who did not cooperate.

Dad looked awful. He was sitting in a bent position on the side of the bed with both hands hugging his stomach tightly. He looked at us but he couldn't answer our desperate questions. His lips looked bloodless and his skin was ashen. Though the house was cool, he sweated profusely.

The fifteen minutes Mama and Grandma spent dressing Dad and walking him down the stairs seemed like hours. As we approached the hospital, Dad uttered his only audible sound other than those painful groans. "Boy, you are the man of the house now, and you have got to take care of your mother," he said in a weak voice.

My mother started crying quietly after Dad disappeared behind the swinging doors with the men in white.

"Mama, you know Daddy is going to be all right," I said, trying to sound like I believed it. She would nod her head up and down in a positive motion and start crying again. I put my arm around my mother's shoulders.

"You know Daddy would be ashamed to see us crying."

The words brought a quiet smile to both our faces. We were still smiling when the nurse informed us that the doctor would be down. Within fifteen minutes the doctor greeted us with a hand shake and told us my father had a ruptured appendix "and could not have lasted another hour."

During the three months he was at home recuperating, the Travis household endured some hard times. During the early 1930's there were no job benefits, hospital insurance programs, social security or unemployment compensation. (Congress passed the Social Security Act in August, 1935.) I tried to fill the void in the family income by taking two newspaper routes. I delivered the morning papers between 5 and 7 a.m. before going to school and the evening papers between 4 and 6 p.m. after school. My $7 per week contribution helped, but it was not enough to feed Dad, Mama, Grandma, Cousin Joe and myself. The landlord permitted us to stay with the understanding that we would pay the back rent once my father was able to return to work.

Grandma worked at being an innovative cook. She stretched the budget down to serving the pot liquor from the greens with corn bread as a total meal, putting us on a greens, beans and hot-water corn bread diet. For four months we had lima beans, cow peas, pinto beans or black-eyed peas with corn bread for breakfast, lunch and dinner; and then she would switch to string beans, turnip tops and cabbage. On rare occasions she prepared boiled turnip greens and we would have Alaga syrup (acronym for Alabama and Georgia) and corn bread for dessert. Grandma was always combining grain (corn bread) and legumes (cow peas, black-eyed peas, etc.) to provide protein for the family.

Dad returned to work in August, 1935. Shortly after that, Grandma and Cousin Joe decided to leave Chicago for McRoberts, Kentucky, to stay with Aunt Della, who was Joe's mother and Grandma's youngest daughter. I was both sorry and glad to see Grandma leave. I was glad because I knew I wouldn't be involved in church activities five days a week anymore. As a matter of fact, I became a church drop-out for the next fifteen years. I was sorry to see her leave because I would miss her presence and good advice. She was very philosophical, and she had a quotation for every problem and occasion. She used to say to me when I suggested that we eat a fourth meal:

"To bed, to bed said Sleepy Head,
wait awhile said Slow,
put on the pot said Greedy-Gut,
let's eat before we go."

After hearing that quotation, I usually went to sleep without a snack. Grandmother was also a stickler about punctuality. She would always say: "Time and tide waits for no man."

Only six months of time and tide had passed before a Western Union man delivered a midnight telegram to our apartment which read: "Mother passed this afternoon . . . come at once." My mother and her sister, Willie, left by train the next afternoon and took my cousin, Frank, and me along. We caught the train at the 12th Street Station for Cincinnati, Ohio, which was the transfer point for trains going into Kentucky. It was my first journey to the South.

It was in the beautiful Cincinnati train station that Mr. Jim Crow kicked me into my assigned corner by refusing to sell me a hot dog at the soda fountain. The next blow occurred when we were herded into a Jim Crow coach, situated - that's right - next to the train's engine. The coach filled quickly, black passengers sitting at one end and baggage at the other. It also sheltered layers of coal dust, soot and a foul-mouthed conductor.

Our Cincinnati-to-Lexington, Kentucky, train stopped at every town and continued to pack Blacks into the Jim Crow car like captives packed into a slave ship in the days of the "middle passage" from Africa. Women, cradling their babies, stood while the conductor occupied four seats for his "office." My mother had Frank and me give up our seats for two of these women, so I rode standing halfway across Kentucky. At Lexington, late at night, we were to catch the double-engine mountain train, which would take us to McRoberts, a mining town.

When we got off at Lexington, we were directed to the rear of the train station where the "For colored only" facilities were located. The ticket and information window there was only manned after the white folks had been served on the other side of the ticket office. The "colored" people's waiting room was dimly lit and much dirtier than the white facility, which was bright, cheerful and clean. The contrast reminded Blacks of their inferior status. It worked.

At daybreak, we saw the train that would take us into McRoberts coming upgrade. The quality of the accommodations on this train "for colored" people was consistent - - our coach was dirty with coal dust and soot, and the conductor's language was just as bad as on the other train.

"McRoberts! McRoberts! McRoberts! The end of the line."

I looked up. McRoberts, sandwiched in a valley between two ugly coal mountains, seemed like the end of my world.

Uncle Ben met us at the train depot wearing his Sunday suit and a sheepish grin.

"Glad you all could come," he greeted us in his Southern drawl.

Uncle Ben's smile was the brightest thing we would see in the mountainous bumpy three-mile ride we took in his Model T Ford from the train station to his home. Uncle Ben was a coffee-colored man with a kind, round face.

The white folks we saw sitting and standing along the road as we drove to the black section of McRoberts stared at us through bloodshot eyes. The leers on their pale, scrawny faces showed that they recognized us as strangers because of our "big city clothes."

Almost every man we saw along the roadway was dressed in faded blue denim, loose-fitting overalls and a bright blue or red bandanna around his neck.

The houses and shacks along the road were painted in a sad rainbow of shades, with the dominating colors being red and white - - until we reached the black people's section, where the houses were unpainted and the wood was rotted. Clusters of black children were playing in front of the shacks and in the roadside gutters. Old black women, wearing red bandannas, watched over the noisy children as they sat in their rocking chairs on the sagging front porches.

"That's the house where Della lives," Uncle Ben said finally, pulling to a stop.

Aunt Della, who had been standing on the porch with some other people I did not recognize, started running down the hill, grinning and crying with her arms outstretched to hug the first one of us she reached. Aunt Della had added at least sixty pounds and a substantial stomach to her frame since her last visit to Chicago five years earlier. Mother and Aunt Willie ran up the hill to meet her. The collision point found three sisters hugging, kissing and crying, joyful at seeing each other, yet saddened by the loss of their mother. Their three-way conversation sounded like a choral counterpoint, with the main theme being a list of names of all the relatives who had arrived for Grandma's funeral.

Travis' maternal grandmother, Winnie Strickland Sims (front row, left) and her daughters pose for this 1914 photo taken in Birmingham, Alabama. With Mrs. Sims are (front row, right) Claudie Crawford, and (back row, left-right) Willie Austin, Mittie (Travis' mother), and Della Story.

When we reached the front porch, I realized the people I hadn't recognized from the road were aunts, uncles and cousins from various parts of the country. After enjoying a moment of pride for having so many relatives, I began to worry about where we were all going to eat and sleep.

Initially, we were only to stay two nights, but there was a spinal meningitis epidemic in McRoberts that resulted in canceling the funeral for five days. On the fifth day we were permitted to have a graveside service for Grandma, because indoor public gatherings were prohibited for the duration of the epidemic.

I had not really accepted the finality of Grandma's death until we stepped out of the funeral cars at the gate of the graveyard. There we began a slow walk up a winding path on a steep and lonely Kentucky hill, behind the pallbearers carrying a pine box. My mind was churning with thoughts about Grandma. Those thoughts made my throat dry, but I could not cry.

Grandma's body was lowered into a dark six-foot hole on the hillside of a Kentucky coal mine, but she will never know how dark it was because her eyes were forever closed.

Uncle Frank, Uncle Russell, Uncle Elliott and Uncle Ben had toiled in the mine holes of Kentucky, Alabama, Illinois and Pennsylvania all of their working lives. They were lowered by cage into the deep dark holes daily. Their eyes were open, but they did not know how dark it was because the nature of their work had blinded them mentally and dwarfed them physically. I reflected on this as I talked with them during that visit.

Four of my mother's five sisters married Alabama coal miners who tried to escape. Each uncle tried to retrace his liberation route nightly for the rest of us during Grandma's five-day wake.

The stories would always begin in the early evening, after the women had cleared the kitchen. My uncles would pull their chairs around the woodburning cooking stove and place large tin cans to the right of their chairs to relieve their mouths of tobacco juice and clear their lungs of the coal-colored spit that always followed their frequent coughs. Every night, as the old iron stove turned fire red, their stories became more intense.

Uncle Elliott was considered the firebrand of the group. Uncle Russell always referred to him as the family Indian because of his reddish complexion and coal-black curly hair. Uncle Elliott's temper seemed to rise with the heat in the old iron stove.

"What took place between you and your foreman in the Alabama Edgewater coal mine that caused you to leave town so hurriedly?" Uncle Russell asked him one evening.

"Nigger! You know what happened!" Uncle Elliott said.

Uncle Russell flinched and stared at Elliott. "All I know is that three carloads of white folks came to my house looking for you. They'd been drinking, and some of them were carrying guns. When they were leaving, I heard one of them say, 'Let's check the freight yard for that coon' "

Uncle Elliott grinned. "The bastards were on the right trail, but they were an hour late. I left the mine running after I hit that cracker on the left side of his head with a methane detector." They explained that a detector was a small stainless steel box half the size of a book, used to test the mine air for gases. "I didn't even stop at the bathhouse to change clothes. I did a one-mile dash in those steel-toed regulation shoes all the way to the freight yard and caught the first thing smoking." He stopped to smile at the memory. "The direction the train was going was not as important as putting the maximum amount of space between me and Edgewater, Alabama," he said.

"I still don't understand why you would start trouble with white folks in the mine," Russell said softly.

"You don't understand!" Uncle Elliott said. "The problem didn't start in the mine but in my mind, when I was born a black male in Alabama."

I sat up at that. The table reminded me of all these discussions my father and his brothers used to have around our dining room table. There was a lot to be learned when the men got to talking like this.

"I resented, as a kid, having to knock on the back steps of a cracker's house to get permission to step up to the back door to beg for a ten cents grass-cutting job," Elliott went on. "My stomach and chest sheltered a silent rage when my young wife had to work in the company-owned shacks of those cracker miners for $3 per week, plus lunch. She cleaned the house, washed and ironed the clothes, nursed their kids on her left breast and ours on the right breast, wiped their red snotty noses and cleaned their dirty chalk-white behinds."

"But nigger mammies have always done those things," Russell said mildly.

"Damn it, Russell! That does not mean that they did not resent having to do them," Uncle Elliott said. "That 'kick me in the ass because I like it' mentality has kept most Blacks in a crap-game kneeling position all of their lives!"

"I still don't think that we should do anything that is going to make white folks mad," Uncle Russell said in a reasonable tone. He was sitting straight in his chair, staring down at his hands with great concentration, as if making a great effort to understand Elliott's rebelliousness.

"I wouldn't have hit that honky if he hadn't threatened to beat my black ass. He wanted me to apologize for implying that he was lying about my work performance."

Uncle Russell looked up from his hands and straight into Uncle Elliott's eyes. After a moment he said, "Always remember that although the man cannot write, he is boss because he is white."

(In many instances, the white mine foreman could not read or write; hence, it was commonplace to see a black laborer with a seventh or eighth grade education assisting his white boss by making out daily reports which required both math and writing skills. In many sections of Northern West Virginia, Ohio, and Western Pennsylvania, black miners held such local offices in the United Mine Workers Union as president and secretary, even though they were outnumbered by Eastern Europeans. It was their proficiency in speaking and writing English that won them the positions.

(Black appointments to the mine committee can also be traced to the language factor. The United Mine Workers contract said all committeemen shall be American citizens, or miners who have made application for citizenship, and are capable of handling the English language comfortably. According to Professor Herbert R. Northrup of the Wharton School of Finance and Commerce, no Black was elected to union vice presidency in Alabama until 1944.)

Uncle Elliott turned to Uncle Frank. "You explain it to him," he said. "You left your kneeling position in the Edgewater mine because you had trouble with your boss, didn't you?" The Edgewater mine, they told me, had a four-foot ceiling, which meant that the miners worked on their knees, using pieces of worn out auto tires as knee pads, as they drilled, picked, and cleaned the rock from the coal before loading it by hand for eight hours daily. The only lights in the work area were the bike-sized lamps on their hats.

"Yes. We moved to West Virginia to work in a new coal mine, but it wasn't because of any racial friction," Uncle Frank said. "We weren't there long before I was recruited to break a strike in a little coal town called Edenborn, near Uniontown, Pennsylvania. The Pennsy mines were the first I ever worked where I didn't have to do any crawl mining. The mines' ceilings there are all six feet or better." Uncle Frank stopped and coughed a long, racking cough. Then he spit painfully into the cuspidor at his elbow. The others turned their eyes away, aware that his cough was getting serious. Uncle Frank was displaying early symptoms of the totally disabling black lung disease, and all were aware of it.

(Several studies in the mid-1930's showed Blacks overrepresented in mine jobs that were both dangerous and unhealthy and underrepresented in the more desirable outside jobs and indirect labor jobs connected with the mines. Of the 2,411 Blacks studied by James T. Lang in his "Negro Miners in West Virginia", only eleven were in positions which, even by the most liberal stretching of the term, could be called positions of authority.

(In a rare instance, a black mine laborer would be promoted to motorman on a mantrip train, used to carry men into the mines and also to carry the coal out of the mines. His brakeman or triprider would always be a Black. Under no circumstances would you find a black motorman and a white brakeman, although the reverse was frequently true.)

Uncle Frank gasped for breath. "My chest feels a bit tight and sore from that black phlegm I just coughed up. Excuse me. I'm going out on the front porch for some air." The others stared after him in silence.

Uncle Elliott turned to Uncle Ben. "Would you let your children follow you into the mines, the way you followed your father?"

Uncle Ben coughed and drank a water glass half full of whiskey in one gulp to clear the old coal dust from his lungs and throat. "Hell, no! I wouldn't put my children in a cage to go down 500 feet under the ground to take the punishment and abuse I took from those redneck crackers they brought in from Mississippi, Alabama and Georgia to supervise the McRobert Mine operation. Those mines were a grave for the living. We only differed from the dead in that we were regurgitated back to the earth's surface every afternoon, only to be reswallowed into its bowels again the next morning."

"So why have you stayed in the mines for twenty years?" Uncle Elliott asked.

"I'm trapped," Uncle Ben answered. "What else can a black man do here?"

Uncle Elliott's laugh was hard. "Nigger! You aren't trapped, you're enslaved. You're enslaved to the company landlord for your shack. You're enslaved to the company store for your food. You're enslaved to the company hospital for your medical care. You're enslaved to the company clothing store for your wife's underwear and your babies' shoes. The corporate master owns you the same as he owns the town you live in, the shack you sleep in, the stores that you buy in, the hospital that you die in, and the graveyard that you'll be buried in."

Uncle Elliott laughed again and looked up as Uncle Frank came back into the room.

"I remember one day in the Edgewater mines when the boss wanted me to be careful and not let a loose rock fall on the mule," Elliott said, his humorous eyes on Frank. "I said 'Yes, sah! But what about me?' He said 'I can always hire another nigger, but I would have to buy another mule.' "

Uncle Frank echoed Elliott's grin. "That philosophy is a hangover from the ante bellum South when the mine operators and the railroad builders found it more economical to hire slaves by the day or week from the local plantation owners rather than to own them."

At that point my mother called me into the adjoining room and said:

"Your father is going to disown us if we don't catch that 6:30 train back to Chicago."

I had a lot to think about as our train made its way to the north again.

Black coal miners spraying a finely powdered rock dust to settle the highly explosive coal dust. Only a small amount of coal dust in the air was sufficient to cause an explosion if set off by a spark or a flame.

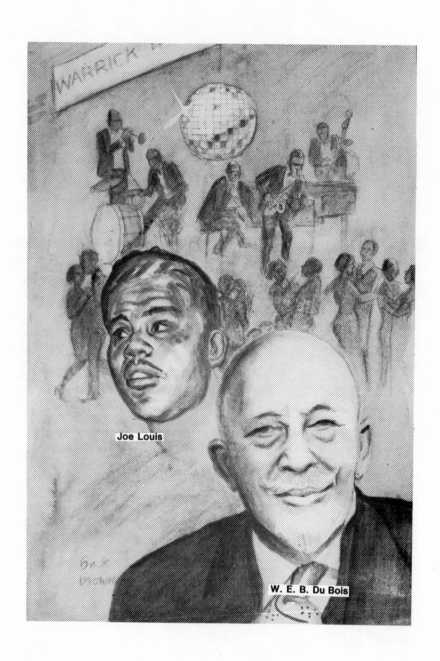

WARRICK

Joe Louis

W. E. B. Du Bois

Chapter 9

DU SABLE HIGH,
CLASS OF '39

There were four of us in Don's Pool Hall on the South Side one Monday morning - Gene Vine, Slim Rose, Eddie Davis and me. We had cut Spanish class to listen to records on the penny vendor: each was to pay for and play five records at a penny a tune.

It was my turn to choose, and I picked Earl Hines' "Rosetta."

Gene's ambition was to be a professional dancer, and he had the agility and style of a natural born tap dancer. All he lacked was the kind of discipline that would have made him practice three or four hours a day. Gene started tapping in rhythm with the song, and the rest of us started clapping to the off beat. Gene kept on tapping to our hand beat after the record was finished, and everybody in the pool hall stopped to watch.

"Man, that was groovy and solid," I said, when he ended his routine. "You ought to try out for the Regal Theatre Amateur Nite or Major Edward Bowes' Radio Amateur Hour."

"You're better than a lot of professional tap dancers," Eddie said.

"Man, I'm not that good," Gene said.

"Come on," I said. "You could be the next Bill 'Bojangles' Robinson if you wanted to."

Gene looked at me out of his sleepy eyes. "Bojangles, ha," he said. He went to the other side of the pool hall and sat down.

The rest of us stood up and stretched luxuriously. It didn't worry us that we were cutting class. We did that a lot. Plenty of times we'd take most of the day off, especially if Gene's mother, a day worker who earned two dollars a day plus fourteen cents streetcar fare, was working.

On those days we'd go over to Gene's apartment and goof off. I would play the piano, and Gene would tap.

We were freshmen at the new Wendell Phillips High School on South Wabash. It was the first new high school to be built in an all-black community in the history of the city, but that didn't impress us. Even at its opening, when I came into the brand new building to find decorators still putting up light green paint in the corridors, the school was jammed. It had been planned to accommodate 2,500 students, but when I started in February, 1935, I was one of 1,300 freshmen in a total enrollment of 3,548 students—all Blacks except for one female white student.

The extraordinarily large enrollment at the new school had been caused by an early morning fire at the old Wendell Phillips High School on East Pershing in January. School authorities closed down the old facility and transferred the entire staff, faculty, records, trophies, students and tradition into a new high school that had no books or supplies. The new three million dollar facility hadn't been scheduled to open until September, 1935. (The name was changed to Jean Baptiste Pointe-Du-Sable 1936.)

The absence of books and supplies gave me the excuse I wanted to hang out at Nick and Angel's Hamburger Grill and school supply store at 4859 South State Street. That's where I took up with Gene and Slim and Eddie. My new friends weren't troublemakers. They just shared with me a general indifference to school.

Slim Rose's highest ambition, for example, was to be able to afford twenty-two cents a day for two packs of Camel cigarettes so he wouldn't have to bum drags or go searching for long butts along the street gutters. He also wanted to have ten cents to get into the Warwick Hall on East 47th Street every Sunday afternoon to do the "jelly," a slow drag with a stomach roll and bear hug, to the music of Nat Cole (the "King" was added six years later) and his Twelve Royal Dukes or Tony Fambro and his Jungle Rhythm Orchestra. The "jelly" was performed best to the slow beat of Duke Ellington's "Mood Indigo," "Solitude," or Hoagy Carmichael's immortal "Stardust."

It was at DuSable that I made up my mind I was going to be a professional musician. And DuSable offered me some opportunities to learn, though they didn't all have to do with classes. Nat Cole, for instance, was a classmate—he was enrolled in the Spanish class we were all cutting until he signed a contract with promoter Malcolm B. Smith to take his first band on the road in March, 1935. I did, however, take Dr. Mildred Bryant Jones' harmony classes seriously. They introduced me to counterpoint and music composition.

Gene was still sitting down, recovering from his exertions, when Slim said, "Clapping my hands and watching you dance has made me hungry. Let's go down to Nick and Angel's and get two sou (nickel) hamburgers with chili sauce and split them four ways."

"I got a deece (dime) for a malted milk shake with four straws," I said.

The others agreed and we headed for the pool hall exit.

Looking west across State Street from Don's front door, we could see the rear of the two-story frame house on 50th and Dearborn where three black men were killed in the street by some white Chicago policemen in 1931 while they were trying to put a 71-year-old woman's furniture back into the apartment from which she had been evicted for being three months behind in her rent.

We strolled the two blocks from 51st Street to Nick and Angel's. The west side of State Street was taken up by two-story brick structures that lacked any socially redeemable character, intermixed with a few frame buildings that looked like they had been nailed together by a bored carpenter lacking plans. The block also had five-story brick walkups with faces that had been masked with wrought iron fire escapes to provide a quick exit from the crowded structures.

Down in the 4900 block on the west side of State, there were eighteen two-story frame structures built before 1900. They were in varying stages of deterioration. Some stood erect, proudly painted in an effort to retain the appearance of their lost youth; others had begun to lean, unmasking their advanced stages of deterioration.

Scattered in between the frame buildings were six vacant lots, weed and rubble-filled gaps once occupied by buildings whose owners had either ceased to care for them or had simply lacked the funds to keep them nice neighbors. The ground floors of the other buildings routinely housed small school supply and candy stores, with the exception of Sam's Grocery and Meat Market at 4960 South State Street and a black-owned eat shop called the D & C Lunchroom at 4904 South State.

As we walked along, Gene and Slim fell into a violent argument about who had the lightest complexion. Eddie and I tried to stay out of it, keeping our eyes on the sidewalk as we walked along. It seemed a silly argument to me, since we all knew the black female slaves' involuntary contact with both white and red men had given Blacks a million variations in skin color. Some very dark Blacks have a reddish hue to their complexion, while others, equally dark, have slight tone mixtures that range from a blue tinge to a brown cast. You might have said Gene was light black and Slim was medium black. But what did it matter? I kept thinking. And do to this day

They were still going on about it when we got to Nick and Angel's. But the place was jammed with students and drop-outs eating hamburgers and hot dogs, drinking pop and smoking cigarettes, so we crossed the street to the D & C Lunchroom, where they specialized in hot tamales and chili.

While the owners, Frank Davis and Samuel Collins, were getting food for us, we continued the discussion about skin color. It had all started the previous day, when we had gone to see the movie "Imitation of Life," starring Fredi Washington, Louise Beavers, and Claudette Colbert at the Metropolitan Theater at 46th and South Parkway. Fredi Washington was a fair-skinned, blue-eyed black woman who played the role of a young black woman named Peola, who wanted to pass for a White. The co-star, Louise Beavers, was both fat and dark-skinned. Her character was Aunt Delilah, the mother who was rejected by her light-skinned daughter.

White folks found the picture both sensational and comforting, because it ended with the implication that any Black who tried to pass for a White would ultimately be conscience-stricken. The picture was also a box office success in the black community because it was the first time that the color caste system among Blacks had been examined in a movie.

Slim and Gene were rehashing the color caste system, not because either of them would ever be able to pass for white, but because they felt that a light-complexioned Black might have some cultural and economic advantage over a dark-complexioned Black. The argument drew the attention of the owners of the shop. Both men were college graduates. Davis had finished Morehouse College in Atlanta, Georgia. He was light-skinned, with straight black hair. Collins was a coffee-and-cream color and had wooly, dark red hair. He had a liberal arts degree from Howard University in Washington, D.C.

"Light-complexioned Blacks have had economic advantages dating back to the earliest days of slavery," Davis said. "Particularly if they have been identified and accepted by the slave master as his offspring in some surreptitious manner."

"Yeah, but a very dark child, the color of Gene or Slim, wouldn't get such recognition even if the master slept with his mother every night," Collins said. "So I think it's silly for you two guys to be squabbling over the smell of the pork chop, as opposed to the pork chop itself."

He went on with a laugh. "That kind of argument is about as productive as bleaching cream. Have you ever thought about the thousands of black women in Chicago who go to bed every night after applying Palmer's Skin Whitener to their faces only to check the mirror the next morning and find out they're as black as they were the night before?"

We laughed with him.

"Those who subscribe to the teachings of Marcus Garvey don't have to keep looking for the elusive emulsified escape that is offered in those cans," Collins said.

"And what were Garvey's teachings on skin color?" Slim asked.

"Garvey did not believe we should make a distinction among ourselves based on a color caste system," Collins told him gravely. "He believed that such a system was evil and worked a great harm to our racial solidarity. He accused one of our major civil rights groups of advocating advancement just for those who were as near to white as possible. He was opposed to anything that resembled a 'blue-vein' aristocracy among Blacks, or what we might call from that movie you boys are discussing a 'Peola' class system."

"What's that about blue veins?" Eddie said.

"There are clubs and churches in Chicago that will not accept as members any black person, no matter what his accomplishments, unless he or she is light enough so you can see the blueness of their veins through their skin."

"Yes," Frank Davis added. "Let me show you a picture from the society section of last week's Chicago Defender. Do you see any dark or brown-skinned girls in that group?" We checked out the picture of young girl debutantes in long dresses. Every one of them had light skin and hair carefully arranged to imitate the loose curls white women were wearing then. "You can safely assume they have all established themselves as 'blue veins' or 'Peolas,'" Davis said.

"But Chicago's 'blue vein' society is really subtle when compared to the one in Washington, D.C.," Collins said. "The way it's flaunted there, in the public schools, private universities, hiring and promotional policies in private business, and in both municipal and federal government jobs is incomprehensible. Your civil service score may get you in the door, but you can forget about a substantial promotion unless you're the right shade of black. And the right shade of black is yellow.

"If you're white, you're all right; if you're yellow, you're mellow; if you're brown, stick around; but if you're black, get back," Collins said. "It's like the owner of the Morris Perfect Eat Shop at 410 East 47th Street, the heart of the 'Black Broadway' in the late '20's and still going strong. He once told me he is partial to real light-skinned girls with 'good' hair, because they make a good appearance and attract the big spenders to his place. That kind of philosophy is shared by a lot of people who hire secretaries, nurses, typists, receptionists. The utility companies have just begun to hire Negroes, and you can bet what kind of looks will get you the job."

"That ain't all," his partner said. "Those color-conscious bastards are perpetuating that propaganda through their children. If a kid wants to marry somebody who is not the right shade, he or she is usually rejected by the whole family. Occasionally a gross difference is acceptable if the prospect happens to be a black professional with both high status and big money. There might also be an exception of the prospective spouse has some other Caucasian feature: if not color, then hair, or if not hair, then maybe blue eyes will be an acceptable substitute."

We studied each others' faces while we munched the last of our food. Then Gene jumped up. "Man," he said, staring at his watch. "I've got to run home and mop the kitchen and make up my bed before my mother gets home."

Later on, I was to regret the hours I stole from school to spend with my friends in this fashion. But at the time I believed my destiny was to be a musician and that the education I was picking up outside of school was superior to anything available in the classroom.

In sharp contrast to my attitude was that of a well-dressed upperclassman I observed in the school. He always seemed to be rushing to some unknown destination, his eyes focused straight ahead. That was John H. Johnson, now president of Johnson Publishing Company, which produces Ebony, Jet, and Ebony, Jr. magazines. He is also president of Radio Station WJPC in Chicago and Fashion Fair Cosmetics.

In April, 1936, the Chicago Board of Education voted to change the name of Wendell Phillips High School to Jean Baptiste Pointe DuSable High School, after the black man who first settled on the land that would later be known as Chicago. The name had been chosen in a poll by the *Chicago Defender*. Second choice had been Alexander Pushkin, the Russian poet and author who was a descendant of a West African adventurer. John H. Johnson was the president of the first class to graduate after the name had been changed.

My own ambitions were taking other directions, though. In Captain Walter Dyett's band and orchestra in room 345, I was having a chance to listen to performances by such great piano artists as Nat Cole, Dorothy Donegan, Thomas Rigsby, Martha Davis, Rudy Martin and John Young.

Music as a profession offered glamour, travel and contacts. And it was a hell of a lot of fun. I can't think of any other business where you can have your cake and eat it too. The price for that is a very high mortality rate among young talented jazz musicians.

At age fifteen, my talents were hardly being sought after by established band leaders, so I decided to organize the best available musical talent in Chicago and start my own group. I learned years later that this was a very sound business principle. I found I had a good nose for sniffing out high-paying gigs, and enough personality—some called it cockiness—to persuade the owner or promoter to give me and my boys the job.

THE MODERN YOUNG MISSES

ANNIVERSARY DANCE

Thursday, July 21, 1938

10 p. m. to 2 a. m.

AT BACON'S CASINO

49th St. and Wabash Avenue

Jack Travis Orchestra

Admission   25 Cents

Semi-Formal

El Feliz Senoritas

request your presence at their

Third Annual Mistletoe Dance

December 26, 1939   *9 p. m. to 1 a. m*

at Bacon's Casino

49th and Wabash

Informal   *Service Fee 25c*

Music by Jack Travis and his Orchestra

featuring Savannah Strong

These announcements are representative of the types of tags worn by high school and junior college students during the 1930's to promote dances.

By early fall of 1935 my band was gigging at least three nights a week. That work record was very good when you consider that the country was in the midst of the Depression. Older and more talented artists were sitting on their hands, talking about the good old days of the 1920's. As a matter of fact, I was working so regularly that Harry W. Gray, the business agent for the Musicians Protective Union Local 208 of the American Federation of Musicians, would come on my jobs and threaten to pull the band off the stand because I was not a card-carrying union musician. In one instance, the band was actually pulled from the stage for playing in a union hall because there was a non-union musician in the group. That one person without a union card was me, the orchestra leader.

On Christmas night, 1935, Gray called me off the bandstand in a loud and crusty voice. The look on his face was both solemn and mean when he asked, "Young man, why are you causing me so many problems?"

"All I want to do, Mr. Gray, is play music," I replied.

"Why in the hell don't you join the union?"

"I tried," I said.

With a flash of anger in his eyes, Gray growled, "What the hell do you mean you tried?"

"Just that," I retorted. "Mr. Musco C. Buckner, the financial secretary and treasurer of the union, told me that I would not be eligible for membership until I had reached my 16th birthday."

"Gray's expression softened slightly, "When will you be 16?"

"Three months from today, on February 25th," I answered.

Gray smiled and said, "I will see you at the local at 3 p.m. on the 25th."

He made a note in his little black book, then turned quickly and walked out of the dance hall.

On my 16th birthday, I joined the union and became the youngest band leader in Local 208. The union card was my admission to adulthood; most of my music associates were five to twenty-five years my

The above photograph of a youthful "Jack" Travis was taken in 1938 at the request of William Samuels, an affiliate of the Associate Artist who was promoting Travis' orchestra for an extensive Midwest tour. Travis has offered the comment that this was the last picture taken of him with hair.

DuSable High School classmates of Travis included such personalities as Nat "King" Cole (top left); John H. Johnson (top right) as he appears today and a youthful rendering of the businessman in 1936; Dorothy Donegan (bottom left), the famous piano artist; Redd Foxx (Fred Sanford) (bottom center), the popular comedian squatting playing the wash tub, and Savannah Strong (bottom right), brilliant song stylist of the 1940's.

The Regal Theatre had a Louis XIV castle appearance and was the center along with the Savoy Ballroom for black entertainment in Chicago from 1927 through the early 1950's (the theatre was shamefully demolished in the late 1970's). Black entertainment attractions such as Duke Ellington, The Mills Brothers, Cab Calloway, The Ink Spots, and Jimmie Lunceford appeared regularly at the Regal. The author personally witnessed lines of people waiting to see these and other artists that sometimes stretched four abreast, from the box office at the middle of 47th Street and South Parkway (King Drive) for a block and a half to 47th Street and Vincennes. The Regal Theatre was an entertainment institution in the black community. Its absence has caused a void in that Blacks now travel 20 to 30 miles to see live entertainment.

senior. This accelerated social aging caused my mother some serious concerns, but my father let it be known that he thought I could handle myself. Time proved him right, because he never found it necessary to put any restrictions on the hours I came home. He understood the life of a musician since he had made several attempts himself at making music a career. My father's only requirement of me was that I call home and give my whereabouts anytime I thought I would have to be out past the time the gig would ordinarily require.

Dad would always say, "I don't want you to call home for my sake, but for your mother's sake. She has a tendency to worry about your late hours."

Late hours became morning and even daylight hours as musicians would congregate for "jam sessions" (an event where musicians from various bands would try to out-blow or out-solo each other) at a different club every morning after work. For example, I saw Duke Ellington, Earl Hines, Cassino Simpson and Art Tatum in a piano playing contest at the Annex Cafe, located at 2300 South State that lasted three and a half hours.

This kind of action was very common at the Three Deuces, located at 222 North State, particularly when Roy Eldridge (trumpet) with side men like Dave Young (tenor sax), Johnny Collins (guitar), Scoops Carry (alto sax), Zutty Singleton (drums), and Truck Parkham (bass) were on the stand. White musicians such as Benny Goodman, Tommy Dorsey, Paul Whiteman and Artie Shaw would pack the place with their side-men every night they were in town, seeking an opportunity to jam and learn what that old black magic called jazz was all about.

Plotnick's Arcadia at 4800 South Cottage Grove Avenue would have a breakfast dance and jam session every Tuesday morning from 4 a.m. until they poured the last person into a cab. The Mid-Nite Club at 3140 South Indiana held the same kind of session on Saturday morning. The Panama Cafe Nite Club at 207 East 58th put on four floor shows nightly, complete with a chorus line, and featured Eddie Coles' band with Nat King Cole at the piano. So did the Dreamland Cafe at 4700 South State and the Cafe Montclare at 2903 South State Street where they put on a red hot floor fhow, plus a special breakfast dance every Thursday morning.

The classy night spots on the South Side during that period included the Grand Terrace at 3955 South Parkway, where Earl Hines and his NBC Orchestra played seven nights a week for eight hours. The evening would start with a half-hour dance set followed by a fifteen minute intermission. The band would come back and play another short dance set and then begin playing the first part of the stage show, which was in three segments, each lasting one to one and a half hours.

The show would include a dozen beautifully costumed "high yellow" chorus girls who would make three to six garment changes per show. In addition, the show would contain top-flight dance teams such as the Nicholas Brothers and the Four Step Brothers, or singles like Bill "Bojangles" Robinson, along with torch and blues singers on a par with Ethel Waters or Lena Horne, plus comedians equivalent to Redd Foxx or Flip Wilson. (These types of productions have not been staged any place in the country, including Las Vegas, in the past thirty years.)

Dave's Cafe at 343 East Garfield and the old Club Delisa at 5512-16 South State featured the band of Albert Ammons (piano) and his

Rhythm Kings. (Ammons was the father of Gene Ammons, a tenor saxophone player, and Bishop Edsel Ammons, both former DuSable students.) Both Dave's and Delisa had above average entertainment that attracted a lot of white folks to the South Side, as did the Grand Terrace. This is only a small sampling of clubs on the South Side of Chicago in the 1930's.

All the clubs had one thing in common, and that was a Jim Crow seating policy in the heart of the ghetto. The best tables in the house were always reserved for Whites. It was a common sight to walk into any of the class South Side clubs and see white folks hogging the ringside seats while Blacks sat on the side and in the rear. If it serves as any consolation, Chicago was still one step ahead of New York's Cotton Club, which was located in black Harlem but did not admit any Blacks unless they were celebrities.

Many a morning, I would get home just in time to change from a tuxedo into school clothing. The fact that I finished high school after such early exposure to show business is attributed to my family indoctrinating me to the need for a high school diploma. (Unfortunately, we believed that a diploma, a degree and education were synonymous.)

Mrs. Mary Herrick, my civics teacher, would occasionally stop me in the corridor and ask, "What do you plan to make out of yourself, Dempsey?"

My reply was always the same, "A musician."

She would smile and say, "Don't you want to back your music up with another career choice in case you change your mind about music as a total lifestyle?"

The bell rang and I went to class without answering that question for Mrs. Herrick, or for myself. The next time we met in the hall, I remember telling Mrs. Herrick that I had the opportunity to meet the ex-heavyweight champion, Jack Johnson, at the new night club he had opened at 3831 South Michigan. She looked surprised, but did not comment.

Mrs. Herrick was one of the few teachers during the entire time I was in public school who actually showed an interest in my activities both inside and outside of the school building. For this reason, I have found it necessary to give her an oral report card on my activities at irregular intervals over a period that has now passed its 44th year.

Nineteen thirty-seven was my best year, financially, in the music business. In addition to a brand new 1937 Buick, it afforded me the kind of clothing I felt a young band leader needed. (The first car I owned was a 1934 Graham Page which was given to me in 1936 by my father.)

A Jewish boy from the West Side of Chicago—Benny Goodman— was directly responsible for my success in 1937 because he made black jazz legitimate by calling it swing and playing it before mass white audiences. Swing was nothing more than warmed-over 1920 New Orleans-Chicago style jazz as played by Louis Armstrong, King Oliver, Johnny Dodds, Erskine Tate, Earl Hines and other Blacks two decades earlier. Benny Goodman took jazz out of her "cat house" environment and put her in a white virginal lace gown and she was received in her country with wild enthusiasm. The *New York Times* solemnly suggested that the craze was getting out of hand, quoting a psychologist on the "dangerously hypnotic influence of swing, cunningly devised to a faster tempo than seventy-two bars to the minute—faster than the human pulse."

My pulse rate must have doubled on the evening of June 22, 1937, because it was liberation night for Blacks throughout the world. My music prosperity permitted me to spend $27.50 (two weeks' salary for a family man working under the Public Works Administration) for a ringside seat at Comiskey Park to see the twenty-three-year old, 197-and-a-half pound Joe Louis deck the 197-pound James J. Braddock for the heavyweight championship of the world.

When Joe Louis knocked James Braddock d.o.a. (dead on his ass) in the eighth round, my head reeled. Even in that state of great excitement, I wondered what my Uncle Otis, the great Jack Johnson fan, would have thought when they raised Joe Louis' hand and announced that he was the new heavyweight champion of the world. I did not have to wonder what the black community thought because the South Side had gone totally berserk, with black people running up and down streets shouting, crying, laughing, and singing as if the millenium had come.

Streetcars could not move because the streets were filled with people from curb to curb. Taxicabs were trying to get through 35th Street by honking their horns and moving slowly down the sidewalks. Whiskey and beer bottles appeared in many hands, seemingly by magic. Huge bonfires were started on street corners, not because black hands were cold, but because black hearts were warm with the feeling of liberation.

The condition of the street would not permit me to liberate my car; I walked from Comiskey Park to the Eighth Regiment Armory at 35th and Giles where the Roy Eldridge and Benny Goodman orchestras were appearing in a "Battle of Swing." When I reached the armory door, I could see Dave Young blowing one of his tenor choruses of *"Lady Be Good."*

There must have been 2,000 people in the hall when I arrived. I worked my way through the crowd to the bandstand to greet Roy, Dave, Zutty, Scoops and other members of the band. Within an hour after I arrived, 5,000 people had entered the armory. The police had to close the doors and stop the band from playing because people were literally hanging from the ceiling. The crowd later went through the ceiling when Benny Goodman's band opened their set with *"King Porter Stomp"* and followed it with *"Big John Special."*

The drive of Gene Krupa's drums and the screams of Harry James' trumpet rocked the foundation of the solidly-built armory. Those white boys were playing black music like it had never been heard before. The Goodman formula for this swing with a beat was that he had some of the best trained white musicians in the country playing the musical arrangements of two of the best black arrangers in the nation, namely, Fletcher Henderson and Jimmy Mundy. The Goodman sound was Black America speaking through a white ambassador of swing.

Wendell Phillips High School, and its successor, DuSable, literally bubbled over with swingers without portfolio. Major H. Clark Smith, musical director at Wendell Phillips, trained some of America's most talented swingers in the persons of Ray Nance (trumpet and violin with Duke Ellington); Willie Randall (saxophones and arranger for Earl Hines); Milton Hinton (bass violin with Cab Calloway); Charlie Allen (trumpet with Duke Ellington), Quinn Wilson (bass and arranger for Earl Hines) and Lionel Hampton; (drummer with Louis Armstrong and vibra harp with Benny Goodman.)

Goodman first heard Hampton play in Los Angeles at the Paradise Cafe in an after-hours jam session. The musical success of the Goodman

Quartet that included Hampton, Teddy Wilson on piano, Gene Krupa on drums and Goodman on clarinet, is legendary.

Major Clark's successor, Captain Walter Dyett, retained the legend with DuSable swingers who became movie, radio and television stars, such as Red (Redd Foxx) Sanford, who appeared in the DuSable Hi-Jinks of 1939; Austin Powell and his Cats and the Fiddle (Powell was both singer and composer); the immortal Nat "King" Cole; and Dorothy Donegan, the jazz piano genius and star of radio, movies, television, and night clubs.

Many talented DuSable swingers' and singers' musical careers were eclipsed by the racist policies prevailing in show business that mirrored white America during the 1930's; those policies manifest only slight modification today. A few of the eclipsed musical talents were Savannah Strong (standing ovation for "At My Beck and Call"); Elizabeth Hunt Moutoussamy (memorable rendition of George Gershwin's "Summertime"); and Bessie Sutton (show stopper of the 1936 Hi-Jinks singing Duke Ellington's "I Let a Song Go Out of My Heart").

The musical and economic mix within the DuSable student body of the 1930's gave it a high educational aspiration level that ceased to exist after the homeowner population living west of State Street was displaced for a public housing community. Prior to the building of the Robert Taylor Homes housing project in the 1960's, there were 312 black homeowners living between 47th and 55th Streets, west of State and east of Federal Street. After the Robert Taylor Homes were completed, the homeowner population had been reduced to twenty-three, according to the 1970 census. The difference was noticeable.

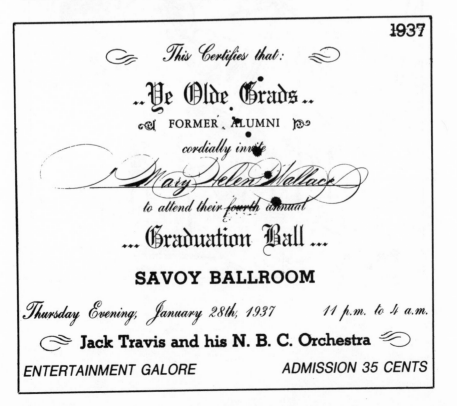

1937

This Certifies that:

..Ye Olde Grads..

FORMER ALUMNI

cordially invite

Mary Helen Wallace

to attend their fourth annual

... Graduation Ball ...

SAVOY BALLROOM

Thursday Evening, January 28th, 1937   *11 p.m. to 4 a.m.*

Jack Travis and his N. B. C. Orchestra

ENTERTAINMENT GALORE   *ADMISSION 35 CENTS*

Chapter 10

MY STREET OF
BROKEN DREAMS

In the weeks before our graduation in June of 1939, the DuSable High School seniors did a lot of talking about the dismal job picture for Blacks. We knew well enough that there were few "clean" jobs for us, other than clerking at the post office or being Pullman porters. There were no black busdrivers or conductors, no black streetcar operators, no black elevated motormen. No Blacks were working in responsible positions in neighborhood banks or in black ghetto branches of life insurance companies or major retail stores. Blacks weren't even able to get jobs as cashiers in the "Bronzeville" drugstore chains.

We knew all that--it was inescapable. We saw the "White Only" job ads for the industrial positions the war had opened up, and we read the "White Help Wanted" signs on the factory gates and hiring halls. The situation was so bad that some of my contemporaries at school even failed courses in order to delay joining that weary march from factory gate to factory gate in search of jobs that did not exist.

I shook my head with the others. But the truth was that I somehow thought it was going to turn out differently for me. Hadn't I been working for years on my music? Didn't I have a skill to sell? I knew that by 1939 jobs for black musicians were drying up, that the craze for "black jazz" had turned to a craze for "white swing" and hundreds of talented black musicians were living off the Federal Arts Project, practicing their craft for an average salary of $55 a month. But what did statistics matter to me, when all I needed was just one job?

My father looked at me with a solemn stare when I talked like this, but he knew he would have to let me face reality for myself this time.

By September, I had worn the soles off several pairs of shoes, trudging from one agency to another in search of that full-time job as a musician. My father grew more and more silent as I told him the stories of my many disappointments.

Then on a Tuesday morning in September, he came into my room and woke me up.

"Boy, if you're going to get a job, you have to be the first one in line at the employment office," he said.

"What?"

"Get up," he said. He watched as I stumbled out of bed and reached for my clothes. "This is how it's going to be," he said. "You can't drive your car until you find a job. I'm going to give you fourteen cents for streetcar fare every day, and fifty cents for lunch money. You understand?"

"Yes, sir," I said.

"Don't spend the lunch money unless you get a job."

"Yes, sir," I said.

Dad had a cousin who worked at the Armour soap works at 31st and Bensen and a friend at the starch factory in the 2900 block on Archer Avenue. They were three blocks apart, so Dad had settled it in his mind that I would visit both places on this first day of serious job hunting.

I walked to 51st and Indiana to catch the streetcar and rode the Indiana car to 31st and transferred to a westbound trolley. The riders were all Blacks talking loudly; some wore blue denim overalls, others wore their Sunday best. When we reached Wentworth, oddly-dressed white folks speaking with foreign accents and smelling of garlic started to fill the trolley. In the six blocks from Wentworth to Halsted, "Big Red" collected an overflow clientele causing both men and women to hang off the rear steps of the trolley and hold the door's center bar and side handles for support.

The air around the Armour soap works was pungent, but not as overwhelming as the smell from the stockyards to the south of 39th Street. Following my father's instructions, I did not go directly to the Armour employment office but walked over the South branch of the Chicago River to the starch factory and waited outside the entrance door. After about an hour, a tall, blond man in white overalls came to the door with a cold expression on his face. "Boy! We ain't hiring today."

I left the starch factory feeling worthless and went back across the bridge to the Armour employment office in a one-story red-faced brick building with about a 30 by 70 feet interior. A middle-aged white man sat at a desk behind a three-foot railing. Facing him were ten rows of wooden benches filled with black and white men, both young and old. The men sitting erect with their eyes focused on the man at the front desk appeared to be new in the job market or had been just recently laid-off. But others sat in a hopeless leaning position, looking alternately at the floor, the walls, the ceiling, and seldom focusing their attention on the man at the front desk. Occasionally the phone would ring and everyone would look up. The desk man would beckon one or two of the bench warmers. Usually they were sent directly to the plant to work without work clothes or rubber boots. I learned that these jobs would only last a half day or sometimes a week, if you were lucky.

I repeated my trips daily to both the starch factory and the soap works for sixty-nine straight days, including Saturdays. Job hunting was one of the coldest, loneliest and most dehumanizing experiences that I had ever encountered. Each day ended as it started except that the soles of my shoes and the seat of my pants became thinner.

My father finally decided my only chance was to buy a job. He was right. I went to the Factory Employment Agency on East Van Buren between Wabash and State. For $10, I got a job as a porter for the Apex Box Company located at 2509 West Cermak Road. The job paid 28 cents per hour or $11.20 per week.

There was only one Black working at Apex. His name was Art and he was a freight elevator operator and order filler. Art had a coffee brown complexion, and a quick smile that displayed his straight pearly teeth. Art was respected by both the bosses and employees alike because of his business-like, no-nonsense attitude. The other employees were either Polish or Italian, mostly Polish women, and the plant owners were German Jews.

With Art's assistance, I made the necessary mental adjustments to perform my portering duties with dispatch. My tasks included cleaning and mopping four two-stall washrooms and sweeping the plant floors continuously throughout the day. After one month on the job, I was commended by my supervisors and subsequently by the vice president of the company for performing my portering chores with both pride and enthusiasm.

My father had taught me early in life not to accept money for any assignment that I did not intend to do well. A laborer at Wilson & Co. he made pulling hams out of vats in a cold room sound like an important and exciting activity.

"I pulled two more vats of hams today than Polock Joe and Mexican Frank who was not even in the running," he would sometimes say.

So positive did my Dad make my attitude about work that he would make me quit paper routes and other odd jobs as a means of punishment for misconduct.

Drawing a weekly paycheck from Apex gave me a very secure feeling and enabled me to make a regular contribution to the family treasurer, Mother. She balanced the housing and food budget, deposited twenty-five per cent of the combined salaries in a joint savings account, and she was the judge of how much Dad and I would be permitted to spend foolishly on the weekends. We both respected her ability to manage our incomes. She was so debt-conscious that she felt that the rent was delinquent if it was not paid seven days before it was due.

My days at Apex went without conflict until Saturday, March 9, 1940. Early that February I had received a call from Zinky Cohn, the business agent for Local 208, the black musicians' union, to put together a seven-piece band for a job at a dance hall. I was overjoyed about the opportunity and the fact that the three-hour gig paid six dollars to each side man and ten dollars to the leader, me. That would almost double my income that week.

All was well that evening until the band started playing "Sunny Side of the Street" and I looked down from the bandstand and saw four white girls from the Apex Box Company smiling and waving. I practically fell off the piano bench, because I knew that Travis the porter could never explain Jack Travis the bandleader to those "ofays." Other Blacks, of course, understood the dual role Negroes had to play in the American scheme of things, but somehow I couldn't bear the idea of explaining that dilemma to Whites.

I could accept my menial job as a porter as long as I kept it separated from my "real" life as a musician, but this sudden collision of the two roles made me feel confused and ashamed. I did not return to my portering position at Apex.

The Apex job was the price I paid for my pride and principle. In retrospect, I think the price was small even though it meant joining 200,000 jobless Chicagoans. I was on the streets two days before I decided I would use the $10 I made on the music gig to buy another job.

This time the factory Employment Agency sent me to the Quality Wet Wash Laundry. The plant superintendent, Emil Gunther, spoke in a heavy Germanic accent as his saucer-shaped blue eyes surveyed me meticulously.

"Can you read and write?" he asked.

"Yes, Sir. I am a graduate of DuSable High School," I said.

"Good did you bring any work clothes?"

"No, Sir," I answered, "But I am prepared to work in the clothes that I have on."

After another quick glance he said, "Come with me."

We walked through the wet steamy laundry room past the men working at the washer, the wringers and then into the dry section where both black men and women were standing in small booths sorting dirty clothes. Some sorters wore homemade masks over their noses and mouths to cut down on the odor of the soiled clothes and the dust. When we reached the drying tumbler at the rear of the building he stopped and introduced me to the operator.

"I want you to teach this young man how to be a bundle boy," Gunther said.

"Come with me, schoolboy," the operator said, turning off the drying machine. ("Schoolboy" was a name that followed me the entire time I remained at the "Big Q.")

I followed Griffin to the bundle racks, where he explained my duties.

"There are thirty-nine truck drivers, and it is your job to see that the bags of wet wash and the packages of finished clothes are placed on the proper racks for them to load on their trucks in the morning and again in the afternoon."

Joe Quinn, a former Notre Dame football star under the legendary coach Knute Rockne, was the supervisor of the truck drivers and the husband of Mary Quinn, my former English teacher at DuSable High. He was a tall, muscular, dark-haired man with a large, oblong head that was set four inches above his broad shoulders. He walked with a fast, wide gait and whenever he came down from his second floor office to check out a complaint about a lost bundle of clothes, he would ask me to accompany him on the search through the laundry racks.

On these excursions I began to attempt to convince Joe Quinn that he should make me a truckdriver.

One afternoon, after I had raised the question for an uncountable number of times, he turned to me and said sadly, "Travis, I wish you would try to understand that if I had the power to hire you as a driver, all of the other drivers would quit."

"All the drivers like me," I said. "I can't remember a single day since I started working here that at least two or three of them have not invited me to join them at the coke machine or offered me a bar of candy."

"Travis, I am sure they all like you as a 'colored bundle boy;' but I am equally sure that they would hate you as a colored driver," Quinn said.

"Why, Mr. Quinn?" I asked. The answer was quick in coming: "Seventy-five per cent of our laundry routes are in the colored community and your presence as a driver would be a threat to what is now considered a well paying 'white man's job,' " he said. He looked at me briefly and then reached out his hand. "I'm sorry," he said. He turned and walked out.

At that moment, I literally could not breathe. I knew then I could never be content with just making an hourly wage of 33 cents or $13.20 per week while white laundry drivers in the green uniforms with the big red "Q" on the back of their jackets made $35 to $50 per week for a lot less work.

On January 15, 1941, A. Philip Randolph, president of the Brotherhood of Sleeping Car Porters, issued a newspaper release suggesting that 10,000 Blacks march on Washington D.C. to demand the right to work and fight for "our country." Randolph believed that this action was necessary because in the fall of 1940, when the national defense program was moving into its second year, over 90 per cent of the holders of defense contracts either employed no Blacks at all or confined them to unskilled labor or custodial jobs. There were less than 5,000 Blacks among the 175,000 trainees in defense vocational programs.

The "March-on-Washington Movement" was tantamount to hitting the "American Mule" on the head. It was the first time that a black leader got President Roosevelt to focus his attention on the need to abolish discrimination in the defense industry and in government employment. By the end of May, Randolph was promising that not 10,000, but 100,000 Blacks would join the march. The idea was spreading like a Southern California forest fire in mid-August.

The White House was not just simply impressed, it was alarmed. It was so alarmed at the thought of 100,000 Blacks marching through the streets of Washington D.C., the citadel of "Jim Crow," that President Roosevelt signed Executive Order 8802 on June 25, 1941, just a few days before the march was to have taken place.

The order was prefaced with a general statement to the effect that there would be no discrimination in the employment of workers in defense industries or in government because of "race, creed, color or national origin." The order also confirmed that there should be no discrimination in defense training programs.

I felt that defense training would be the gateway to the millenium for millions of Blacks. At least I hoped it would be for me. Executive Order 8802 seemed too good to be true.

Sixty-five defense plants listed in the "want ad" section of the daily newspapers but only two companies even allowed me to fill out applications. The rest said that they had filled their trainee quota and suggested, frequently with a smile, that I try again next week, next month, or next year. By this time I was wearing my heart on the bottom of my feet, and each step I took started a rhythmic "there ain't no hope" feeling pulsing from the soles of my feet to the crown of my head.

The weight of my heart made my shoes so heavy that I had to share my burden with both my father and mother. In spite of our closeness as a family, my parents had not realized how seriously I was taking my inability to get more than menial employment. It was then Dad suggested I go to see Alderman Earl B. Dickerson.

Dickerson, now an alert 90-year-old, was then at the height of his political career and had just been appointed by President Franklin D. Roosevelt to the newly-formed Fair Employment Practice Committee. I went down to his office at 3507 South Parkway without an appointment late one afternoon and after an hour wait, I was invited into the inner office.   "What can I do for you, young man?" he said.

"I would like to be an aviation engineer or mechanic."

"Have you had any training or experience in either field?" Dickerson snapped.

I described my job experience and told him of my eagerness to have a job.

"Son, your feelings about the subject is not enough. You need training or experience, and it is helpful to have both," he said.

I told Alderman Dickerson about my experience looking for jobs at the defense plants while he made some notes.

"My committee is investigating hundreds of complaints like yours. I am going to suggest that in the meantime you go over to the Armour Institute at 3300 South Federal Street (formerly Armour Avenue) and see if they are offering any aviation programs in which you might enroll," he said.

Following his suggestion, I went over to the Armour Institute of Technology, which had merged with Lewis Institute the year before, to form the Illinois Institute of Technology, but found it did not offer courses in aviation defense work. However, a small white-haired gentleman said, "I understand there are some being offered at the Wendell Phillips High School."

I went directly to Phillips and enrolled in a four-month, 40-hour-per-week, government-sponsored aviation mechanic program. The instructor, a very attractive bronze-colored aviatrix named Mrs. Willa Brown, was part owner of the Coffey School of Aeronautics, the school that issued the completion certificate upon my graduation from the course.

When I received the aviation mechanic certificate on a Friday afternoon, I knew I had my hand on a direct passport into the defense industry. The thought of becoming a defense worker filled me with so much hope that I could not sleep more than two hours per night for the next three nights.

Monday morning I got up and was fully dressed by 3 a.m. In the process of releasing the burglar latch on the front door, I awakened my father, who turned on his bedroom light, looked at the clock and shouted, "Boy! ...don't you know it's just five minutes after three?"

"Yes, Sir!" I answered.

"Where are you going this early?" he muttered.

"To get a job. I want to be the first in line at the defense plant employment office."

"Good luck," he said and turned out the light.

At high noon, my employment world was still dark. The bright rays of hope that my aviation mechanic certificate gave me gradually dimmed with each job rejection.

"We ain't hiring no boys today." "We won't need any mechanic trainee for at least nine months." "You are over-qualified for our present position opening." "We already got one colored fellow working here as a

(Left) Known as the "elder statesman" among civil rights leaders, A. Philip Randolph, the master strategist, was for many years the head of the Brotherhood of Sleeping Car Porters and later, also served as president of the Negro American Labor Council. Randolph was one of the major forces behind the 1963 March On Washington. (Right) Chicago Alderman Earl B. Dickerson, after his appointment to the Fair Employment Practices Commission in 1941.

Willa Brown (right) and Lola Jones standing in front of their biplane at Harlem Airport outside Chicago where Brown ran an aviation school in the 1930's.

washroom attendant." That comment had a familiar ring.

When I returned home after dinnertime that evening, my father was sitting on the front steps smoking one of his favorite three for ten cents El Producto Cigars. As he exhaled the smoke from the cigar he smiled and asked, "How did things go today?"

"No good, Dad," I replied. "The same old 3-6-9." (The phrase comes from the policy "dream book" and means "shit.")

Reflecting a look of understanding, Dad said gently, "Sit down, son. I heard some good news at the stockyards today. They're hiring new men in my section of the Sweet Pickle Department and also on the beef killing floor at Wilson's. I understand they are also hiring at both Swift and Armour."

"God Almighty," I said. "That means I can go to work with you in the morning."

"Nope!" Dad said. "I don't want you working at Wilson & Co. As a matter of fact, I didn't want you working in the stockyards, period. But since the Yards appear to be your only option, you should go to the Armour & Company employment office at 43rd & Packer first, and then go down the street about a half a block to Swift & Company."

The next morning my feet hit the floor when Dad's Big Ben clock alarmed at five o'clock. Mother was already in the kitchen fixing breakfast and preparing brown bag lunches for both Dad and myself. I was excited because I was about to become part of the Packingtown (Stockyards) that my Dad, Uncle Otis, and Uncle Joe always talked about.

On a hot summer day, an east wind would cause a diluted version of the foul smell and brown mist from the fertilizer plant to descend upon Chicago like a smog from downtown to Morgan Park and from Ashland Avenue to Lake Michigan. My father warned me not to accept a job in the fertilizer plant because I would not be able to get the odor out of the pores of my skin. The permanent body stench would cause one to become a social leper like Dad's friends "Stinky" Davis and "Funky" Mose. The odor was so terrible that these men had become outcasts and Dad never saw them anymore. In spite of the very real handicaps of these jobs, black workers were sometimes forced to take them because they were all that was available to them.

The fertilizer fumes were dominant among the many smells crowding my nostrils as I walked through the stockyards, along with the sounds and smells of the thousands of hogs and cows being herded into the killing rooms through the overhead runways, criss-crossing the brick-paved Packingtown streets. In addition, there was the scent from the rancid blood of dead animals along with that of the animals' waste, added to the rank flavor from dirty and sweat-stained clothes worn by the work gangs.

Animal cries from the area made Packingtown both ugly and somber on the brightest of the sunniest days.

At the Armour Employment Office, I found at least 100 men, both black and white, waiting for the employment manager to open the door.

Finally, a broad-shouldered, big-faced old Irishman stepped outside of the door. It seemed that more than half the fellows knew the Irishman and many of them started shouting "Big Mac" and waving their arms to get his attention. He stood there for several minutes looking over the human herd before he started beckoning for those individuals he intended to employ that day. Although I was almost at the rear of the crowd he beckoned for me (I attribute my luck that day to my six-foot height).

"What kind of work can you do?" he asked me when I reached the front.

"Any kind," I replied.

He gave me a yellow slip and directed me through the door behind him to the doctor's office where I was checked for heart trouble, tuberculosis, hernia, and venereal disease.

Then I reported to the time-keeper's office in the Sweet Pickle Department in my high-top rubber boots and brand new blue denim overalls, with fifteen other black laborers. A short, reddish-skinned man in a dingy gray smock stepped out of the time-keeper's office and motioned for us to encircle him for instructions. "Mexican" Frank was his name and he introduced himself as the assistant foreman. Assistant foreman was the lowest official supervisory position in the plant. (No Blacks had achieved even this lowly rank in the stockyards' seventy-five year history, although Blacks did sometimes act in an unofficial capacity as a gang "strawboss.")

Our gang was assigned to pull floating, half frozen bacon bellies out of a long tank and then load them into pushtrucks. This job was cold and wet. How my dad performed this task with enthusiasm for forty years was beyond me then—and is now.

My Dad and Uncle Joe once explained the routine for black work assignments in Packingtown, saying, "Black folks cannot be permitted to work with finished meat products." Aunt Mary, naturally, asked, "Why not?"

Plant visitors and foreign guests come to the room where bacon is being handled for packaging and they would be offended, if they saw black hands touch something they might eat, was the reply.

"That's ridiculous," Aunt Mary said. "Black folks have been handling food for white folks as long as I can remember."

"I understand how you feel, Mary," Uncle Joe said. "But I overheard a superintendent in a long white frock say to an assistant superintendent, "We must be scrupulous along sanitary lines, and only white hands are fit to touch the meat. We could hire Negro women, but their hands would have to be washed almost every hour and we would have to manicure them."

"Mary, I could not believe my ears," he laughed.

Dad interrupted: "The oleo (margarine) department barred Negro women although no hand touched the butterine in the course of packing. At the same time, Negro men pack pails of the same butterine, which not only is shoveled into the receptacles, but must often be molded by black hands into a workable mass. This is allowed because the white public does not see this action. The walls in the butterine room are painted white and the workers are clad in white, and the public relations men thought that the plant image would be prettier if the workers were white."

With my eyes still blinking from all the whiteness, I said, "What chance does a black man or woman have of getting one of those clean jobs wearing a white uniform or frock?"

Dad answered calmly, "None! Unless there is a strike or a war."

That conversation took place just fifteen days before the Japanese bombed Pearl Harbor on December 7, 1941.

The USS Arizona was one of the more seriously damaged United States ships at Pearl Harbor on December 7, 1941. Many of the more than 2,000 officers and enlisted men killed at Pearl were buried alive in ships like the Arizona.

Chapter 11

WORLD WAR II

"The colored folks have bombed Pearl Harbor! The colored folks have bombed Pearl Harbor!" yelled Willie "Pretty Stockyard" Cole as he rushed through the front door of Nelson Sykes' Brass Rail Saloon at 329 East 47th Street.

For several seconds everyone in the barroom was silent when Frank Williams, who had just finished swallowing his shot glass of Canadian Club Whiskey, said in a loud guttural voice: "Nigger! What the hell you been smoking?"

That question tore up the barflies and guys who responded with everything from a tee-hee to a belly laugh. Everyone, that is, except "Pretty Willie," who was standing in the middle of the floor waving his arms for attention and shouting, "I'm serious as a barrel of rattlesnakes. Look! I'm crossin' my heart on my mother's grave. The Japanese have just bombed a place near California called Pearl Harbor."

A drunk named "Broke" Hunter standing at the end of the bar interrupted Willie's shouting with, "I know the white folks are going to give me a steady job now."

"Amen," replied "Fat" Clark. "I recall my father tellin' me how much overtime money colored people made during the last big war."

By this time Nelson Sykes had turned the table model Zenith radio up full blast and the voice of President Franklin D. Roosevelt was heard saying, "On December 7, 1941—a date which will live in infamy—the United State of America was suddenly and deliberately attacked by naval and air forces of the Empire of Japan. Very many American lives have been lost. As Commander in Chief of the Army and Navy, I have directed that all measures be taken for our defense. Always will we remember the character of the onslaught against us. . . ."

In the summer of 1941, as the Japanese were invading the French colonies of Indochina, the United States drew the line and embargoed first scrap iron, and then oil. Pearl Harbor was inevitable and its timetable predictable. The Japanese would have to go to war before they ran out of gasoline.

"Baby the Pimp" Bell distracted our attention from President Roosevelt's radio speech when he shouted, "Bartender, I'm buying two rounds of drinks for everybody in the house." Bell then raised a water glass of VO 90 proof whiskey above his head and said in a very slow and solemn tone, "Remember Pearl Harbor."

The freeloaders' immediate response to Bell's drinks on the house was drowned out by the roar of the Englewood "L" express train thundering overhead on its nonstop route past 43rd, 47th, and 55th Streets enroute to its stop at the 58th Street elevated station. The smothered acknowledgements to "Baby" Bell's toast were certainly not unanimous. Some Blacks experienced a vicarious pleasure from the thought that "Charlie" was getting his ass kicked by some "colored" people. (There was a small black sect on the South Side known as "the Moors" who were actually pro-Japanese.)

Three days after Pearl Harbor, Germany and Italy came to the aid of Japan and declared war on the United States. On December 19th, the Congress of the United States extended military conscription to include men between the ages of 20 to 44. Thousands of white men had begun to volunteer for service in the Air Corps, the Marines, the Navy, and the Army the day after Pearl Harbor. Black men were not permitted to volunteer for any duty except the Army and kitchen (mess) duty in the Navy.

At the same time, American industry responded to the call by literally opening up thousands of new plants overnight. These factories ranged from huge shipbuilding yards employing masses of people, to tiny one-man operations in the basements of private homes. Many of the plants in the union stockyards were on triple shifts. The magnates of industry and big business were recruiting Whites for the clean, new, high-paying war jobs, while the dirty, low-paying stockyard and steel mill jobs were being offered to Blacks. Low-paying or otherwise, there now existed a thirst for black laborers that had not been paralleled since World War I. And as white men and women left the cleaner jobs in the stockyards for positions in the defense industry, Blacks were pulled in as their replacements at Armour & Company, as well as other industries.

Although I had worked at Armour & Company only a little more than a month, I was transferred from the sweet pickle department to the canning department. This assignment was considered a cleaner and steadier job. The symbolic significance of the departmental transfer was that I was instructed to dispose of my blue denim overalls and wear white denims because I would be handling sealed cans of processed meats that would ultimately reach Army and civilian markets. Handling canned meats had a side benefit because I was soon introduced to an old timer in the department named "Kiddo" Hamilton. One day at lunch, Kiddo said, "Why do you bring a cold lunch from home everyday when you can have a hot one on the house?"

"What do you mean?"

"Kid, buy yourself a five-cent loaf of bread and I will show you how to eat well for a week."

The next day at lunch Kiddo took me over to the south end of the department where there were some hot pipes running along the wall. Kiddo had tied ham, sausage and Spam to the pipes earlier in the day so that at lunch time the meat would be red hot and juicy.

The delicious times lasted for about a month before I began to have problems with my sexual drive. Needless to say, I had suffered some embarrassment and I was in a dilemma about my love life. I first shared my delicacy with an older lady friend who guaranteed she had a cure for my distress. However, before trying her remedy, I reluctantly told my father about my recent experience. He literally fell out of his chair laughing and said, "Boy, are you trying to tell me you are all used up at age 21?"

I looked at Dad without replying. He then seemed to recognize that I was serious and stopped laughing.

"What have you been drinking?" he asked.

"An occasional bottle of beer."

He pondered with a serious look on his face and asked, "Has anybody been cooking for you other than your mother?"

"No!"

"Your problem must be related to something that you are eating or drinking," Dad persisted. "Think, boy! What have you been eating or drinking within the past month that is different than your diet of three months ago?"

"Oh! Oh!"

"Oh! Oh! What?"

"I have been eating stockyard meat with Kiddo Hamilton everyday."

"What kind?"

"Canned Army-ratio Spam and sausage."

Dad broke into hysterical laughter that was so extensive I thought he was having a convulsion. Finally he stopped laughing and wiped the tears from his eyes and said, "Boy, don't you know that they put saltpeter (potassium nitrate) in that soldier meat so they won't have no nature, and that is the answer to your problem." Dad began to laugh again and this time I joined him.

"Son, there ain't no such thing as a free lunch," Dad said between laughs, "and I am going to suggest that you 'brown bag' it from now on, the same way I do."

I followed Dad's suggestion and my delicacy straightened up in a little less than a week. I stopped hanging out with Kiddo at lunch after I quit the Armour meat diet. I started "brown-bagging" it and sitting out on the curbstone. When the weather wouldn't permit, I'd sit in the locker room and eat. One day, to my surprise, I saw a middle-aged man who looked just like Erskine Tate, the great band leader of the 1920's and '30's, sitting in front of a locker about ten feet from mine. The gentleman looked both unfriendly and ill-tempered. His partially bald head was large enough to accommodate a seven and three quarter inch hat. He had a strong Indian-red complexion and his face was filled with hundreds of small pockmarks (possibly the product of some childhood illness.) His eyes were large and piercing. Several days passed before I asked John "Stormy Monday" Ransom who that sour-looking fellow was who had the locker down from mine . John came over and cautiously whispered, "Man! That's Erskine Tate, one of the finest band leaders Chicago ever produced!"

I couldn't believe my ears. Why would a man who had reached his summit in music be working as a laborer at Armour & Company? You would not have to be Duke Ellington to know that racism afflicts all black musicians. The good ones and the mediocre ones suffer in one black kettle of Jim Crow. Without further hesitation, I walked over and introduced myself to Tate. He didn't appear pleased at all to meet me until I told him I had attended Willard Elementary School with both his daughter, Evelyn, and his nephew, Emmett, and also, that I was a member of Local 208 of the Musician's Union. That broke the ice. He smiled and invited me to sit down on the bench beside him in front of his locker. I had hardly sat down when the lunch whistle blew for us to return to work. As I left, Tate said, "Come around at noon tomorrow and we'll talk about music."

The next day we ate and I had an opportunity to tell Tate that my mother had taken me to the Vendome Theater at 31st and State to hear his band accompany such great blues singers as Mamie Smith, Bessie Smith, Ethel Waters, and Mae Alix. Tate appeared delighted and said, "I believe I had one of my greatest bands during that period because both Louis Armstrong and Earl 'Fatha' Hines were sidemen in that orchestra. There are others who will tell you my best band was the one I took into the Metropolitan Theater at 46th and South Parkway."

I simply nodded to Tate's statements because between the ages of 8 and 10, when I saw him at both theatres, I was not equipped to make a musical judgment on the merits of either band. (Live bands were used in the theatre pits to set the mood for various scene changes in the old silent movies. The band would be given a new music script with each film. There would be several themes, eight to sixteen bars long. If the band leader held up one finger, the band would play the love theme, two fingers would signal the villain theme. Most theatres in black ghettos had a lone piano player.) Tate and I became daily lunch companions for the next several months that I worked at the "yards."

On Friday afternoon, August 7, 1942, when I arrived home, my mother told me she had put a letter on the dresser for me.

"Who would be writing me a letter?"

"Since I didn't open it, I would suggest that you read it and see."

I opened the envelope and the first word I saw in bold type was "GREETINGS." The letter continued, "You are hereby notified that you have been selected for training and service therein. This local board will furnish transportation to an induction .... You will there be examined, and, if accepted . . . you will be inducted into the land or naval forces. Failure to report subjects the violator to fine and imprisonment."

As I sat on the bed staring at the letter, mother yelled from the kitchen, "Who was the letter from?"

"The draft board."

"The who?"

"The Army, Mama."

Mother rushed into the bedroom and snatched the letter from my hand. She read the letter twice and said, in an utterance that sounded like a prayer, "I know 'Uncle Sam' is not going to take my only child. I know 'Uncle Sam' is not going to take my only child."

"Mama, the 'man' wants some cannon fodder and he ain't making no exceptions."

My world came to an abrupt end when I reported to the induction center where I passed the physical examination. I was then ordered by my draft board to report back on September 9, 1942, to be transported from the board to the Illinois Central Station at 12th and Michigan Avenue, where I would board a train for Fort Custer in Michigan.

The last ten days before I left for the Army were spent partying with my friends. The best times consisted of "joint hopping" from the Keyhole Lounge at 39th and King Drive to the Red Moon Lounge at 61st Street, four doors west of South Park, and the Wonder Bar on 63rd, three doors east of South Park. Sometimes we would cover as many as fifteen taverns in one night. The night before I was to leave, Claude Jenkins gave a party in my honor at his mother's home at 59th and Prairie. He had invited about twenty fellows who included Charlie Murray, Joe Simmons, "Jelly" Martin and Milton Turner. The party broke up about 4 a.m. and several of my friends had to walk me home.

I had only been in bed an hour when Dad awakened me to wish me good luck and to ask me to write. An hour later, Mother shook my bed and said, "It's time for you to get up and go to the draft board."

I didn't realize it immediately, but my mother's face looked as if she had been crying all night. At that moment, she was putting up a brave front. She had packed a big suitcase for me. I looked at her and said: "All I need, Ma, according to the instructions, are a few personal items such as a toothbrush, a comb, and a change of underclothes."

She responded in a soft, tearful voice, "You have got to have two pairs of pajamas." Mother reluctantly began to unpack the suitcase. She lifted each piece from the bag as gingerly as she would have lifted a baby. As she touched each garment, she would repeat: "Why do they have to take my only child? Why do they have to take my only child?" At this point she started shaking and screaming: "Why, Lord? Why are they taking my only child?"

I said, "Mother, I don't know," and started crying myself, uncontrollably. Without saying goodbye, I dashed out of the kitchen door and down the back stairs, sobbing loudly and screaming, "Mama! I don't want to go! Mama! I don't want to go."

At 8 a.m. sharp the draftee bus was loaded and ready to go—with or without me. The thirty-five minute bus ride from the draft board on Garfield Boulevard (55th Street) north down Michigan Avenue to the 12th Street train station mentally took less than five minutes. My mind was absorbed in the past. It was not until I boarded the train an hour later with a group of about 100 draftees that I began to feel like a cow among a herd of stockyard cattle being led to slaughter by a belled goat. (The stockyards used trained goats to lead herds of cows to the slaughter house. The goat would then return to the cattle pen to lead another herd. A single goat would lead several thousand cows to their deaths daily.) The herd instinct helped deliver the cows to the killing floor. What was delivering me? Was it loyalty? Was it fear? Was it propaganda? Was it the opportunity to become a first-class American?

"Battle Creek! Battle Creek!" yelled the conductor.

"Follow me," shouted our group leader as he waved his arms toward the front of the train. After we got off the train we were instructed to jump into the Army trucks that were lined up to take us into Fort Custer. Within twenty minutes, I was standing in the street in the company area of the 1609th Service Unit. The "old" soldiers (three days in service) were laughing and shouting, "Shorty got your gal and gone" from the balcony and windows of the type of double-deck barracks that would be my home for the next four years. We were left standing in the streets for about ten minutes before a tall, slim, shifty-eyed man came out of the barracks and for several minutes looked through the draftees as if they were transparent.

Travis' first military home was Fort Custer in Michigan. Pictured here are recruits standing in formation in front of their barracks at this installation named for the famed Indian fighter.

He then said: "I am 1st Sgt. Hammond. We are going to process you through this reception center within three or four days and then you will be shipped to another camp for your basic training."

At this point he was distracted by a draftee who was talking. He said to the recruit, "What's your name, soldier?"

"John Rose," the recruit replied.

The sergeant wrote his name down and said: "Soldier, if I catch you with your big trap open again, I am going to make you think hell is paradise." Hammond gave Rose a hard stare and then turned and walked back to the center column where he announced that Buck Sgt. Willie Moore would be in charge of taking us to the warehouse for our G.I. (government issue) clothes and then to the dispensary for immunization shots.

We had just returned to the barracks with two duffel bags of Army gear when Moore blew his whistle for us to fall in formation in the street directly in front of the barracks for the retreat, a ceremony signaling the lowering of the flag at sundown. At the end of the ten-minute ritual, we were told to fall out for chow (withdraw from formation to eat.) The "old" recruits ran to be the first in line at the mess hall. When I found out what was happening, I was about two hundredth in a line of 350 men waiting to eat. A young soldier standing in front of me fell to the ground. Luckily, someone standing nearby recognized that it was an epileptic seizure and rapidly placed a stick in his mouth to prevent the disabled soldier from biting his tongue.

The first meal and the first night in the Army were uneventful except that I almost fell off the top of a double-deck bunk as I turned in my sleep. The next morning I was awakened by a thundering voice on the loud speaker: "Ha, ha, ha, ha, I am the Shadow. Since the Shadow sees all and knows all, the Shadow can see you laying there on your big, black a--. Ha, ha, ha, get up! Get up! Get up! Every swinging d--- let your feet hit the floor and your a-- hit the door for reveille."

That afternoon, as we stood at attention for retreat, Hammond, accompanying Major Peterson, did an inspection of the troops. When they reached me, the major stopped and asked me: "What's your name, soldier?"

"Private Dempsey J. Travis," I replied.

Hammond interrupted, reprimanding me: "Goddammit, soldier, you always say 'sir' when you are speaking to an officer."

I replied, "Yes, sir!"

Peterson then asked: "What did you do for a living as a civilian?"

"I was a musician, sir!"

"Did you get this soldier's name, sergeant?" the major inquired.

Hammond replied: "I did, sir." And they both stepped briskly down to the center of the parade ground to take their position in front of the troops for retreat. The next day I was called to the orderly room and told by Hammond: "Soldier, you have been selected to be a member of the permanent personnel of the 1609 Service Unit."

That was my first break, in that it meant that I would be stationed at Fort Custer and that I could go home every weekend after I finished my twelve-week basic training. My second break came when I was asked to organize an orchestra to play for the Friday and Saturday night U.S.O. dances in Battle Creek. The gig paid three dollars a night per man. Everything was going smoothly until one Sunday Hammond asked me: "What did you bring me from your last trip to town?"

"What?"

Hammond responded in a harsh tone, "You heard me."

I asked: "What was I supposed to have brought you?"

"A pint of Grand Dad every time you play a dance."

That meant that I would be giving Hammond one-third of my salary for the privilege of playing music. That was, as my father used to say: "Too much sugar for a dime." My pride and conscience would not permit me to swallow Hammond's strong-arm tactics. I immediately made the top of Hammond's "people-to-make-miserable" list. For instance, if the last train for Chicago left at 9:45 p.m., he would issue my pass to commence at midnight. On Thanksgiving, a girlfriend came to visit me from Chicago, and Hammond refused to let me leave the camp until midnight when everything in town was closed. He further restricted the pass to a 5 a.m. return for reveille. Hammond was such a son-of-a-bitch that I was forced to take refuge on several occasions in the non-commissioned officer's room and literally weep. The other alternative would simply be to illegally destroy Hammond.

The legal destruction of Private Travis was on the top of Hammond's May agenda. When I returned to camp from a weekend pass in Chicago on Monday, May 10, 1943, Hammond had executed his most fiendish scheme—I was put under house arrest the moment I entered the barracks.

"Guards, you have made a mistake," I pleaded, "I am not late. I wasn't due back in camp until 0700." The two guards simply shook their heads and kept their hands on their guns.

After about an hour, Hammond walked into the barracks with a sar-

(Below) Travis and Marion Bridges in the summer of 1945 at Aberdeen Proving Grounds; (Right) Dempsey J. Travis in uniform in 1942; (Bottom) Travis pictured with his mother and father in late October, 1942 in front of their 1941 Buick.

donic grin and said: "I have orders in my hand to ship you to a port of embarkation."

All my feathers fell. I knew Hammond had the noose around my neck and was about to pull the trap door. Hammond then gave the guards the following instructions: "Keep this soldier under close surveillance and don't consider this assignment complete until Private Travis is placed on the troop train, and the train is out of your sight."

"Attention!" the guard shouted. "Right face, forward march." The three of us marched off to the train in cadence. Enroute, soldiers on the street stopped and stared at me as if I were a common criminal.

The troop train that I was placed on was loaded with black men who had just been released from the stockade (Army prison). Most of them had been convicted for AWOL (absent without leave), desertion, and other military offenses. Sending soldiers overseas prematurely was one method of controlling and punishing the incorrigibles.

I had never even missed bed check. But getting on Sgt. Hammond's list was enough to make me an incorrigible. He had nailed me to the cross.

DIARY OF A RETURNING HERO

**"THOSE GERMAN PRISONERS WOULDN'T
EAT IF I ALLOWED YOU TO SIT NEAR THEM!"**

Chapter 12

CAMP SHENANGO

The extent of segregation and discrimination in the armed forces through World War II is something that has been conveniently left out of the history books. And the full viciousness of the situation was something I had disregarded during my relatively privileged time at Fort Custer.

Comparing Fort Custer to Camp Shenango, Pennsylvania, is like comparing the high rise public housing complex of Cabrini-Green to Lake Shore Drive's rows of luxury high rises on Chicago's lakefront.

From the moment I stepped off the train with the others at Camp Shenango, it was borne in on me that as a black man, I had no status, no rights, no dignity, no claim to human treatment. For a lot of us, the hellishness of Camp Shenango was symbolized by the mud which engulfed our feet and ankles as we got off the train. It was a slimy mud, it was a smelly mud, it was a mud that consumed you mentally without incarcerating you physically. It was a mud that could drive men mad.

Maybe ten per cent of the soldiers at Camp Shenango, a huge installation where thousands of soldiers were being processed to be shipped overseas, were Blacks. They kept us out of the way as much as possible. The Blacks' barracks, about a mile and a half from the main gate, over by the woods, was like a separate little Jim Crow ghetto on the post. Though conditions at the post were bad for all the soldiers, black and white, for Blacks they were simply unspeakable.

We could not use the white PX—the only PX—or the white recreational facilities. For us there were no roads, no movie theatre. It was as if I had suddenly been thrust into one of my relatives' stories about the Old South: Blacks were supposed to efface themselves, to wait around for Whites, not to get in the way, to literally get to the back of the bus.

Later on, I became aware that Shenango had some German prisoners of war, and they were treated better than black American soldiers. They were allowed to use facilities we could not. It was as if it was we who were the enemy aliens.

Other unofficial "enemy aliens" had their own troubles during these sad times.

One hundred and twenty thousand men, women and children of Japanese ancestry, 70,000 of them American citizens, were confined to internment camps for varying amounts of time during World War II. Yet, more than a million persons of German and Italian ancestry living in the U.S. at that time remained free, although a few were also incarcerated. Throughout the course of the war, no Japanese-Americans residing in the U.S. were ever charged with espionage or sabotage. Reparations for these persons, hustled out of their homes, businesses and family lives with as little as a day's notice and able to take only two suitcases of belongings with them, is a topic now being debated at hearings held in various places of the country in late 1981. Forty years—to the year—after the bombing of Pearl Harbor.

But back to Shenango.

The food was bad. Army food is bad, of course, but this was no joke; it wasn't possible to eat it. Bad meat, undercooked, or watery "shit on a shingle"—it seemed like every meal was a new outrage.

I remember on the third night I was there I went to the mess hall—a separate mess hall for Blacks, of course—and found men jumping up and down on the tables, stomping the food in their trays into the table tops. I had been sent to a madhouse, and I knew then that I was going to have to think carefully about ways to retain my sanity. I couldn't escape through a movie or a 3.2 (alcohol content) beer in the post exchange, because there were no such things in the "colored" section of the camp. And Blacks were not permitted in the white area except on official daytime business.

Even if you needed medical attention, you were suspect if you showed your face on "their" side of the camp. Once I was sent to the hospital because I had hurt my foot in obstacle course training. A white, middle-aged doctor with full colonel rank asked me, without a smile or an examination, "Boy—what's your problem?"

"My right leg and foot are in pain."

"Your what?"

"My leg and foot have been hurt, sir."

"Where is the blood, nigger?" the doctor said.

"The injury is internal and didn't break the skin, sir."

"Boy!" he snarled, glaring at me. "A nigger's feet are supposed to hurt. Don't you show your black face in this hospital again trying to goldbrick unless you're bleeding."

By the fourth week of my time at Camp Shenango, the authorities, worried by the presence of the large number of black soldiers being shipped in daily, opened a makeshift post exchange in a one-story barrack and a small theater for black troops. We had to attend the tiny movie house in shifts.

But by that time, there was a mood of simmering resentment on the post. We didn't know at the time, but that was true at camps all over the country. During the spring and summer of 1943, outbreaks of racial violence between black and white soldiers occurred at at least nineteen camps across the country, from Mississippi to New Jersey, from North Carolina to California. In addition, soldiers on leave in several cities were involved in racial violence. The exact number of soldiers involved in these incidents was never recorded; in fact, the Army did its best at the time to keep the incidents out of the papers. By all accounts, the outbreak I was to witness at Shenango was one of the bloodiest.

At camps all over the country, Blacks were experiencing the same kind of treatment I was. Years later, Mrs. Mary Herrick, my old teacher from DuSable High, would share with me some letters from classmates of mine, written during the war.

"Oh, yes, about that incident you heard over the radio," James Armand wrote from Camp Van Doren in Mississippi. "One of the boys down here in the Infantry went into town and got shot by a town policeman. It has quiet(ed) down now. They talk about shipping all the North boys back up North. I hope so, but I doubt it." The soldier added a footnote: "P.S. You don't have to worry about me fooling with these crackers down here in Mississippi. They are crazy as hell."

James Norman wrote from Greensboro, North Carolina: "Do you know I entered a drug store (Walgreen's) in Greensboro, and they refused to serve me. I naturally have heard of discrimination but I didn't think that applied to soldiers. It makes you stop and wonder sometimes why we are fighting."

James W. Hopson had his eyes opened when he left his station at Camp LeJeune, North Carolina, for a day trip into Washington, D.C. "The cafeteria in the Capitol building has a unique way of discriminating. The signs on the doors read 'Senators and Employees,' but our guide told us that it was a public restaurant and that the signs were put there for other reasons. We, of darker hue in the group, knew what that reason was. After leaving the Capitol we visited the United Nations Service Center across the street from the Washington Terminal. We must have been the first Negroes to ever go in there, for we met wild-eyed stares and even the Negro employees seemed to be surprised.

"However, everyone was very cordial afterwards. I have termed Washington as the dividing line of the nation. South of it one enters a strange world with Middle Age customs. North of it one sees a nation struggling to make the meaning of freedom a reality."

The immediate cause of concern to the Camp Shenango authorities was that Blacks were trying to receive services at the white post exchange and to gain entry at the white movie theaters. These young men needed something to do besides playing blackjack or poker all night and day.

Some black soldiers shot craps on doubled blankets spread out over the latrine floor within an arm's reach of men using the latrines. Sometimes the gamblers would shout in chorus, "Roll those dice, baby needs a new pair of shoes, and daddy needs some money to make honey with Bonnie." Sometimes a kneeling crap shooter would look up at a soldier sitting on the toilet and growl, "Cut it short and mix some water with that shit."

The morning of July 14, 1943, was hot and dusty. I said to "Kansas," my upper bunkmate who hailed from that great state, "Let's stay in the barracks and play cards until it's time for the movie."

"Okay," he said, "if the game is draw poker with five cents as the limit."

Kansas was in good spirits that day and talked non-stop about his plans as we played cards. He had an undergraduate degree from an Eastern college and planned to go to medical school when he got out of the Army. Kansas maintained his cheerful manner in spite of all the miseries of life at Camp Shenango. The only thing I ever heard him complain about was the commanding officer--white, of course--who refused to select him for an Army special training program, which would have allowed him to enter medical school while still in the Army.

The hours passed quickly, and we didn't stop to go to lunch because we had heard that they were serving a dish fondly called "dear old Billy goat." At 5:30 we hit the chow line and then went directly to the theater that had been set up for Blacks. The line already too long for us to catch the first show, and we started to change our plans and go into a small town, Sharon, Pennsylvania, about twenty miles from the camp. But Kansas was against it. "Let's wait until Saturday and go into Youngstown, Ohio, where we can ball," he said. So we waited around to catch the second show.

When we came out, there was a large group of Blacks milling around in front of the theatre. We went over to see what was going on.

"A black soldier just got both eyes kicked out because he tried to buy a cold beer in the white post exchange," someone in the group told us.

Another black soldier screamed, "Let's go down there and get those cracker bastards!"

Kansas and I were staring at each other, wondering what we should do, when six open Army trucks pulled up, filled with white military police carrying M-1 rifles and double-barreled shotguns aimed directly at us. On signal the Whites turned out all the lights on the east end of the ost and opened fire on the unarmed Blacks standing in the middle of the street. We all tried to break for cover, but it was too late. The screams and cries of those who had been shot pierced the hot July night air.

I was knocked to the ground by a blunt force. I saw Kansas lying near me. I didn't realize I had been shot until I felt a warm, sticky substance soaking my pants leg and shoulder. There was noise and confusion all around me, and then silence.

The Army ambulances pulled up within a half hour. Medics with flashlights stepped over the wounded bodies, lying on the ground as thick as flies, trying to decide who was dead, who was alive, who warranted a trip to the hospital or the morgue. When they reached me and Kansas, they motioned for the stretcher bearers with their flashlights.

"Can you walk?" a medic asked me.

I tried, but I was too numb to move. The medic turned me over and said to another medic, "This nigger has been shot three times." Then they turned their flashlights on Kansas. "They got this one in the head, but he'll be all right."

What did they mean? Did they mean he would be all right but I wouldn't? As I lay there preparing to die, my thoughts were not of heaven or hell, but of hate. I was cursing the darkness, and I was bleeding with hate.

On the way to the hospital, I heard the ambulance driver say to the medic, "Why the hell do we shoot our own men?"

"Who said they were men?" the medic said. "We shoot niggers like rabbits where I come from."

At the hospital, Kansas was rolled into a small room and I was left on a cart in the corridor. After a few minutes a doctor rushed into the little room. I could see him lift my friend's eyelids. He put a stethoscope to his chest, and the last thing he did was try to straighten his legs, which were in a bent position. They wouldn't straighten out. He put out the lights and closed the door.

Kansas was dead.

I came out of sedation at daybreak, amidst the groaning of a ward full of young soldiers who had been wounded the night before in the Camp Shenango riot. I learned later that the violence was still going on--it lasted three days, with soldiers breaking into the supply dump to get guns and ammunition.

In the bed to my left was an eighteen-year-old kid whimpering for his mother, his doctor, anybody. I tried to get out of bed, but the lower part of my body was paralyzed. I joined his cries, by screaming: "Help me! Help me! I can't move!"

Two orderlies rushed over and checked my pulse.

"Don't worry," one said. "Your legs will be all right."

He was pushed aside by an important-looking man in a dark blue serge civilian suit.

"Excuse yourself for a few minutes," the man said. "I want to talk with this soldier."

He leaned over my bed and asked, in a soft voice, "How are you feeling this morning, young man?"

"Awful."

"Who shot you?" he said. He pulled a small black book from his pocket and made several notations in it.

"What?" I asked.

"Did you have a gun?"

I didn't answer. I turned my head away in disgust. The man leaned closer. "Soldier, I'm here from Washington to help you," he whispered. "You must cooperate."

I turned my head back to look him straight in his saucer-shaped hazel eyes and said, "How?"

"I thought you might help me catch the radical Communist troublemakers," he said in serious tones—and with a straight face.

"They were all white fascists dressed in the United States Army's green fatigues," I whispered. "Both the fascists and their guns spoke with a Southern accent."

The man gave me a puzzled glance and made a few more notes. Then he walked away.

Later on I was awakened from a nap by the voices of a team of doctors discussing my condition at foot of my bed. Without saying anything to me, the physician in charge pulled down the sheet, turned me on my stomach and began jabbing his fingers in the center of my back just above the buttocks.

"Do you feel anything?"

"Yes!"

That response must have coincided with his diagnosis, because he turned and said to the others, "He'll walk again."

The Camp Shenango riot didn't make the newspapers in Chicago. The only way my parents found out what had happened to me was through the Red Cross. On Wednesday, they were walking down the corridor toward me. Dad was wearing his important facial expression, the one that complemented his million-dollar stride. When Mother spotted me her face beamed like a well-lit Christmas tree.

I was literally choking in an effort to hold back the tears. Mingled with the tears of joy at seeing my parents again were some tears of grief for my friend, Kansas, whose body was lying on a white table in the hospital morgue waiting to be shipped in a flag-draped pine box to his family,

I had a rough convalescense after that. My temperature rose until I was shipped in an ambulance over bumpy roads to the Veterans General Hospital in Butler, Pennsylvania, a fifty-mile drive. I was to have an operation there, and I was given a private room on the top floor of the hospital. But the first person to visit me was not a doctor, but the blue-suited man I had met earlier at the base hospital in Shenango.

"I hope your trip was comfortable, and I'm sure you'll find this private room an improvement over the crowded ward back at the base hospital," he said.

I nodded.

"Don't discuss the Shenango situtation with anyone in the hospital. Do you understand?"

I nodded again. He raised his right hand, parted his first and second fingers in a Winston Churchill "V for Victory" sign, said "good luck," and left the room.

My surgeon, Lt. Col. Richard Babcock, was a ruddy-faced, partially bald man with a very infectious and charming personality. Within a few days after I entered the hospital, he had me feeling as if he and I were in an undeclared war against the world. Col. Babcock knew my private room was not a privilege, but a prison in which to keep me quarantined to prevent the spread of a contagious virus called "niggeritis." He also knew that my operation could not be performed until the Red Cross was able to locate enough Negro Type A blood plasma in their segregated blood banks.

Moreover, the colonel was wise enough to know if I were ever able to escape from my hospital room, I would be treated as an untouchable by the white patients.

"Don't take any books or papers in that room, Mary. They put a coon in there yesterday who can't read or write," I heard a white woman hospital employee outside my partially closed room door say one day. Several days later I caught a little white lady in a Red Cross cap peeking into my room.

"Hello, there!" I said. "Won't you come in?"

She blushed, smiled sheepishly and stepped into the room, extending her hand.

"I'm Mary. I came up to see if we could do anything for you."

"I don't know, but I would certainly like to get out of this bed."

After lunch the next day, Mary came up with a wheelchair that had been ordered by Dr. Babcock and offered to take me for a ride. But out in the corridor we got such stares of hatred and gasps of disapproval that I said, "Let's go back to the room."

Mary was only five feet tall and weighed less than 100 pounds, but she had a lot of guts, and she arrived daily for my ride after that. The

Aberdeen Proving Grounds, 1944: Dempsey J. Travis pictured in the A.P.G. Exchange with award he retained during his Army career for best operated Post Exchange. This picture was never printed in the Post newspaper because it would have caused racial tensions.

stares continued until one day she rolled my chair down to the hospital auditorium, and I played a couple of jazz numbers on the piano during the recreation hour. After that I started to have some friends, and some of the white soldiers even began offering to replace Mary as my wheelchair pilot.

One day we were within 200 feet of my room when a tall, grim-faced soldier in a purple robe and white pajamas jumped into the wheelchair's path with both arms stretched out like a traffic cop. The man grabbed the arms of the wheelchair, and both Mary and I were about to panic. He burst into a loud laugh. "My buddies and me have decided to take .turns chauffeuring the piano player around," he said. The big soldier introduced himself as Pfc. James Messina from Newark, New Jersey. Mary, recovered by this time, thanked him for his offer, but her face flushed as she added sharply, "Soldier, you could have offered your services in a fashion that would have been less threatening."

Jim, one of eight children of an Italian family, had completed his junior year at Rutgers University a month before he was drafted into the Army. Sometimes he would try to equate the prejudice against Italians with that against Blacks, but I kept telling him, "Jim, you can get that monkey off your back if you remove the vowel 'a' from the end of your name and change your church. Man, that would make you an instant WASP."

"Travis, you got the right name and the right church. The only thing wrong with you is your color," he said.

"Some of you Italians are dark enough to pass for colored," I would say when Jim tried to get too hip. And I teased him that that might be because Hannibal and his Carthaginian troops from North Africa had occupied Italy for fifteen years from 218 B.C. to 203 B.C.

I had two successful operations, but the third was postponed several times. Lt. Col. Babcock and the other surgeon, Col. Cohen, disagreed over the risk involved in removing the bullet fragments from the lower part of my back. Babcock thought such an operation would cripple me permanently. Cohen disagreed. Babcock resigned from the case, and Col. Cohen went ahead and performed the operation—successfully.

I had a thirty-day leave in Chicago—which my mother and I spent writing letters to the President, U.S. Rep. William T. Dawson and U.S. Senators Scott W. Lucas (Dem.) and C. Wayland Brooks (Rep.) from Illinois to try to get me discharged.

Back at the hospital in Butler, I was told I had been reassigned to Camp Shenango. I protested to Col. Cohen that I was still having trouble walking. He looked at me piercingly. "Soldier, that limp you have attempted to perfect in your right leg is a fake."

"Sir!" I protested. "It's excruciating for me to have to walk on this leg."

"Don't worry, soldier," he said. "With your I.Q., you aren't going to have to stand. We're going to arrange for you to sit for the duration."

It didn't work out quite like that, but it was close. When I got back to Shenango, I found that some changes had been made. The official name of the post had been changed to Camp Reynolds, and a large service club had sprouted in the black area of the camp. Further, the color bars had been lowered, and Blacks were allowed to attend the main movie theatre in the white area. All this was done to cleanse the air of the racist stench that had hovered over the place after the riot.

In June, 1944, having given up all attempts to get discharged from the Army, I was shipped to Camp Lee, Virginia.

The train had a three-hour layover in Washington, D.C., and I had a good opportunity to witness Jim Crow with no clothes on. Everything was racially separated, from water fountains to soda fountains. Even the taxicabs were separate. Blacks could only ride in cabs owned or driven by other Blacks, and black cabs weren't permitted to enter the horseshoe curve in front of Union Station. Women, men and children had to carry their luggage a block to get to transportation.

Racism was so contagious in the District of Columbia that black people were practicing it on each other. On the Capital Transit, a circular advertising rooms for "light-colored folks only" was distributed.

Roy Eldridge, the black trumpet star with the Gene Krupa Orchestra, received double pay for not appearing with the band at Lowe's Theater in Washington. The Howard Theater on Florida Avenue was the only movie house with live, top-flight black stage shows. They featured such bands as Jimmie Lunceford, Claude Hopkins, Baron Lee, Lucky Millinder, Duke Ellington, Andy Kirk, Erskine Hawkin and Count Basie. I saw most of the same name bands with the U.S.O. shows during my tour at Camp Lee.

After the Washington exposure I didn't find Confederate Virginia as bad as I had expected. My survival mechanism made quick adjustments to a less subtle form of American apartheid. I found the seats at the back of the bus and the "for colored only" waiting rooms in the train stations offensive, but not unbearable.

Back at the post, the black Army's heavily-shoed feet marched left-right, left-right, in the hot Virginia sun. The drill sergeant would lead the platoon in an ad lib lyric to a World War I melody:

"Virginia is a helluva state,
Parlez-vous;
Virginia is a helluva state,
Parlez-vous;
Virginia is a helluva state,
The asshole of the forty-eight,
Hinky, dinky parlez-vous."

As we continued our march, we would sing:

"They say this is a white man's war,
Parlez-vous;
They say this is a white man's war,
Parlez-vous;
They say this is a white man's war,
Well, what the hell are we fighting for?
Hinky, dinky parlez-vous."

The exhilaration of marching was preparing a positive feeling of esprit de corps for when we went overseas. But I wasn't going. My I.Q. score got me selected out to attend the Quartermaster School for Administrators. I was sent to Aberdeen Proving Ground in Maryland, over my protests, with the company commander telling me, "I received a special order from Washington stating that you are to be sent to Maryland for the duration of the war, not overseas."

Major Sloan, the company commander at Aberdeen, asked me to organize a band for the company. I accepted with genuine joy.

"Good," he said, in his booming Texas accent. "You can do that in your spare time. Right now, I want you to type."

"Sorry, sir, I don't know how to type."

"Private Travis, you can learn." Major Sloan reached into his bottom desk drawer, pulled out a typing book, and handed it to me. Then he told his company clerk to give me a desk and a typewriter. Within thirty days I had become a self-taught fifty-words-a-minute typist.

Maj. Sloan made me assistant manager of the Colored Post Exchange, then manager, and finally I became area manager over three post exchanges, including the first large integrated post exchange at Aberdeen. In that position, I won the first prize weekly award for the best-operated Post Exchange. I continued to win the weekly contest for two straight years. The Army took my picture, but did not run it in the post newspaper as was usually done. The executive officer in charge of post exchanges told me, "Travis, we just can't afford to print this. It would offend too many people. I hope you'll understand."

So my Army career ended in relative prosperity: I got a promotion to Technical Sgt. Fourth Grade, and, along with the bi-weekly salary I received as exchange manager, I was making double my sergeant's pay. My father was a great lover of cigars, and I used to send him at least two boxes of the best smokes each month.

I liked to think about him back in Chicago, smoking my cigars and bragging to the neighbors about his son. I liked to think about that, and about how it was going to be when I went home.

I had adopted New York's Harlem as my new neighborhood on most of my weekend passes. Each of more than 100 train rides into New York

City always revealed something new. Harlem was New York's most visible neighborhood from the train because the railroad tracks were not covered. New York City's political power brokers in the 1930's decided to cover the railroad tracks in the white communities out of funds from the New Deal Westside Improvement Program; however, they did not feel such an amenity was necessary in Black Harlem. Uncovered tracks meant that Harlem's Blacks living between 125th and 155th Streets near the railroad had to endure the never-ending sound of clashing steel from the conjugating railroad cars. The intermittent moans and squeals of the cows and pigs being railroaded to the killing floor punctuated their Harlem days and nights. Floating through every open window were latent cases of silicosis germinating from the railroads' constant spewing of soot, smoke, grit and grime. Harlem was the coal mine of New York City.

The economic deprivation that prevailed in the Harlem mine, in spite of the war boom, caused thousands of black women to line up six mornings a week in the "slave markets" of mid-town Manhattan and the upper Bronx. White housewives were bidding for their services in 1944 at auction prices ranging between twenty-five and thirty cents per hour with the cost of the noon meal deducted. White trade unions made sure Blacks would have to work for such slave wages by denying them union cards, thus adding to their handicap to compete for better jobs.

The economically depressed noon-day Harlem transformed into a free-spending, glittering showplace each night under the Harlem moon before the clock struck twelve. Downtown white folks came uptown nightly to slum, get high, and sometimes fly. Every night, the Savoy Ballroom, 133rd and Lenox Avenue, Smalls' Paradise Cabaret, 135th Street and 7th Avenue, and the Elks Rendezvous, 133rd Street and Lenox, were loaded with white folks who wanted to see or learn to do the latest dance crazes, such as Peckin, Trucking, or the old Lindy Hop. Harlem at night in the 1940's was very reminiscent of the night life on the South Side of Chicago during the 1920's and '30's. Harlem's Apollo Theatre's 1890 architecture was not comparable to the Louis XIV castle appearance of Chicago's Regal Theatre. But the talent at both theatres was the same. Black entertainers rotated from black ghetto to ghetto in the fashion of the old Circuit Court judges.

My desire to return to Chicago was often forgotten when I saw talented former DuSable High School entertainers such as Ray Sneed, Jr. performing his famous exotic dance at Smalls' Paradise, or got a wave of recognition from John Young, the pianist, as he played "Foggy Bottom" with the Andy Kirk band on the stage of the Apollo Theatre, or encountered the famous pianist, Dorothy Donegan, as I caught her act at the Howard Theater in Washington, in concert at the Walnut Theatre in Philadelphia, or backstage at New York's Zanzibar Cabaret when she appeared there in the Cab Calloway Cotton Club Review.

Mid-Manhattan's thirty-six legitimate theatres afforded me the opportunity to balance my jazz interest against the best in live theatre. During the 1944 theatrical season, I caught Paul Robeson, the original genius for all seasons, in his powerful and poetic performance in the title role of Shakespeare's "Othello" at the Shubert Theatre on 44th Street west of Boardway. "Carmen Jones," Billy Rose's black version of George Bizet's opera, was the best musical on Broadway that year and I saw it at a Saturday matinee for the grand price of $2. "Anna Lucasta" was presented by the American Negro Theatre at the Library Theatre located in Harlem at 103 West 135th Street for a subscription price of seventy-five cents per seat. "Anna" is the story of a Polish family written by a white playwright. The tragedy, the comedy and the drama of the black experience in Harlem, mine, as expressed by Langston Hughes, Claude McKay and James Weldon Johnson, had not penetrated the Broadway stage by 1944. (Richard Wright's *Native Son,* a Chicago-based novel with a stinging social commentary, reached Broadway in 1941.)

"Black folks are happy folks and that's why they are not seen in serious roles in the movies or on the stage," said Art Mills as he leaned on the clover-shaped bar at Smalls' Paradise.

"Bull shit," I responded. "How can you be happy when the man is constantly kicking your ass?"

Art retorted, "Haven't you ever seen a white man kicking a nigger's ass and the nigger was laughing?"

After a brief reflection, I responded, "Yes! I have on more than a few occasions. However, none of them were laughing because it was funny. They laughed in self-defense. A laugh was sometimes the only weapon the nigger had to save his pride. Particularly, if it meant the end of his job or his life."

At this point I walked over to the jukebox and put in a nickel to hear the Mills Brothers and Ella Fitzgerald's rendition of "Into Each Life Some Rain Must Fall." I played that song twenty-three times and Art said, "Man, aren't you tired of hearing that song?"

I replied, "For some unknown reason I can't stop playing it."

Art said, "Are you having trouble with your old lady?"

"Nope!" I replied, "but I think I will call my mother. I haven't talked to her for two months."

I placed a collect call to Chicago and the first thing my mother said was, "Where are you? I have been calling Aberdeen trying to reach you for two days to tell you we had to rush your father to the County Hospital."

I hung up the phone abruptly and called Sgt. Morris Brown for a special pass to go to Chicago. He told me I could go directly from New York and that he would mail my furlough papers directly to my home. I caught the New York Central's "Pacemaker" that afternoon and arrived in Chicago on Saturday morning, December 16, 1944.

I went directly from the train station to the County Hospital. Dad's fear of the County Hospital and its alleged "black bottle" for colored folks meant he had to have been critically ill to consent to going there. My arrival at Dad's bedside confirmed my suspicions. They had tubes hooked into his arms and his nose. I had been in the ward for more than an hour when Dad opened his eyes, beckoned for me to come closer, then touched the sergeant's stripes on my Army uniform, smiled without saying a word and closed his eyes again.

Since Dad was on the critical list the intern permitted me to sit by his bed throughout the night. The only sound Dad made all night came from a heavy roaring in his chest. At 5:48 a.m. Sunday morning he opened his eyes and said, "I didn't think you would get here in time." I didn't respond. I simply touched his hand and smiled. Dad looked at me through his weak, watery eyes and said in a soft but audible voice, "Boy! Take care of your mother." Seconds after he spoke those words his eyes seemed to reel back into his head, and his mouth snapped open as if his jawbone had become unhinged. My father was pronounced dead at 6:03 a.m. Sunday, December 17, 1944.

My Aunt Willie invited Mother and me over to her home at 5336 South Wabash after the funeral. We stayed through the Christmas holiday. Christmas without Dad was a bust. Aunt Willie's excellently-prepared meals fell flat on my taste buds. Her expensive imported whiskies did not even give me a buzz. My spirit was so low that a street curb seemed high.

Aunt Willie's son, Frank, said, "Man, you are going to grieve yourself to death. Uncle Louis (my father) would not dig your mood at all. Let's get the hell out of the house and go and drink with Daddy-O-Daylie, the rhyming bartender, down at the DuSable Lounge. Hey! We can also check-out Floyd "Guitar Blues" Smith's Trio." (The DuSable was located on Oakland Boulevard, about 100 feet west of Cottage Grove in the basement of the DuSable Hotel.)

To our disappointment, we found that Daddy-O had moved his talents to Charlie Coles' El Grotto Supper Club at 6400 South Cottage Grove in the basement of the Pershing Hotel. The twenty-five block trip South to hear Daddy-O's rhymes and to see him do tricks with the ice cubes gave me the first real laugh I had during my furlough in Chicago.

The next day we decided to go downtown to see the World's Champion Joe Louis' wife, Marva Louis, the new singing sensation. She was accompanied by my friend, Zinky Cohn, the piano wizard, on the stage of the Rialto Theater at State and Van Buren. (The Rialto was a famous Burlesque theatre that changed its policy from strip tease to all black stage shows in the fall of 1944.) Thursday, December 28, 1944, marked the first time in my twenty-plus years of visiting the Loop and its theatres that I had ever seen such a large army of Blacks outside the boundary lines of our South Side black ghetto.

Our Allied Armies had pulled up along the German Siegfried line in December, 1944, when Hitler launched his last fanatical counter-offensive of the war. So effective was the Germans' offensive that all the troops were forced back some fifty miles, almost to the sea.

The tides turned in January, 1945, when the Allies retaliated with a renewed offensive. The Soviets had also begun a winter offensive. By the end of February, the Soviet Allied troops had moved westward within thirty miles of Berlin. The American and British troops were advancing eastward. Victory for the Allied troops was in the air when President Franklin D. Roosevelt died suddenly on April 12th, 1945, in Warm Springs, Georgia. Although most Blacks had been denied the right to cast a vote for Roosevelt in the four times he was elected President, they reacted to his death as one would react to the lost of a close friend or relative. (Roosevelt served less than three months in his fourth term.)

I arrived in Washington, D.C. from Aberdeen, Maryland, on Saturday, April 14th, to visit with relatives over the weekend. The train station was jammed with dignitaries of all types awaiting the 10:30 a.m. arrival of the Roosevelt Funeral Train. Black and white folks stood integrated on both sides of the streets, sidewalk deep, from the train station to the Capitol. Many of them were openly weeping. The hot and humid Potomac weather made waiting for the funeral procession onerous. It was heartbreaking to stand there among a throng of Blacks and Whites who had become unified in tears over a fallen leader. The vibrations of my

Marva Louis, former wife of the late "Brown Bomber" Joe Louis, a singing sensation in both Chicago and New York during the '40s.

Zinkey Cohen, renowned pianist, was musical director and accompanist for Ms. Louis. Mr. Cohen can best be described as a consummate musician who accompanied, other than Marva Louis, such stars as Ethel Waters, Eddie South, the Black Angel of the violin, Staff Smith and Jimmy Noon just to mention a few.

heartbeat seemed louder than the clop, clop from the hoofs of the six white horses that pulled the caisson carrying President Roosevelt's flag-covered coffin. The moans from the crowd as the coffin passed were subdued by the drone of planes overhead, and the humming from the motors of the slow moving black limousines.

The War moved swiftly in the next twenty-five days. The German government surrendered unconditionally at General Eisenhower's headquarters on May 7, and May 8, 1945, was declared as V-E (Victory in Europe) Day. Less than 120 days after Roosevelt's death, President Harry S. Truman issued an ultimatum to the Japanese to surrender or face "prompt and utter destruction." Truman waited a week and on August 6th, 1945, his promise of destruction fell out of the sky in the epoch-making form of an atomic bomb over the city of Hiroshima in Japan. The city was obliterated: 75,000 to 80,000 people were killed, and thousands more permanently injured. On August 14, Japan agreed to surrender. One hundred and fifty days later, on February 2, 1946, I surrendered my uniform at Indian Town Gap, Pennsylvania. The captain at the "Gap" separation center told us that we had thirty days to get out of uniform and into civilian clothes. Within thirty hours after I left the "Gap" I was back in Chicago standing on the corner of 47th and South Parkway in a ready-made double-breasted cocoa brown suit. The real world that I was about to grapple with was unlike the civilian utopia I dreamed about during my forty months and twenty-three days stay in the Army.

This 1946 photograph of the corner of 47th Street and South Parkway (now King Drive) is truly symbolic. During this period 47th and South Parkway was the cross roads of the black community. If one stood on the corner for three hours, he/she could see people they had not seen for years.

Chapter 13

FACING FACTS

"Black boy! You can't read, you can't write, and you can't do arithmetic. All you can hope to do is succeed as a common laborer, at some task that requires a strong back and a weak mind."

Those were not the exact words in the letters I had received from Roosevelt, DePaul and Northwestern Universities, but they might as well have been. They all meant the same thing: I was being rejected. I could tell myself that I knew I had talents, that I had even managed to experience success in that unlikely setting, the segregated U.S. Army, but none of it mattered. I felt utterly destroyed.

It didn't seem to help to reflect that my rejection might have more to do with my color than with my potential. After all, I knew that DePaul and Northwestern had strict quotas for both Blacks and Jews. But my anguish and shame at being rejected by Roosevelt was far greater.

Roosevelt was quota-free. It had emerged on April 17, 1945, spawned by protests over the bigotry of the Central YMCA College. That was after Dr. Edward J. Sparling, president of the YMCA college, had refused to give the board of trustees a black head count, since that would have meant establishing quotas for the education-hungry black veterans returning from the war. At that time, tuition fees for all students at the college were the same, but Blacks could not use the YMCA swimming pool or other athletic facilities in the Association Building at 19 South LaSalle Street.

In February, 1946, however, Roosevelt represented hope for black veterans, and many of my buddies were heading downtown to attend.

I was left out. In spite of all my ambitions and the new sense of adulthood that I had brought with me from the Army experience, I was too dumb to attend. My feelings can best be described in a blues lyric I composed:

> "If you don't believe I am dead, baby,
> Just try calling me on the phone.
>
> "The man done buried my mind,
> And my body is all alone."

Those notices from the university authorities convinced me I was a deadhead, since I had flunked their exams. I took it all very seriously, and I went back to my pre-war job at Armour. I was rehired with veterans' preference as a "Georgia mule." The preference helped, because 30,000 members of the United Packing House Workers' Union had just returned from a strike called January 16, 1946, against post-war cutbacks in jobs, hours and wages.

A "mule" unloaded the boned hams from the end of a conveyer into a two-wheeled "Georgia buggy" and then pulled the buggy, in the manner of a harnessed animal, to a scale a hundred feet away. The work was hard, demeaning and boring, and my unhappiness grew. Only the lunchbreaks provided any mental stimulation at all, as twenty or so other "mules" and I would gather around to talk about black issues. I liked to talk about what I was already calling my "Negro Agenda."

For example, there was the question of black folks who had lived around 61st and 62nd Streets and Calumet since the early 1930's but who still weren't permitted to go to the White City Roller Rink at 63rd and Calumet until 1946. It took picket lines, bloodied heads and many arrests before they were let in.

We talked about the incident when Cab Calloway, the internationally famous band leader, was beaten over the head and had a finger broken when he tried to see Lionel Hampton and his orchestra at the "white only" Pla-Mor Ballroom in Kansas City, Missouri. The Stevens (later the Hilton), the Sherman House and the Congress Hotels in downtown Chicago refused to accommodate the National Negro Museum and Historical Foundation for a planned celebration of "Negro History Week." The downtown hotels in Chicago, and most restaurants, did not allow Blacks to sit and eat, either.

One day I hauled my "Georgia buggy" over to the scale. The white man, in a white frock, wrote down the weight on a white piece of paper and slapped it on top of the load of dead hams in the buggy, just like he always did.

"Pull that load to the Sweet Pickle Department and rush right back and get another one," he said.

As I was chugging along following the orders, the department superintendent stopped me.

"If you don't quit, we are going to fire you in two weeks. Your noontime discussions with the men are causing morale problems in the department," he said.

"What are you talking about?" I asked.

"You know," he said, and he walked away.

I quit the stockyards in March, 1946. I knew that kind of work held no hope for me. Instead, I decided to take a chance on self-employment. I had taken an accounting correspondence course during my army years, and now I decided to set up as a tax consultant, filling out tax returns for the members of Rev. Victoria Pitts' storefront church at 2216 South State Street.

That work brought about a change in my self-image. It gave me so much confidence that I enrolled in two courses at Englewood Evening Junior College, where there were no entrance requirements and the registration fee was only five dollars. With the help of my high school friend, Dustalear Cook, who had become a Chicago schoolteacher, I passed both courses with better than a "B" average.

That summer I tried a more ambitious venture. I leased the Pershing Ballroom in the Pershing Hotel at 64th and Cottage Grove for four separate dance dates. I booked a popular recording act, the "Cats and the Fiddle," headed by Austin Powell, for the first date.

The Pershing Hotel was the site of Dempsey Travis' first musical flop as a dance promoter. This established hotel housed the famed Pershing Ballroom, and was the largest hotel of its type owned by blacks until the mid-1940's. The Pershing was the home base of the renowned pianist, Admad Jamal. The El Grotto nightclub which was located in the basement was one of the class spots of its time featuring such artists as Earl "Father" Hines and the late Ivy Anderson, Duke Ellington's songstress.

It was a flop. I had a partner, a man I had admired because he had a college degree. But only 420 people attended. I had personally sold 390 tickets, and my college-educated partner had sold thirty. We assigned our three remaining dates to the Adams Brothers, two local dance promoters, and dissolved our partnership.

But then I was even more determined to get an education. I took the placement examination at Wilson Junior College and was told I would have to take remedial reading and English. Not understanding just what I was letting myself in for, I stopped at the next table and registered for American Literature 117.

While I was standing there, I overheard two teachers in a heated discussion over who was going to share an office with a new appointee to the English department. A bespectacled male teacher was telling a red-headed woman teacher, "Okay, I'll share my office with her. I learned to understand them through my military experience in World War I." The woman gave a sigh of relief. It became clear as I listened that the "them" they were talking about was Henrietta L. McMillen, Ph.D., the first Black appointed to the English department in the Chicago Junior College system. She later became head of the English department for both Wilson Junior and the Chicago Teachers' College.

Oh, those "thems," I thought. It was a word that curdled the human sensibilities of all those Blacks who made history by being "firsts" and then had to suffer the curse of being thought of always as exceptions to the "thems."

In the remedial reading class, on the first day, the instructor paced back and forth in front of us and then delivered a little speech that has echoed in my mind ever since.

" Now, I think I should start this class by telling you that if you have gone this far in life and still have to be assigned to this remedial reading class, you'd just better face the fact that you're not going to make it. The cards of academic life have been stacked against you. My statistics show that only one out of every 200 people who are enrolled in this class graduate from college with an undergraduate degree. Eighty-five per cent of you present today will not survive your first college year."

Dr. Witney E. Smith's statement set my brain whirling with mad promises to myself that I would be that one out of the 200 to graduate from college. But the promises didn't seem at all realistic when I was brought up sharply against a terrible and unexpected obstacle: I could not read. Oh, sure, I could work my way through application forms and letters and so forth, but as far as doing more sophisticated reading, the type of thing I had to do if I was to have any hope of staying in college, I was floundering. And I hadn't even understood, when I graduated from high school, how handicapped I was.

In the remedial reading course, I struggled painfully through high-school-level texts, reading every page one word at a time. But in the "Lit" class, for which I had so casually signed up, I was required to read one book each week and write a comprehensive report about what I read. I quickly discovered that this was far beyond me. I spent ten to twenty minutes on a single page, staying up until early in the morning.

"Why don't you go to bed, boy, and get some sleep?" my mother would call.

"Mama, there is no time to sleep. I have got to learn to read."

"You're ruining your health."

"Mama, how can I have a healthy body with a hungry mind?"

"Suit yourself," she would answer as I returned to wrestling with Hawthorne or Thoreau or Sinclair Lewis.

When Dr. Ernest Ernst read my first book report, he threatened to throw me out of the class. He thought it was a joke. I protested that it was not and told him I was willing to do it over and over until it was acceptable to him. He let me stay in the class provided I came to his counseling office on Mondays, Wednesdays and Fridays to review my work.

"Dr. Ernst, what did I do wrong?"

He shook his head. "Well, you just didn't understand what you read. Why don't you try again?"

I had no resentment. I just kept trying.

About the eighth week into the semester it paid off. I was inching through a book by Theodore Dreiser, one word and one phrase at a time, when suddenly it clicked! It became clear—it all fell into place. The phrases rolled together into sentences, and the sentences rolled into paragraphs of thoughts and ideas.

I let out a loud yelp, and my mother tumbled out of her bed and came running—she must have thought I had injured myself somehow.

"Great God A'mighty, Mama, I can read!" I said.

Not long after that, I had a similar spontaneous experience in writing. It had been almost impossible for me to express myself on paper in a logical fashion. If you cannot grasp ideas logically when you read them, you certainly cannot explain and recreate them. If Dempsey couldn't read, you can be certain he would not be able to write.

In December of 1946, I was trying to put together a letter to the Veterans Administration, complaining about the fact that I had never received a disability check for my service-connected disabilities. Like magic, I discovered I had written eight full pages in less than an hour, describing, giving reasons, and drawing conclusions. Before that time, it would have taken me that long to compose two poorly constructed paragraphs. I had learned to read, and now I had learned to write! I was 26 years old, and at that age discovering the written page was a euphoric experience. Unearthing the potential of a mature mind is a powerful instrument for change.

My studies suddenly became easier. In spite of the facts of the negative society around me, I was able to keep the spirit to fight past my obstacles. Other students in the remedial reading class did not, and they succumbed in the first academic year, as Dr. Witney E. Smith had predicted.

But I knew you had to keep the spirit, even in the face of incidents like the one that occurred when Thomas Leonard tried to buy a small can of aspirin for a headache in Sam's Tap Room at 1034 East 43rd Street. Thomas was refused service and was subsequently shot in the stomach by a member of an anti-black Oakland-Kenwood area mob. Three of his friends were brutally beaten by a white mob of forty men. The Blacks were all arrested and taken before Judge Charles Daugherty on Jan. 3, 1947, in felony court and held on counts of assault with intent to kill.

It was spirit that propelled Jackie Robinson to run the bases of liberation for Black America when he was called to play in the major leagues on April 9, 1947. And it was spirit that rocketed me through Wilson Junior College in sixteen months instead of the usual twenty-four. I received my diploma on January 30, 1948.

My Wilson diploma was a quick passport to Roosevelt University, the fountainhead of democracy in higher education. Of course, Roosevelt didn't have much competition. In 1948, the spirit of brotherhood that permeated the walls of the University was unlike anything I had ever experienced. Every morning when I stepped inside the University's walls I was enveloped with a feeling of hope for black people in America. However, each afternoon when I stepped outside the University's doors onto Michigan Avenue, I was jarred back to the realization that Roosevelt University did not mirror the real world.

Daily, as I walked north on Michigan to catch the bus going south, I looked at the tall, white-owned office buildings and said, "Those buildings don't even have black smoke coming out of the chimney." I knew that Blacks did not have a "toenail hold" on the financial fortunes of America, and I decided I was going to work for change since the status quo was simply unacceptable to me. At the time I believed that I could best work for change through classes in law and politics.

In my classes at Roosevelt I met some brilliant young Blacks. There was Gus Savage; Harold Washington; Oscar Brown, Jr., writer, actor, producer and singer; Robert L. Kimbrough, now a dentist; Frank London Brown, author of *Trumbull Park;* Mark Jones, Circuit Court Judge, Cook County, Illinois; and Clarence Towns, also a dentist.

Savage, Washington, Oscar Brown, Jr., Frank Brown, Bennett Johnson and I were all sitting on the floor in a temporary housing trailer project at 57th and Perry, the home of Gus and Eunice Savage, when we all agreed, after much debate, on a single "Black Agenda." One of the planks in the Agenda was that both Gus Savage and Harold Washington should run for Congress. Gus agreed to run from a West Side district and Harold agreed to run from the South Side.

It has taken thirty-two years to fulfill a commitment that sounded like a "pork dieter's" dream. The six men who sat on the floor that night were dreamers all right, dreamers who have continued to support each other financially and spiritually over the years—in days of both feast and famine. Unfortunately, there was an abundance of famine and very little feast. Both Gus and Harold took their seats in Congress in January, 1981, representing the 1st and 2nd Congressional Districts in Illinois. Both the 1st and 2nd Congressional Districts are expansions of the restrictive covenant areas occupied by Blacks prior to 1948.

What Congress refused to achieve legislatively, the United States Supreme Court did—when it ruled in Shelley vs. Kraemer on Monday, May 3, 1948, that racial restrictive convenants were unenforceable.

The next morning Mr. Richard Hill, Jr., lawyer and the former president of the first black-owned national bank in Illinois, the Douglas National Bank at 36th and State Streets, gave me and his son, Oscar, who became an attorney, a ride to Roosevelt University. Mr. Hill turned around in the driver's seat and held up the *Chicago Tribune* that he had just bought from the newsstand at Garfield and Michigan. "What does this headline on restrictive covenants mean to you and Oscar?"

Both Oscar and I gave vague answers about Jim Crow housing that did not satisfy Mr. Hill. As Mr. Hill drove north on Michigan Boulevard he explained: "Colored people can live in the 61st block on Rhodes with the full sanction of the law. The covenant suit pending against Mary A. Green at 6439 S. Maryland, brought by Vivian McCormick, 6435 Maryland and Bessie McGray, 6417 S. Maryland, to enforce a covenant against Negroes living in that block will be dismissed.

"As a matter of fact," he continued, "all race restrictions in every state of the Union and in the District of Columbia have been struck down as a result of the Supreme Court decision. Every race restriction recorded against real estate in Cook County is now meaningless. They can be tossed out as scraps of paper." Neither Oscar nor I said a word until Mr. Hill stopped the car at Roosevelt University, where we thanked him for the ride.

I was thinking hard about the decision and what it would mean to black people. I had always been more or less aware of housing and the problems it presented and the human toll that segregation had taken in Chicago. In spite of my failure to be aware of the case as it went through the courts, I understood its importance. And, of course, I was well aware that the postwar period had been one of acute housing shortage, with a resulting acceleration in tension between Blacks and Whites in many areas of the city.

By April of 1949, for example, a simmering situation burst into violence in Park Manor. Jesse Howell's home at 6958 South Prairie was burned; a Ku Klux Klan cross was planted on the lawn of Ruth Minor's house at 215 East 70th Street; and a roving gang of white hoodlums smashed windows at the home of Mrs. A. Carter at 7023 South Vernon.

Both the Federal Housing Administration and the Veterans Administration supported the racist climate for years after the 1948 Supreme Court decision on restrictive covenants by refusing mortgages to Blacks moving into white areas such as Park Manor, Chatham, South Shore, Kenwood and Hyde Park. The Veterans Administration made funds available through the G.I. Bill to educate black minds, but under the same bill it was working, in practice, to exclude Blacks from needed housing, most spectacularly in the suburbs. These kinds of governmental inconsistencies kept pushing me toward a career in law.

Quite by accident, I launched a career in the field of housing, instead of law. At the home of Theodore McNeal, Jr., at 4640 South Michigan Avenue, in the Rosenwald Building, Moselynne E. Hardwick, my fiancee from Cleveland, Tennessee, Mae Robinson, McNeal's mother, Eugene N. Robinson, his stepfather, and I started talking about housing during dinner one night. Mrs. Robinson said, "I understand you plan to enter law school this fall after you graduate from Roosevelt University?" I told her I had been accepted at the Chicago Kent College of Law.

"I guess you will go into criminal law?" she said in a less than enthusiastic tone. "I think your personality is more suited to dealing with happier situations," she said.

"Like what?" I asked.

"In the field of real estate, you would be dealing with families buying homes or possibly young couples renting their first apartments. You must admit that people in those categories create a better working environment than someone who might be on his way to breaking into a jailhouse."

Moselynne and I discussed Mrs. Robinson's suggestion extensively after we left the dinner party. Mrs. Robinson had put something on my mind, and I enrolled in a real estate principles course at Roosevelt the following week as a career hedge to supplement the income from my G.I. bill while in law school.

In August, 1949, three major events took place. I asked Moselynne to marry me; I received my Bachelor of Arts degree from Roosevelt University (thirty-two months from the day I entered Wilson Jr. College); and I passed the Real Estate Broker's exam.

I formally opened my first real estate office when I proudly hung my real estate license in a third floor bedroom on August 17, 1949, at 5428 South Indiana, where I lived with my mother. September was just as eventful because at high noon on September 17, 1949, Mose and I were married. One week later I entered law school. In 1949, I had achieved my 1946 three-year projection. I finished college, married a beautiful, loving girl, and entered a profession.

This photograph was taken by the author of his wife
Moselynne in the Fall of 1950 one year after their marriage.

Chapter 14

DON'T STOP ME NOW

I had chosen the 1949 recession as a time to go into business, and things were tough. For awhile I shared an office in the afternoons, since I was attending law school in the morning, with an attorney named William Hughes, over the old State Theater at 3509 South State. The agreement was that I wouldn't have to pay my half of the rent until I earned my first real estate commission. Three months later, I had not earned a single commission, and few prospects were fighting for my attention. Then Attorney Hughes, who worked full time at the post office at night, moved across the street into the Binga Arcade building at 3460 South State to share offices with several other part-time lawyers.

Since he had taken the desk, chairs, telephone and telephone directory, for several months I used an orange crate for a desk and a tin scrub bucket for a chair. On the rare occasions when I had appointments with clients with wallets intact, Attorney Horace Galloway, who leased the suite, would let me use his front office.

One day Dr. Allen L. Wright, M.D., a 1939 DuSable classmate who now practices medicine in Chicago, paid me a surprise visit. He found Travis, the real estate broker, sitting on a pail behind a wooden box. His face did not reveal any surprise at what must have been an incongruous sight.

"What do you have to sell in Douglas Park?" he said.

"I have a deluxe yellow brick three-flat, with three six-room apartments with two baths in each unit, at 1641 South Drake Avenue."

"That sounds like something I might be interested in. When can I see it?"

"Any time you want. But we'll have to take the streetcar, because I don't own a car."

Dr. Wright drove me over to see the property. A few days later we saw it again with his wife, Alyce. They bought it. It was my first sale. The commission was $1,240, which was more money than I had ever had in my life at one time.

When Moselynne came home from work that evening I had placed the big check in the middle of the bed, where she couldn't miss it.

"Baby! You can quit your job now and come home and take care of our business," I said.

Moselynne's typing ability proved a real asset to our enterprise. She would type twenty or more letters every day to property owners in the Douglas Park area, soliciting property for sale. Then she would type an equal number of letters to the 3,416 owners and tenants being displaced by urban renewal on the 100-acre Lake Meadows Development Site, from 31st to 35th Streets, from King Drive to the Lake. Douglas Park properties were attractive to these displaced families, because the $3,000 to $5,000 in equity they received from urban renewal represented a good down payment for West Side properties, providing the buyers weren't too old to qualify for a mortgage.

I got to be very good at matching South Side people with West Side housing. Many Blacks chose Douglas Park because the West Side Jewish residents being displaced by black South Side immigrants never reacted violently, as did the Irish and Poles on the Southeast and Southwest Sides. The Jewish homeowners in Douglas Park were so cordial toward me that I would sometimes get up enough nerve to ask them why they were moving.

"We're moving west to California," they always said.

I thought it was strange that so many people from the same area would be moving to the West Coast. Later on a Jewish friend told me that Skokie, Illinois, and California were synonymous. In the west area of Hyde Park, the Jewish sellers would always tell me they were moving south to Florida, when they were in fact moving north, to Lake Shore Drive or Highland Park, or Chicago's very, very white North Shore.

Searching out mortgages for Blacks displaced by urban renewal in 1950 and 1951 was more exhausting than driving a 1923 Model-T Ford non-stop from Chicago to California. The Ford would ultimately reach its destination, but the displaced family frequently would not find its mortgage. Major white Loop banks and savings and loan associations were not interested in making loans to black borrowers. The two very small black-owned savings and loan associations didn't have enough money to meet the demand. And angry Whites were wildly demonstrating at City Hall against seven sites in white neighborhoods that were being proposed for subsidized housing for low-income displaced Blacks.

But at the same time, white speculators were having no trouble getting mortgage money from life insurance companies and savings and loan associations to exploit black homebuyers through contract sales. It was common for Blacks to buy homes on contract from speculators at prices that had been marked up 200 to 300 per cent. Contract selling was a common practice in Chicago into the early 1970's. A successful lawsuit filed by both the Westside and the Southside Contract Buyers' Leagues slowed the practice. The land contract is intrinsically a good document. It was the white speculators' exploitive use of the instrument which gave it a slaveship stench.

Human exploitation in any form is vicious. Exploiting an economically and culturally disadvantaged people in their efforts to seek basic shelter is vile. I starved the first nine months I was in the real estate business because I refused to become a "bird dog" for white speculators and their white and black lending sponsors who were plundering the black housing market with land contracts.

I had been a licensed broker on a bare survival diet for almost a year before I met Henry Banach, a man of Polish ancestry, and another named August Saldukus. Through Banach, I was able to get loans for Blacks through the Polish-controlled Universal Savings and Loan Association on the city's Near South Side. Saldukus was president of the Midland Savings and Loan Association. During my first years in the business, these two institutions made 99 per cent of my loans. I was delighted with the arrangement, because ultimately all my people were able to get deeds instead of contracts. Both institutions charged a five per cent service fee plus six per cent interest annually. These prices were bargains, since the other money available demanded a 10 per cent cash service fee up front, plus 6 per cent per annum.

The magnitude of the discrimination in the mortgage market was—and is—obvious when you consider that the average white buyer in that period was paying a 1 per cent or less service charge, with an interest rate hovering just above 5 per cent. Some institutions were paying brokers a 1 per cent finders fee for every white borrower who qualified for a mortgage.

That discrimination, and the oppressive effect of the land contract on the black community, made it evident to me that the only way a black man could survive in real estate and serve his people was by creating a source within the black community to use some of that community's own wealth. So I began to dream about what was to become the Sivart Mortgage Corporation, the conduit needed to achieve that objective.

Sivart, as a mortgage banking institution with its roots, purposes—and dreams—in the black community, could tap the billions in black savings being held by white institutions in the form of pension funds, insurance premiums, time deposits and savings certificates. But there were many obstacles that had to be surmounted, and finally getting the thing underway was to take years.

In 1951, Chicago was a city deeply divided by the most overt racist practices, so much so that when I spoke of my Sivart dream to people like my mother, they shook their heads and said I was hopelessly out of step. Black lives in Chicago at that time were still clouded by one report after another of outbreaks of racial violence.

On June 8, 1951, Harvey Clark Jr. ventured into the white suburb of Cicero, the most vehemently defended bastion of white racism in the Chicago metropolitan area. Clark and Maurice Scott, Sr., who owned the moving van that was carrying Clark's belongings, were greeted by several members of the Cicero Police Department when they arrived at 6139 19th Court in Cicero, where Clark had rented a third floor apartment.

"You niggers have no moving permit, and you can't move your nigger junk into this building," was their "Welcome Wagon" salute.

In the middle of the afternoon, George C. Adams, Harvey Clark's attorney, who was a Creole of black, French and Indian ancestry, received a telephone call from the janitor at the Cicero building. The janitor told him the police had halted Clark's move-in. Adams got hold of Maurice Scott, Jr., the son of the moving van owner, and the two sped off to Cicero in Adams' car.

When the car pulled up at the address, Scott saw a policeman holding a gun at the back of his father's head and kneeing him forward. Scott ran over to them, and another Cicero cop put a gun to his head, while white women crowded around to deluge his face with layers of thick, frothy spit.

National Guardsmen in fighting gear during Cicero Riot, 1951.

Clark and his lawyer, with the aid of two attorneys for the National Association for the Advancement of Colored People (NAACP), Ulysses S. Key and George M. Leighton, obtained an injunction against the Cicero police from U.S. Federal Judge John P. Barnes. The injunction allowed Clark to move his furniture into the apartment a month later, on July 10, but it did not abate the racist rage in the breast of the Cicero mob.

Only a small knot of Whites watched the move-in, but by 9:30 the following night, the pack had grown to a growling mob of some 5,000 people, more than half of them women. The family never was allowed to occupy the apartment. During the night, teenage hoodlums broke into the building and threw Clark's furniture, clothing, and other personal property out of the third-floor windows. Each time a window was broken or an object was hurled out, the mob would roar in delight. The roars amplified to a frenzy when the Cicero rioters began to lynch the Clark family—symbolically—by setting fire to the furniture and clothing that had been thrown to the ground.

By the second night, the atmosphere in Cicero was one of a raw carnival without masks, a mob in search of a collective orgasm of racial hatred. The mob was still there, howling and jeering, on the third night, but that was the night Police Chief Konovsky and his men went home, leaving the Clark family's possessions to the mercy of the good white citizens of Cicero. Law and order for Black America had failed.

Finally, at the urging of Alderman Archibald Carey and the Cook County Sheriff, Governor Adlai Stevenson sent in the National Guard to quell the disorder. It took 500 bayonet-wielding Guardsmen to end the incident. It was the first time since the bloody Chicago riot of 1919 that a Governor had to send troops into Cook County. A $200,000 lawsuit was filed in Federal Court against Cicero's town officials for violating the Constitutional civil rights of the Scotts, Edwards, and the Clark family.

The protective legal umbrella the NAACP put over the Clark's civil rights case was one of the reasons that I became a paid-up life member of that organization in the fall of 1952. Paying out a lump sum of $500 for a civil rights membership in those dark economic days was not a small thing for me—or for the NAACP. The organization had only 88 fully paid life members nationally and 133 subscribing life members in 1953, compared with 20,000 fully paid life members and 33,000 subscribing life members in 1975, according to Beatrice Steele, Chicago NAACP Life Membership Chairman.

So a new life member in those days was very important, so important that the executive secretary, the legendary Walter White, would fly from New York City to the city of the donor to personally present him with a life membership plaque. I will never forget my own presentation. The Life Membership Committee of the Chicago Branch of the NAACP arranged a meeting for the occasion in the Wendell Phillips High School Assembly Hall. At the last minute, Walter White was called to Washington D.C., and he sent in his place his assistant, Roy Wilkins.

I found it curiously hard to speak before this friendly and expectant audience about my conviction that civil rights and my own life and quest for economic success were inextricably intertwined. I had been working out my ideas on this for years, ever since I first began to listen to my father and his brothers talk about the situation of Blacks in America around our dining room table. Nevertheless, my voice quavered as I spoke.

In contrast, the Whites who crashed bricks through the front window of Donald Howard's apartment at 10630 South Beasley on August 6, 1953, were having no such difficulty in expressing themselves. They weren't saying, "Welcome to the National Association for the Advancement of Colored People," nor were they saying, "Welcome to Trumbull Park Homes." They were shouting:

> "Coon, coon, you came too soon,
> You and your kind should go to the moon."

The siege of Trumbull Park was the longest and most costly racial incident in Chicago history. In the late summer and fall of 1953, as many as 1,200 policemen patrolled the area around the 427-unit Trumbull Park project on some days.

My friend and fellow Roosevelt University alumnus, the late Frank London Brown, was a tenant in Trumbull Park. I lived his terrors daily. He would call and tell me that he was coming to visit if he could get the "Black Mariah" to pick him up. Blacks leaving Trumbull Park for any purpose had to be transported out of the area, for their own protection, in a dingy, black patrol wagon that reeked with strong, offensive odors left over from its usual function of ferrying drunks and criminals. The police would give their passengers the option of being dropped off at 95th and State Streets or 95th and Cottage Grove, which were the southern boundaries of the "Black Belt" in 1953. To get back into Trumbull Park, Frank would have to call Essex 5-5910, and the paddy wagon would pick him up again at one of those two points within twenty to thirty minutes—maybe. Not surprisingly, visiting among Blacks in Trumbull Park was discouraged by the Chicago police.

Nearly thirty years later, I could not trace the exact route of the "Black Mariahs" when I visited the area, because expressway construction had eliminated some of the streets. But I found that in addition to Blacks living in the project, others had bought private homes on the east side of the 106th block on Beasley. I talked to a white man, about 65 years old, who told me, "The doctor said I had high blood pressure and a bad heart, and I would have to live with these ailments the rest of my life. The way I look at it is, if the good Negroes in this project don't try to marry my grandaughter or molest my wife, I'm resigned to live with them as neighbors as long as there is breath in my body."

Dempsey J. Travis is pictured here in his offices on the 2nd floor at 412 East 47th Street in 1951 along with members of this first sale force. Left to right: Robert McGee; the late Willie Wright; Dempsey J. Travis; Theodore McNeal; Edward Spraggins and Eugene N. F. Robinson.

Pictured are Mr. and Mrs. Donald Howard of 10630 South Bensley on August 6, 1953, boarding up their windows after thugs had terrorized them in a brick throwing escapade.

Mr. Howard and a friend are escorted into a "Black Mariah" by Chicago Police.

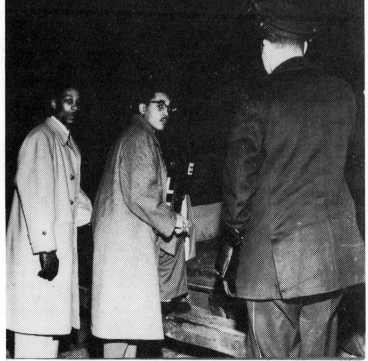

Standing - Left to right - Congressman Harold Washington, Congressman Gus Savage; the late Willie Wright, Attorney Lawrence Haliburton and sitting are Mrs. Travis, the author' mother and Henry G. Fort, a former member of the Nat "King" Cole orchestra. The group is gathered in the kitchen of Mrs. Travis's home at 5428 South Indiana Avenue during a holiday party in 1952.

Chapter 15

CIVIL RIGHTS STRUGGLE - NORTHERN STYLE

In 1954, a lot of things were beginning—just beginning—to change for Blacks. And I had my problems too.

I was hospitalized with a mysterious disease for four months. The doctors, although they admitted they did not know what was wrong with me, recommended surgery. I insisted they confer with me first. So, one morning, two cheerful young surgeons appeared in my room carrying a large anatomy chart and explained in lay language how they were going to proceed.

"What do you expect to find after you open my stomach?" I asked.

They looked at each other and then at me. "We're not sure."

"Then it's an exploratory operation," I said.

"Yes. But it's the only way we can find out exactly what is wrong with you."

I asked them to give me a half hour to make a decision. When they returned, I had called my wife and mother to come to the hospital to help me dress and check out.

The doctors were shocked. They warned me I was making a mistake and that I would never be readmitted to Billings Hospital, the prestigious University of Chicago hospital on Chicago's South Side. The threat didn't disturb me, because it sounded to me like such a readmission would give me a quick entry into the cemetery.

I was at home for two weeks, physically sinking, when I got a letter from the head of internal medicine at Billings, asking that I call him. I was readmitted as an outpatient, and a young internist finally found the cause of the trouble, diagnosing it as "obstructive jaundice." The symptoms had not been produced by cancer, as they had thought.

"Boy, are you lucky," my wife said when I told her the news.

"Baby, I'm lucky in more ways than one," I said. "I'm lucky in having you as my wife, and I'm lucky that God gave me an opportunity to re-examine my life and the world around me during the four months I've been on my back."

It was unfortunate that I had to go through such a crisis before I saw the finiteness of life clearly: that is, that time for Dempsey was not eternal. As simple as that observation might appear, most of us seldom confront those realities in the earlier years, or we would not misuse our time and our bodies in the ways we do.

Most young Blacks shy away from thinking about the effective use of time in accomplishing career goals. As a matter of fact, many of my friends attributed my illness to overwork. They kept reminding me that I had worked hard—too hard, they said—in organizing the Travis Realty Corp. in 1949, the Travis Insurance Agency in 1950, and the Sivart Mortgage Corp. in 1953. I had overtaxed my body by age 34, they said.

Nonsense!

But there were more things to think about other than the personal problems of Dempsey Travis. Too much was changing for Blacks during those months.

The May 17th, 1954, Supreme Court public school desegregation ruling in Brown vs. Board of Education of Topeka monopolized my attention during my hospital stay. Was it possible, I wondered, that the old "separate but equal" principle the Court had enshrined in the 1886 Plessy vs. Ferguson decision, but had now been overturned, could be dismantled? Could it be done for education in a housing market that was, as I well knew, intensively segregated? I did not see how it could. I thought that the housing issue should have been dealt with first, or at least simultaneously, with the public school issue. If there had been a mobile black housing market in the 1950's, when there was a great desire among Blacks to integrate, it's obvious that there could have been Blacks in every neighborhood school without the devastating drawn-out problems that have plagued American education ever since the 1954 decision.

The desire to integrate and to bury the black identity was very strong in the 1950's. For example, the Board of Directors of the National Negro Business League at its 1954 convention at the Parkway Ballroom in Chicago seriously considered deleting the word "Negro" from its title. The Chicago Negro Chamber of Commerce later changed its name to the Cosmopolitan Chamber of Commerce, and the national organization dropped the word "Negro" from its title. Both organizations lost members because of strong minority opposition, and the Chicago Chamber split into two separate bodies, the Cosmopolitan and the Negro Chamber of Commerce.

Black organizations, in their search for a new identity, were receiving their signals of change in the civil rights struggle from two geographically and culturally separate locations: the United States government in Washington, D.C., and the movie industry out in Hollywood.

From Washington, the winds of change were measured in three U.S. Supreme Court desegregation decisions: housing in 1948, railway dining cars in 1950, and schools in 1954. And, in 1949, Truman's Army integration policy was implemented—and subsequently followed by both the

Navy and the Air Force.

Out in California, the "Black Sambo" and "Farina" images were finally under attack in the Hollywood Hills. The Clarence Brown adaptation of William Faulkner's "Intruder in the Dust," starring Juano Hernandez, shot on location in Oxford, Mississippi, showed the Black American in a new positive image—one that had never been seen on an American screen. "Dust" was followed in 1956 by "Young Man with a Horn," which co-starred Juano Hernandez with Kirk Douglas. Then came a series of Sidney Poitier movies that appeared to indicate that America was finally ready to integrate.

In many ways it seemed a time of hope, yet the steady drumbeat of flare-ups of racial violence continued to backlash those hopes.

On Sunday, August 28, 1955, Emmett Louis Till, a fourteen-year-old Chicago boy, was kidnapped at pistol point from his uncle's home in Money, Mississippi, and then murdered. The child was kidnapped by Roy Bryant and his half brother, J. W. Milam, for making a "wolf whistle" at Mrs. Bryant, an incident that the two men alleged had taken place four days earlier. Till's water-swollen body, with one side of his face beaten to a pulp, a bullet hole in his head, and a cotton gin fan lashed to his feet, was fished out of the Tallachatchie River near Greenwood, Mississippi, three days after he was kidnapped. Till was the 575th recorded lynching victim in Mississippi since 1882.

The all-white Mississippi jury manifested no higher thought for a black boy's life than for a rabbit's life when they acquitted Roy Bryant and J. W. Milam of the Till murder and kidnapping, even though the half brothers had admitted taking the boy from his uncle's home. Deputy U.S. Attorney William P. Rogers said in a television interview, "We just have no authority to step into a state if we think there is a failure in the administration of justice."

It was the knowledge of that kind of failure of justice that made Rosa Parks' refusal to move to the back of a Montgomery, Alabama, bus on December 1, 1955, more than a matter of risking going to jail. By defying a white bus driver in the cradle of the Confederacy, Mrs. Parks had said that she was willing to die.

It was a time when even the smallest acts of everyday living could call upon a black person's deepest reserves of courage and heroism. Even a man like Dempsey Travis, real estate broker on the South Side of Chicago, who dealt with such mundane matters as mortgages and real estate closings, had to draw courage from such figures as Dr. Martin Luther King, Jr. Dr. King's effective and moving oratory generated the adrenalin that thousands of Blacks needed to make an early commitment to protest passively but to work actively for civil rights.

The civil rights revolution that grew after Mrs. Parks' arrest changed American's open violence toward Blacks into a more subtle form of racism. But in the struggle against Jim Crow, Dr. King and many of his followers paid the full price for their commitment. That price was violent death. They gave their lives so little black girls and boys, in the North and South, would never have to raise the question asked in the poem of my late friend, Langston Hughes:

"Where is the Jim Crow section
On this merry-go-round
Mister, cause I want to ride?
Down South where I come from
White and colored
Can't sit side by side.
Down South on the train,
There's a Jim Crow car.
On the bus we're put in the back
But there ain't no back
To a merry-go-round!
Where's the horse
For a kid that's black?"

Fighting Jim Crow housing in 1955 could best be described as a grim merry-go-round. I scrambled around the clock seven days a week in an effort to remove the obstacles between the black community and a mortgage market anchored in racism.

I felt myself very alone in my fight until I met George S. Harris, president of the National Association of Real Estate Brokers, a black real estate organization known as Realtist and a counterpart to the National Association of Real Estate Boards, which excluded Blacks from membership at that time.

"Travis," Harris told me in the fall of 1955, "your efforts are like a minnow trying to change the tide of the ocean. I'll show you how we can lick this problem if you join NAREB and become a part of an orgnized effort that's fighting for democracy in housing."

I accepted Harris' invitation and went to New York that year to an NAREB convention. There I met many successful young black realtors, such as Q.V. Williamson of Atlanta, Georgia, who became the first Black elected to the Atlanta Board of Aldermen since Reconstruction; William Harps of Washington, D.C., the first black member of the American Institute of Real Estate Appraisers and later its president; and S.B. Odell of Oakland, California, a wealthy real estate developer and broker. We all shared the same goals. And George Harris proved to be a master parliamentarian and orator. Seeing him in action was an inspiration. He became my mentor and friend until his death in September, 1980, at the age of eighty-two.

I came back from New York fired by the idea of working with the Dearborn Real Estate Board, the Chicago affiliate of the NAREB, as a powerful voice for black housing in the Chicago metropolitan area. But I was impatient. The slow parliamentary pace of the group irritated me, because I couldn't help thinking that Chicago could burn down—it seemed to have a knack for it—while we were exercising ourselves over Robert's Rules of Order.

I felt we needed new leadership and an active plan to deal with racism in housing. But the group was very much bound to tradition and the way things had always been done. For instance, it was a tradition that the first vice president should succeed to the presidency of the Dearborn Board.

The day before the election, I polled the "young Turks" in the group for support for my own candidacy for the presidency. The old guard was surprised and displeased when I won by two votes. They considered my

Frank London Brown was the speaker at the first installation banquet of Dempsey J. Travis as President of the Dearborn Real Estate Board.

Photographed in 1957, are left to right: George S. Harris, President, National Association of Real Estate Brokers; Dempsey J. Travis, President, Dearborn Real Estate Board presenting award to the late Elmore Baker, Founder of the Dearborn Real Estate Board; following the the unidentified gentleman to the right of Baker is Attorney George Crank, the late J. Goodsel Jacobs; Ripley B. Mead, Jr.; Anthony Quarles; the late Bert Williams; seated left to right are James Summerower; Chester Dixon; Albert Johnson, and John Edelen.

move both rude and rash. I considered that rudeness and rashness are sometimes necessary when confronting vicious and pervasive problems like racism in the housing market.

My first five months in office were hell. Some members threatened to resign from the board. There was no staff. I had to use my own staff and financial resources, not exactly those of a Rockefeller at the time. The tide turned in May of 1958, when four of my "young Turk" allies and I packed the Parkway Ballroom with more than 700 people for my installation banquet. It was at this point that I began to get the attention of the white and black press in Chicago and my presidency of the Dearborn Real Estate Board allowed me to make some noise about the serious issue of Jim Crow in insurance.

"Quarantine the niggers" was a gentlemen's agreement within the insurance industry that had become 90.5% effective by late 1959. January, 1960, found black people who lived on the South and West Sides of Chicago being red-lined by 285 of the 310 casualty and fire insurance companies operating in the State of Illinois.

Black homeowners and tenants living within the "off limits" area were slapped with fire and automobile insurance rates that sometimes exceeded 700 per cent of the amount charged Whites living in identical housing and driving identical cars in other sections of the city. Black markets for high-rated, sub-standard insurance policies were created by mass cancellation of the standard-rated insurance policies held by those living in the "black-lined" areas.

Prominence in the black community was not an immunity against discrimination by the insurance industry. Among my insurance clients who were affected by the mass concellations were Earl B. Dickerson, president of Supreme Liberty Life Insurance Company; Dr. N. O. Calloway,

(left to right) **Attorney Robert Tucker, Adlai E. Stevenson, III and Dempsey J. Travis.**

president of the Chicago Urban League and, also, president of the Medical Associates; Kit Baldwin, president of Baldwin Ice Cream Company; and Irving Mollison, a South Side resident and a Federal Claims Court Judge in New York.

The underwriting practices that permitted insurance companies to cancel or reject insurance policies based upon the color of one's skin as opposed to the merit of the individual risk made me furious. As a young businessman, I took a fighting position on the side of the black community rather than the "go along and get along" attitude adopted by many of my business contemporaries. My stand-up posture did not enhance my business with Blacks or endear me with the white insurance establishment. The only bottom line compensation that I received from fighting against injustices was the ability to look in the mirror each morning while shaving a face that reflected a feeling of contentment for having been on the right side of Blacks' struggle for civil rights.

My presidency of the Dearborn Real Estate Board is best described in a book titled: *Negro Politics: The Search for Leadership* (1960, The Free Press), by Dr. James Q. Wilson and Henry Lee Shaltuck, professor of Government at Harvard University. Dr. Wilson said:

> "Dempsey J. Travis, a real estate broker, is a young and energetic businessman who has sought to organize Negro real estate and insurance men into a campaign to alter a policy of fire insurance companies that results in an inability to insure properties in Negro areas against fire losses. His energy has carried him to the presidency of the Dearborn Real Estate Board, a professional association of Negro real estate brokers, and to the vice-presidency of the Chicago Insurance Brokers Association, a group of Negro insurance men. Efforts by Negroes to halt and reverse the series of fire insurance cancellations on the South Side of the city brought Travis to the forefront as an organizer and spokesman. The stake of the Negro businessmen in the issue was clearly a tangible one, since property and insurance sales are severely hampered by this inability to obtain fire coverage at a figure near the manual rates . . . . Travis, with a few others, held a series of meetings among interested parties in the Negro community, and then met in conference with the Mayor and the state director of insurance, attended by insurance company representatives. The issue was quickly seen by Negro leaders such as Travis as a racial one, and he alleged in a newspaper interview that "290 insurance companies are practicing Jim Crow."

My first term as president ended successfully and I was re-elected to a second term without opposition. In 1970, I was drafted to serve a third term as president. I became the first person other than the founder and first president, the late Elmore Baker, to serve as the president for more than two years in the Dearborn Board's forty-year history.

Here Travis shares a light moment with the internationally renown prize winning artist, Charles W. White.

Chapter 16

FRONT LINES

The Chicago Branch of the NAACP had more than 50,000 dues-paying members in 1959, and it was the largest branch in the country. The presidency of the branch carried a lot of national prestige and responsibility, and it was a highly coveted office.

Yet to serve as president of a professional or civil rights organization required both a personal commitment and a great financial sacrifice. And sacrifice was what some fellow members of the Chicago Branch of the NAACP were asking me to do when they urged me to run in the election of October, 1959.

Left to Right: Dempsey J. Travis, Al Raby, and Dr. King at press conference in 1966 held at the Liberty Baptist Church where Dr. King announced a $4.5 million FHA commitment that had been made available by HUD. The first building rehabilitated under the commitment was 3410 W. Douglas Blvd.

I refused to consider the initial request, because I did not feel I could afford to be away from my fledgling business for an additional year, having just completed two years as president of the Dearborn Real Estate Board. Moreover, I had recently been elected to the first vice presidency of the NAREB (National Association of Real Estate Brokers) at their convention in New York.

However, in the interim, I met Dr. Martin Luther King, Jr., and Daisey Bates, the pillar behind her late husband, L.C. Bates, who was the key black leader in the 1957 desegregation battle at the Central High School in Little Rock, Arkansas.

The sacrifice I was being asked to make was miniscule compared to the way Dr. King and Daisey Bates were laying their lives on the line. It was with them in mind that I agreed to accept the nomination and run against the late Gerald Bullock, a schoolteacher and civil rights organizer.

The election contest that year was hard-fought and very political. On the night of the election in December, 1959, the Dunbar High School auditorium was jam-packed with 3,400 paid-up members, both Blacks and Whites, and an additional 2,000 people overflowed into the street. Ballots were cast after nominating speeches were made. I will never forget the "Blue Stocking Candidate" label that the late State Rep. William Robinson hung on me in his powerful address for my opponent.

The ballots were hand-counted all night, and I did not know until late morning the following day that I had been elected president of the largest and most powerful NAACP branch in the country.

My election to the presidency of the Chicago branch of the NAACP gave me a broader base from which to continue the struggle I had begun as president of the Dearborn Real Estate Board against the practice of insurance "Jim Crowism" in hearings before the State Senate Committee, the State House Insurance Committee and in the offices of both Mayor Richard M. Daley and Joseph S. Gerber, the state insurance director. In the struggle with the insurance giants I sometimes felt like a small boy crying in the wilderness. However, I learned that if people cry long enough, their eyes will ultimately clear, and they will see that the solution is not in crying but in fighting back.

Never had a black social club responded to the financial needs of a civil rights organization as did the Winsomettes, headed by Bernadine Washington, who presented a check in the sum of $3,000 to the NAACP in May, 1960. The following month, the Chicago Branch of the NAACP, sparked by the new consciousness of black oppression in both the North and South, had the most successful Freedom Fund Dinner in its history, netting the organization $31,000. Thurgood Marshall, NAACP chief legal counsel and currently United States Supreme Court Justice, was the speaker for the event, which was held on June 17, 1960, in the Morrison Hotel. Marshall told his listeners, who included Chicago Mayor Richard J. Daley, "If we are going to fight segregation in housing in Georgia, we are going to fight it in Chicago."

The fight for freedom in Chicago became a reality to me when I received the following telegram from America's two foremost civil rights leaders:

```
LU LU
western union                                      Telegram
```

LLCQ15 SA001
S NNY049 NNZ48 LONG BOOK NYZ48 NL PO UUX NEW YORK NY 10
DEMPSEY TRAVIS   1960 JULY 11 AM 12 2S
414 EAST 47 ST CHCO
WE ARE REQUESTING YOUR COOPERATION IN AN IMPORTANT UNDERTAKING.
WE BELIEVE A MIGHTY VOICE MUST BE HEARD AT FORTHCOMING POLITICAL
CONVENTIONS DEMANDING ELEMENTARY JUSTICE FOR THE NEGRO. WE
PLAN TO COME TO CONVENTION AND NEED YOUR HELP. EACH PARTY MUST
REPUDIATE SEGREGATIONISTS WITHIN ITS RANKS. CHICAGO HAS HISTORICAL
OPPORTUNITY TO UNIQUE CONTRIBUTION TO CIVIL RIGHTS. COURAGEOUS
SOUTHERN STUDENTS AND MILLIONS OF DISFRANCHISED NEGROES LOOK
TO PEOPLE OF YOUR CITY TO REPRESENT THEM BEFORE CONVENTION.
WE URGE YOU AND OTHER COMMUNITY LEADERS TO COOPERATE WITH US,
IN ORGANIZATION OF NON-VIOLENT "MARCH ON THE CONVENTIONS MOVEMENT
FOR FREEDOM NOW." LOS ANGELES LEADERS BEING CALLED UPON FOR
SIMILAR ACTION. JOAN SUALT, HUNTER ODELL, AND NORMAN HILL IN
CHICAGO AS OUR REPRESENTATIVES TO ASSIST YOU IN CONVENING COMMUNITY
COMMITTEE TO IMPLEMENT OUR SHARED OBJECTIVES. PLEASE WIRE READINESS
TO SERVE ON COMMITTEE TO COOPERATE WITH US AND REPRESENTATIVES
IN ACHIEVING OBJECTIVES OF THIS PROJECT
   A PHILIP RANDOLPH & MARTIN LUTHER KING JR 312 WEST 125TH
ST NEW YORK 27 NY.

The initial meeting of the Chicago March on Conventions Committee assembled in the Blue Room of the Parkway Ballroom and was called to order on June 21, 1960, at 3:55 p.m. by Bayard Rustin, executive assistant to A. Philip Randolph. Some Chicago leaders attended. Rustin expressed appreciation for the presence on the part of those community leaders in the hall and introduced A. Philip Randolph.

In his remarks, Randolph, often called the father of the modern civil rights march, discussed both the purpose and program of the "March on Conventions Movement for Freedom Now." He stressed the importance of the march in Chicago and in Los Angeles as a demonstration on the part of black people and their supporters in the labor movement and liberal movements for a strong civil rights platform for each of the two conventions.

"This demonstration shall be a protest against the conspiracy of silence on civil rights and the piecemealness which characterizes both the Republican and Democratic parties," said Randolph. Randolph, who had been called the most dangerous man in America by President Woodrow Wilson, said the "March on Conventions Movement" would emphasize the need for a Presidential Executive Order to implement court decisions ending segregation in housing and the guaranteeing of the right to vote. He wanted the march in Chicago to be a huge, mass demonstration that would leave no doubt that black people stood firmly behind their leaders in the demand for an end to equivocation on the civil rights question.

In addition to the insurance "Jim Crow," there was job "Jim Crow," housing "Jim Crow," and graveyard "Jim Crow," as evidenced by the sign, "For Caucasians Only," on the gate of the Oakwood Cemetery at 67th and Cottage Grove. I believed that the solution to the insurance "Jim Crow" could be reached through housing integration.

At an NAACP Board meeting in January, 1960, three days after I was installed as president, I outlined a plan for integrating suburban housing. The Board approved my integration idea, and invitations were extended to 127 suburban village officials in Cook, Kane, McHenry, Lake, Will and DuPage Counties to attend a one-day conference to be held in April, entitled, "A Blueprint for Democracy in Housing." Cooperating organizations for the conference were the American Friends Service Committee, the Chicago Urban League, and the Union of American Hebrew Congregations. Members of these same organizations joined me in the cold north winds of February on the picket lines in support of a national boycott against F. W. Woolworth, S.S. Kresge, S.H. Kress and W.T. Grant stores for continuing their policy of refusing to practice "Democracy in Eating" at the lunch counters in their Southern stores.

The morning session on "Democracy in Housing" was held at Roosevelt University, and the luncheon and afternoon sessions were held in the Blackstone Hotel. Both sessions were packed with people who did not need the lesson: 350 white and black liberals who were closely identified with the Civil Rights Movement. Only eight of the 127 village officials who were invited attended.

The meeting, the first of its kind to be held in Chicago, was a monetary success but a media flop in terms of getting the integration message into the right ears. The messages were many, coming from such authorities as Dr. Louis Laurenti, a professor from the University of California who discussed his new book, *Race and Housing Values;* Dr. Curtis D. MacDougall, professor of journalism at Northwestern University's Medill School of Journalism, who talked on "Exploring the Race Myth;" Dr. George Grier, of the research division of New York State's Commission Against Discrimination, expounded on his book, *Property Values and Race;* and Dr. Dietrich C. Reitzes, of George Williams College, gave a dissertation on "Changing the Climate On Integrated Housing." In addition, there were many other national authorities present who spoke supportively for ethnically mixed housing.

The suburban refusal to respond to our effort told me again that white folks generally did not want to hear anything about living next door to black folks. Deerfield, Illinois, typified the 1960 suburban racial mind-set when they voted to have a green park rather a dark-skinned neighbor.

Civil rights for Blacks in Chicago in 1960 were still in the Dark Ages. Racial flare-ups were constantly taking place in at least a dozen public high schools. Bands of white teenage hoodlums were waging a campaign of harassment in the schools and in the streets.

Private business schools in the Loop did not have a race problem like the public schools, because they simply did not admit Blacks. Mary L. Jackson, of 400 South Hamlin, and Mrs. Rachel Hawkins, of 2124 South Drake, who were both employed as secretaries at the Navy Pier University of Illinois Campus, were denied admission to the Moser Evening School on East Jackson Boulevard because they were Blacks. The reason for denying Blacks admission was given by Mrs. Paul Moser, president of the school, who politely said, "We never have."

At the co-chairmen's meeting on June 30 at the Parkway Ballroom, additional nominations for co-chairmen who had accepted as of June 30, 1960; Willoughby Abner, Lemuel Bentley, Gerald Bullock, Julia Fairfax, Ishmael Flory, Rev. A. Lincoln James, Charles A. Hayes, Theodore A. Jones, A. R. Leak, Attorney Odas Nicholson, Rev. Owen D. Pelt, Rev. E. P. Pettigrew, Sterling Stuckey, Dempsey J. Travis, Josephine Walker, Ralph Wright, Rev. Stroy Freeman, Attorney Rufus Cook, Ald. Leon Despres, Curtis Strong, Dr. L. H. Holman, Brenetta Howell, Dr. Robert L. Kimbrough, Rev. William Lee Lambert, James Wright, Theodore Green, Hon. William H. Robinson, Augustus Savage, Rev. Curtis Barge, Earl B. Dickerson, Kermit Eby, V. C. Crowder, Rabbi Jacob Weinstein, Aaron Aronin, and Kale Williams.

But there were some happy notes in a sour time.

Rustin, Randolph's heir apparent and the architect of the 200,000-plus-person march on Washington in August, 1963, explained the importance of a large demonstration in Chicago to follow the demonstration in Los Angeles at the Democratic Convention. The Los Angeles committee was planning a demonstration of 5,000 to 10,000 people, and we were urged to set similar goals for Chicago, lest the implication be left that the black leadership was concentrating on the Democratic Party and endorsing the Republican Party.

" 'The March on Conventions Movement' is a demonstration against the do nothingness of both parties," said Rustin.

In the question and answer period, Randolph, with characteristic quiet dignity, made clear that the March Movement welcomed and solicited the cooperation of black Republicans in Chicago, especially those who would be delegates to the Republican National Convention. As to future plans by the march movement, Randolph said, "We will cross that bridge when we get to it." For the entire period leading up to the Convention, the emphasis was to be on mobilizing the maximum number of people to take part in the demonstration.

Nominations for additional co-chairmen for the Chicago Organizing Committee were made from the floor. Twenty-four nominees were accepted, representing a cross-section of groups and organizations in Chicago. The meeting decided that ten additional co-chairmen would be nominated at the meeting of co-chairmen scheduled for the following week.

In his deep, Harvard-accented baritone voice, cultivated during his many years of orating on the street corners of Harlem, Randolph urged the selection of a coordinator to centralize the responsibility for the overall march. It was the consensus of the meeting that at the co-chairmen's meeting the following week, a coordinator would be selected, and that presently an interim convenor of the co-chairmen's meeting should be selected. Upon nomination by the Rev. Owen Pelt, I was unanimously elected as the interim convenor, and next was unanimously elected as general march coordinator.

Thousands of sign-up cards were printed to get people to pledge their support and participation in the rally and demonstration. The job performed during the next seventeen days by a small staff of five, which included Timuel D. Black, Norman Hill, Bennett Johnson, Joan Suall, and Carl Fuqua, executive secretary of the Chicago branch of the NAACP, in bringing together support groups for the rally and march was monumental.

The afternoon pre-convention "March for Freedom Now" rally held Sunday, July 24, 1960, in the Liberty Baptist Church at 4853 South Park, packed the church and then spilled over into the streets. Some 5,000 supporters heard remarks by Roy Wilkins, New York Governor Nelson Rockefeller, and A. Philip Randolph. And nearly 4,000 supporters attended the West Side evening rally held at Stone Temple Baptist Church at 3622 Douglas Boulevard and heard both Dr. Martin Luther King, Jr. and A. Philip Randolph.

At 4 p.m., July 25, 1960, the demonstrators assembled in front of Rev. Louis Rawls' Tabernacle Baptist Church, 4130 South Indiana Avenue. At 5:10 p.m.—sharp—more than 10,000 marchers, by a police count, stepped off proudly enroute to the Amphitheatre at Root and Halsted, the site of the G.O.P. Convention.

Sharing the front line of the march was Dr. Martin Luther King, Jr., A. Philip Randolph, Ralph Abernathy and Dempsey J. Travis. Right behind us were the student sit-in leaders: Diane Nash, Bernard Lee and Marion Barry, now mayor of Washington, D.C. The Chicago march was the largest of its kind ever held in the country. We marched north on Indiana and west on 39th Street singing to the tune of "I've Been Working on the Railroad:"

> "We've been marching on the vigil
> All the live long day.
> And we'll be marching on the vigil
> Till Americans change their ways.
> Can't you hear our plea for freedom?
> Rise up so early in the morn.
> Can't you hear our plea for freedom?
> Put Civil Rights in your platform!"

That fine hour faded quickly on Sunday afternoon, August 29th, when I was called by a Chicago newspaper reporter and told about a wade-in by the NAACP Youth Council, which included forty black and ten white sympathizers, at Rainbow Beach, between 75th and 77th Streets and the lake. Blacks had previously refrained from using this beach because over the years they had been unrelentingly molested by both lifeguards and white bathers. The black youths' objective was to prove that Chicago had a chance not to earn the title of the most segregated city in the nation, and also that Chicago must permit its black citizens to wade in the blue waters of Lake Michigan. But the NAACP could not prevent the violence that was to follow when 21-year-old Velma Murphy, of 9216 South Parnell, was hit with a rock. Gangs of white youths, some armed with stones, despite the presence of ninety-six policemen, followed the autos of the demonstrators who left the beach at 77th Street to as far west as 79th and Stony Island.

My civil rights objectives had not been accomplished when I decided not to seek re-election for a second term as NAACP president. I had been a truant from Travis Realty Company, Sivart Mortgage Corporation and the Travis Insurance Agency for three years, two as president of the Dearborn Board and one with the NAACP. I felt a longer absence would destroy my small business enterprise.

Unattended businesses generally go into a holding pattern before they fold up and disappear. Black businesses too often just instantly self-destruct. My business had neither self-destructed nor disappeared, but it was fading fast. Sales volume at Travis Realty Company for the year 1960 dropped 40 per cent from the previous year. Sivart did not receive an authorization from the Federal Housing Administration to act as loan correspondent mortgagee for the Chicago Metropolitan Mutual Assurance Company until August 1st, 1960, which meant few, if any, F.H.A. loans could be generated and closed before January 1st, 1961.

My insurance sales suffered the same disastrous results as the real estate sales. The price I paid for participating in the civil rights movement came within a hairline of destroying my business career.

The white establishments called me a demagogue, and my black business peers privately called me a fool, a fool for investing my time in what they considered unrelated black problems.

•

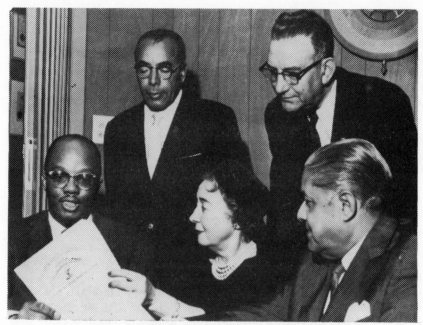

Julian Black, former manager of the late Joe Louis
transferring his interest in the Julian Black Realty
Company to the NAACP. Dempsey Travis, President of the Chicago Branch of the NAACP accepting the presentation. Mrs. Julian Black is pictured
in the middle. Shown also is Aaron Payne, lawyer
for Joe Louis and Black, along with George S. Harris, President of Chicago Metropolitan Mutual Insurance Company.

May, 1960: Presentation to Sammy Davis, Jr. at
Winnsomets NAACP Fund Raising Affair at the old
Chicago Sheraton Hotel. Left to right are Harry
James, band leader; Dempsey J. Travis, Sammy
Davis, Jr. and Daddy-O Daylie.

Pictured at meeting to discuss NAACP Freedom Fund Dinner in 1960 are left to right: Dempsey J. Travis, president, Chicago Branch NAACP; executive secretary of the Chicago Branch, NAACP, Rev. Charles Fuqua; Freedom Fund Dinner Chairman, Attorney Earl. B. Dickerson, and Mayor of Bronzeville, Cora Carroll.

Nearly 4,000 supporters attended the West Side evening rally of the Chicago Conventions Movement held at Stone Temple Baptist Church on Sunday, July 24, 1960. Pictured are Dr. Martin Luther King, Jr., and Dempsey J. Travis, general coordinator of the Chicago March Committee. This picture was taken moments after Mr. Travis had introduced Dr. King to the packed church.

To this day, I cannot differentiate between economic problems and civil rights problems—they are irrevocably saddled with each other, more-so in this country than anywhere else on Planet Earth.

Pictured at a 1960 NAACP rally are from left to right: Dr. Martin Luther King, Jr.; Fred Shuttleworth and Dempsey J. Travis.

Chapter 17

RAISING THE
"COTTON CURTAIN"

In the 1960s, John Fitzgerald Kennedy turned on the light at the end of the housing corridor for Black Americans. Lyndon Johnson kept it burning but Richard Milhouse Nixon turned it off in the 1970s.

The 1960s mark the real beginning for black participation in the housing market without most of the traditional restraints that had been imposed by both the private and public sectors. Black home ownership in Chicago increased from 36,667 in 1960 to 74,219 in 1970, a staggering 103 percent in one decade. The executive order for equal opportunity housing signed by President Kennedy on November 20, 1962, was a proclamation to both friend and foe that all federal agencies were directed to prevent discrimination because of race, creed or national origin in federally assisted or federally owned housing.

The precedents for fair housing, which had been ineffective, included: The Civil Rights Act of 1866 ("All citizens of the U.S. shall have the same right in every state and territory, as is enjoyed by white citizens thereof, to inherit, purchase, lease, sell, hold and convey real and personal property."); the 1917 U. S. Supreme Court (Buchanan vs. Warley) which held racial zoning ordinances invalid; the 1948 Supreme Court Decision (Shelly vs. Kraemer) which held racial restrictive covenants judicially unenforceable; the Housing Act of 1949, whereby Congress made the National Housing Policy Declaration: to realize as soon as possible the goal of a decent home and a suitable living environment for every American family.

Upon signing his Executive Order, President Kennedy made this statement:

"It is neither proper nor equitable that Americans should be denied the benefits of housing owned by the Federal Government or financed through Federal assistance on the basis of their race, color, creed, or national origin. Our national policy is equal opportunity for all and the Federal Government will continue to take such legal and proper steps as it may to achieve the realization of that goal."

The Order called for an end to discrimination in the rental or sale or use of government-owned and operated housing and of housing provided, after Nov. 20, 1962, with the aid of federal loans, advances, grants or contributions, or with the assistance of loans insured, guaranteed or otherwise secured by the credit of the federal government. That Order was, of course, designed to open up a large segment of the housing market to minority group home-seekers and turn a pressing need into an effective demand.

At the time the Order was issued, openly-voiced dismay and fearful projections of imminent social and economic catastrophes were plentiful. But the dire circumstances did not materialize.

Home building did not collapse, and builders and lenders did not panic. They went right on building and financing homes at one of the highest rates in history. Those who had hoped for some kind of social revolution were equally without satisfaction.

There were results, however. In the week ending Nov. 30, 1962, the first full week in which the Order was effective, the FHA department of the Housing and Home Finance Agency (one of HUD's predecessors) said it received new-home mortgage applications at a rate of about 199,000.

More revealing are some totals available from the spring of 1964. Under the various federally assisted programs, including the VA, some 600,000 units were either completed or approved; about 800 urban renewal projects were underway or in planning.

New housing subject to the Order included: FHA mortgage insurance applications for new units as of November, 1963, totaling 282,500, units, of which 191,700 were single-family and 90,800 multi-family; and, in addition, the FHA held 70,000 units acquired through foreclosure for sale or rental on the newly opened market. The VA, during this period, reported requests for 100,000 units subject to the Equal Opportunity Order.

And then President Kennedy was assassinated.

The Housing Proclamation of the New Frontier was implemented and expanded with the legislative skills of President Lyndon Baines Johnson's Great Society.

The United Mortgage Bankers of America Inc. (UMBA) was organized in Chicago in 1962 because Blacks were not admitted to membership in either the Mortgage Bankers Association of America or any of its local subsidiaries. The history of UMBA parallels the Kennedy and Johnson administration because prior to the Kennedy election and the appointment of Robert C. Weaver as the first Black Federal Housing Administrator, there were no Black mortgage bankers. As a matter of

Plaque presentation to Dr. Robert C. Weaver, Secretary of the United States Department of Housing and Urban Development by Mr. Dempsey J. Travis, President and Chairman of the Board, United Mortgage Bankers of America. The ceremony was held at the Mid-Winter Meeting of the UMBA in the Waldorf Astoria Hotel, New York City, February 12, 1964.

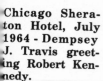

Chicago Sheraton Hotel, July 1964 - Dempsey J. Travis greeting Robert Kennedy.

Officers, directors, and charter members of the United Mortgage Bankers of America. Picture was taken February 18, 1963, at the Americana Hotel in New York City during the first Mid-Winter Meeting of UMBA. Seated, left to right are: J. W. Robinson, senior vice president, Houston, Texas; Dempsey J. Travis, president and chairman of the board, Chicago, Illinois; Joseph T. Bickers, secretary, Atlanta, Georgia; and Robert L. Hughes, assistant secretary, Kansas City, Missouri. Standing, left to right are: James Lynch, Chicago, Illinois; M. J. Anderson, Austin, Texas; G. W. Gates, St. Louis, Missouri; C. W. Calloway, Atlanta, Georgia; George Haley, Kansas City, Missouri; Millard Robbins, Chicago, Illiois; George W. Crank, General Counsel, Chicago, Illinois; Jesse Johnson, Jr., Denver, Colorado, and Q. V. Williamson, Atlanta, Georgia.

New York City, 1970: seated left to right: Franklin D. Roosevelt, Jr.; M. J. Anderson of Austin, Texas, and Dempsey J. Travis.

fact, Blacks could not enroll in mortgage banker courses which were limited to members of the white trade association. I was finally admitted to the MBA School of mortgage banking with the direct aid of the White House in 1966 and graduated in the class of '69 at the age of 49.

Mortgage banking is the primary vehicle for channeling FHA & VA housing investment dollars from major insurance companies and pension funds into the black community. The need for Blacks to participate became obvious when one considers that between 1947 and 1960 the government insured more than one million mortgage loans for veterans in suburban areas, and 800,000 for veterans in the cities; 99.5% of all mortgage loans approved for northern cities were for white veterans. The V.A. and F.H.A. loans made to Blacks in the city were a direct by-product of a campaign initiated in 1953 by the National Association of Real Estate Brokers (NAREB) entitled "Democracy In Housing."

NAREB was pushing for legislation to enable F.H.A. and V.A. to make direct loans to Black home buyers in as much as all other lending avenues were closed. The local Dearborn Real Estate Board, under the presidency of Robert N. Landrum, set up a series of meetings and workshops advocating and supporting the national position.

Out of this dual action came a compromise called the Voluntary Home Mortgage Credit Program (V.H.M.C.P.) enacted as part of the Housing Act of 1954, which marked the first formal governmental recognition that minority citizens needed special assistance to equalize their opportunity to obtain home financing.

Although President Dwight Eisenhower supported the V.H.M.C.P. concept and brought attention in his housing message to Congress on January 24, 1954, to the fact that "many members of minority groups, regardless of their income or economic status, have had the least opportunity of all citizens to acquire good homes," the V.H.M.C.P. was a flop because it had to depend on the same lenders who had denied blacks loans through the regular sources.

Mechanically the program worked as follows: a black home buyer had to be humiliated and rejected by three lending institutions. Once this had been achieved he could file an application in the Regional V.H.M.C.P. office which was located in the old Federal Court Building on Clark and Adams. The regional office would in turn circulate his application among lenders who had agreed to participate in the program. This ritual (by my experience) could take from six months to a year to find out you had been rejected.

Having sent ten black families through this sand-burning experience, Travis Realty Company dropped out of the program. It was after this experience that the Travis Realty Sales Force decided to organize the Sivart Mortgage Corporation in order to circumvent this mortgage bottleneck. We did not achieve our objective because the Federal Housing Administration would not approve an application for a black mortgage banking company in 1954.

Access to capital was, in 1962, and remains today the primary thrust of UMBA. During its first years, the members of UMBA conducted door-to-door campaigns in their own communities, and conducted an extensive survey nationally in search of economic input for their black communities through mortgage financing. Speaking before church and civic organizations throughout the nation, the first members used strategy that ranged from street picketing and conference room confrontations to legal action.

Results began to surface, when in February, 1963, a $10 million commitment was made to three of UMBA's member companies by the International Ladies Garment Workers Union, headquartered in New York City. Prior to this major breakthrough, the sole source of funds for black mortgage bankers was from black life insurance companies.

In rather rapid succession, a total of $50 million was made available that year for mortgage money from banks and savings and loan associations based in New York City. Visits to 63 banks, 48 life insurance companies, and 10 savings and loan associations in New York City and in Washington, D.C., made by some forty black mortgage bankers and real estate representatives, added impetus.

UMBA used what was described by its first president, Dempsey J. Travis, as "quiet persuasion." It urged white-owned financial institutions to consider these facts: 85 per cent of the savings of Blacks were in major white financial institutions; some 38 per cent of black families, as compared to 62 per cent of white families, were homeowners; the number of black households with more than $5,000 income a year rose almost twenty-fold between 1950 and 1960 from 43,000 to 766,000, and yet the majority of black households were still substandard dwellings although the owners could afford reasonably-priced houses.

An additional stimulus to the minority housing market came in 1967 when the insurance industry launched its unprecedented $2 billion urban investment program. At the same time F.H.A. changed its policies and announced its intention to insure single family mortgages in blighted areas. With these major innovations and policy changes UMBA realized what in actuality would have been a wild dream seven years earlier.

In 1969, the Federal National Mortgage Association (F.N.M.A.) appointed nine Blacks and one Spanish-speaking mortgage correspondent, thus giving a big thrust to the black mortgage banking industry. However, at the same time, national priorities shifted and the alliance between HUD and the insurance industry faded with the change of administrations. Although the nation was still sorely in need of low and moderate cost housing, President Nixon refocused his commitments and priorities toward black capitalism and moving disadvantaged Blacks to the suburbs. In 1969, when Nixon took office, there were five black mortgage banking companies in Chicago. In 1981, Sivart Mortgage is the only one left in this city. Nationally, the liquidations of black mortgage bankers have been equally disastrous, with their number having been reduced from fifty to seven.

While all this progress was helpful, there were still many blanks to fill in. As always, it helped to backtrack and re-evaluate the past in order to proceed forward.

The need for a black-controlled mortgage company was evident when you consider that in 1960 more than 3,200 Chicago families, mostly black, were displaced by urban renewal and the city was given a quota of 2,000 Section 221 government loans. Only three such loans were made for homes within the city during 1960, according to the Community Conservation Board, the issuers of the loan certificates. John L. Waner, area director of FHA in Chicago, commented: "Unless the lenders liberalize their practices in making loans to the minorities, there is a strong possibility that the government itself will move in."

I knew that a government that had not permitted a black mortgage banking company to squeak through its racist-laden bureaucracy until 1960 would not intervene in the mortgage market on behalf of minorities. Hence, Sivart Mortgage Corporation became the vehicle for opening the doors wider to the FHA mortgage market.

The Sivart mortgage banking presence in Chicago not only raised the "cotton curtain" between the black community and the FHA, it also created jobs for Blacks within the mortgage banking industry in "lily-white" companies that had never considered a Black for a job or mortgage application previously. The John F. Kennedy "New Frontier" philosophy, and the appointment of Robert C. Weaver, created a political climate that permitted Sivart Mortgage Corporation to exist.

The Washington political climate of FHA was six years ahead of the national mortgage banking industry in accepting Blacks among its ranks. In 1960 it was impossible for a perceptible black man or woman to gain membership in either the Mortgage Bankers of America or any of its local chapters. A denial of membership was also a denial of the right to participate in the only educational programs in mortgage banking being offered in the country.

Recognizing that I could not survive in the mortgage banking field without black support, I suggested to Charles L. Warden, president of the National Association of Real Estate Brokers during the annual meeting in Boston, Massachusetts, on August 20, 1961, that a commmittee be formed for the purpose of surveying the lending practices of the life insurance industry, whose premium proceeds were regularly invested for use by mortgage bankers. A survey of some 25 major life insurance companies was completed and a report was made at the next annual convention which was held in Dallas, Texas, in August, 1962. The survey would become a meaningless stack of papers if we did not create an institutional vehicle to follow through and implement our findings. Therefore, on August 14, 1962, I made a plea before 500 real estate men and women at the Dallas convention to join me in setting up a black mortgage banking association that would be an arm of NAREB. A formal breakfast meeting of twenty real estate brokers was called on the morning of August 15, 1962, for the purpose of discussing the preliminary oganizational structure of the new mortgage banking association. I was selected temporary chairman.

The next meeting of UMBA was held October 13, 1962, in Chicago at the Sherman Hotel. At that meeting I was elected both president and chairman of the board. It was decided that a survey be made of lending institutions in New York City in February, 1963 in order to determine their lending practices toward minorities. Two hundred questionaires were mailed out, and the ninety-three institutions that replied and agreed to an interview included fifty-five savings banks, thirty life insurance companies, seven savings and loan associations, and one pension fund. Four hundred million dollars in oral commitments were made by the savings and loan industry, but none materialized. The life insurance industry made no promises, and thus had no commitments to keep. This was also true of the mutual savings institutions.

To get commercial banks to finance a FHA mortgage commitment from a black life insurance company was almost a hopeless task. The unwillingness had to be racial since the principal of a FHA loan is fully insured by the U.S. government. The 100 per cent guarantee did not carry much weight with Jerome M. Sax, executive vice president of the

Exchange National Bank of Chicago, who stated in a letter dated July 14, 1960: "After reviewing the report of the Sivart Corporation and your own personal statement, we are agreeable to interim financing on your FHA mortgage loans up to $15,000. These loans would be 30 to 60 day loans and would be personally endorsed by yourself and Mrs. Travis."

Sax's letter takes on more significance when you consider the fact that the Sivart Corporation statement reflected a liquid net worth in excess of $100,000 and yet Sax wanted additional collateral in the form of the personal signatures of my wife and myself to guarantee the government's 100 per cent guarantee. I sincerely believe that Sax thought he was being benevolent or he would not have ended his letter in the following manner: "May I also say that it is a pleasure to do business with people like yourself."

Sax's offer to do business was one that I could afford to refuse.

In the 1960's, people like me were probably considered to be excellent candidates for the funny farm when we appeared at a major bank asking for a $500,000 line of credit. I will never forget how I had to verbally wrestle with Norman M. Alperin, the chairman of Drexel National Bank at 3401 South Martin Luther King Drive, to get a $60,000 line of credit. That hassle should not have been necessary because my family had banked at Drexel since 1900, and I, personally, since the late 1930's. Finally, on a cold January morning in 1962, Alperin, with his board's approval, agreed to extend Sivart Mortgage a $100,000 line of credit. The condescending tone of Alperin's voice when he made the credit offer offended me so deeply that I stormed out of the bank empty-handed, never to return except to close out my accounts.

The cost of maintaining black pride and personal dignity can be extremely high.

For three months I walked the streets of downtown Chicago daily in search of a bank that would extend a line of credit to Sivart Corporation. One afternoon while sitting in my office at 414 East 47th Street with both hands clutched about my head, G.H. Wang, a friend and former Chinese ambassador, walked in. With a startled look on his face he said, "Mr. Travis, what is hurting you?"

I reluctantly told him the Exchange and Drexel Bank stories. He shook his head and said, "I want you to meet my friend Mr. Humphrey, chairman of the Central National Bank of Chicago."

On March 21, 1962, I met Humphrey and he, in turn, arranged for G.H. Wang and me to meet with the senior officers of the bank. Within eight days the bank had approved a line of credit for $200,000 with the understanding that we would transfer all bank balances controlled by the Sivart Mortgage Corporation to the Central National Bank. The working relationship was excellent. Before the end of the 1960's, our line of credit had been extended to $3 million at Central National Bank.

I succeeded in opening the banking doors, with the help of a friend, before I could unglue the passage to educational preparedness in the field of mortgage banking. It was not until the fall of 1962 that a school sponsored by the Chicago Mortgage Bankers was opened at Central Y.M.C.A. Junior College at 119 South LaSalle Street which actually allowed black enrollment. Charles A. Tatum, my executive assistant, and I jumped at the opportunity to enroll. We became the first graduates of the Central Y.M.C.A. Mortgage Banking School on June 17, 1963. The educational opportunity for Blacks was so unique at Central "Y" that

Marion Jordan, an UMBA member, commuted to Chicago weekly by plane from Kansas City, Missouri, to attend two Monday evening classes in mortgage banking.

Prior to my enrollment at Central "Y" my only educational exposure to mortgage banking had been derived from reading newspapers and real estate trade magazines. It was my need to fill an educational void that prompted me to write President Lyndon Baines Johnson and request that he intercede on my behalf to gain membership in the Mortgage Bankers of America. President Johnson assigned his White House counsel to investigate my allegation. After an exchange of letters and calls between the White House and the MBA, I subsequently received a MBA membership application in the fall of 1965.

Now what I needed were two active members as signatories. I visited a dozen mortgage banking offices and each one offered some senseless reason for not being willing to put his name on the line for a black applicant. Finally, I asked the president of the largest and most respected name in the mortgage banking industry to sign. I told him that the president of the United States was interested in seeing my application processed. He blurted out, "To hell with the president." I left his LaSalle Street office and walked slowly down that canyon-like street wondering if the whole world were anti-Black.

I was ready to give up when I remembered having met Harry Gottlieb, a mortgage banker, at some social function. I went directly to Harry's office in the Inland Steel Building at Monroe and Clark and handed him the application. Harry looked at the application and said, "You are a red hot number, Travis. However, if you were white I would sign this application. Therefore, I am not going to let the fact that you are black change my behavior." Harry suggested that since I banked at Central National Bank that Marvin Reynolds should be the second signatory, and he was. I was finally admitted to the MBA School of Mortgage Banking at Northwestern University in the summer of 1966 and graduated as the lone black mortgage banker in the class of '69 at age 49.

Never too late? I've never been much of a fan of that depressing cliche.

Members of the National Association of Real Estate Brokers are pictured in this 1968 photograph taken in Philadelphia congratulating Ms. Diahann Carroll on her performance in the play, "No Strings.' Ms. Carroll and Dempsey J. Travis are shown in the center.

Former Governor Otto Kerner of Illinois and Dempsey J. Travis at the Bismarck Hotel in 1961.

Pictured in this 1968 photograph, left to right are: Dr. James Buckner, Vice President Hubert H. Humphrey, and Dempsey J. Travis. This photo was taken in July at the Blackstone Hotel, Chicago.

Dempsey J. Travis with secretary of HUD and former Governor of Michigan, George Romney.

The West Side erupted after Dr. Martin Luther King, Jr. was assassinated on April 4, 1968, in a Memphis, Tennessee motel. National Guardsmen are shown marching through the burning area. They were among the 6,000 called to active duty by then acting Governor Samuel H. Shapiro in 1968. The tall building in the foreground on the right is 2400 West Madison (Madison and Western).

Chapter 18

THE CONTRACT
BUYERS LEAGUE

It is possible to look back on the 1960's as a decade of hope, especially after the Nixon administration cut off many of the avenues of opportunity in the early '70's. But it was also a time of gut-wrenching despair as the country was wracked again and again with bloodshed and rioting.

My own feelings of frustration and horror at some of the events, during that critical time when America was finally trying to come to terms with its legacy of racial bigotry, manifested themselves in painful episodes of psychosomatic physical symptoms. Again and again, I would awaken at dawn, clutching my chest and screaming for relief from the excruciating pain that was throbbing through my body. I was in the mouth of a devil with a thousand teeth, I recall telling my wife on one occasion when my scream of pain awakened her.

The first time I experienced these symptoms was on Friday, Nov. 22, 1963. It is the curse of all my generation to remember exactly what we were doing on that day. I was driving south in Markham, Illinois, with Albert Brown, a real estate client and a fellow graduate of DuSable High. We had graduated together in June of 1939.

"John F. Kennedy, the thirty-fifth President of the United States, has been shot," a voice on the radio said. And then, only moments later, the voice said, "The President is dead."

I pulled the car over to the curb.

"Man, I feel sick. My body is throbbing with pain," I said. We sat for a few moments. "I'm sorry. I just don't feel like showing any houses."

Brown nodded. I made a U-turn and drove back into Chicago. I dropped Brown off and went directly home.

"You're home early," Moselynne said. I was too agonized to answer. I walked into the bedroom and sat down in a chair in the corner. I began to weep uncontrollably. Moselynne came in and stared at me in wonder. She hadn't heard the news. She didn't understand what was wrong with me until I finally managed to gasp, "Why did the young President have to die such a violent and senseless death?"

Kennedy's murder foreshadowed a decade that was to be filled with years of fears, tears and grief. The weeping Memorial Statue of Abraham Lincoln drawn by Pulitizer Prize cartoonist Bill Mauldin captured most Americans' mood. It wasn't only Black Americans who were thrown into paralysis, but we had a special cause for bitterness. John Kennedy had been our "white" hope. In him, for the first time, we had seen the possibility of an America not plagued with racial inequities.

These hopes were devastated and travestied through the decade in the successive assassinations of Malcolm X, Medgar Evers, Dr. Martin Luther King, Jr., Robert Kennedy, Fred Hampton, Mark Clark and hundreds of others who died in the struggle for black liberation.

The last time I saw Dr. Martin Luther King, Jr., alive, was in August of 1967, in San Francisco.

I was in town for a National Association of Real Estate Brokers convention when Q.V. Williamson, who was president of the association, asked five directors to go with him to the airport to meet Dr. King's plane. We stood waiting as he walked off the plane, accompanied only by a fellow minister. Here was the acknowledged leader of Black America, a Nobel Prize winner, hated and reviled as much as he was loved, a fearless center of controversy for years—and he walked in alone, with not a single security guard. My heart almost stopped beating. We must all have had the same feeling, because the six of us immediately encircled Dr. King and briskly walked him through the crowded airport.

I think each one of us was thinking during those moments that we were eight walking targets.

That evening, I talked for the last time with Dr. King. He laid out his plans for the Southern Christian Leadership Conference's Poor People's Campaign for the following summer. It would be directed, he said, at establishing a base for economic development, with emphasis on jobs, housing, education, and the medical needs of the poor. All this was to be accomplished through direct subsidies from the federal government. It was an ambitious plan, and some were urging him to move more slowly. But I think most of us had the feeling then that we had to move while the country was still listening to black people. We knew how difficult it is to get your messsage across when nobody is listening.

At 7:30 p.m. on Thursday, April 4, 1968, I was sitting in my office at 840 East 87th Street. Again, I had the radio on. A voice broke into the programming: Dr. Martin Luther King, Jr. had been killed in Memphis, Tennessee. It was less than eight months after our meeting in San Francisco. Dr. King had become an unguarded target in the gunsights of James Earl Ray.

In the twenty-four hours after Dr. King's death, rioting erupted in 125

American cities. Nationally, 69,000 troops were called out to suppress the predictable violent reactions to his death. The riots caused 46 deaths, 2,600 serious injuries, and 22,000 arrests. The recordable property losses exceeded $100 million.

In Chicago, acting Gov. Samuel H. Shapiro called 6,000 National Guardsmen to active duty. Areas of the West Side went up in flames.

As I stood in my office at 87th Street, I could see the sky redden as fires swept through the West Side. The spectacle of a grieving, frustrated people turning its anger and horror on itself was enough to make you weep. There was fear, too, of course: the fear that the violence would go on and reach into every area of the city.

The schools let their students out at before noon that day, and as I sat in my office, I could hear the sound of shattering glass as they went down the commercial street breaking windows. Only a small door in our building was kicked in: apparently the word was quickly passed that this was a black business.

Though black middle class areas escaped the worst of the violence, the riots only further divided the city. Mayor Richard Daley proved that Chicago was seething with racial hate when he issued his famous order to his police to "shoot to kill or maim" any looters. Black organizations vocally protested that obviously racist order.

The damage the rioting did to the black community in Chicago—and elsewhere—is inestimable. White businessmen, including large chain operations as well as small Jewish merchants, never rebuilt in areas that had gone up in the riots. In the other black areas relatively untouched by the violence, fear of the future made them move out. The closing of commercial establishments, many of which have never fully rebuilt by black merchants, spurred the redirection of black shopping out to all-white suburban areas.

Without Dr. King, and with the memory of the racist horror that had stilled his voice, black leaders floundered. There were many voices, articulate voices with strong ideas of what needed to be done, but it was difficult to regain a unified sense of purpose. Still, the work went on, and more and more Blacks were talking about the economic issues that had always been my concern. Today, the Arab-owned businesses are a primary source of question marks on the black community. And tomorrow???

A National Black Economic Development Conference was called in the month of the first anniversary after Dr. King's death on April 25th, 1969, by the Interreligious Foundation for Community Organization (IFCO). I delivered a paper on housing at the Conference which was held in Detroit. It was subsequently published in the April, 1970, edition of *The Black Scholar* as, "The 1970 Homestead Act." It has since been re-published in a book entitled, *Contemporary Black Thought: The Best From The Black Scholar, 1973,* and again in a Department of Housing and Urban Development funded edition of *The Black Scholar* released in December, 1979. The following are brief excerpts from the article:

"Historically, because of our position of servitude, we were never permitted to be counted among the landed gentry. When land in America, during the late 18th century, was selling for 8 and 9 cents an acre, most black people in this country were in shackles and chains or prohibited, by law, from becoming landowners. In those few instances where we were permitted to buy, the absence of security was always present because of the fear of being dispossessed by an angry white individual or mob. Many instances are recorded in history where Blacks had to leave land, home, and personal effects in the middle of the night, simply to escape with their lives.

"The 1785 Ordinance of the Continental Congress set the price of land at a dollar per acre, plus expenses. It was usually sold in sections of 640 acres each and larger quantities were sold, by negotiations with the Congress, at a few cents per acre. Such cities as Cleveland, Cincinnati, and Marietta were developed by The Ohio Company, which purchased 1½ million acres at a price of 8 to 9 cents per acre in 1787. If we compare the price The Ohio Company paid for its land with the current prices of from $500 to $800 per acre for raw farmland, and $2,500 to $3,000 an acre for land adjacent to metropolitan areas, I think we can readily see that some new economic innovations will have to be applied if the black man is ever to participate in the mainstream of our capital development.

"Regrettably, our founding fathers and their successors never saw the need of a land reform act that would include the black brother. Even though Blacks fought in every battle, including the American Revolution, when land grants were given to soldiers in lieu of pay, the historians have yet to find any recorded documentation showing that black soldiers participated in the 1776 G.I. Bill."

Julian Bond, the very young Georgia State Representative, delivered a brilliant paper on politics. Fannie Lou Hamer, the Mississippi Civil Rights Leader, gave a fiery and passionate address on voter registration.

An unexpected main event took place in the early evening on April 26, 1969. By the time I arrived at the hall with my tape recorder, all the seats had been filled by the 500 community leaders who represented every major city and civil rights organization in the country. I opted to sit on the floor near the lectern, as opposed to standing in the rear of the auditorium. After about a half hour's wait, a tall muscular young man stepped up to the lectern dressed in a faded-blue denim overall. He had a head covered with a voluminous shock of black curly hair, and reddish brown skin that gave him an Indian appearance. The man was James Forman, director of international affairs for Student Non-Violent Coordinating Committee (SNCC), and a fellow Roosevelt University graduate.

Forman electrified the hall with a gusty delivery of his Black Manifesto, which demanded restitution from both the Christian churches and the Jewish synagogues. His speech was constantly interrupted with applause, footstamping, and emotional shouts of "right on, brother" and "power to the people." This was the first time I had ever become emotionally part of an audience that had been lifted into a mental state which bordered on mass hysteria.

Here is part of what Forman said:

"We, the black people assembled in Detroit, Michigan, for the National Black Economic Development Conference, are fully aware that we have been forced to come together because racist White America has exploited our resources, our minds, our bodies, our labor. For centuries we have been forced to live as colonized people inside the United States, victimized by the most vicious, racist system in the world. We have helped to build the most industrial country in the world.

"We are, therefore, demanding of the white Christian churches and Jewish synagogues which are part and parcel of the system of capitalism, that they begin to pay reparations to black people in this country. We are demanding $500,000,000 from Christian white churches and the Jewish synagogues. This total comes to 15 dollars per nigger. This is a low estimate, for we maintain there are probably more than 30,000,000 black people in this country. Fifteen dollars a nigger is not a large sum of money and we know that the churches and synagogues have a tremendous wealth and its membership, White America, has profited and still exploits black people. We are also not unaware that the exploitation of colored people around the world is aided and abetted by the white Christian churches and synagogues.

"This demand for $500,000,000 is not an idle resolution or empty words. Fifteen dollars for every black brother and sister in the United States is only a beginning of the reparations due us as people who have been exploited and degraded, brutalized, killed and persecuted. Underneath all this exploitation, the racism of this country has produced a psychological effect upon us that we are beginning to shake off. We are no longer afraid to demand our full rights as a people in this decadent society."

I came back to Chicago with my brain reeling. Reparations for past inequities was not a new idea in America, but this was the first time that any Black had demanded financial restitution from religious institutions. The boldness of Forman's message sent us all away on an emotional high.

But back in Chicago, things had to be fought out on a much grittier level.

I had been concerned ever since I started in the real estate business over the way Whites exploited Blacks by selling them houses on contract, without a mortgage. I knew that such contracts were often terribly inflated, with legal provisions that meant the buyer—so desperate to get out of the black ghetto that he often failed to fully understand what he was getting into—could lose all interest in a home he had been paying on for years by missing a single payment. The heartbreak that such a situation could cause was graphically demonstrated just a few blocks from my office in 1970.

Some 1,000 families in this situation had banded together to fight the injustice by withholding their payments and putting them in escrow to try to force renegotiation of contracts which were clearly unjust. For example, one man had signed a forty-one-year contract in 1960 for a South Side home at the price of $31,950, with a down payment of $3,500 and monthly payments of $227. An appraisal valued the house at only $25,000, and the Contract Buyers League figured he eventually would have paid around $85,000 for it. By 1970, when the man joined with about 430 other families in withholding his payments, he had paid more than $20,000 in taxes, principal and interest. If the League did not succeed in challenging the contracts in court on the grounds that they violated an 1866 Illinois statute barring racial discrimination in the sale of property and exploitation on the basis of race, he stood to lose every penny of that investment.

I read about the Contract Buyers League's efforts with a mixture of admiration and apprehension. These people were protesting a terrible evil, but they were doing it at the risk of devastating retribution. Poor families who had been exploited all their lives, they stood to lose an investment of half a lifetime's work in many cases. I had no reason to believe that the courts would sort this thing out and rectify the injustice.

That was why on the day it was announced the Cook County Sheriff would begin evicting those families from their homes, I drove over to South Eggleston Avenue and stood in a crowd watching the spectacle of twelve families' belongings being carried out and set in the mud. The sidewalk and streets became filled with rocking horses, beheaded dolls, baby carriages, rolled-up bedding, dining room tables, refrigerators, sofas and television sets. There were also paintings of Dr. Martin Luther King, Jr. and John and Robert Kennedy heaped up in the mud and unseasonable snow of April, 1970. The watching crowd, kept back by burly police officers, added their tears to those of the ex-homeowners.

I didn't sleep more than two hours the night following the evictions. Every time I closed my eyes I saw the expressions of the weeping women and children. Standing helplessly by their sides were their men, wet-eyed with anger, watching their life savings and dreams being boarded up and plastered over with "keep out" signs.

The following day the Rev. Jesse Jackson called and asked me to attend a Saturday morning Operation Breadbasket meeting. There he introduced me to Sidney Clark, South Side chairman of the C.B.L., and I also met Louis Diamond, president of Midstate Homes, Inc., the contract seller of more than 100 homes on the South Side. Universal Builders, holders of more than 500 contracts on South Side homes, was not represented at the Breadbasket meeting. Contract buyers had been evicted from seventy of the Universal homes, and some of those homes had been fire-bombed and dynamited. The contract buyers and the sellers were in a stalemate that seemed to offer no way out but violence.

To avoid further bloodshed, I began to meet with Louis Diamond to try to find a way out. He had displayed to me some sensitivity to the plight of the contract buyer families. We met for several hours, just the two of us, for nine consecutive days, and finally we thought we had a solution: Diamond agreed to reduce the contract principal on the unpaid balance by fourteen per cent, providing the contract buyers agreed to pay their delinquencies, and only *if* I was able to find mortgages with a below-market interest rate with no discount cost to either buyer or seller. The agreement was designed to save an average of $5,000 for each participating contract buyer.

I had pledged to do the impossible. I had promised to obtain seven per cent mortgages in a tight money market where the prevailing interest rate was eight and one-half per cent.

I knew that the economics of my proposition would not make sense to any business institution, and therefore I packaged it as the social issue it was. I made calls to two black-owned banks and two black-controlled insurance companies in addition to four white lending institutions and asked each to commit $100,000 in mortgage money to the Contract Buyers League families. Within forty-eight hours George S. Harris, president of Chicago Metropolitan Mutual Assurance Co., had committed $100,000, as had Al Boute, president of Independence Bank, Earl B. Dickerson, president of the Supreme Liberty Life Insurance Company, and Harold

Algar, president of the Seaway National Bank.

The instant response of the four black institutions delighted me. It was different with the white institutions. They showed no sense of social obligation to the contract buyers. They saw no reason to make seven per cent loans, and that was that. One Loop banker, though, indicated he would participate at an eight and one-half per cent rate plus a five per cent discount! Having gained the backing of the black lending institutions, I was able to negotiate an additional $3.5 million mortgage commitment with Oakley Hunter, president of the Federal National Mortgage Association, headquartered in Washington, D.C.

Members, family, and friends of the Contract Buyers League burn a facsimile of a real estate contract belonging to Charles Davis, a contract buyer and Co-Chairman of the Contract Buyers League. The ceremony was held to commemorate the first mortgage financed under the Contract Buyers' agreement coordinated by Dempsey J. Travis.

My efforts in the Contract Buyers League is best reflected in the following editorial:

Chicago Tribune

FOUNDED JUNE 10, 1847
CHICAGO TRIBUNE, TUESDAY, AUGUST 18, 1970
WHERE THERE'S A WILL

Thanks to the enterprise of Dempsey J. Travis, a mortgage banker, and the help of other black businessmen, the stalemate which has resulted in the eviction of a number of contract buyers of South Side homes has been broken.

For more than a year, members of the Contract Buyers League have been withholding payment from the firms from which they bought their homes as a protest against what the buyers regard as unfair contract terms. They say that racial discrimination denied them access to conventional mortgages and forced them to sign the contracts. The companies have responded by evicting non payers.

As Mr. Travis assessed the situation, "Nobody is making any money and everybody is losing." Most of those evicted are without homes. The sellers are not collecting any money, and the vacant homes are being vandalized. It was a dispute which could easily bring more tension to an area already surfeited with tension . . .

Mr. Travis has thus done a good deal to heal a festering sore and showed that even some of the most troublesome problems can be solved. "As a black businessman," he said, "I believe I have an obligation to the black community. I gain my living from the community, and I should do what I can to help the community." If all Chicagoans, black and white, had this attitude, the city would be a lot better off than it is.

Chapter 19

READING THE OBITS

My father had never managed to have breakfast with Mama and me since he usually left the house shortly after 5 a.m., except on Sunday. This particular Sunday he had his face buried in the funny papers and my mother and I were gabbing away.

"I dreamed last night that I was going to be rich and Daddy wouldn't have to work anymore." I must have been about nine years old.

My mother smiled at me—the kind of smile a mother gives in response to a childhood fantasy.

My father folded his paper abruptly and looked at me.

"Everybody wants to be rich, boy," he said. "You concentrate on getting that food into your mouth and then worry about how you're going to get through this day without getting a spanking."

"That was a true dream," I said. "That dream was as clear as the day is long, Daddy. I figure it's just a matter of working hard."

My father snorted. "Your mother and I, and your uncles don't know nothing but hard work."

I took a few bites of an apple. "I understand that," I said. "It's just— well, if a person really sets out to be rich, you know, and plans and works at it, well, it might happen outside of a dream. Mr. Charles Murray across the street is rich. Why not me?"

My father smiled, shook his head, and picked up his paper again. "Okay, millionaire, it sounds easy as pie," he said. He then rubbed me on the head and said, "Maybe your dream might come true."

My father's attitude toward my business plans turned out to be a common one. Years later, when I was scouring around the city in search of new opportunities, I often got that funny little headshake from people. They thought I was crazy. Didn't I know a black man's chances of making it were razor slim?

No, I didn't know that. Once I began to see how the business world worked, I couldn't get the idea out of my head that black-controlled businesses could bring more and more Blacks into mainstream America. As I got more formal education about America's history and the workings of commerce, it only seemed like a more reasonable proposition, not less.

I couldn't see any conflict in Blacks riding on the wagon of commerce that they once pulled.

At first, of course, I got into business to provide a comfortable living for my family. But the millionaire lifestyle that many successful businessmen adopt has always seemed alien to me.

I think one reason for that is that my success has been a double satisfaction. Not only was I making enough money to support my family in comfort, but I was proving wrong all those prognosticators who predicted I would never make it. I'm afraid a black person in America is going to be able to get that double satisfaction for a long time to come.

In the 1960's, when a lot of privileged Whites were taking notice of Blacks for the first time, it became obvious that there was a basic misunderstanding. White college kids by the thousands were suddenly breaking with their parents' establishment and turning their back on the Mercedes cars and the Caribbean cruises and all the other trappings of success. They expected to turn around and find in the black man a humble, simple, non-materialistic person upon whom to model their new lives.

They were shocked, then, when they found out that that's not what we Blacks were all about at all. It's very well to give up your Mercedes and your mink coat when you know you can have them if you just reach out your hand. But we had never had that. We had lived poor, and we knew what it was like: it was rotten. We wanted to experience the good things. Maybe not forever—but just once!

It was thinking about that kind of thing that made me realize my attitude toward material success would always be bound up with my feelings about the situation of Blacks in America. Very early in my career—when my success was still pretty shaky—I got myself involved with social projects that didn't seem to have a lot of potential for contributing to my personal economic gain. But I found that a person who goes out of his way to empathize with others and make opportunities to show social concern—and still survives the first five years in business—will build a solid foundation for a very successful enterprise. That's because the enterprise will then be important to a lot more people than just yourself.

It may be that some will interpret your empathy as weakness and your social concern as naivete. But you can count on your God-given barracuda instincts to balance the scale.

Some time in the late 1950's, I remember sitting in the Chicago Title & Trust with Circuit Court Judge Kenneth Wilson. Wilson turned to me with a smile and said, "You know, Chicago is fortunate."

"Why is that?"

"Because a guy with your talents could have decided to be a con man

Presentation of the First "Black Enterprise Magazine Award In Finance" by Vice President Nelson A. Rockefeller to Dempsey J. Travis and Mrs. Travis at the White House, February 21, 1975.

Session of the Presidential Task Force on Urban Renewal. Picture taken at the White House, 1970.

Washington, D.C., 1970: First Black Caucus Joint Session with United Mortgage Bankers of America; pictured left to right are: Willis Carson, president, National Association of Real Estate Brokers; Congressman Parrin Mitchell; Dempsey J. Travis, president of United Mortgage Bankers of America; the late Congressman Ralph Metcalfe, and Congressman John Conyers on Capitol Hill.

...und-breaking ...mony at Lake ...ve Village, ...ch, 1970. Pic-...d left to right Dr. A. L. Rey-...ds; Bishop H. ...mas Primm; ...or Richard J. ...ey; Dempsey J. ...vis, and John ...er, area direc-...United States ...partment of ...sing and Urban ...elopment.

Pictured are Donald Walker and the Rev. Jesse Jackson making presentation of first "Black Businessman of the Year" award to Dempsey J. Travis. Photograph taken December 3, 1970.

President Jimmy Carter and Dempsey J. Travis in the East Room of the White House, Washington, D.C., December 20, 1979 following briefing and luncheon meeting.

instead of an honest businessman. And you know what? I think you could sell the Golden Gate Bridge."

I laughed. "You've got something there," I said. "You know, I could talk a fellow out of his shoes if I wanted to. Sometimes I've had to restrain myself."

Joking aside, Wilson had a point. A lot of black youngsters grow up with the wheeler dealer, the drug pusher and the pimp as the only models of economic success that they know. And that's very unfortunate.

Business success requires single-mindedness. You can't permit yourself to be distracted by any scheme that will conflict with your objective. The commercial goal must be in the front of your mind constantly. This requires a discipline that costs more in personal sacrifice than most people are either willing or able to make. The aura of success is sweet, but the price is never cheap.

The successful men I know and have read about were all clock watchers. The pure sociologist seldom survives in business because of his unwillingness to watch the clock of commerce. Social experiments can go on forever, whereas a viable business plan had better be finite. Time is a tool that must be used carefully, because there is no lay-away plan for holding its hands.

I use to try to convince my marketing staff of this principle. At the beginning of each sales meeting, I would designate someone to read aloud the obituaries of some recently deceased prominent citizens. I wanted to cure my salesmen of the disease of procrastination, which they all suffered from to a degree. Since I know that disease is contagious, I still read the obituary column daily as a reminder that my own time clock is finite.

I try to invest my time the same way I invest my money. I spend very little on small talk or small thoughts. I want to make it yield intellectual or monetary benefits. On lucky days, it yields both.

Time must be made to adapt to the work to be completed. I never let myself sit at a desk with four hours of work to be completed in an eight-hour time frame. I either fill the extra four hours with a new task or leave the office in search of a new business opportunity.

Those things are true for anyone, black or white. But Blacks face some special hurdles if they want success. One is plain fear, and I don't discount it. There are still plenty of things to be afraid about in our lives. But I think too often we give in to that fear without really knowing what we're afraid of. We opt for security before we really know what we can do.

The one thing my mother and my wife always agreed on was that after I got through with junior college, I should go into the post office and get a nice secure job, with a nice, secure paycheck. They had my best interests at heart, and they weren't discounting my abilities. They just thought the world was going to prove too much for me. Even so, I still wanted to take a few risks. If I'd taken their advice, I'd probably be the best letter sorter the post office ever had—but I sure would have missed out on a lot of fun.

Many young Blacks see that they're in a trap, and they get so angry and frustrated that they become paralyzed. I'm not saying they're wrong about that trap. It still exists.

I recognized that trap very early in my life. I decided the idea was not to step on the spring so it would close on you. That's a kind of sixth sense you develop that I can't quite explain. At Camp Shenango, I stepped on the spring. I was in the wrong place at the wrong time. But it hasn't happened since.

I know about the rage many Blacks feel about their situation. I recognize that, too. But I never let it overwhelm me. If I let that kind of rage build in me, then I'm dying. I can't sit back and make a program of hating Whites. I've go other things to do.

Reading, combined with an ongoing educational program, is a top prerequisite for operating a successful business. During my first twenty years in real estate I always carried at least ten academic hours in evening courses each year at schools like Roosevelt University, Central YMCA Junior College, the Illinois Institute of Technology, Chicago Kent College of Law, and Northwestern University. I always read ten newspapers daily including the Chicago papers plus the *Wall Street Journal, American Banker, The Washington Post, The New York Times* and the *Christian Science Monitor*. I still fit in at least five newspapers daily, two books a month, and a dozen trade journals, as well as at least two five-day educational seminars a year.

Academic training, combined with experience, taught me how to look at an almost devastated piece of real estate and see a gold mine instead of a disaster. The first lesson I learned was never to buy other people's paint. I've saved as much as 300 per cent by fixing a wreck myself instead of paying a much higher price for a painted doll.

I'm an early riser and always have been. I found this one common thread among all the successful men I've known or read about: they're not sleepers. I've always had a high energy level, and a long time ago I decided I wasn't going to worry about standing out or being different. When people tell me to slow down—and for some reason, somebody is always telling me that—I tell them to speed up.

President Lyndon Baines Johnson asked me to participate in the White House Conference, "To Fulfill These Rights," in 1966. President Richard M. Nixon asked me to join his Housing Task Force in writing the 1970 Housing Bill. President Gerald Ford brought me into both his energy and inflation think tanks. Vice President Nelson Rockefeller presented me with the first Black Enterprise Award in finance at the White House in 1975, and President Jimmy Carter asked me to a White House briefing and luncheon in 1979.

I've met and shared the dais with then-Presidential candidate Ronald Reagan at the Executive Club of Chicago. I remember that everybody was saying he'd never get to be President. He was just an out-of-work actor, and he was too old, they said. And now Reagan is sitting in the White House getting ready to cut his 71st birthday cake.

Blacks spend so much of their energy fighting nightmares that very little is left to spend on following their dreams. I know that looking at our situation can be downright sickening at times. But there's another side of it that we ought to look at sometimes, too. With all our handicaps, we've increased our income from $50 billion annually in 1960 to $127 billion in 1980. There were more than one million Blacks attending college in 1980, as compared to a quarter of a million in 1966. We have a multitude of black elected public officials throughout the land, and mayors in a number of major cities like Atlanta, New Orleans, Detroit, Los Angeles and Washington, D.C.

The first black president of the United States has already been born and will be elected before the year 2000, providing the rest of us build on the legal victories of the '40's and '50's, the Civil Rights struggle of the '60's, and the political victories of the '70's.

I remember that when I was 38, a lot of my friends thought I had reached the high point of my life with my election to a second term as president of the Dearborn Real Estate Board. They knew how important that was to me, and I guess they expected that from then on I'd be taking things a little easier.

One of those friends was the late Wilbur Slaughter, a fellow realtist. He was a copper-colored, quaint-faced man. One late afternoon before a Dearborn Real Estate Board meeting he glared at me with his piercing, intelligent eyes and said, "Boy, are you lucky! This has got to be the zenith of your real estate career."

I only smiled at Slaughter's remark. But inwardly, I was saying to myself, "Man, are you wrong. This is nice, sure. But there is going to be a lot more to my life than this."

And there was.

And there will be more.

Dempsey J. Travis and the late Roy Wilkins at a press conference in New York City at the Waldorf Astoria Hotel in 1973.

Part Two:

VOICES FROM THE PAST
AND THE PRESENT

Alice Blair

Alice Blair, 57, is deputy superintendent of the Chicago public schools. In more than 30 years since entering the system as a teacher, Blair has served in a succession of administrative posts.

"Fifty-first and Dearborn was a bunch of shacks, in terms of what we lived in. We didn't have hot water—and the houses were torn down for slum clearance in order to build Robert Taylor Homes. But in those shacks, there was something different from what is there now."

Alice Blair

When I was a child in the school system, most of my teachers were white, and they didn't particularly like me, or like us or like black youngsters. But in order for those teachers to teach or remain as teachers, those youngsters had to achieve. They had to teach a certain body of material; they were measured by the amount of that material I mastered. If I didn't master it, I didn't get promoted. When my brother finally graduated from elementary school he was equally bright and equally literate, but he had to remain until he mastered that body of material.

Now expectations have changed. I don't want to say unions prevented administrators from demanding teacher performance in terms of teaching youngsters skills. But it was that, I think, plus the fact that we weren't all herded together—we weren't all poor and on relief. So there was a variety of images of how people could live in the schools we attended.

I started school in 1929 in kindergarten; at that time we were approaching the Depression, and my family moved every year. Through about the seventh grade I was in a different school in every grade. Whenever the rent was due, my mother packed up and moved to another apartment, as many other people did. As I look back on that, I don't know that was such a disadvantage. I began to sense early what was a good teacher and what was a good school. There were schools that I went to where I knew more than the youngsters in the class. Then next time around when we moved, I didn't know as much. And so I began to really be very sensitized to what was a good school at a very early age.

My mother played policy, as it was called in those days. She won some money, and she took that money and put it on a down payment on a house on Dearborn, 51st and Dearborn. That was the first permanent place I had to live in. By that time I was a freshman at DuSable. For the four years, we stayed on Dearborn, and I worked in the school office as an honor student. Later, under the old National Youth Administration (N.Y.A.), I got paid six dollars a month, which helped get me through high school. Helped buy my clothes, helped my mother and stepfather. My mother worked in a laundry, and my stepfather was a cook at the old Harding Restaurants. There were three of us—my sister and brother and I—and that was the way they maintained us.

Fifty-first and Dearborn was a bunch of shacks, in terms of what we lived in. We didn't have hot water—and the houses were torn down for slum clearance in order to build the Robert Taylor Homes, the largest public housing complex in the country. But in those shacks, there was something different from what is there now. Because in those shacks along that street were all kinds of different levels of people. Some were in poverty, and some were affluent. Because Blacks just couldn't move all over Chicago. Some of those frame houses were fixed up beautifully, because people had the resources to fix them. Blacks were hemmed in by restrictive covenants.

Judge Earl Strayhorn's mother-in-law lived at the end of the block and she was a teacher at Farren. Judge Earl Strayhorn and his wife lived on Dearborn for a period of time. The mother-in-law I always admired. She was always well dressed when she passed our house going to Farren to teach. The Whites (a black family) owned a lot of little stores and businesses. They had a grocery store on the corner.

So that was what was different about Dearborn Street when I grew up and Dearborn Street now, with the Robert Taylor Homes. Now, from 75 to 78 per cent of the people receive some form of public assistance. I think it is unfair, that it was a political decision to do that. By so doing, we have taken away the success images, and we cause those children to see nothing but poverty. We give them no desire to do things better.

When I finished high school there were just no plans for me to go on to college, because my family didn't have any money. This was in 1943, the beginning of the war. But I was a member at that time of the Cosmopolitan Church. Rev. Mary Evans was the minister of that church at that time. They took up money and paid my first year's tuition and bought me clothes for the first year at a Presbyterian school in Knoxville, Tennessee.

It was the first time I met with real segregation, where you rode in the rear of the bus and Blacks didn't sit past a certain place on it. That was my first experience with that, on leaving Chicago and going South. I had been lectured when I left home by my grandmother and mother, that I was going to the South. For me, at 18 years old, this was just a terrible, frightening experience.

But I did very well in that setting for about seven months. Then I went into the town of Knoxville to do some shopping with other students from the campus, and when we got on the bus the Whites had begun to sit in seats that were ordinarily for Blacks because the bus was so crowded. Blacks had to stand. I understood that that was what I had to do. So I had a conversation with one of the other students. Then a white woman passenger turned to me and said, "Nigger, don't sit down beside me." She was sitting next to the middle door that you go out of.

I began saving spit before we got to my stop, and just as I stepped off that side door, I spit in her face. She screamed and yelled, and the bus driver stopped the bus. I was chased on campus and had to hide in the dormitory. The matron of the dormitory said none of the girls were out that day. But someone told her who had done it, and then I was restricted to the campus.

I decided I wouldn't go back South after that year. I felt bad about the church sending me and then learning I had behaved so badly in terms of this experience and caused the school so much trouble. It did cause them some trouble.

I had heard a recruiter on campus talking about the WACS (Women's Army Corps Service). They said you could go on to college. It appealed to me, because I felt I wouldn't have to be dependent on anyone. My family wouldn't have to support me. I could put in these two or three years in the WACS and earn my college credit that way.

When I came home, I didn't tell my mother about that experience in Knoxville, nor did I tell the church. I enlisted in the WACS. I was stationed in New York, at Staten Island. I was what they called an information educational specialist. I was trained to teach men to read and write before they went overseas to Europe. This was a port company where they loaded the ships, so they weren't as careful in terms of their screening of men, because they used brawn rather than brains. But when the men went overseas they had to be able to write and read. I taught them, and that probably was the beginning of my philosophy about teaching people to read. All people can learn to read if given a reason for it. These men, although they were adults, learned to read and write. This was an intensive program, and they had eight weeks to learn. It was a phonics program. And the men did learn to read and write in eight weeks because they had to. They had to report to those classes, and the Army could make them do that. If anything has given me the belief that all children can learn, given the right incentive, that experience did that.

When the war was over in Europe, I went out to California, though I still remained an information educational specialist. I gave the orientation lectures when the men came back from overseas. This was the kind of experience I had in the Army. I also worked at night as a post librarian, and I took United States Armed Forces mail order courses. I accumulated around nine to twelve hours that way. My goal was to finish college, so I spent my off-duty time doing that.

When I got home I entered Roosevelt University on the G.I. Bill. In between, I got married and had children. I went back to school after each child. Later I divorced. I started doing social work and took education courses. I finished my degree on the G.I. Bill while I was married. I was getting money with dependents. When I got my divorce, I applied for the social work job. None of that was planned.

Later, I took education hours at night, because teaching was paying more than social work. I didn't have any reason to feel I was going to be a great teacher or anything. The fact was that I had two children to support, and teaching at that time was paying something like $2,400 a year, which in 1951 looked like a lot. So I went into teaching.

I got a bachelor's degree in 1951, a master's degree in 1961, and a doctor's degree in 1978. I tried to rear children and yet continue to go to school. It took that length of time to get all the degrees. It has taken me thirty years to get from teacher to principal to deputy superintendent. Though everybody says I have risen rapidly in the Chicago school system, that is not the case at all. They know I have worked at every level, rather than moving straight from teaching to the deputy superintendent's job. I have done everything in between.

I was district superintendent in District 13, which takes in the Robert Taylor Homes. When I became district superintendent, my office was in

DuSable High School. I had graduated from DuSable. And I was supervising the elementary school I graduated from, Farren. I was supervising the elementary school where I started school, Burke, and I was supervising the various schools that had made a difference in my life. Yet they weren't making a difference any more in the lives of most of the young people. It wasn't because there had been such outstanding teachers or outstanding administrators in that district when I was in school. It was the home environment that had changed, because so many poverty people were being herded together.

Scattered-site housing would have done much more for black people than herding all of them together in a Robert Taylor concentration of poverty, or a Cabrini Green, the city's second largest housing project. I was just as poor as these young children—my father died, and my mother worked. But it was different. That is why District 13 was so important to me. I felt it was a mission.

DuSable High School was important to me. I said when I came there, "This high school has got to change. The kids cannot walk through the halls with hats on, can't smoke pot, and there has to be an atmosphere conducive to learning." You start that with the administrator. That's what I believe happened with the schools when I was going to school: there were some things set down by those above that said there are certain skills these youngsters have to learn or stay here until they learn them. There was never any belief that we couldn't learn them, over a short or long period of time. As nasty and dirty as we might have been, the teacher never assumed that we couldn't learn to read, write and compute.

I went to DuSable with the belief that those youngsters didn't have to behave that way. They wanted to behave differently. I just accepted no excuses. I didn't accept the idea that the fact that because they came from Robert Taylor Homes meant they couldn't behave any differently. I immediately announced that I also came from that community and went to that high school and was just as poor, and we didn't behave that way. I immediately set a tone that sent a message to the administrator, a message to the teachers, that things were going to be different here, or the administrator wasn't going to be there any longer, nor were the teachers. It was just that simple and dramatic. I was willing to do whatever I had to do to make a difference.

Within three weeks you could see the climate changing. There were some physical things that had to be done, and I began to worry people about the rehabilitation, the windows. The school had almost no windows at the time I came there. So I began to worry the people downtown who had to do with that. I was persistent in terms of getting the physical plant repaired and made attractive. Then I began to talk to the local politicians and secured a track field for the youngsters. With them seeing my involvement in trying to make things better there, the youngsters felt good about coming to that school. I certainly felt very pleased about the way things were going when I left, and I am sure it is going to continue that way.

At the Beasley School, right in the middle of Robert Taylor Homes, we tried another program. It was an attempt to try to put together what had happened to me. Put together a variety of youngsters, rather than all of them poverty youngsters. If you could put white youngsters in, if that could be worked, I thought that would be a good idea. But integration was not my initial interest. My interest was getting a principal who believed in children, getting a group of teachers who believed in the children, and identifying youngsters in the district who were being lost in the other schools and had demonstrated potential so that they wouldn't feel locked into their environment, where even though they had potential they didn't want to achieve much higher than their neighbors and didn't want the kids to think they were sissies because they did well. The peer pressure was so important. If they were in a school where everybody was doing well, it would raise the standard for those youngsters—and that, in fact, occurred. They continue to live in Robert Taylor or in the area around Robert Taylor, but they are achieving as well as students across this city in privileged areas. I had done it years before, though I was very poor: I achieved at a school because there were those around me achieving. So that's happening at Beasley, and that's why.

Every time they publish the reading scores, one of the only black schools in the city that's always one of the top schools in reading is Beasley. Beasley continues to be up there in the ten or twelve top schools. Then when people look and see Beasley at 52nd and State, they want to know what's going on. I have discovered people don't care where the school is if their youngsters are going to achieve. If it's a good school and the kids are safe, they don't care where it is. When I left the district, there were at least 1,000 kids on the waiting list for Beasley. There are 1,200 children there now. Close to maybe 150 of those are white, over ten per cent white. It certainly can be duplicated. It bothers me they don't have a design like it for the integration plan. But I am in a different capacity now, so I can't determine what other programs will be similar to it. I just hope it continues to be a top-notch school. I think with the parents seeing what can be done, they are not going to let it deteriorate.

Let's look into the future, now that you are deputy superintendent working with Chicago's first black superintendent of schools, Dr. Ruth Love. Tell me what you see happening.

We're very excited about what's going to happen, if the schools stay open and the political structure supplies the money. There have been terrible financial crises in the last few years, of course. But we are ready to go in terms of improving the educational programs for the children. The system will be graded in the old fashioned way--first grade, second grade and third grade. That wasn't the case during the last ten years in Chicago. We are back to the basics. We have got a promotion policy now that if the kids don't learn at the first grade level, they stay there until they do. That did not exist before.

We have developed handbooks for teachers, telling them what ought to be taught. We developed scope and sequence charts containing the entire program of the elementary school. Teachers can paste it on the wall and see exactly what they are supposed to teach in every area. Not only are we giving that to the teacher--we are giving that to the parents. We have developed a new report card that tells parents exactly what the youngsters are doing in school. We put a separate section for effort, rather than grading them high in achievement because they try hard.

All of this has happened since Dr. Ruth Love, the new Chicago superintendent of schools, has been here. In addition, we have developed a program called Mastery Learning in Reading, where the youngsters have to complete a number of units to move on to the next group, and they are tested on that. That is a citywide program; there has never been a uniform program throughout the city.

In terms of teachers, we are going to have to take what we have and upgrade their skills. At least we can give them the ability to teach the basic skills and develop the kind of staff development programs we need in house and with the universities that will train them on the job. What we have done in the past, when we have found teachers unsatisfactory, was to grade them unsatisfactory and then transfer them somewhere else. It is an arduous task to fire teachers. We have decided when a teacher has been marked unsatisfactory, we will work with the universities, try to send them back to school, as businesses do, for six months, with the universities working with them and bringing everything they have to bear. Some of these people haven't been back to school in twenty years. There is no rule in Chicago that forces people to take courses every so often. If they graduated twenty years ago, they can teach, without ever upgrading their skills. The in-service we provide just isn't adequate for making them better. We have just completed the proposal, and the universities are very excited about it. Why wasn't this done before? The universities will keep us abreast of what they are doing. We're starting out very modestly in the fall of 1981 with sixty teachers, if we can get funded.

The next thing we came up with is called "adopt a school." The businesses criticize us all the time and say we are not doing our job. So we are saying. "Come in, help us and adopt a school." We are putting all the high schools up for adoption, and we are permitting business people to identify those things they have to offer. We're not asking for money, we're asking for people to tutor--if a graphic arts company came in and worked with those students who asked for graphic arts. So far we have been overwhelmed by the response. Major companies have come in already and adopted a school. Again, new and different. So I feel very up about what's going to happen in this school system.

Are drugs a major problem among black students?

Drugs are not new to the black community. I think it's more of a new phenomenon of the suburbs. Most of the children at DuSable get a cheap high, because they can't afford the hard drugs. They may be high on wine. We had drugs when I was going to DuSable; drugs that are now in the suburbs were at DuSable in the '40's. My locker-mate overdosed in 1942. It's never listed as the number one problem by the principals.

The number one problem is gang recruitment. We moved away from that for ten years or so, but now it has returned. The gangs are a vehicle for robberies and selling drugs and so forth. We are writing a new discipline code and a policy for dealing with the gangs. I personally don't think the gangs are a school problem: they are a problem for the law enforcement officials. The youngsters are ready to be taught if we can control the outside forces.

We do not do that.

Alvin Boutte

Alvin Boutte, 52, is chairman of the board and chief executive officer of Independence Bank at 7936 S. Cottage Grove Ave., the largest black-owned bank in the United States.

"As a black man in this country, even today with all the things that have changed, some attitudes are not changed. The black man finds himself isolated, no matter who he is. There is a relationship with the white businessman downtown, but it's a limited relationship."

Alvin Boutte

I had a magnificent father who seeded my mind with all kinds of ideas, things I could succeed in if I tried. My father was a working man, and probably smarter than I am today. He was self-educated. He finished grammar school, and then he had to go to work to support the family. But he never stopped reading. He was a constant reader.

Because he was a reader, I became a reader. I can remember my room at home full of books. I read about things I had never seen or never comprehended. So that opened my eyes and brains to many possibilities.

Young people now have many more opportunities than we had, and that's the way it ought to be. But I think they will have to take advantage of all the opportunities presented to them. One of the things that helped me was reading. I'm an avid reader today. I was an avid reader when I was 13 and 14 years old. I have been into many black households, both affluent and otherwise, where I don't see magazines, books and newspapers.

I think people need to open books and their minds to things they never experienced. They need to prepare themselves to get as much out of the opportunities that are available as they can. In any case, almost everyone has some opportunity. They should take advantage of it, and next try to make a concentrated effort to improve their reading habits. They need to read more about a variety of things, things they may feel they'll never get involved in. The knowledge alone will help you, will open new worlds you can't imagine exist. I don't see enough of that.

I went to an all-black school, a parochial school called Sacred Heart.

Since integration, all the schools in Lake Charles, Louisiana, are integrated, but I hear that the best school in the city happens to be Sacred Heart. It had tremendous discipline. They were very tough, but in a very positive way. It was a good school, now that I can put everything in proper perspective. We had two black teachers, one a physical education teacher and the other was an English teacher. This was in 1944 or 1945.

The first time I really competed against other people, other than Blacks, was after I had finished high school and finished college. I got a lieutenant's commission after completing Officer Candidate School. I finished second in a class of 220 people--only five were Blacks. I didn't have any idea what I knew. And that experience gave me real confidence. I had been totally educated in black schools--I finished college in 1950 with a degree in pharmacy. I was 18 years old, and I had a degree in pharmacy, but I couldn't take the board because they said you had to be 21 years of age; thus I couldn't practice.

When I got out of the Army, the first thing I did was sit down and try to decide where I wanted to live. After much thought I knew I didn't want to go back to Lake Charles. I knew I wanted to live in a large city where there was a large group of Blacks.

The first place I went was California, but California didn't have reciprocity laws, so the examination I had taken in Louisiana, which I passed, didn't apply. They had a rule you had to go to school there at least a year and then take an examination. So California was out. I decided I was going to try New York.

I was passing through Chicago. I didn't know a soul here. I had never been here in my life. I stayed here for two or three days and drove around the city. I have been here ever since.

I had accumulated some money in the Army, and I decided I was going to find a job so I could save enough to buy a business. I saw an ad in the newspaper about a man who wanted to sell his drugstore. I took a look at the store, and I liked it, but I had never run a drugstore or even worked in one. I made a deal with him that he would give me a job for one year, and I would give him a deposit to buy the store. His name was Tom McCauley.

The first thing I learned was how he operated the store, but I didn't just do that. Maybe he wasn't operating it properly. So I used to go out and visit other stores. I used to leave the store at 4 p.m. and come back at 7 to close up at 10 p.m. Between 4 and 7, I always went to two or three stores to find out what they were doing. I made a concentrated effort to find out what systems other people were using and their value. Then I went to business school at the University of Chicago to learn some basic principles I didn't get in pharmacy school. At that time I didn't think I needed an MBA, but I took courses I knew would help me. And I started a five-year plan, what I was trying to do with my life. I developed it in stages.

I bought that store, and in two years another store. I wanted to develop a drug chain like Walgreen's. I believe there was a market in those days. The drug stores in those days had one of the highest returns in the retail business. It was difficult to lose money in it. But the industry changed. I didn't change; it was the industry that changed and made it impossible and much too risky for what I wanted to do. It became a highly regulated business as third party payments came into the picture in the late '50s. Sometimes you wouldn't receive your funds for months. In addition, they had really reduced the prices on a lot of things. The market was much thinner than it had been before.

A person in that business not only would have to have working capital, but have to have sufficient capital to replace whatever they sold for as long as three or four months. It made it a much more capital-intense business. The regulatory system and the federal government began to allow discount stores, which had just come on the horizon, to sell 60 to 70 per cent of the goods that drugstores sold exclusively up to that time. These things made a material difference in drugstores, and that's why you don't see many today. I had an opportunity to sell in 1968.

George Johnson and I had a nominal amount of money invested in the Independence Bank, which wasn't doing very well. It had had four presidents in its first five years. There were a variety of reasons why it wasn't doing well, including a lack of training and a lack of leadership. Our reputation was at stake with this bank, even though we had only a small amount of money in it. I think when we organized the bank, we both had invested $60,000 to $70,000 apiece. For a bank that's small.

Our conclusion was that since I had sold my business--I was going into business with Johnson Products--that I ought to go into the bank and learn the banking business. So in 1969, I was elected chairman, and I have been here ever since.

We decided to construct the building at 7936 S. Cottage Grove the first year we organized the bank. We knew that in order for us to develop credibility, we had to show the public that we could make a physical difference in the neighborhood. The bank was started in 1964, along with our sister bank Seaway.

We're located in Chatham, which is a marvelous community that lost its last institution, Chesterfield Savings and Loan, in 1963. Really, we came into the market to fill the vacuum that would have existed. Many communities were not as fortunate as Chatham and didn't get a replacement institution, and the record shows that they suffered.

At first we were going to build a building we could afford to house only the institution, which was a very small community bank. But we decided to wait to build a substantial building, one that would have permanency. We wanted it to be a role model for the other property owners. We feel we can totally develop this entire block and really make it one of the most beautiful blocks on the South Side. It will be an encouragement and stimulation to other people around. We expect to have tours, young people coming in to look at this bank. Our second idea was to build a building with another relatively large black-owned business, a black insurance company, but the legal ramifications made that impossible, so we had to scrap that one. So it took us years to finally build.

I am very concerned about capital formation. Black people have so many tremendous problems developing an institution. They have so much difficulty with the formation of capital and bringing together capital. Everybody loves our bank and seems to feel that it's worthwhile having it, but in order to have a bank, you must have a substantial amount of capital. And that must come from people.

Most black businesses, as you, know, are under-capitalized. Black people are in the developing stage where they want businesses owned exclusively by themselves. They have difficulty convincing other Blacks to pool their money together. We've had that trouble for years, and so have other black institutions. It's substantially the same today as it was 20 years ago.

About 18 months ago I went to try to raise $2.5 million in new capital. The bank had grown substantially and required new capital to support those deposits. I went to the conventional capital markets that all businessmen go to: the investment banking houses, Salomon Brothers, and large insurance companies that have done business in this area for years, Metropolitan, New York Life and Equitable. We said, we have developed this institution to the point that we have X millions of dollars in it, and we want other investors to be involved. Essentially we were turned down by all of them. Not just them, but some of those liberal organizations like the pension funds. In 1980, they used about 64 per cent of their disposable funds to invest in various corporations around America, but we knew they hadn't made any investments to black-owned or black-controlled companies. We were not successful with them either.

It's a problem that must be corrected if we are to develop substantial institutions. It's probably racism or a combination of what they perceive as a risk factor, a risk they are not willing to take. They are reluctant to invest in institutions located in certain areas. It's a highly sophisticated "redlining." The truth is we have never been able to overcome that.

We did raise our money, primarily in our own community. This is the third time we were involved basically with the same people. We also raised some part of it in the large white corporate community in Chicago.

We had a bond issue that was sold independently, developed by Saloman Brothers of New York. Instead of pledging real estate as collateral for the bond issue, we put up various government securities, which made the bond issues a cinch to sell. Salomon Brothers sold the bond issue without any trouble. The price we paid was significantly lower than the market. As a matter of fact our bonds were rated AA by Moody's and Standard and Poor. As a matter of fact our rating is higher than the City of Chicago.

The most important time in the history of black banking will be the next one to three years. We are in a consolidation period now. The methods of doing business today require huge pools of capital. Not just banks, but other big companies are trying to merge. Black businesses, especially black banks, must introduce stages of consolidation, because there is an economy of scale there. It serves the best interest of the stockholders, and utimately it serves the best interest of the consumer.

The banking laws that let bank holding companies hold more than one bank must be fully utilized. The record shows that Texas did this six years ago. Seven years ago Texas had roughly 1,000 commercial banks, and after the new laws were put into effect, today they have about 345 banks. It's dangerous for us, because we could end up an island in the middle of the sea of huge financial resources. If we do, we will not continue to prosper. All black banks must start talking to each other. We have seven groups here with a tremendous amount of capital, and we should pool our resources together. We do not have to be under one umbrella--there could be several umbrellas. Black institutions have to pool their capital to survive, or they will be gobbled up. Black financial institutions are going to behave like all financial institutions right now: try to find a marriage partner to consolidate their capital with other capital, to create an economic entity so that they have more power and more leverage.

Our business is not just with the people of Chatham, though that's our primary market. It would be a serious mistake for the people of Chatham to make demands on us we cannot fulfill. Our philosophy is not to do that. Black people need institutions that have sufficient strength. We have brought in more capital to Chatham by far than we have taken out. Chatham has had a neat experience as compared to Woodlawn. Chatham had capital flowing into it from Whites, funds to be used for housing and whatever.

What is your experience with white businessmen?

Let me give you an example. My wife and I and our little boy went to an affair. There were only four Blacks there, and we ended up talking to each other.

As a black man in this country, even today with all the things that have changed, some attitudes are not changed. The black man finds himself isolated, even the rich or the most successful--no matter who he is. There is a relationship with the white businessman downtown, but it's a limited relationship.

Whites regard us as a special market. That's a new word coined five or six years ago, but it's so descriptive. That has not changed very much, whether you live on Lake Shore Drive or wherever. That has not changed.

It doesn't mean we are not doing more business with Whites, but the basic problems are still there. More white people today will accept the idea that all Americans should be equal under the law. That has changed dramatically in the last 15 to 20 years. Just look at Chicago Fest (Chicago's summertime lakefront festival, sponsored by the city.) Look at the crowds. We are at the same location, but we are not together.

Johnny Brown

Johnny Brown, 33, is president of Brown's Tire Corp., which has three locations in Chicago, two in Cleveland, Ohio, one in Birmingham, Alabama, and one in Atlanta, Georgia. Brown holds a master's degree from Governor's State University and has taught in the Chicago public schools. Originally from Alabama, he is one of 12 children born to a sharecropper.

*"Whites do not necessarily select just one individual to be like. Many times their fathers are successful, and they don't know what **unsuccessful** means. . . . It was very difficult for me to select a role model, in order for me to become a businessman."*

Johnny Brown

My father was from a proud family. He was a sharecropper in the South, and with his brothers, lived and worked on a plantation. Whatever they had at the end of the year, were able to get a profit from, they shared that 50-50 with the owners. They had to do all the work and buy all the equipment, but once they harvested the product and took it to the city and sold it at the end of the year, then they had to split 50-50.

My father decided to move from rural Hale County in Alabama to a little town called Demopolis. My father moved there and got a job at the local cement plant. It was a unionized plant. Blacks got the worst jobs and Whites got the best jobs. He was in the union, and they did pay the union scale.

It was like he was in business, the way he talked about it; he discovered sharecropping was not the right type of business to be in.

I was born two years before he decided to move from the rural area to the city. I am from a family of twelve children. I am the seventh child out of the twelve.

I remember when we were hired out to pick and chop cotton, when we were living in Demopolis. We were paid $2 per day—$2.75 maximum. That was in the '60's. This was before Dr. Martin Luther King, Jr. made his famous march to Selma, Alabama. We were still doing that for $2.50 to $2.75 per day—not per hour.

I guess the business end of the Browns came when our father died. I was a junior in college. My brothers and I made a commitment. We decided we all would finish college. This is one thing they expounded on in the South. We made that decision ourselves. We also made a decision that our mother wouldn't have to worry about working again. She was doing housework in the South.

We used to all go back home for get togethers. During the Fourth of July week in 1967, we all decided to go into some type of business. A year later, when we met back in Demopolis, we decided to try to pool our money to find some type of business to go into. The way it worked was that black business people were selected by white businessmen for business. Willie Mays was a Black chosen to go into business, but because he was not a businessman he was unsuccessful. So we were told that we were not the right type to go into business. For example, we were interested in opening a tire company. But instead we were offered a gas station. But I did not accept that.

Some of the boys were in Cleveland, Atlanta and Chicago. We were interested in starting a business anywhere. The way it ended up, we pooled some money, which amounted to about $19,000 between the six of us. We could not get a Small Business Administration loan—we were turned down by the SBA. So we put the money in the bank.

I finished college and went to Governor's State and got my Master's degree. Afterwards I started teaching school at Burnside Elementary School in Chicago. In addition I got a job at Goodyear Tire in the afternoon changing tires. I continued through the summer and eventually got a position as a salesman up front; the door was opened. This is how I got involved in the tire business.

The $19,000 was initially used as good will money. Goodyear said, "We will take this money, realizing you cannot get an SBA loan, and take the chance." Because at the time the store, at 85th and Cottage Grove, was losing money, and the timing was right. They had a decision to make. They could close the store, but they had an eight- or nine-year lease on the store. Rather than pay off that lease, they decided to take a chance on Johnny Brown.

I bought the property two years later. The other brothers were investors initially, but the money was refunded. When I say $19,000, we had to wait over a period of time, because all the people had a use for their money. So they helped get me started, but they weren't partners. I have a brother and a sister working with me now. One brother has his own architecture firm in Atlanta.

When I first went into the tire business in 1970, when the store changed from Goodyear to Johnny Brown's Tire Company, the last thing they said to me was, "You are getting it now, but in six months we will be getting it back. You people just don't know how to run businesses."

A white man said this to me, because you don't see a lot of Blacks in the tire business. It is a very hard, everyday business. It's a very high risk business, too—you know what the insurance rates are like. If one of the guys puts some brake shoes on a person's car and he goes out two hours later and hits someone because the brakes failed, I am reponsible. It's a hard business and a continuous grind. There's never any real relaxation—most of us don't want it, either.

Goodyear at that time had 1700 stores. I felt like, if they can run 1700 stores successfully, Johnny Brown could run 17; that was my goal.

I was not only the first Black in Illinois to have a dealership, I was the first black Goodyear dealer in the country. I was the fifth independent Goodyear dealer in the country. There were a lot of obstacles. I did not have any financing, so I didn't have the credit line. I was almost at a point where I sold four tires and had to go to the district to pick them up. In my business, if you are going to be successful, you must stock over $300,000 in the store. The stock is due in thirty to sixty days. If I put $50,000 worth of stock in the back room, I could not run the business five days. But this didn't stop me.

What ignited me is something James Baldwin said a long time ago, which I've kept in my mind. Baldwin said when a person acts, he commits himself. When you commit yourself, in many cases you endanger yourself. You are either going to be proven a liar, or you are going to carry through what you said you would do. He also made a comment in one of his earlier books: "If you go outside during the daylight, all the stars are affixed in the sky just like they are in the evening. They are there, but we can't see them." Blacks have always been like that, not seen during the day, and in fixed positions at night.

What I have found with the black consumer is that when he walks into the store, he wants to be treated first class. I don't let him stand. If he has a complaint, I take care of it immediately. What I do find is that if he has a complaint and you don't handle it right away, you will not be given a second chance.

My business is dirty, but I try to keep it immaculate. If it is dirty, the black consumer will walk out, 95 per cent of the time. If you want to compare the Brown Tire Company with a Goodyear store or a Goodrich store, it is immaculate. I know it is first class. Nobody says, "I can't go to his store because his store is not clean or his mechanics are not first class or his people do not treat me first class."

There are not a lot of black businessmen to be role models to younger Blacks. When we see one of our Blacks accomplishing something, we try to relate that to ourselves, and a lot of times we just try to do the same thing—like barbecue places. We have more than we will ever need. We say: "Leon has been successful, so I know I can operate a barbecue place." Or a car dealership, we flood the market with car dealers. We become competitive with one another instead of competing with white businesses.

Take Johnson Products. We see that Johnson is successful, so a lot of people are getting into cosmetics. We should be diversified. Sometimes this causes hardships and forces others to go out of business. If you would go downtown, you would see a lot of successful white businessmen. Whites do not necessarily select just one individual to be like. Many times their fathers are successful, and they don't know what *unsuccessful* means. They have the money, cars, yachts—all the good things. It was very difficult for me to select a role model in order for me to become a businessman.

Most Blacks in high school, college and graduate school are not looking at a particular individual at that point. They are busy trying to be successful in college. You find some of our own successful businessmen are not educated, I mean in a formal sense.

Success comes with devotion and seriousness. Most of the successful black businesses are right here in Chicago. We also find some businessmen who make a mistake not identifying with their people. If the Black is buying his products, he must show the Black he is concerned about him.

When we were on the plantation, animosity existed between the house niggers and the field niggers. In the end they had to come together for a cause to better their conditions, the lightest ones in the house and the darker ones in the field. When a cause comes up, you must have some communication between the ones in the house and the ones outside. I never will disengage myself from the lesser class, even if I become super rich.

William Y. Browne, 84, is president and owner of the Riley-Browne,
Inc. Realty Company at 658 E. 63rd Street. He is a member of the Chi-
cago Real Estate Board and was the first black president of the South
Central Real Estate Board.

"Bartlett had a host of salesmen dress up, and they would go to the white people with these handbills and would tell them that Negroes were coming, and if they didn't sell the property at a sacrifice, they wouldn't get anything for it."

William Y. Browne

We didn't have anything like race riots in Chicago until 1918. Prior to that time black and white people lived together. Blacks lived at 52nd and Ingleside and at 63rd and Drexel. There were isolated areas where they lived in two- or three-flat buildings together up to the 1930's. And back in the early 1900's there were instances where Blacks and Whites lived in the same building, and there weren't any racial problems. We lived on the 3700 block of Dearborn, and we lived with Whites, around 1908 and 1912.

The strikebreakers were the ones to cause the problems. They were not used to urban life, and they didn't know how to live like people in the North. It created a racial barrier for those people to get along with the other people. That was part of the beginning. In 1919, there was the race riot.

Ed Morris was supposed to be a multimillionaire Negro lawyer at the time. He had very little colored practice—it was practically all white. He represented at one time a number of the gamblers here in Chicago. He bought property down on Dearborn Street. He had the Morris flats at 27th, 36th and 37th and Dearborn. They were nothing but six-flat buildings, but they were front and rear buildings with steam heat units. I'm talking now about 1910, 1913, 1915.

Back about that time things began to change. Negroes began to move into better areas. The great majority lived west of the tracks, west of State Street. Then they moved to 36th and Forest Avenue, which later became Giles Avenue. None lived out on Grand Boulevard—they were all wealthy Whites who lived on Grand. After Negroes surrounded them on Prairie and Calumet on one side, and Vernon on the other side, the Whites began to move away, and Negroes got into some of those houses. One of the first was Dr. George Cleveland Hall. He was one of the better known surgeons of Provident Hospital. And Dr. R.A. Williams. He had a big real estate business at that time, and he owned all of that property in the 4500 block on King Drive, on the west side of the street.

He had at that time what was known as the Royal Circle of Friends. He came from Arkansas and he had a large real estate office on 31st and Cottage Grove.

The Royal Circle of Friends was a fraternal organization that had chapters across the country. It was a powerful group until the 1950's. It had extensive South Side real estate holdings and provided such services as insurance to its members.

Back at that time Jesse Binga and Oscar DePriest were the leading real estate men in Chicago. Jesse was the first because he had a private bank and real estate office. And Oscar was a politician. He was a County Commissioner.

The people that I worked for were managing property for Riley Green. He was the best known undertaker we had in Chicago at that time. He was a real black fella, with lots of money and dignity.

First Grand Boulevard became an integrated area and then an all-black area. It moved rather rapidly because right down in that area they didn't do any bombing. The Whites were predominately Jewish, and they didn't resort to the bombing of Blacks coming in. So they moved all they way from 35th Street to 51st Street. The Jewish synagogue was at 46th Street and King Drive, which is now a Baptist Church. There were very wealthy Whites who were all in that area.

We Negroes first began moving east of the tracks on State Street shortly after 1900. The Frederick H. Bartlett real estate firm bought up lots of property; he went through that whole area. George F. Harding owned a lot of property there—he was quite a politician around Chicago. He owned all the property on 33rd and Rhodes Avenue, Vernon, and over to Cottage Grove. But south of there was this property that Bartlett owned.

Bartlett had a host of salesmen dress up, and they would go to the white people with these handbills and would tell them that Negroes were coming, and if they didn't sell the property at a sacrifice, they wouldn't get anything for it. So these white people, who had never had had any contact with Negroes, sold to Bartlett.

They sold two-flat buildings for probably $1,500 or $2,500. And then Bartlett doubled the price and sold the buildings to Negroes with a $300 or $500 down payment, or whatever they could pay. After he completed the sale of that area, from 35th to 39th Streets and from South Park to Cottage Grove, then he built Lilydale in the 95th Street area. And that was a Negro area completely. He built some very shoddy frame houses and sold them.

And Bartlett's company was partially responsible for the use of restrictive covenants in some areas. Together with many others who picked it up later, they found it possible to sell property to foreigners coming into this country by telling them that there was a restrictive covenant on it. They would be protected for life against Negroes coming into their area. And most of them felt that there was a great value in this restrictive covenant.

So Whites were living in that area, and Negroes were coming in. And Whites didn't know how to deal with them too much.

Take the 4700 block of State Street, and 4800 on the west side of the street. Binga would lease the whole block for one-third the gross rental price, and then he would pay the taxes or insurance, or maybe he would do both. And then he would sub-rent it for whatever price he could make. Big profits. Thirty-sixth and Forest (Giles) is a block of property that was called the Binga flats, and they were rented to people.

I think truthfully, as I remember, Binga and DePriest leased instead of buying because they were just interested in getting what they could out of it. Binga could afford to buy the buildings. Remember, he had his private bank. So I don't believe money was his problem. Because he would enter into a five- or ten-year lease and take over the entire responsibility. Binga and DePriest were able to lease property from people who had other interests besides their buildings. Binga and DePriest did a lot of managing for themselves, and they were the leading ones who had money.

When I started in business I had a six-flat apartment building, and I ran it on the same basis. I rented the building from a Dr. Jennings. It was located on 29th Place and Prairie Avenue. Every three months I paid him $270. I bought the building in 1921 and kept it for ten years while I was building up management.

I got $45 a month from each tenant, and then I had a rear building that I got $25 from. But you see, I don't think I paid my janitor but $8 or $10 a month, and coal was always $6 or $7 a ton. So you see I was able to clear a little over $100.

I went down to 39th and Prairie where the Springer subdivision was, and I went to their office and rented the store at 39th and Indiana for $25 a month. Springer said he wasn't going to rent the store to me, but the carpenter who wanted it didn't come in. So he gave it to me, but not without letting me know that he felt that I wouldn't be in the store more than thirty days.

I remember when I was a kid they called people kitchenette kings and queens. Were the white people involved in this?

Some Whites were. Most of them had business in the colored areas.

Before we had the Depression, people were paying $90 and $100 a month. All of a sudden the bottom dropped out, and nobody was able to pay any rent at all. Five- and seven-room apartments were too big to pay rent for, and they then divided them and rented them in sections. First they rented rooms.

Rooming was the principal source of income for people. There was a time when we felt the roomer was important, because he helped to pay the rent. We preferred tenants who owned a piano because we knew they wouldn't move out overnight.

And of course there were clauses in the lease. No canned beer could be brought through the front door. They had to bring it in the back way or we would cancel the lease--this is what was called "rushing the can." They could buy beer by the bucket, and as soon as they drank one they rushed out for another. And the smell was objectionable to others, follow?

Pearl Franklin Smith was a kitchenette queen. She was one of the first persons who took an apartment that she rented at 39th and Indiana and divided it up in small apartments. She put keys on the doors. If people had roomers, why, then you didn't have to lock anything. But if you had kitchenettes, why, you locked up whatever you had around.

In many instances, there was only one bathroom and one kitchen. In the beginning they were allowed certain periods to use the kitchen.

They could use the bathroom whenever they wanted to.

A seven- or eight-room apartment was divided up for three families. The rent from the three families in the apartment was more than enough to cover the cost of the rent. Much more than what the rental would have been if they had rented to one party. The reason they didn't rent to one party was because they couldn't find one party that was responsible enough to handle it. Before the city began to put restrictions on kitchenettes, they began to abuse the privilege: a seven-room apartment might be occupied by seven different families.

Kitchenettes, I must say, were one way to deteriorate the property value of the building. Let's say where you could make $400 or $500 off your apartments in a six-flat building, they would make $1200 and $1500 off the same kind of a building, if it were rented as kitchenettes.

What was your experience with Blacks going to downtown hotels in the early part of the century?

The experience was very, very bad. I know Louie Anderson in particular, who was the alderman of the Second Ward, who couldn't go up on the elevator in the Palmer House or the Sherman or any of the downtown hotels, on the front elevators. They had to use the freight elevators. In those days, also, you couldn't sit on the first floor of a theatre--you had to sit in the balcony.

What did Black folks do for mortgages back in 1910?

Back at that time there were no mortgages available to Blacks. The white mortgage houses said that they would make a mortgage, but they had no market for them. The white people would not buy the mortgages.

So they bought property that was already under mortgage, because 90 per cent of the real estate investment property or private home was on a mortgage. As long as they paid it or a prepayment or an annual prepayment they would renew that mortgage. They would put down the payment ranging from $500 to $1,000, according to what they had, if they weren't people who had cash, because there were no colored racketeers back then.

I bought my house with a 12 per cent mortgage on it in 1920. Then one year I got a notice telling me to pay it off, and I was not able to pay them off until after the Depression. They gave me a 60-day notice to pay $1,200. That was a lot of money.

When the stock market fell and nobody had any money, so they foreclosed and took property back. They took it from Whites as well as Blacks. And at that time the Reconstruction Finance Corporation came into existence, and that was a life saver during the Depression of the 1930's.

Earl B. Dickerson

Earl B. Dickerson, honorary board chairman of Supreme Life Insurance Co., has been affiliated with the firm since 1921. Born in Canton, Miss., he is a graduate of the University of Chicago Law School, a former Chicago alderman and a founder of the American Legion. As a lawyer, his numerous courtroom victories include Hansbury vs. Lee, et al, a celebrated "restrictive covenant" case which opened up 26 blocks on Chicago's South Side for Blacks. He has served on a Presidential Commission on Fair Employment Practice, and has been affiliated with numerous professional, civic, educational and civil rights groups and associations.

"We have proven the case that we can live like princes, but let's not forget our origins."

Earl B. Dickerson

It had to be about 1964 or 1965, in this building, at 48th and Chicago Beach Drive. Now, get it right. We had invited people to discuss Dr. Martin Luther King, Jr. And I asked, "How many of you are willing to contribute to this organization for a period of a year to help support the efforts of Dr. King?" I started off with $100 a month. A large number of Blacks in there gave $100, and then some only stuck to giving $50.

What I am trying to get at is, what project do we have before us that we can promote and in which we can involve black millionaires now? The time is ripe again. It cost me $750 that night, and I said, "God damn it, the brains that I got would keep me from starvation. God damn it, we're not going to go into slavery because of some shit."

I want people to understand the preservation of neighborhoods. I was on the Southeast Commission. The Marshall Field Foundation gave $75,000 to the Southeast Commission to make a survey of the area and tell about the kinds of buildings they were going to put up and so on, and it had to be an integrated area. Whatever you do, they said, you have to let people in on the basis of their status, not on the basis of their race and color. After they made their first year survey, then they gave another $75,000 to the same purpose.

I just don't want black people to be uninformed about where the action is. I don't want them to think the action is in Schaumburg when it's really on 22nd Street.

I was the first Black to buy in the Hyde Park/Kenwood area. I bought that place, 5027 Drexel, in the spring of 1948. The trend is that Whites are buying back into that area.

What's happening out there is this: In the area from 50th Street, the University of Chicago is still eager to protect that area. They get these professors and encourage them to buy houses in that area. They are persuading them to buy houses in that area in order to make sure the flanks of the University are protected. And these white people are coming in and buying these homes.

I don't blame these people. One of the greatest influences in my whole life is the University of Chicago, which contributed to my success like nothing else. It's been my life, and my association with it has been tops. I am on all the committees. That doesn't influence me, except that the recognition I get is good.

Look more closely into the finances of this area. See the houses that are about to be sold. The trouble is that too many Blacks who have money are not intellectual enough to give a damn about living in the University area.

I want you to do this. I don't want you to join that procession of Blacks so black that their every move is based on the idea that there is a movement against Blacks, to keep Blacks out. There is no campaign now, and I have been on the Southeast Commission since it started in 1952. There has never been in that organization any desire to keep Blacks out. What they want to do is preserve the community. Now if you measure up to those on the board, well then, sure, you're welcome. But why bring in somebody, whether he's black or white, to destroy the community? Therefore, it's harder on Blacks, because sometimes they don't measure up.

Did you know Jesse Binga?

He was a mean son-of-a-bitch. You know I knew him. He ought to know me speaking from the grave. Binga was a crook. He used all the means he could on people. He had no sympathy at all.

When I was a boy, I lived with the Crawleys, in 1907. There was a man trying to get work for me on Saturday from members of St. Mark Church. This fellow was the janitor of this building on 37th and South Park, that big brown building. Whites lived there. On Saturdays, I used to go with this fellow—he looked like a white fellow but he was colored—and wash windows for the white people in that block.

Blacks moved into this block, the 35th Street block, going out to 37th. I think Blacks lived up to 4400 Parkway (formerly Grand Boulevard and now King Drive). That was the covenant, and they had a lawsuit, and we obeyed it. And down the line from 35th Street on out, you see, in the blocks of 35th, 36th—all those were white folks living in places that I remember as a boy. All the way out, Whites lived on Grand Boulevard. And then this house was bought at 4420 Grand, I think it was, and they had a lawsuit on that. And finally, the real movement of Blacks moving in the Grand Boulevard area got a stimulation.

Did you know about Blacks being brought into the stockyards as strikebreakers?

Yes, that was done, but not too much. That was before, in 1937, I think, when the Weisner Act went into effect. That laid the foundation for labor to get a stronghold on the working people. Before that time we not only found out in Chicago, but all over the nation, that these manufacturers and people like the stockyards people would bring in these Blacks and others to be strikebreakers. But that didn't last too long, and it was very sporadic. It didn't go on every day.

There were the little strikes between 1918 and 1924. The Pullman strike was the biggest strike. It was tremendous. And then, of course, there were these sporadic strikes where they were bringing in these people from outside. And they were not able people. And then, of course, Blacks were not admitted into the union.

They were called strikebreakers because whenever they were employed, they couldn't get in the union. So they called the Blacks strikebreakers, and they blamed them for their situation and all the turmoil.

Then and now, I have always insisted that Blacks be respected wherever we go because in the highest industrial society in the world we have made good. You and I in the 3 per cent class. Three out of 100 is not bad, is it, Dempsey?

And you and I have proven the case that we can live like princes, but let's not forget our origins.

Alfreda M. Barnett Duster

Alfreda M. Barnett Duster, 77, is a retired social worker who has long been active in organizing programs directed at helping and encouraging students to stay in school. The daughter of writer and civil rights activist Ida B. Wells, she is a graduate of the University of Chicago.

"People knew then and all the way up to now that Marshall Field's didn't want our dollars, and they would make it clear to you. So mother heard about it and went down there to test it out."

Alfreda M. Barnett Duster

My father came to Chicago in 1869. My mother came to Chicago in 1892 or 1893 for the World's Fair. They decided to get married. He did some faithful courting and they got married in 1894.

There was not a single black family east of State Street, and they bought a house at 3234 Rhodes. Now, there wasn't violence then. It was 1901 or 1902. We moved in, and when mother would come out on the porch, the neighbors would shake their rugs and bang their doors shut.

There was some antagonism between the teenagers on 31st Street, where there were Whites who decided to fight the incoming Blacks. Blacks dared not cross Wentworth Avenue on the west and State Street on the east, or they got beat up. And any Whites would get beat up too, if they were found in Blacks' territory. We're talking about the 1920's—well, a little earlier than that, before the 1919 riot.

The Blacks' housing in that area was very poor. Mostly frame cottages. They were put up before the city said you couldn't put up any more frame cottages. That area along there—with our folks not keeping up the property—it deteriorated.

But from the very first going, the South Siders always felt they were better than the West Siders, and there was no love between them. And the people on the West Side didn't come to the South Side too much, and the people on the South Side hardly went over to the West Side at all.

Around 1890, everybody lived downtown, what is now considered the Loop. From Lake Street to 22nd Street. That was what you might call the city limits. Everybody, Whites and Blacks, lived there. When white people got wealthy, they moved south to Prairie Avenue. That used to be the "Gold Coast" for a while. Now the colored people, they moved south, moved west of State Street, and white people, of course, kept all this property over here. That's Michigan, Indiana, Prairie. That was predominately white.

Everybody hated to see the last black man leave his holdings in the Loop. The last one I remember I heard about now was the Boston Store on the corner of State and Madison. But it's a matter of money that he just couldn't refuse.

My father graduated from law school in 1878. But the time I can remember, that's early 1900's, there was only one building in the Loop that would rent to black lawyers. That was 184 West Washington, and the black lawyers who wanted an office in the Loop had to be in that building. The first group that was able to break out of that building, the big lawyers, went to 166 West Randolph, and before long they could rent any place.

As the black population moved south, they moved south along the west side of State Street, and as I say, in 1901 or 1902, my father was the first to buy over there. They would take a section and build it up, just like now. When a lot of Blacks moved in, the Whites moved out. And, of course, there was such a demand for houses that they would fill up in a hurry. When one section was filled, they would work in the next section. So that 35th was the dividing line, and then 39th Street.

Now, in 1919, there was a white woman who owned a place at 3624 Grand Boulevard, which is now King Drive. She got a lot of harrassment from her neighbors for one thing or another, so in retaliation she put a black family in that house, which was the first black family on King Drive. The family was that of Richard B. Harrison, the famous actor. So, when my mother heard about this, she contacted this white woman and bought the house at 3624 King Drive from her.

Shortly after that, Dr. R.A. Williams came from Arkansas. He was the head of the Royal Circle of Friends of the World, and he came here to establish a branch. He bought and got options to several pieces of property from 35th all the way to 37th.

When the riot came along in July of 1919, one of the persons that helped keep people so they wouldn't get killed while the fighting was going on lived at 4404 King Drive. I don't remember the name of the people who lived there. Blacks had already moved up to and past 47th Street. The first black family to move south of 47th, and again to break the tradition, was the same Richard B. Harrison family.

During the Depression days there were some pretty weird stories of how, in order to pay for these buildings, people had to take in roomers and get any amount of money they could. To give you the picture, my mother bought the house at 3624 Grand Boulevard, a three-story, fourteen-room house. Four baths, Italian marble, sink and all for $8,000. Now in the meantime, Vernon Avenue to Cottage Grove—our people moved all in there—and it was a very nice neighborhood. Maude Hudland and her family were there, and they were one of the first settlers in Chicago.

I was born in Chicago at 3234 Rhodes Avenue, September 3, 1904. I went to Douglas School and Flower Technical School and then Wendell Phillips High School. Then I went to the University of Chicago. At that time, all one needed was a diploma from high school to go and register. I graduated in three and one-half years, before I was 20 years old. I got my bachelor's in philosophy degree from the University in 1924. I worked for my father in his law office and then I married Ben Duster.

I had five children: Benjamin, Charles, Donald, Alfreda and Troy. I stayed home with my children, and I worked with them. We didn't have any money. By this time the Depression had come along, and so I knew they couldn't get to college except with a scholarship. So after they came in from school and played for a while, we would work. It paid off because every one of my children graduated first or second in their class. This was my answer to no money.

All east of Cottage Grove from 35th Street to 63rd Street remained white for a long, long time because of the boundaries. It wasn't until later, when the pressure got too great, that they let Blacks move into the area. Now 63rd—west of Cottage to King Drive, and from 60th to 63rd—that area remained white until the late 1940's.

In east Woodlawn—there weren't any Blacks over there until 1948 or '49, when the boys came home from the war with some money. I understand that a pianist named Mrs. King didn't put her money in the bank during the Depression, but bought some buildings and rented to the Whites. When the boys came home from the war she put up a sign saying, "For Rent to Colored." After she rented, she decided to turn it into a co-op.

I had my house at 32nd and Prairie for twenty-five years. Members of the block fought the city when they tried to come in there (to condemn property), because at that time the laws said they had to buy 60 per cent of the land before they condemned the other 40 per cent of it. When it first came up, we got together as a group and vowed not to sell, so they couldn't condemn. But they got laws passed which now let them take people's land. Those laws didn't exist in the beginning. They bought it and let it sit for fifteen years. They just put up a senior citizens' building right across the street from the Douglas School recently.

Do you have any theory on the color consciousness of black people, you being a sociologist?

Yes. From the beginning of the slavery days, the Whites told the colored that the house niggers were better than the field niggers, and they did more for the house niggers and so on. This is how they got an opportunity to read, because the white children would leave their books around. The mistresses would teach their own slaves how, and sometimes the slave men would have to take care of their master's property, so that's how some learned. That's why the light Negroes thought more of themselves. So anyway, in Chicago, there got to be a blue vein club— you couldn't belong if you couldn't show blue veins in your arm. Sadie Gray Mae refused to join any sorority because of how critical they were about the color of your skin.

Can you tell me anything about the problems Blacks had in using downtown hotels in the early days?

People like Paul Robeson could go anywhere. Paul stood on his "here I stands" and was firm until any person could go and stay and/or eat at the hotels. It did happen that those who were of lighter skin had better advantages, and they thought they were better because they were lighter, just like the white people actually believe they are better because they are white.

All I can say is, as long as there were not so many of us, we didn't have a problem. There was no other place for Whites to go, and as far as I know there wasn't any problem. I was talking to a group of retired waiters who said that the Edgewater Beach (Hotel) put them out overnight. They were all fired. They blanketed them all out because they would get a couple of ladies, or they would come in drunk and so on.

There's a story about my mother and Marshall Field's, when they wouldn't wait on her. People knew then, and all the way up to now, that Marshall Field's didn't want our dollars, and they would make it clear to you. So mother heard about it and went down there to test it out. In order to make her point in the store, she picked up some men's underwear and put it over her arm and started out of the store. She wasn't shoplifting, because it hung so high off her hands. Then the men came over, and that's when they had objections raised to their policy.

John Jones, a tailor and wealthy black merchant—the Chicago Historical Society has a big ten-foot picture of Jones and his wife--was the man who broke the "Black Codes" in Chicago. You know, black people could not buy property, could not vote, couldn't buy land. Nothing. He was elected to the state legislature to lobby to break the codes. This was long before my father came here, and my father came here in 1869.

Mother was really concerned about her people. I don't know what she would do if she looked at them today. She really felt that her race deserved all that she could give it. She was concerned about the conditions that held them down, and she was going to do something about it. She knew Frederick Douglass personally. She had talked to him and had been to his home. My mother was the oldest of eight children. She was from Holly Springs, Mississippi. Both her parents were slaves.

My father died at the age of 84 in 1936. My mother died in 1931. He lived five years after her death, and he lived with me.

Somebody needs to march into our community and create the desire for a decent neighborhood instead of marching to tear down another one. We should try to help our people, not to ruin our own communities, because the ruin of our own communities is part of the thing that causes prejudice about moving into a new neighborhood.

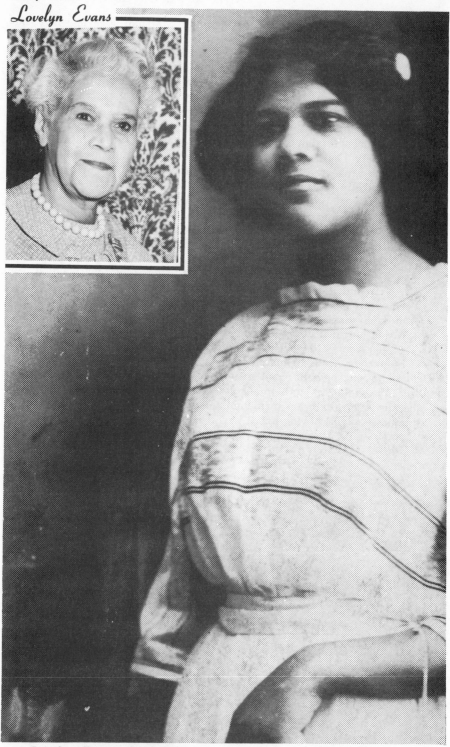

Lovelyn Evans, 86, served for many years as personnel director for Campbell Soup. She is retired now, but she remains active in the local and national Republican Party.

"Sometimes some stupid white folks would come by and say to my mother, 'I hear you married a nigger.' She would tell them, 'Don't come by here and try to borrow that nigger's money, 'cause I ain't going to give it to you.'"

Lovelyn Evans

My father, Joseph Miller, owned the Miller Buena Park Fireproof Warehouse Moving Company. He came here in 1888 from Baton Rouge, Louisiana.

He started out with one horse and one wagon. He acquired more vehicles as his business grew. We were at Halsted Street and Bradley Place, and then we moved to Grace and Evanston Avenue. We had a one-story office there. Then in the back there were the barns, and we lived in the adjacent house.

When the business was more successful we moved to 4015 Broadway. We started out with a one-story office, and we lived in the back, I think for a year. Then my father built this large warehouse. It had fur storage, open storage. We lived on the top floor in a seven-room apartment in dad's new elevator building. It was called a penthouse.

At the warehouse, my father had a crew of thirty integrated workmen. Swedish, Polish, Negro, German.

The clientele were all rich people at that time. There was nothing but fine homes. They lived in Buena Park and they would have townhouses on Lake Shore Drive.

Then there was Mr. Mueller, who was one of the leading architects here. His daughter, Sylvia, had a picture of George Washington that she loaned to the Art Institute. And the only one who could bring it to the Institute was my father. That's the kind of reputation he had.

My mother was strictly a German, and my father was a Negro, but with some Indian in him. They had very few friends. Both sides of the family were not happy with the marriage. Both families felt they had been disgraced by this marriage. But we never had any trouble. My father was strict on being honest about it.

Sometimes some stupid white folks would come by and say to my mother, "I hear you married a nigger." She would tell them, "Don't come by here and try to borrow that nigger's money, 'cause I ain't going to give it to you."

We are just as racist as the white man. I experienced it later on. I got the same kind of treatment my mama did about her marriage.

I was raised in the Presbyterian Church on Addison and Broadway. We went to Sunday School there. There was no colored around. Later on I began to want to see somebody looking like me. I guess you call it the call of the wild. We began to meet Earl Dickerson, Ruth Pollard, (daughter of Fritz Pollard, All American from Brown University), some of the Negroes' heroes. You had to pass inspection.

My sister went to Howard University. She was five years younger than me. Her allowance was $150 a month to throw away. It was a lot of money, you better believe it. When you think about it, the salaries were $12.50 or $15 a week--that's white and black.

We had very wonderful dancing schools, and you could meet your friends and not worry.

They used to call Lake Shore Drive "the Esplanade." And I would drive down there with my horse and buggy. It went from Grace to Diversey. My father had a horse that he showed at the South Shore Country Club, around 1908. I met Mrs. Jarvis Hunt. She had colored grooms.

We were called the privileged nigger class. Did you know that in those days we had a Polish lady who did the washing, because my mother was in the business with my father? We had white workers, and they never thought anything about working for colored.

What changed all that was all the colored people coming to town and bringing their funny ideas with them. When A.L. Foster moved to Glencoe, there was a great deal to do about he was the first colored to live there, but the Bakers have been living there ever since I could remember. You didn't have a mobile society like you have now. If you didn't have a horse and buggy, then you weren't out on the street.

After I got married we lived at home for awhile. Then we had an apartment on Victor, around 1917. Negroes were living all over the city. All over, upstairs, downstairs. There weren't that many colored people here at that time.

The first place I ever lived on the South Side was 3406 South Park. Now you can take a stone and throw it into the Drexel Bank from where I lived, right at 34th Street.

Bishop Archibald Carey and his family lived around the corner on Vernon. That was an elegant area back then, in the early '20's. South Park started about 22th Street and come to 35th Street. When you crossed 35th going south, that's Grand Boulevard.

Dr. Cleveland Hall lived at 3408, right next door to me. And a Dr. R.A. Williams came from the South with a lot of money, and he bought a six-flat at 3524-46 South Park. Across the street Bill Bottoms owned the most fantastic three-apartment building that had ten rooms, three balconies, a music room, library, living and dining, who knows how many rooms for the bedrooms. Nothing but millionaires lived there.

Our folks have a way of naming something. So they called Grand Boulevard "Boulevard Denege." The colored named it that.

On the South Side you had places like Al Kierney's. It was a beer garden at 35th and Calumet. Nothing but big spenders were there. White, strictly white. We couldn't afford it, even though it was a black area. That was in the community when I first moved there. As soon as it became predominately colored, they all moved out.

The same thing happened to Ernie Henderson's chicken shack. He had the best of clientele. They came from all over to spend money at 47th and Indiana. He started in the basement cooking over a two-burner stove, and then he got famous. That was in the mid-'30's.

There was a very fine tailoring shop called Finchley's. The story was they didn't want any Negro trade, but Ernie bought every one of his suits there. He had 365 suits, one for every day of the year.

Then there was Smiley the caterer. He was a very strict colored businessman, and he had all the rich parties to cater to. I don't think Negroes could afford Smiley.

Mrs. Fannie Emanuel was the social leader, and she was dark brown. You didn't qualify according to color. It wasn't like it was in Washington, where it was very color-conscious. You didn't have to have money, either. It was character. Mrs. Emanuel was the lady who would blue-pencil your name, and nobody would invite you.

We didn't drink, and you better not be caught smoking. Very strict social code. If your mother was not married to your father, you were out. If you were not decent and honest, and your mother didn't know my mother and their family, then you were out. Very strict.

It was later when that color foolishness started out. It was when we got a large influx of colored people that it seemed like the social morals changed. That early Chicago society was hateful.

I had contact with a great many prominent men: Julian Black, John Graves, Louie Thompson, Max Graves, Theodore Holland. Those are some of them.

I thought Marcus Garvey was nuts. I remember when he came here with that "go back to Africa." And W.E.B. DuBois—he was a very elegant man. When I read he was embracing Communism, I dropped him.

Paul Robeson was a fine man. I was so sorry he went to Russia. He would have had his ambition to sing in the Metropolitan Opera come true if he had only waited.

I wanted to tell you about Grace Lyceum and Quinn Chapel. We would have literary societies with Paul Lawrence Dunbar, Roland Hayes and Abby Mitchell. We had a wealth of talent here. Grace Presbyterian Church and Quinn Chapel fostered that.

Then the Mushmouth Johnson family made their money from gambling. They opened up this place called The Dreamland at 35th and State. Very high class.

Jesse Binga was a very proud, stern man. Every holiday he had a very exclusive high-class party, and you had to be somebody very elegant to be invited. You didn't have to be light to go to those parties. His wife was dark. And you could be dripping in mink, but if you didn't have character, you were nothing. People called Jesse Binga hateful, but he was a man that had money.

I was at the Campbell Soup Company for twenty years. I started in as a clerk, and then I was reluctant to go to work because I didn't like working in factories. Elmer Henderson (of FEPC) told me that he thought that I owed it to myself and to the race to take this job where they never had colored before. It took me three weeks to decide. I went there, and he told me he had been considering a woman from Northwestern, but I seemed to have good common sense. I said I would think it over. They called me and said they weren't going to hold job open any longer. So I took it, because I would be a pioneer and open some fields for some other colored people.

My association with Campbell Soup was one of the most informative, educational experiences that I had ever had. We had Indians, Greeks, Polish, Germans, etc. We all got along, because Campbell said, "There will be no segregated washrooms or lunchrooms. Everybody is going to get along." Other companies had segregated washrooms because they were afraid of what would happen.

I did recruiting one year. We were only paying fifty-five cents an hour. Our people worked up from labor and production, and now they're all over the place.

Paul J. King, executive director of United Builders Association of Chicago, has been active with the Congressional Black Caucus Brainstorming Group, the Cost of Living Council, the National Association of Minority Contractors and a Small Business Administration task force on government-funded construction programs. Active in construction affairs involving minority builders across the country, King is a speaker and lecturer on construction and related topics at universities, conventions and builder s groups.

"I like the idea that when my son came home from Georgetown University he was reading Macus Garvey in one hand and the Wall Street Journal in the other hand. I like that combination."

Paul King

In 1968 there was an organization called the West Side Builders, a black group of contractors that was being helped by Brenetta Howell and Garland Guice, who were with the Chicago Economic Development Corporation (CEDCO). I was always interested in organizations and people, which is why I am active in Alpha Phi Alpha fraternity, which has been one of the best experiences of my life. In 1968 Garland and Brenetta were able to get a grant from the Department of Commerce, and they wanted to have somebody that was a contractor and had a college degree run the program. I was a member of the group, and I had graduated from Roosevelt University, so I won by default. At that time you got $10,000 a year for being full-time director, and they allowed me to continue my contracting business with the stipulation that if I got over a certain threshold I would make them aware.

This group had come together with the intention of focusing on certain issues affecting black people. Through some fortunate circumstances they chose the construction trade unions; in 1969 it was recognized that the white unions were ignoring Executive Order 11246 which required that contractors doing federal work must not discriminate, must take affirmative action.

In 1969, Blacks were the heaviest minority. Our focus was on shutting down work in order to force contractors to comply with the law and take more Blacks into their shops. Now, the contractors made the point they had union bargaining agreements, and they were not the problem--the unions were the problem.

What we did was physically go shut down jobs. We had at that time the involvement of the Disciples, the Vice Lords, the Black Stone Rangers and Breadbasket, which at that time was led by Jesse Jackson. It was a very interesting group of people. I have never seen a group of black people organized so effectively, especially considering we had all these powerful egos.

The guys who were members of the gangs would turn up 300 to 400 strong in the morning and attack a construction site--nonviolently. The first demonstration took place on July 23, 1969. It was on Douglas Boulevard on the West Side, where some urban renewal work was going on. There were no black contractors and very few black workers on the particular project. It was enough to make anybody cringe. Here you are in the middle of a black neighborhood, and a white contractor is doing the work. I think they had one black sub-contractor. That gave me an opportunity to picket that job, to shut the job down, and we ran all the people home.

When the TV and the press came, they found me, because I was the head of West Side Builders. I had some words ready for them right away. That's what got me started. Emotion and true sensitivity got me started: the arrogance of somebody who builds and does not give any work to the sub-contractors who are black. The fact is that we did have the leverage of the law, and black workers were being excluded. That was the first demonstration.

And I have to admit flat out, through all the aggravation that has been attributed to the gangs, in this particular context they were meeting at seven in the morning until seven at night, sometimes all the way until two in the morning. They had representatives or one of their leaders at every meeting. They actually put the troops out in the field. They were the ones who gave us the numbers when we went to demonstrate. As for the Urban League and the NAACP and the other civil rights groups, they were out to lunch. I suspect they weren't with us. It was a demonstration where numbers and bodies counted. At that time the guys from the gangs were youngsters, teens. Some of them wanted jobs that were supposed to come out of these demonstrations. I think there is a message that I would draw from it: there is a positive force in all people. If you identify and work with it, it will contribute to what you are trying to do. There was an accord that was struck with those people that may not be possible today. I think this is one of the things that black people in Chicago must be very careful about: not to write off a group of our own people as being hopeless just because they don't demonstrate the behavior or qualities that we want to see or are comfortable around. There is something in all people that could be a positive force.

I think you have to separate the person and his opportunities from the person and his emotions and the person and his philosophy. You have to remember that with all the education you might have, with all the advantages, you are still black in a white nation. There is a portion of me that was fortunate enough to be born into a family that is still together, cohesive and supportive. I was fortunate enough to have a father who was in business, who displayed for me an example of independence and tenacity.

My father is in the wholesale produce business. His is the oldest black-owned distribution business, run continuously over the last 35 years. I have got the firm 8A certified--that's a program under the Small Business Admmination which allows firms that are deemed socially and economically disadvantaged to get contracts without bidding. If I am successful he will be able to get government contracts to supply produce to Army bases, Veterans Administration hospitals, the Department of Agriculture and other federal agencies that buy fresh fruits and vegetables. I'm also in some negotiating to get P. King Produce into a position where it will have space for trade at the international port and space for local distribution at South Water Market.

My father gets up at three in the morning to go and take care of his business. He gave me the example of concern for his wife and children. My mother gave me an example of what to look for in a wife by being much concerned for her children. My mother didn't have an education past the high school level, but she saw that I learned how to play the piano and understood opera before I was 12 years old.

I say all that to make the point that one is fortunate to have all of these things. But education and family background are supposed to prepare you to do something more with it. I became kind of a rough character when I acknowledged the racial discrimination that I saw in certain areas once I got involved. It was just so blatant that I started raising hell.

You live in Chicago, you know Chicago. We can talk about many things which are a source of irritation.

I was in the construction industry. I worked for my uncle while I was in high school, at DeLaSalle High School. When I got to college I wanted to make some money. I remember I made my first $100 in one day by getting four painters that were out of work to do some work that I had contracted. I made $100 more than I had to pay out, so I was hooked. So I went into the painting business a year after I was out of college. I was 23 years old. I fumbled around making and losing money. I had too much freedom, not being tied down to a job. Rearing my first kid after being married at the age of 22.

I have been speaking to college kids lately, at Florida A & M University and in Atlanta. I think there is hope for some young people. But I am seriously disturbed with the people that are my age and a little younger. I just don't see that potential mobilization that was there in 1968 and 1969. Of course the solutions are much more obscure. When you look at this economy—inflation, recession, falling of the dollar, energy and all that stuff—it is basically a political, moral kind of a deal.

My oldest boy goes to Georgetown University—he's a freshman. So I gave him some going away advice. I told him to be cool with the concept of God, cool with his family, and then study business and finance. Be cool means to be right. Understand it, get a grip on it and handle it. These are three of the most powerful forces in your life.

Most people are hopeless or oblivious or otherwise out of it and don't understand what's happening to black people. I don't know, maybe the train has left the station, and it isn't going to come back. I had some ideas on how to reach the people in places like Robert Taylor Homes, before the train left, but now it's gone. If you have a ratio of three kids per apartment in some of the projects, where are these people going to live when they become teenagers and out of the jurisdiction of their parents? Where are they going to work? I don't know, unless somebody establishes a reservation somewhere in some suburb that will accept them. Provide a method and an incentive to go out there and live. There is a bedroom shortage in Chicago—you almost have to go to Oak Park to look for housing. If you've got kids, what's going to happen? Especially when the job market is so strict in terms of being service-oriented or high-technology-oriented. Neither area has been geared to those people in those projects. The Hispanics—Cubans and Puerto Ricans—and the

Vietnamese are taking up the service jobs that used to be available. The goddam Arabs are taking over your business in the black neighborhoods.

Some black people don't recognize the serious threats that we are under: the re-emerging of the Ku Klux Klan, Blacks getting shot in Buffalo and Utah. I am talking about alcoholism being the third biggest killer among Blacks. Dope the kids are on. The destruction of families. I think our race is under severe attack. If the people don't realize that, they are at a different level, and we don't have anything to talk about.

But I am big on Chicago. I am the first generation born here—the rest came from New Orleans. I like Chicago. I've got a nice house. I understand Chicago. I think Chicago's racism is clear. First of all, I think as a city it will prevail. The black private sector idea may be in motion by that time.

I like the idea that when my son came home from Georgetown University he was reading Marcus Garvey in one hand and the Wall Street Journal in the other hand. I like that combination.

I think there will be some positive action going on with the kids calling their own shots. I think also that there will be a much larger black underclass. That groups of Blacks are in serious trouble, and that group will be much larger. I cannot see the miseducation that's occurring in those public schools not having an impact. This impact will be visible when they will be in decision situations.

In this period we are seeing a group of people seriously being manipulated by the media. You will find the people divided up into two groups: the ones that read books and the ones that do not. We're getting an indication of what they plan to do in the future, to try to separate us on the basis of the so-called class distinction. There is one class being black and being discriminated against. Within that class of Blacks, you have differences in perception, differences in opportunities and differences in lifestyle. But I don't think basically that a black person who doesn't have any serious bad habits such as addiction to drugs or alcohol—his taste and my taste are not fundamentally very different. I think there are some basic characteristics which do not change regardless of your education and economic conditions. I believe that that community of interest is stronger than any other thing that can separate us.

I got a lot of press on one notion: I said black leaders have failed. Look at the current headlines and you can see some credence in that remark.

I think in the concept of leadership you have to develop a few things. We have to have a black private sector, businessmen with money supporting black private institutions so that we can train leaders. We have no training from generations of black leaders. The black private sector should support an ideology which will generate black leaders. We've got to have an independent source of money to promote an idea.

I don't think there is anyone as a black leader who can encompass the aspirations and interests of all black people. I think that day has gone. My sister marched with Dr. Martin Luther King Jr. At that time he was speaking of a broad moral issue which all of us could be represented on.

Now it is very different. We take very different views about issues that once might have been accepted by most Blacks. Like "symbolic" busing to get black kids an education is all right with me, but on the real side I don't think there is anything inherently beneficial in busing unless it's learning to get along with the race that is in the majority. As far as education is concerned, that can be provided in a black school. Both of my boys went to Howalton Day School at 47th and Dearborn. Both of them tested right into St. Ignatius, a Catholic high school with a strong academic program. Competition for entrance to the school is keen, and students must take a rigorous examination to be accepted. My oldest boy left St. Ignatius and got a scholarship to Georgetown University. But his basis was a black private school right there on 47th and Dearborn.

The point I am making is that we are diversified in our thinking, and we are diversified in our interests. You take Dearborn Park, an expensive "new town" being built next to the Loop. That means something very threatening to you and me, from an ethnocentric point of view. We think we see a trend to mix that neighborhood in such a way that a ring spreads that will keep Blacks from controlling that land. To others, it might mean improving land values on housing to the south, where Blacks are still living. But we see things differently.

We can't have one person leading us because we have too many different interests. There should be a black leader in business, surrounded by black leaders in special business groups. We can take a look at the white models: you don't have one leader getting into another leader's specialty. They recognize special interest groups and organize around them. I think it is possible to achieve that once people are able to see some advantage in coming together. That's a very difficult thing to deal with: coming together.

When you talk about leadership, I think of the Blacks who serve on corporate boards. What kind of feedback do you get about what they are doing?

I think your question is very good, but I will go one step farther and include those black elected and appointed officials who sit on prestigious and influential boards. I see no tangible positive influence, unless they give some symbolism for grammar school children who might be impressed by that.

Let me give an example. Our family has a currency exchange on 55th Street at Prairie and the El. Two blocks over, on 55th and Michigan, is a currency exchange owned by a Jewish man. They mail state checks to the currency exchanges so the people can pick them up instead of being ripped off in the mailbox. The currency exchange benefits, because the people will cash their checks and the exchange will get a fee. At my mother-in-law's exchange she may get five checks a month, whereas the white owner gets hundreds.

I took this problem to the black man who signs the checks. He referred me to another black man who is head of the agency that disburses the checks. Both of these men are my friends. Both are my fraternity brothers. But they couldn't do one damn thing about helping me make some money.

I went to DeLaSalle High School. All the mayors of Chicago prior to Jane Byrne went to DeLaSalle High School except maybe Cermak. I knew the late mayor (Richard Daley) on an intimate basis. I knew his kids. They helped me to make money, based on our 25-year-old relationship at the school, and I helped them to make money also. The Irish Catholics I knew were on a basis of friendship. They helped you make money and you helped them make money.

This is not so with our Blacks in these elected positions. I won't say that about every one of them, but about 99 per cent of them. What's wrong with us is that we can't create any leverage to make somebody else some money. Something is wrong when our people get on these boards in those positions and then don't help other people to make it. We've got three Blacks on the Chicago Housing Authority board. I am cordial with two, but so far as stroking a path to help make some money, I have not seen it yet. I am talking about getting legal contracts.

Corporate boards could be positive for Blacks, if those memberships meant doing more business with Blacks or implementing some policies to move Blacks into higher ranks.

But I'm tired of Blacks getting positions where they don't handle the money. We don't have any Blacks in charge of the Department of Public Works or the Department of Streets and Sanitation. We usually get jobs like Human Services director or superintendent of schools—somebody else handles the money.

There is a tremendous void in Chicago, period, in terms of leadership or movement-type people. We have so much in common between us. Why can't we get together to make some money? Stepping aside, the same applies to the whole leadership concept.

People don't have anything really to say. I don't honestly know that many black people who have anything going on that's really all that conversation-worthy. If you have got a group of people who don't recognize the plight that we are in, you are talking from two different levels.

Jewel N. LaFontant

Jewel M. Lafontant, 59, is a lawyer and life-long Republican. A native Chicagoan, she was a founding member of the Congress On Racial Equality (CORE). She has been an assistant U.S. attorney and also served in the U.S. solicitor general's office. She was the first woman ever to argue a case before the U.S. Supreme Court as a deputy solicitor general.

"Well, I don't know about this tokenism. People say to your face, 'They selected you because you are a good-looking woman' or 'You are a twofer.' It means two for one—a Black and a woman—and I laugh about it. But they are serious. I can't look into the person's mind, why they selected me. All I can say is, 'Thank you.'"

Jewel N. LaFontant

My grandfather was born in Coffeyville, Kansas, and received his education at Oberlin College and went to Oberlin Academy. After he finished Oberlin, he went to the University of Indiana to become a lawyer. My grandfather was named John B. Stradford. He was born September 10, 1861. His wife, my grandmother, also finished Oberlin Academy.

Oberlin was on the Underground Railroad. It was the first college to have co-education, to have females and males. It was also the first white college to admit Blacks. Since both my grandfather and my father finished Oberlin College, I was destined to go to Oberlin.

Growing up in Chicago, my father felt I shouldn't date or have "company" until I was 21 years old. He didn't let me out of his sight. I thought I wanted to go to school down in Nashville, at Fiske, or Howard University. But he wanted me to go to Oberlin because of the great history of the school, and because it was a great school. He was a firm believer that you should not go to a school just because it was a black school. But you would go to the school if it happened to be black and was the very best. In those days, the colored schools didn't measure up to a school like Oberlin, and not very many white schools did either.

He used to say, "You don't go to college to have fun or get married. The fact that it is all white shouldn't bother you. You are not going there to socialize anyway—you are going there to get the best education you can get." It was the same way in law school—I was going to compete on Whites' terms.

We lived at 4937 Washington Park Court. I went to grade school at Willard, and I graduated from Willard. I went from there to Englewood High School. The only school in our district that I could have gone to was DuSable, and my father and mother were opposed to that. They felt they were trying to create a separate situation for all black children.

I was enrolled for one day at Hyde Park High School, and the principal put me out. He said I was supposed to go to DuSable. I was finally admitted at Englewood. My dad would drive me to school every day. Englewood wasn't a bad school. I finished in 1939, finished Oberlin College in 1943, and finished law school at the University of Chicago in 1946.

I'm not aware of my African heritage on my father's side, but I am on my mother's side. My grandmother was the offspring of a Scottish-Irish man and a slave.

My grandfather was born in Versailles, Kentucky, and located in Alexandria, Indiana, in 1900, when he was about 29 years old. He established and conducted a hotel there, achieving considerable financial heights. Natural gas was the chief wealth of the community, and evidently he was on some prosperous land. But when the supply of gas became exhausted, he lost a fortune as Alexandria became a deserted village. From there he went to Tulsa, Oklahoma, where he built another hotel called the Stradford Hotel which had a library. During the Tulsa riots, around 1920, he was bombed out. While in Tulas it's said he amassed a fortune over $150,000. In those days that was a fortune.

His hotel was burned to the ground, along with forty-four square blocks of Negro property. He fled to Kansas to save his life. Extradition proceedings were initiated to bring him back to Tulsa, claiming he had killed some white folks. He had been indicted for rioting. They said he was a crazy nigger. My father defended him and kept him from being extradited. My grandfather always gave my father credit. "There are not many sons who could have saved their father's life." But another thing—even when he was in Tulsa, the white people hated him so. He headed a movement of Republicans in a Democratic Tulsa, and with his movement he was responsible for the Republicans taking over, it must have been in 1920.

Then, when my grandfather came to Chicago, he practiced law with my father. He also had a barber shop and a candy store on 51st Street near King Drive. But he did have an office with my father. They didn't get along very well.

My father never worked while he was in school. His father had enough money to put him all the way through. When he married my mother, my grandfather would send him $200 each and every month. Two hundred dollars a month was a lot of money.

My father was a brilliant man. He finished college when he was 16 and got a master's degree and finished Columbia Law School by the time he was 20 years old. He went from Columbia to Tulsa to join his father and then left, because he couldn't stand the racial prejudice. He would brief the law and try to argue the cases, and then the white judge would say, "I hear what you say the law is; but the law is as I see it." He left with my mother and brother and came to Chicago.

He was quite a billiard player. He earned a lot of money playing billiards all through college. I was a good pool player, too. I was brought up on the pool table. He was a champion pocket billiards player for the city of New York. He was a member of the Colored Amateur Billiard Players Association.

My father practiced law in Chicago. Because the American Bar Association didn't admit Blacks, he and three other lawyers founded the National Bar Association. He became its president in 1932.

He was an orator and a labor lawyer. He represented the Brotherhood of Sleeping Car Porters. He and A. Philip Randolph were very good friends. Milton Webster, A. Philip and my father were very close. I always remember A. Philip Randolph as being handsome and quiet, whereas Webster was bombastic. Not a good-looking man, but a powerful man. His daughter and I were close friends. My father was responsible for the founding of the Brotherhood of Sleeping Car Porters union. I have seen speeches of his where he was actively involved in pressing for workmen's compensation for the workers.

A. Philip was instrumental in my father being considered for the Virgin Islands' judgeship. He wrote letters to the President and the Secretary of Commerce saying Stradford was a brilliant lawyer who could represent all the people. He didn't get it; his good friend Judge William H. Hastie was chosen. My father played poker every Saturday night, and it would go until Sunday morning. Both he and Hastie were at one of these poker parties when the word came Hastie had been seleted. He was happy for him, because they were very close. But even in those days, the Eastern establishments were considered above the Midwest-- Hastie taught at Howard University.

My father was always in the forefront of civil rights organizations. So much so that when I was up for appointment as assistant U.S. Attorney, the one thing in my background that was going to prevent me getting the job was the fact that my father was active in the National Negro Congress. That group, along with many other black groups, was pushing for equal employment, in the '30's and '40's. My father became the president of the Congress. There were people in the organization trying to turn it around, like they tried to turn the NAACP. The National Negro Congress turned out to be Communist-related, and as late as the '50's they were trying to hold that against me.

In 1955, I became the first black woman to be appointed an assistant U.S. attorney for the District of Illinois. I had sense enough to know that if I had been rejected, I would be damned for the rest of my career. A fellow named Ira Latimer—and this was after the McCarthy days— had been a Communist. Former Communists were confessing that they had found the light, and they were exposing other Communists. Latimer wrote the FBI and told them that Jewel Stradford Rogers was a Communist, which was an untruth. I had to overcome that. I did overcome it, because I could point to the convention of the NAACP in Atlanta where Communists tried to come in, where they tried to get other organizations to merge with them. I had fought and voted against it.

In addition, I had debated publicly with Latimer and exposed him as a fraud. I had to show all this information to the F.B.I. I showed them minutes and got affidavits. I don't remember all I had to do.

The U.S. attorney for the District of Illinois wanted to hire me and was very helpful. He took my papers in; and I was approved. My father was a union man, he was never a Communist. Being a Republican helped in disproving the allegation of communism. I have always been a Republican, as were my grandfather and father.

If we got poor grades, my parents would always say, "Never use race as an excuse." We never did. We never described people by color. "Get the very best education you can get," they said. Money wasn't really a goal, but education could be useful in breaking down barriers. I think the biggest thing wrong with America today is racism.

My father founded the National Bar Association for black lawyers to get together, exchange ideas, and learn. He helped found the Cook County Bar Association in the 1930's because Blacks were not admitted to membership in the Chicago Bar Association. That meant you didn't have access to a good library or any facilities.

Tell me about your growing up on Chicago's South Side and more about your family.

My family was very friendly with Carl Hansberry, who was a real estate man in Chicago. He was very well-to-do. Hansberry bought a two-flat at 61st and Rhodes. He'd been living before that down on South Park. Blacks hadn't lived between 60th and 63rd between South Park and Cottage Grove. My father represented him when he bought the building. I remember we were sitting in the front room of Hansberry's apartment, when bricks came through the window. The Whites filed suit to get the Hansberrys out, and my father represented the family. I was a little girl. My father brought in the Supreme Liberty Life as one of the defendants in the suit, I guess because Supreme Life had made a mortgage for the Hansberrys. My father was the main lawyer. The lawyers from Supreme Liberty Life were Earl B. Dickerson, T.K. Gibson, Jr., Loring B. Moore and Irwin C. Mollison. Dickerson was the one who finally argued the case. My father was very unhappy about it, and the Hansberrys were unhappy about it. My father had labored with them through all the dramatic days—the case had gone on for years. The Hansberrys knew my father had done most of the work and wanted him to get the credit.

When the decision came down, one of the papers said, "Attorneys C. Francis Stradford, Earl B. Dickerson, T.K. Gibson, Jr., Irwin B. Mollison, and Loring Moore, acting in concert for various clients, have gained a unanimous opinion from the United States Supreme Court upsetting a residential covenant barring Negroes from certain areas. It seems to have been the brief presented in the case of Mr. and Mrs. Carl Hansberry, represented by attorney Stradford, which swung the court."

The Hansberrys were the real defendants, and my father prepared the brief. Having argued many cases in court, I know the person who argues the case, which is the glamorous part of the law, gets the credit. You are up there for a half hour or forty-five minutes, but the bulk of the work has been done before you get there.

I knew playwright Lorraine Hansberry. She was about four years younger than I. Her sister, Mamie, and I were about the same age, and we were good friends. Lorraine was considered spoiled. She was the only one in the family born to affluence; all the others could remember when they were poor. By the time Lorraine was born, the Hansberrys had a chauffeur, fur coats and cars. Lorraine was very smart. She was often impatient with her older brothers—she thought they were silly. She was very quiet and a little stand-offish. I was shocked when she turned out to be a brilliant playwright. She always wanted to be a doctor. I never thought of her in the theatre or being a writer.

In Oberlin, I became president of the Cosmopolitan Club, which was a group of people interested in international and civil affairs. I had grown up thinking you were supposed to be a leader and make things better. When I went to the University of Chicago, I was one of the founders of CORE (Congress on Racial Equality). We got involved in sit-ins in the early '40's, before it was popular. There was a restaurant called Stoner's, it must have been on Wabash downtown, that didn't serve Blacks. We would get a mixed group together and go there and sit down, and we wouldn't be served. We would sit right at the window so the other people walking by could see us. They would serve us eggshells. I remember there was a crippled white fellow with us, and they would kick him. They really abused us. Then we would turn around and file a lawsuit.

I was on the legal redress committee of the NAACP. We filed lawsuits against the various restaurants, and we ran Stoner's out of business. I developed an attitude when I went into places where people didn't want me because of my color. I felt sorry for them because I knew we people were beautiful and we were right. They were ignorant people. So you got a joy out of going places where you knew they didn't want you. I remember my father said that when he went into court on the Hansberry case, the judge said from the bench, "I wouldn't go where I wasn't wanted." You hear Blacks saying that now. Our attitude was never that way. But if you played into their hands, you didn't go where they did not want you, and then you were not sharing in what this country had to offer.

I am not very hopeful where race is concerned. I think at the top levels there will be more interaction and more achievements. I think that will keep growing. But at the lower levels, I am almost in despair and wondering when the explosion is going to come. The attitudes between the races are worse than ever.

I serve on a number of corporate boards—Trans World Airlines, Continental Illinois Bank, Equitable Life Insurance Co., Equitable Holding Co., Bendix Corp., Food Fair, Foote, Cone and Belding Advertising. These are powerful companies, and you can do a lot.

For instance, you take Food Fair. Each board is different, like human beings. Some are more sophisticated than others, and it takes you a little while to figure them out. The same thing applies to a judge: I used to go watch a judge for a week--study his reactions, determine what pleased and displeased him before appearing before him. A company on whose board I serve was reorganizing. They would come to the meetings and say how they were hiring people in the new community.

"Since you have hired all these people, how many Blacks did you hire?" I asked.

"You know, Mrs. Lafontant, we have a hard time. We just haven't had any black applicants."

"What have you done to reach the black community?"

"We put it in the local papers."

"Why don't you try to find out about their organizations down there? By the way, did you know there is an Urban League down there?" I said.

"No, I didn't know."

I didn't leave it at that—I found out that the fellow who is in charge of personnel for the state of Florida is a black man. I didn't know that, and they certainly didn't know it. I got the information and put the company in touch with this gentleman and shortly afterwards, Blacks were hired.

There was an article in one of the New York papers recently accusing the Blacks on corporate boards of being selfish and not doing anything for their brothers. They generalize and say that about all Blacks on corporate boards, but they have not done their homework. I guess they wanted us to be like that. They want to say, you are not deserving, rather than try to find out if you have done anything.

The problem I find with people who criticize you, not knowing, some-times—I feel they are trying to find an excuse for themselves not being where you are. I understand it. Sometimes it makes you very lonely.

Two people start out the same, but one succeeds and one doesn't. The one who doesn't has to live with himself, and he has to rationalize why he isn't where you are. We can't bring ourselves to admit that someone else is smarter than we are or someone else is more deserving than we are. I think it is human nature.

You have two different groups: people who are happy for you, that you have achieved, and the others who are critical of you—they have other motivations that are not always justified.

I have people say to my face that the only reason they selected me is because I am a Black. "You are just a token." I have gotten so it doesn't hurt me. Not only Blacks say this to me. A white judge said it to me from the bench one day. Richard Ogilvie was running for gover-nor, and I had been selected to give the speech at the $100-a-plate Mc-Cormick Place dinner. I am in the middle of a hearing, and the judge said from the bench, "Why did they select you?"

"I suppose they thought I would give a good speech," I said.

He said, "No, they selected you because you are a token."

Well, I don't know about this tokenism. People say to your face, "They selected you because you are a good looking woman" or "You are a twofer." It means two for one—a Black and a woman—and I laugh about it. But they are serious. I can't look into the person's mind, why they selected me. All I can say is, "thank you." It is up to me to turn tokenism into something real.

In 1960, when I was selected to give the nominating address for Rich-ard Nixon—I don't know how my name came up—I got a call that I would give a seconding speech. I wasn't a regular delegate—I was select-ed as a delegate-at-large. I don't know how it happened or why. I had worked awfully hard. I got the notice either that morning or the night before—no notice to speak of. I wrote my whole speech under a hair dryer. You would think that you are censored, that they prepare your speech for you or read it; none of that happened. I gave the speech like I wrote it.

When I was selected to travel with then Secretary of State Henry Ca-bot Lodge as his civil rights advisor, I received that call while I was at the National Bar Association in California. I was called to the telephone, and over the telephone they asked me, and I said yes.

A lot of time, if you go public, you kill yourself. I went through that when I was young. I enjoyed seeing my name in the paper, and then people start shooting at you. That's what I feel about Blacks with these corporate boards. It is one thing for people to say you are a token, but I find I get it more from black people than others.

When I went to the Solicitor General's office in 1973, I became chair-man of the federal women's programs for the whole Department of Jus-tice. Women were really mistreated in government, as were Blacks. When I left there in 1975, I went as a representative to the Internation-al Women's Year Conference in Mexico. There was a group of black and white women there who were using obstructionist tactics, and they were just raising sand and accusing all of us who were delegates of not being sensitive to issues of poor people and black people. They said we were just middle class. One vocal woman was a CORE Representative.

White people are afraid of black people in large numbers. They just fold up. When I had to get up to speak, I brought it right down front. "You are talking about not being sensitive to black causes," I said. "I am one of the founders of CORE. I dare you to say this to me." The American government gave me credit for turning things around. The women apologized to me.

The thing that bothers me most about our black people is that we don't support each other. Here I am standing up as a representative, and I am the only Black there and they choose me to attack. I had to fight and scramble to get where I am. And the fight isn't over.

Louise Quarles Lawson

Louise Quarles Lawson, 63, is president and chief executive officer of Illinois Service Federal Savings and Loan Association of Chicago, the second-largest black savings and loan association in the United States. She was the first woman to serve as president of the American Savings and Loan League.

"I tell our employees they have a unique opportunity: the one thing you don't have to deal with is color. That's a major plus. If you are working here, you should want to be what I am."

Louise Quarles Lawson

When the war ended in 1945 I was working in Chicago, for the Labor Board. When the war ended the job ended. I was working in a temporary position, a temporary civil service job. My unit head at the War Stabilization Board told me about a job at Illinois Federal--he was a friend of the late Robert Taylor, and Robert Taylor was executive secretary of Illinois Federal Savings and Loan Assn., and Robert Taylor had put out the word he was looking for somebody. Taylor is the only Black to ever be appointed to the chairmanship of the Chicago Housing Authority, and the Robert Taylor Homes were named for him.

He interviewed me at Illinois Federal, and he said, "Fine, I would like for you to talk with Sidney Brown--he is our attorney. By the way, are you from the University of Chicago?"

"No," I said. I guess he thought I was because the man who referred me to him was from there.

"Where are you from?" Robert Taylor said.

I said, "Mississippi."

He nearly died. He had his feet up on the table, and he was smoking a cigar, and he almost choked on the cigar. He jerked his feet off the table and nearly swallowed his cigar. I really started feeling mighty put out about it. "What's wrong?" I thought.

All I could see was myself setting under a tree eating watermelon with no shoes and a straw hat on! He really put me down. So then he said, "They need somebody, that's one thing, so I'll let you go and talk to Sidney Brown. Whatever he decides is all right with me." I went to see Mr. Brown, and he said, "I don't know why he said that--he's from the South, from Alabama. So don't let it bother you." And that's how I got started.

I was born in Fort Gibson, Mississippi, which is between Vicksburg and Natchez. I went to grammar school in a little Delta town called Friar's Point, across from Memphis, Tennessee, until about the fifth or sixth grade. Then I moved back to Fort Gibson because my grandparents lived there, and I went to the laboratory school connected with Alcorn College. For me it was good. We had a principal who had a master's degree from Columbia University. At the time she came we were dis and dat kids, very country, as country as we could be. She brought some culture into our lives and some positiveness.

I don't want to talk about what year that was. I'll put it to you like this: it was when I was in the sixth grade, 500 years ago. You had to do your work. She brought you up to a level, and I think I got my basic start from her in trying to reach for something. Miss Jenkins, from Dallas, Texas. She was the most sophisticated lady I had ever seen in my life. She was a nice woman, and you wanted to win her respect, but she really put you through some changes to win it. I do other people that way myself, now: not much nonsense, and you don't need to waste time with people trying to figure out what they want. If they want something, they ought to tell you.

I went to college, and when I was a freshman I was Miss Alcorn, and in my sophomore year I was Miss Alcorn. Alcorn is in Lorman, Mississippi, and it is a university now. When I finished college I went to Tuskegee to work, and I met a fellow and married, and we moved to Winnipeg, Canada. He was in the Army. And then my mother, who lived in Gary, Indiana, became ill, so I came down to Chicago and brought her over so I could take care of her. And that's when I was working for the Labor Board.

After I talked with Robert Taylor, I was really upset. I didn't know too much about Chicago anyway. But Mr. Brown calmed my nerves down, and through the years he became my mentor. He said, "Don't get upset about that--most people who have done anything are from the South." Before it was done with, Mr. Taylor had really laid the stuff on me, but I wouldn't have missed working for him, because I think I would have been much weaker. If I had worked for a kind person, like me, I would be all messed up--I would have thought life was easy. He would work you to death.

He demanded so much for so little. I was getting $150 a month. Besides my other work, I was going to churches on Sunday and talking to people about opening savings accounts. He thought that because I was from Mississippi, I would understand the preachers better: I could talk that talk. So I was just working myself to death. I would go home at one o'clock in the morning, trying to balance the books and be back at nine a.m. I didn't know anything else but work. Two of us worked in the office. We were doing $80,000 to $100,000 in new deposits and waiting on people in those old crammed offices in the Rosenwald Building at 62 East 47th Street.

This was in 1946. We had assets about $365,000--we were not at $500,000 yet. I earned $4,800 then, and I wanted a raise. So he had a neat way of approaching me, and he approved $200 a year! Mr. Taylor said, "We had our meeting last night, and guess what--I bet you never dreamed when you were in Mississippi you would be making $5,000 a year."

I said, "What I never dreamed in Mississippi was that I would be working this hard, either."

I wouldn't take it--it was too insulting. They went back and gave me more money. I think they gave me $5,500. That was absurd too, especially when they wanted me to think it was so good.

Robert Taylor was a very unique man. He could make anything big or little, the way he said it. If you wanted to spend $2,000 on furniture, he would make it sound like all the money in the world; but if he wanted to spend $10,000 for a study, he would say, "Oh, well, it will only cost $10,000..." I learned a lot from him. Whatever he wanted you to be, he could carry you there. He was a master politician. Every board is that way: they know how things will work out before you get there.

I had no authority to call meetings of the board, but Robert Taylor would tell me to call them up to meet tomorrow, so I would call. So one night we had a meeting with A.W. Williams, who was chairman of the board, and he looked at me and said, "I want to tell you something, young lady--I'd like to be asked if I've got the time to come to a meeting. I am busy, like everybody else." So Robert Taylor looked at me and said, "You didn't call him in time." I was so outraged I got up and left them sitting there. Mr. Brown came out, and I said, "That's just too much. He knows I don't call the meetings, and I'm not going to take all this flak about that. Why didn't Mr. Taylor say something?" Mr. Brown said, "Don't you understand? He was talking to Taylor."

I didn't understand any carrying on like that. I came from a simple life, not a sophisticated life, not where I am looking at you and talking to someone at the other end of the table.

When Mr. Taylor died in 1957, George Walker became the executive secretary and I became the assistant secretary. Then Mr. Walker left in 1965, and I became secretary. Then the business really hit the fan. I expected to be named managing officer--I was the assistant manager, and everybody got upset. The directors didn't want a woman to be that. They made it clear I wouldn't be it.

They got Mr. Brown to come into the office and stay a couple of hours every day, but he thought this was all silly. He insisted that they find somebody who knew more about the savings and loan business than I did, because I had been there since 1946, and this was 1965. To this day it is very difficult to get people that know anything about savings and loans, especially managing officers. So they looked and looked. It was kind of rough right through there, because I was really insulted and really hurt because they didn't want a woman to do it. Then on the other hand, I told myself, "I have done enough whining, and I better get busy and hold it together the best I can." Then they didn't even come in the office. Archibald Carey was the president then. Not only was he a male chauvinist, but the rest were, too. They didn't come in for a while. "Let's see what will happen and see her fall on her face." They weren't going to give any assistance. They got downright hostile about it.

Then I called a couple of ministers, and they got a breakfast together and told me that I could bring anybody from the office I wanted to, and they would help in developing the association. You know, I needed traffic in the worst way, because I had to prove that I could do it. But then Mr. Carey say, "You don't need to go--John H. Sengstacke and I will go. Thank you for telling us." But when I told the minister who had gotten the others together that I wouldn't be able to come, he said, "I will just call it off until you can come." So then Mr. Carey agreed to take me along, and the minister said, "We will turn the meeting over to Mrs. Quarles, because she wants to talk to us about something." But I said, "Our president is here," and I let him talk.

And then when we opened our new building, they didn't even let me get introduced. Carey didn't want anybody to get the notion I was going to do anything there. I became president after he left to become judge, but by then he was my biggest booster.

In 1975 I became president. Usually whoever is the managing officer becomes president, and A.W. Williams decided to quit as chairman of the board. One day he came in and said. "I made a decision, and do you want to hear what it is about? I think I have a candidate for president."

They pulled so much stuff I thought it could be Jack the Ripper. So I said, "Not really. Whoever it is is okay."

So then he wrote my name on a little piece of paper. Before I could get my breath, he said, "I think I would like for my son to be on the board." I had to pay a debt right away. It was so I would vote for him and go along with him. His son was 23 years old, and I had never heard of a 23-year-old kid being on a board.

Even though our association is relatively young, I think we have done as well as any other small association has done. We have moved up from the fourth to the second largest black-owned savings and loan association in the country. Our assets are $96.5 million. The Family Association of Los Angeles is the largest in the country--at last report, they were at $117 million. We are supposed to pick up Morgan Park Savings and Loan, and then we would probably be at $100 million, and we would be the only black savings and loan association in Chicago.

I've done some interesting things. I was the first and only woman president of the American Savings and Loan League in 1973. The Carter Administration offered me the position of executive vice president of GNMA (Government National Mortgage Association). I was going to take it--I stayed in Washington off and on in 1977. I was dumbfounded when I heard about it. I told my board, "Guess what--somebody called from Washington and offered me a job there." They said, "Oh, really?" No enthusiasm or nothing. Then when I said, "I'm going to Washington for interviews," they figured I'd never get it. Then when I got a letter saying I was selected, that's when I began to get some respect.

When they couldn't find me from time to time, they believed me. I had leased an apartment in Washington. To get me to stay they raised my salary and went back and paid me pension for all the years I had been there, which could have been done a long time ago. And since then I haven't had trouble with salary raises.

Did you know we are the only savings and loan association that has had any net profit, for the most part, for the past six months? I went to a meeting last week out at Oak Brook. There were ten associations, and not one had a net profit for the first six months of 1981. We never have been invited before to anything they had. They are trying to start a service corporation with a group of savings and loans where you can pool your resources. They invited us because we made income and they didn't--they wanted to see how we did it. We are 21 per cent equity. So we are just doing our own thing. We are not making too many loans, because it doesn't make any sense, because nobody can qualify. We are investing our money in short term. We ended up with about $200,000 net profit in that, which is not all the money in the world, but most of them had none.

I have been working since I was eleven years old, telling people I could do things that I couldn't, and finally catching on to it. My mother was a strong, determined woman, and so I guess I picked some of that up. I told a lady I could cook--she had a little boy and a grocery store, and she hired me. My first meal was Swiss steak and cherry pie and peas. I put some flour, salt and pepper in, browned the meat, put some water on it and boiled it. You know how tough Swiss steak is. I made a cherry pie with a pound of butter, and nobody could pick it up. A can of peas that was a can of water. When they came in they couldn't eat that meal. She was a nice woman, and she said, "You don't really know how to cook." I thought I did, because I had helped my mother cook for a white family for many years. The lady said,"Let's start over." I learned. I really can cook now. I don't like to be last in nothing.

I tell our employees they have a unique opportunity: the one thing you don't have to deal with is color. That's a major plus. If you are working here, you should want to be what I am.

Customers have a feeling that black or other businesses don't know how to treat their customers. We have to refute that by the fact that we do give good service. You can't take personally things that a customer may say to you.

There was a little girl from Rockford, and she worked for us about three years. She was a disbursing person. She did a good job at it. Another girl who was working for us was going with a fellow who was into something. She lived with him, but she backed off and put him on this other girl. She was so flattered at the attention that she fell for him. She was on vacation, and came back on Tuesday, left on Wednesday with $12,000 of our money. He told her to bring it on Tuesday and they would put it back on Wednesday. It turned out she didn't turn up the next day, and we couldn't open our vault. The slicker told her to jam it and everything until she got back. The safe people had to come out and spend all day getting it open.

They found her in back of the police station dead, shot through the head. I think they knew who did it. We got our $12,000 back, and we didn't press charges. Some people thought it was so cold. We didn't go to the funeral or send flowers. I said she took her flowers with her.

People ask me why we don't have more employees. We talk to a lot of people, but you can't hire everybody you talk to. They don't pass the basic honesty test. I guess it's a sign of the times. Almost everyone out of 12 we tried recently had taken something from somebody, something that would let the people who analyze the test know that we would have trouble if we hired them.

Parents have got to take a stronger stand than they do. You have to train your kids like I was trained. Right is right, and something else is wrong.

I took some courses at the American Savings and Loan Institute. I started in 1947, and for the first few years nobody spoke to me but the instructor.

One time the instructor got so carried away, teaching real estate law. He brought a document to the class. It was just after they had removed the restrictive convenants. "I found a document that will keep them out," he said. All the white students were running up there. "This is the instrument you need to use."

After they all sat down, I said, "Now tell me how to get in, since you are the instructor." He had forgotten I was there. I reported him, and we got all kinds of apologies. They always forget you are there. It's another example of racism. It's the same kind of thing we face in trying to integrate the schools. How else can you account for the fact that Chicago schools have not been integrated in the 27 years after the 1954 supreme court decision? It is absurd to think they need more time to get their act together.

Robert Lucas

Robert Lucas, 56, is executive director of the Kenwood-Oakland Community Organization (KOCO). An active worker in the early days of the Congress Of Racial Equality (CORE), Lucas led the famous march into Cicero, the Chicago area's most integration-resistant suburb, in 1966.

"I remember being involved in school boycotts around 1961 because we felt Ben Willis, who was then superintendent of Chicago schools, was containing Blacks in so-called 'Willis Wagons.' As you remember, if a school was on the border, so to speak, between the white and black community, he would contain the Blacks in the 'Willis Wagons' — mobile units stuffed into playgrounds."

Robert Lucas

I came to Chicago in 1942. I lived with my mother who had come here to seek employment from Rosieburg, West Virginia, when I was 17 years old. I finished high school at Wendell Phillips evening school and after that, in 1943, I went into the Army. I came out of the Army in November, 1945.

Did you have any unusual experiences in the Army?

Oh yes, I had some unusual experiences in the Army. I remember just prior to us going overseas, I was stationed in Fort Knox, Kentucky, and I'd had training to be in the infantry. However, as we came out of basic training, the Secretary of War decided that there shouldn't or wouldn't be any Blacks in combat, or at least there wouldn't be in any large numbers. So, in spite of the fact that we had been trained as infantrymen, we were sent to Fort Knox, Kentucky, and put into the Quartermaster's Corps . . . as truckdrivers. And I remember, as they were preparing us to go overseas in May of 1944, I remember the company commander assembling the company and saying to us, "You know, you may be treated differently in this country, and suffer from some aspects of racial discrimination, but what you need to keep in mind is that you know you're better off than other minorities in the world." You know, that kind of talk has never made any sense to me at all and it still doesn't. Some Blacks still fall for that line that they're better off in this country than they are in South Africa; obviously they are. But you don't compare yourself with South Africans, you compare yourself to your white counterparts, and then see how you measure up.

But, anyway, other than listening to the company commander making that kind of statement, I remember another unusual experience in Europe. Our company became a part of the famed "Redball Express" and our job in Europe was to keep the third army (Patton's army) supplied with ammunition. And I remember one day as I was returning from taking ammunition up to one of the army divisions on the way back, I saw a line of white soldiers in the field with shiny, brassy messkits. The reason I am making this point is that we had been on rations—K-rations, C-rations, what have you—for about thirty days. K-rations was the stuff that came in cardboard boxes, cheese and crackers and so forth; and C-rations was more like corn beef hash and stuff in cans, and the D-rations were chocolate bars. The reason why we were doing that is that we had been told that the food had been sunk in the Atlantic Ocean by the German U-Boat. Of course, we were in a segregated army and we just assumed that that went for all of the troops who were in Europe, whether they were black or white. And so we accepted it. But when I saw these guys in the field with the messkits, that suggested only one thing. A messkit is like a skillet with little compartments, like a metal plate. That there was hot food being served. So I parked my truck and I dashed toward the food and the mess sergeant saw me coming and he beat me to the punch, so to speak. He beckoned to me to come up to the front of the line because he read my face. He knew what was on my mind, that I was going to get some food or die trying. And so he beckoned me to come to the front of the line and he loaded me up with food and then I went off by myself and ate the food, but I could hardly wait until I got back to the company to report to my fellow soldiers what was going on.

Your fellow black soldiers?

Some of my fellow black soldiers became rather irate, but most of them accepted it. So what do you know; that's the way things are and there's nothing we could do about it. But, anyway, from that point on, that just totally destroyed my faith in the country and so it destroyed my faith in the so-called sense of fair play. I have rebelled in my own way. For instance, after taking ammunition up to the front, I would take my time coming back; and then stop and fool around, because I knew they couldn't prove anything and I always had a good alibi.

I got out of the army in November, 1945. And I came back to Chicago and fooled around to the first of the year, hung around 47th street, mainly where Blacks usually hung around, 43rd Street, 35th, and I went to work the first of the year. I went to work in a factory out in Argo — and I worked out there for three months and then I got fired because I refused to work overtime. The second job, I went down to the Polk Street Freight Station. During that time you could always get a job at the freight station because Chicago was the center of the freight business, the steel mills and the stockyards. So I went down to the freight station and worked down there about nine months but I didn't like the way Blacks were being treated, so I organized Blacks down there and got fired. In January of 1947, I enrolled in Roosevelt College, which was then at 231 South Wells Street, and I spent a year at Roosevelt College. But I always wanted to play football and they didn't have football, so I left Roosevelt in 1948 and went to Wilson Jr. College and got involved in basketball and football. I got there too late to file for basketball, so I hung around until the fall semester at Wilson and applied for the football team and I think I should have made the team. But the coach was so prejudiced, he said I would be used in the second team, and I thought I was good enough for first team so I quit. I spent a year at Wilson, which is a two year college. I left Wilson and got a job in a Post Office as a clerk. Around May of 1949 I got disgusted with civilian life and the way Blacks were being treated in Chicago and I decided to go back in service and make a career of it. So, in May of 1949, instead of going back into the Army, which was my mistake, I went into the Marine Corps and stayed there from May, 1949, to May, 1950, and they gave me what you call a general discharge — it wasn't an honorable discharge, and it wasn't a dishonorable discharge — the reason for the discharge was that I was not compatible with the services.

Were the Marines integrated at that time?

Yea, well that was right after President Truman had issued the executive order to integrate the armed forces, so they were beginning to integrate and the reason why I couldn't make it in the Marines was they wanted to make a messboy out of me, and I refused to do that. They had two kinds of jobs — they had what they called general duty for Blacks, and that had to do with some sort of service work where you just fool around on the base and maybe work in the supply house or maybe cut grass, and they had what they call the mess part of it, this was strictly where you were waiting on officers and shining boots and serving officers. And that was with two years of college. So anyway, I left the service in May of 1950 and came back to Chicago and attempted to get back into the post office. I didn't right away, so I went to Detroit to see some relatives. I worked at the post office over there and got tired of Detroit and came back here in 1952 and had some odd jobs at the Ritz Bowl at 43rd & Indiana, and so I worked down there setting pins while I looked for a good job. I finally got a job at the Merchandise Mart, but in 1954 I went back into the post office and stayed there until 1967.

The conditions in the U.S. Post Office for Blacks were deplorable, to say the least, despite of the fact that Blacks were in a clear majority down there and Blacks had much more education than Whites. So the average White down there then wasn't really from Chicago; they were usually from southern Illinois or Iowa or one of the neighboring states and they usually had about 12th grade education and a lot of them were off the farms. But these were the guys with all the best positions; these were the guys with the supervisors' positions. In fact, there was a large number of Polish people there too, urban Poles who lived in the city. So it was really the farmers and the Poles and Eastern Europeans who were really running things at the post office for the most part, and had all the supervisory jobs, in spite of the fact that Blacks had all this education. A lot of Blacks, like myself, had two, three and four years of college, but couldn't really get promoted. What always bothered me was the fact of how content the Blacks were and I would always attempt to talk to some of the clerks about, "Hey, why don't we do something about this?" in so many words, and they would say "Well that's the way things are," and some of them would talk a good game but that's as far as it would go. So, I first started raising cain inside the post office about why Blacks weren't promoted and just about the general working conditions. I was really motivated at that time. Around that time Dr. Martin Luther King Jr. had started in. I had read Paul Laurence Dunbar, Richard Wright and some others I was reading . . . James Baldwin was coming to be known and I was also reading some of his books so I was really motivated by two people at that time, Dr. King and James Baldwin, and so that motivated me to really protest.

Baldwin really talked about the contradictions in this country. You know, here's the Constitution and, of course, Blacks weren't considered free, until the so-called Civil War, and after the 13th, 14th, and 15th Amendments, these Amendments supposedly made Blacks free and equal, and yet by 1955 and 1956, we still weren't. Baldwin really spoke from my point of view; Baldwin spoke of those glaring disparities in the country and was always trying to pique the conscience of America to make it live up to the founding fathers' plan. Baldwin talked about the three-fifths of a man and the fact that over Jefferson's protests, the slavery thing was left in Declaration of Independence, in order to appease the South. At least that's the way I interpreted what Baldwin was saying.

And so, I guess it was in 1959, I was looking around for something to do, in addition to working at the Post Office, and I heard about the Congress Of Racial Equality (CORE). I joined CORE, which at that time was in units, the strongest of which was over at the University of Chicago, and I joined CORE in Chicago where most of the officers in the organization were Whites. In the local, as well as in the national organization, most of the officers were Whites and from 1959 to 1960 we had meetings. When students sat in in Greensboro, North Carolina, CORE got real active in the sense that we began to support the Southern Movement.

For example, when students were sitting in Woolworth Stores in the South, we would picket Woolworth's stores here in the city to support the Southern demonstrations. Later, the national CORE got involved in the freedom riots—around 1961. We picketed bus stations and various targets in the North to support that effort. What I'm saying is that CORE, by the time I joined it in 1959 until about 1963, primarily was supporting what was going on in the South with SCLC and other groups. Then, in 1963 the movement came North and CORE helped to pioneer the movement in Chicago, and I think it was also true of the movement in New York too.

CORE itself went back to 1942. CORE was formed right here in this city by James Farmer, believe it or not. I think they had some cafeteria sit-ins in Chicago in 1942 over in South Kenwood where there were restaurants that Blacks couldn't eat in. They sat in there and also in restaurants in the Loop where they weren't welcome at all. In the summer of 1942, CORE left Chicago and went to New York, which at the time supposedly had a more favorable climate for those kinds of things. At least you could get more support from the liberal Jewish community. But about 1963, when we really got active here after we stopped supporting the Southern Movement so much, it was really about the subject of school integration. I remember being involved in school boycotts around 1961 because we felt Ben Willis, who was then the superintendent of Chicago Schools, was containing Blacks in the so-called "Willis

Wagons." As you remember, if a school was on the border, so to speak, between the white and black community, he would contain Blacks in the "Willis Wagons"--mobile units stuffed into playgrounds. That was to keep from integrating the schools. About 1963, CORE decided to take it on as a project. There was a school around 61st & Stewart in Englewood, and the School Board had stepped up its containment policies using Willis Wagons to keep from integrating Blacks. So we picketed the schools around 61st & Lowe for a number of days, a very dramatic protest.

It was dramatic in terms of the kinds of thing we got involved in. For example, people volunteered to break the law by blocking up streets. I remember one woman climbing a flagpole, an Indian woman by the name of Sybil Bearskin; and some black guy climbed some pole out there and stayed up there for quite a long time. And police came and arrested them and we surrounded the pole to keep the police from arresting these people—those kinds of things. So, finally we decided to really dramatize the need for school integration in the city, so in the summer of 1963, we had a sit-in at the Board of Education. Chicago policemen weren't used to Blacks behaving that way, so we were able to continue a sit-in for two or three weeks. I used to come from work, sit there for four or five hours and then go home and go back to work, because the police really didn't know what to do with us, so they let us sit in. Finally, two or three weeks later, they decided to arrest us and those issues brought the movement to the City of Chicago around the first of August. CORE began to organize and mobilize people for the march on Washington; as you remember, that was August 28, 1963. We participated very heavily in the march on Washington and I remember we were on a train and it seems to me one coach was made up of about fifty CORE and about half of the delegations were white. About forty per cent of those in the sit-ins were whites. CORE was very much integrated until 1965, really all the way up to black power movement of 1966. Then whites began to leave CORE in 1964, and finally in 1966, they just about left altogether. There were a few still around CORE in 1967, but 99 per cent of them had left in 1966. The reason they left in 1964 is because Blacks inside CORE began to flex their muscles—what I mean to say by that is they said Whites can be in the organization, but because the civil rights movement was for the advancement of Blacks, Blacks ought to be in the leadership. And at that point, some of the Whites began to leave the organization because they could not be the leaders any longer.

A lot of us were at that time being motivated by Malcolm X and I was taking the position that Blacks ought to be in leadership and Whites ought to be in membership. The black nationalists in CORE felt Whites should have left as early as 1964--at that point all Whites should have left. The way we were defining nationalists in those days were people who were leaning towards the teachings of Muhammad and Malcolm X. Then there was . . . I love the New York tradition, the Harlem tradition that talked about separatism—there was some from Marcus Garvey's persuasion, and some from Malcolm X's school of thought, and some just believed separatism was the only way out. Then there were a lot of nationalists who believed that this country would be ultimately integrated, but Blacks needed to get themselves together, and that made sense in those days. But you still find Blacks, supposedly educated Blacks, who are nationalists—you still find Blacks, as late as 1981, talking about we got to get ourselves together. To me, I think it's a cop-out, a sort of an escape valve; it gives the appearance you are doing something, but in reality you aren't. They're still up in an auditorium talking about we got to get ourselves together. I guess I make these kinds of statements because primarily I'm an activist—I believe in doing things and I don't have much patience with people who talk and talk and talk.

At what time did you organize, you came to my attention with this march on Cicero? It seems that Dr. King turned around and didn't go to Cicero, and you decided that you were going to go, and you organized the march. Tell me about that, what year was that?

Triple CO (CCCO) was made up of various community organizations like black civil rights organizations, community organizations, church organizations and so forth; the purpose of the Triple CO, as we called it, was to coordinate the civil rights activities in the City of Chicago and focus the activities on a specific target, which I think worked quite well for about three years, from 1963 to 1966. It really was started by some of the so-called militant Blacks. Charles Davis, a black public relations man was the first convener, and at one point Rev. Arthur Brazier, with TWO (The Woodlawn Organization), was a convener. The convener who became the most prominent and more remembered, however, was Al Raby. He was a convener from 1964 until the fall of 1966. I would remember CORE being the most active group in Triple CO.

From 1963 to 1966, we really boycotted the Board of Education and a lot of people got arrested. One time James Farmer came in, and Dick Gregory got involved with CORE; he had been involved with Dr. King down South, and when Gregory got involved in Chicago he got involved through CORE. Then finally, in 1966, I guess in Mayor Richard Daley's estimation, Ben Willis became what they call a political liability, so Daley with his control of the Board, told the Board not to rehire Willis because of the marches and those kinds of things. Willis was finally driven from office.

That's one of the reasons I think that Blacks are losing now; they aren't really willing to put in; you know they do a lot of talking, but we are losing the things that we gained within the last twenty-five years. We aren't willing to use energy to protect those things. An example: Mayor Jane Byrne (in 1981) took two of our guys off the school board thus reducing Blacks to three, and then put on two white women and there was not a whimper; Blacks grumbled and mumbled among themselves but nobody even went down and said to Byrne, you can't do that. Nobody said a word and I think that's one of the reasons why people are sort of running over us. Anyway to get back to the subject of marching in 1966, we marched on the Chicago Post Office for a few months. We really started. . .The objective was to get more Blacks promoted and improve the general working conditions in the Post Office. Our first demonstration was at the Christmas Party of 1965. During that time, it was customary for the postmaster to have a gigantic Christmas Party where the establishment was involved, usually someplace like the Amphitheatre or a sports stadium like that. I remember that the Urban League had done some really good research, something about the number of Blacks who were in the Post Office and the lack of supervisory positions, and had given the research to the Chicago Postal Alliance. Those brothers were kind of conservative, but there was a woman in

CORE who was also the secretary for the Chicago Postal Alliance, and she brought the research to a CORE meeting. We looked at it and we used that research to raise the questions about good working conditions and we brought it to the Christmas Party. It was held at the Chicago Stadium, and it was cold, about ten below zero, and everybody was saying it was really too cold to be demonstrating and it was too cold to march. But we picketed this party at the stadium, about twenty-five of us, and we passed out leaflets at this Christmas Party, and a lot of Whites as well as Blacks were shocked because they thought up until that point that Blacks really had it made.

They were shocked to know that Blacks were being treated that way and shocked to learn there were so few Blacks in supervisory positions. We didn't go inside, but that sort of put a damper on the whole Christmas party. Not many people participated too enthusiastically. But in the early spring in 1965, there was a CORE meeting and we decided to picket the Post Office, which we did for about three months every day. I was surprised because a number of postal employees participated in the picket.

Right after that large numbers of Blacks got promoted. Some people gave me credit, some gave CORE the credit -- the point is it was accomplished and we didn't care who got the credit. As a matter of fact, we'd like to believe as a result of that we got our first black postmaster, Henry McGee, who had been working for years and finally got promoted to postmaster, by U.S. Sen. Paul Douglas around 1967

About that time we're talking about picketing the Post Office in 1966 and the Triple CO had invited Dr. King to town. When Martin first came to town he got involved with the slum movement, the organization was called The Movement To End the Slums; but Mayor Daley went up to him and we were about to be co-opted, so then the leadership of the Freedom Movement, the SCLC, decided to march in the white community for open housing. The public always thought we were marching for open housing, but the truth of the matter was that we were marching in the so-called white communities on the North, Southwest and Southeast sides to dramatize racism in the North that was a hidden agenda. But we had to tell the public we were marching for open housing, although we knew that wasn't really politically possible at that time in Chicago. Dr. King and his staff looked at the Cicero marching threat as the kind of thing to hold over Mayor Daley's head, Dr. King and his staff must have announced at least four times publicly they were going into Cicero and it was more of a threat than anything else. We thought that might threaten Mayor Daley and force him to meet the objectives of the marches.

They wanted Mayor Daley to open up the housing in Chicago.They felt he had the power, and he did. I think if had he met those objectives he would have been defeated in 1967. Blacks wanted open housing and wanted the City Council and Mayor Daley to use his office; he could control the Democratic Party -- really to pass a city ordinance -- saying Blacks can live, work and play anywhere they want inside of Chicago. That's really what they wanted and were trying to get Daley to do. If you remember in late July or early August of 1966, the city was really becoming polarized, the tension was thick between the white and the black communities as a result of the marches and the way the marches were seen.

You had already had the Southeast and Southwest side marches?

The Southwest side and the Northwest, we'd had those already and the races were really polarized. You could almost feel the tension in the air. We just went into the various communities -- we went into Marquette Park and that's where Dr. King got hit by a brick. We went into what they call Chicago Lawn -- that's around 3200 West on 63rd Street -- and we went into Gage Park, which is west of Damen on 55th Street. Those were some of the community areas, and in the Northwest and Southeast side we went into poor white and Latino communities. Anyway those marches produced the polarization I'm speaking of, and the tension was really so thick you could feel it, you could almost cut it with a knife anywhere in the city. You know you could see it, you could feel the hostility in the faces of Blacks as they looked at Whites and vice versa, and so the city fathers reached a point where they had to do something about that. Chicago's Archbishop John C. Cody, who had been supportive of Dr. King, began to say to Dr. King that we needed to sit down at the table, and even some of the conservative black leadership felt the same way, they really believed that maybe Martin needed to stop.

And I also remember that in 1966 when Dr. King was here, that's when they had a rebellion of sorts on the West Side. I guess that was the first time since 1919 that Blacks had really rebelled. Finally, the businessmen, really the power structure, finally had a meeting at the Palmer House and they invited a bunch of civil rights folks -- Dr. Martin Luther King was there, Al Raby, a lot of people were there, John Sengstacke, publisher of the *Chicago Defender*. A lot of people were there. And that was the first time I had come face to face with the power structure -- Mayor Daley was there, as were the City Corporation Council, Archbishop Cody, Bill Lee, the labor leaders, etc. I mean this was the first time we had talked with the power structure and this was the first time the establishment gathered in one room. At that time, Blacks rebelling was somewhat of an enigma to the power structure; they weren't really used to that.

So they were asking us ways to stop this. And I remember this, and it always bothered me: most Blacks weren't really asking for anything. Usually when Blacks have Whites on the run, so to speak, their demands are very weak. Here are all these white men from these various institutions in the city sitting in this room, and they believed that at any moment this rebellion was going to spill over into the Loop and destroy all their stuff down there and they were rightly afraid. Yet you had Blacks in the room from the Urban League and from the Triple CO, and even Dr. King, and nobody really knew what to ask for, nobody really made any demands of any significance.

I remember I got up and I said one of the reasons for the rebellion was because of social conditions and I ran down the whole list; and I was ignored at that time. I was known as a renegade anyway, and I was ignored; and it was at that point that the white leadership members felt they could not trust me. But it was at that same point that the black leadership felt that Dr. King could no longer be trusted, he wouldn't be involved in these kinds of meetings. And I remember that out of that meeting at the Palmer House, all the Blacks could think to ask for, and Bill Berry asked for it, was for some portable swimming pools. They said the reasons why the Blacks were rioting is because these little kids wanted to get cool under these fire hydrants. Bill Berry got up there and in a sense he was begging these Whites for a portable swimming pool. And they respected Bill. As a result of that, we got the portable swimming pools . . .

Then that was the bottom line?

That was the bottom line, yes. These white men were afraid to death of Blacks and they could have gotten almost anything that was reasonable. The SCLC had made all these threats about marching in Cicero and we were getting feedback -- Blacks who were working in Cicero (none lived there, of course), they were being beat up by Whites because of SCLC, making these threats. They didn't believe anything was going to happen and they were complaining because Dr. King was making these threats and not carrying through with them. If you remember, a young, high school kid had gotten killed that year, seventeen years old and he was looking for a job, and we were angry about that. So we had talked about the first summit conference which -- the whole purpose of the summit conference was Dr. King had a set of demands -- and the demands were stated that, well, if you meet these demands, we'll stop marching. They really couldn't agree.

They had really agreed to nothing really. They had an agreement, but the agreement really wasn't worth the paper it was written on. The agreement did say in a kind of vague, off-handed way that Blacks would be able to live throughout the city, but, Dempsey, there weren't any teeth to the agreement-- there was no way to enforce it. And I believe that Dr. King wanted out. I mean it was a face-saving kind of thing, Dr. King and the freedom movement really wanted out.

Out of Chicago?

Yeah, and Mayor Daley. There was a lot of pressure on Daley. Whites were beginning to say, "Hey, you may not be re-elected," and so Daley got what he wanted. Daley was the only one that really won, but the Whites won too and the Blacks got nothing. Dr. King had a face-saving thing, but I believe until this day that Martin was ill-advised; he just had the wrong cats around him.

I was a Chicago CORE chairman then, and I was also part of the national action conference and a regional chairman. So I said to the press and to the world, in the morning I'm going to call a CORE meeting and I'm going to urge CORE to go to Cicero. We did have a CORE meeting and the executive council decided to go, so we went to Cicero on September 4, 1966.

I said we were going to march in Cicero without the National Guard and with or without a permit, and that changed the complexion of everything. And the press said, "Well, what about the people?" I said, "I'll go if I go by myself," and that motivated Blacks and that put the Whites on the defensive. So within hours, the National Guard was promised and the town attorney agreed to give us a permit. So, on Sunday, September 4, we met in Franklin Park -- Franklin Park is on Chicago's West Side near Cicero -- this was our assembly point and we moved off.

How many people did you have out there?

I don't know how many we had when we went in. A lot of people caught up with us. What really happened to a lot of people, the march was really called for 1:30 in the afternoon and it was 1:30 and there weren't enough people there to suit me. So the youngsters said, "Bob, it's 1:30, it's time to go." I said, "Well, let's wait a few more minutes. And then I saw some people had started moving and I was reminded that during the march on Washington, the leadership got restless -- I don't know if you know this, but we started moving before Dr. King and A. Phillip Randolph -- and they had to catch up with us. So we stepped off on time; a lot of people weren't there, so they had to run to catch up with us. We came out of Cicero with 193 people.

What I should mention here, the day that I went, the Sunday that we marched, at that point I was living at 6421 South Laflin and my family was out of town, which was good, because I don't know what would have happened to my wife had she been here. But my family was out of town; my wife was out of town visiting her brother, who was making a career in the Navy. She had both the kids with her, so I was sort of a free agent. The march made me a nervous wreck, all kinds of threats but, anyway, Dempsey, what I think is very important here is that Dr. King called me up that Sunday morning. It must have been about 8 o'clock. Martin, you know. I was shocked. I was getting a call from "de Lord." I was pleased but also shocked to think that Martin would call a little old guy like myself. Martin said, "Bob, I understand that you're going to Cicero," and I said, "Yeah Doc, we're going." He said, "Well, I'd like to talk you out of it but I know I can't, but since you're going you have my blessing." You know I thought it was really big of him and that really made me feel good. I went and there wasn't any bitterness at all because he said if you must go, you got my blessing. I know the guy really meant it, because I knew him and I could tell the way it came over the wire. So, as I said, we went and of course we told the public we were going for open housing because you had to have that kind of rationale, otherwise people would say you were a fake. But the hidden agenda was we just wanted to let white folks know we were not afraid to come over there. White folks were beginning to feel that they had the niggers afraid to come over there.

And that had to stop.

There were four or five guys all taller than me, and I'm six feet, one inch tall, four or five guys as we left Franklin Park surrounded me. I don't know who the guys were and since that time I've seen one of those guys and I actually didn't know who they were before, until two or three years ago I saw one of those guys. But they thought that probably I was going to get killed and I'm pretty sure they were sort of my bodyguards.

The Chicago Tribune called it the march that returned the bricks. Whites would throw the bricks and miss us, and the young Blacks would catch them in baseball mitts and throw them back. It was quite a march.

Well, let me ask you this Bob, what . . how did that change your career? How did you get involved in KOCO (Kenwood-Oakland Community Organization)?

After I came out of Cicero I was still at the Post Office. The Post Office began to pick, pick, pick, and so finally in October of 1967, I was fired, strangely enough by a black guy. I mean the white postmasters had sort of gone along with me. It was McGee who fired me. What I was fired for didn't really make any sense. I guess the supervisor who I was working under claimed that I had gone on a break and stayed five minutes over or something, instead of staying just ten minutes. I was so angry then I wanted to make a career out of civil rights, not a professional, that's different. I wasn't thinking about being paid, I just felt I had more time to work in the movement and that we could get more done. So, I was hurt for a few days but after three or four days, so much stuff was going on and I stayed active and pretty soon you forget about it. You just learn to live off less.

So I went over to KOCO in November of 1969. Curtis Burrell, who then was in the leadership position and also Leonard Sengali, who had some type of affiliation with the Black P Stone Nation, was also involved. But, anyway, I was hired in November of 1969 to coordinate a leadership training program. The organization had gotten funds from the Rockefeller Foundation to develop the business leadership inside of Kenwood and I was hired to implement that program. The Stones were put out. I guess Burrell put the Stones out of KOCO. When I went to KOCO, the Stones were really part of the staff. There were three or four guys that were really part of the staff; Mickey Cogwell was my aide; Andre Small who is still around, and a couple of others. As I said, there were four or five of them that were active, and Burrell put them out at gunpoint around May in 1970. A year later, to make a long story short, the Board accused Burrell of having lost the perspective of the organization and so they got rid of him in May of 1971 and that sort of threw things in chaos. Burrell took the organization to court and the judge examined the constitution and said the constitution was too vague and ordered the organization to rewrite the constitution and then have an election and so forth. The constitution was rewritten, there were several meetings, and the constitution was finally ratified in February of 1972, and the election was held in March of 1972.

About forty community people approached me and asked me to run for chairman, so I ran for chairman of KOCO in March of 1972 and I served as chairman from May 1972 to April of 1975. KOCO originally started around 1955 as a social service agency. Around 1968, KOCO got involved in some hardware stuff, they set up the Open Development Corporation that rehabbed the building at 46th & Lake Park. Later, we built the health center at 43rd & Vincinnes, also sponsored by KOCO. Around 1977, we decided that we had to go into redevelopment in a real big way, so we got money from the city and we had a plan for North Kenwood Oakland. Around that time, the organization took over eight or nine buildings in the community that Whites had milked and now were no longer making any money. They had left them. The tenants came to us and asked us to manage the building, so we went to the corporation and got ourselves appointed as receivers. So the organization between 1975 and 1977 was appointed Receiver of about ten buildings by Cook County Circuit Court. At this point, we have about six or seven buildings in the HUD Section 8 program. In spite of Reagan's cutbacks, we hope to rehab those buildings.

We haven't given up.

Seated left to right: Ripley B. Mead Jr. on the lap of his grandfather Edwin Ripley Mead, George W. Mead, great-grandfather, settled in Chicago in 1849, standing is Ripley B. Mead Sr. who died in December, 1975, at the age of 84.

"That's how they got started buying property. Because they would get a good fella, Jewish fella, that would sell a piece of property on a contract. Just like they do now."

Ripley Mead, Sr.

My uncle, Adolphus Harris, started in the real estate business in 1903. They ran that real estate business when they weren't on the road. My uncle was running on the railroad at that time, on the Chicago & North Western. He had a parlorcar that ran from here to Lake Geneva.

Most of the states in the West were dry, and this fella named Jim Wright, he was running on the road as a Pullman porter. And he would stop up there on State Street, say around Van Buren, and pick up a lot of those cheap paper suitcases, and he would go to State and Madison and fill the suitcases with loose miniature bottles of whiskey. He would go down to the train, where I would meet him and carry the stuff up on the train. And I put as high as ten cases on the car, and he didn't have one passenger in there.

By prearrangement, a guy would get on somewhere in the dry states. And Jim would say, "Take that suitcase and get off." It looked legitimate. That's how the whiskey got out there, and it made money.

Now my uncle, Adolphus Harris, used to go up there. At that time, the white people didn't pay any attention to Negroes. They only had the parlor car between Chicago and Lake Geneva during the summer, and he would buy the car out every day, and then when the man came along, like the Mitchells and the Lytton's from the Hub Clothing Store and all those people, he would have his seat ready to have them pay him by the month for the seat. He would buy the car and rent it to rich people. And they just had a seat.

That's how they got started buying property. Because they would get a good fell, a Jewish fella, that would sell a piece of property on a contract. Just like they do now. That's why all those people got that.

And that's what closed the Binga State Bank, too. You see, he was trying to finance the contract buying. The banks in those days went in for mortgages, and what they had was stocks also. It was frozen assets that closed the bank, because Binga had the advantage of going to those people and giving them mortgages.

But when the Drepression hit us, it just wiped the bank out. You see, we didn't have automobiles and jewelry and all these personal things to make a loan on. So the only thing the bank went in for was real estate.

Well, I started with Jesse Binga in about 1907. I was collecting rent. Of course you can't say this now, but he was one of the original block-busters.

Binga was a huckster, they call it. And then he got into business some way or another. There is something else that helped him out. There was one particular building that I know about, that we lived in at the north-east corner of 50th and Wabash. McKey and Poague was the manager, and they were afraid of colored people. So Jesse Binga used to rent that 24-flat building for $150 a month. Binga had to pay the taxes and insurance and keep the building up. I'm talking when I first worked for him in 1907. He had that building, but it wasn't his first building. He was at 36th, 37th and State Street, and colored people then didn't go much past 39th Street.

We got our own building at 2312 to 2428 Wabash. The red light district was down at 22nd Street. That was whites, and we would see that we got the buildings they turned over to colored. Most all these women from that area worked on what was known as the line. They were working women, maids. There were white prostitutes and black maids. People like Chicago Mayor Bill Thompson and all those were there, and there was a saloon on the corner at 22nd and State called Wings. It was one of the places that hired colored waiters. You know, they used to make a lot of money at that time, back in 1906 and '07.

Binga had a connection with the First National Bank. The Binga State Bank. See, we used to clear through the First National. Binga brought a Model T truck. They didn't have any Brinks service. And I used to take the money down to the First National in that truck. And somebody always went with me, and he had a sawed-off double barreled shotgun. We used to go down Michigan Ave. in this little truck. The police would always chase you off Michigan.

Renault Robinson

Renault Robinson, 40, is a member of the Chicago Housing Authority board, appointed by Mayor Jane Byrne in 1980. He is one of the founders and executive director of the Afro-American Patrolmen's League.

"Brutality, first of all, still takes place. There are no ifs, ands or buts about that. There is still a bunch of foolish, ridiculous, sadistic white police, and just a few Blacks now who still engage in that kind of treatment. But for the most part it's not as wholesale as it used to be, where they just ran roughshod over you. Now they have to worry a little bit about who they're grabbing, and who they're pushing around."

Renault Robinson

Housing is at a premium now, especially multi-family dwellings. People cannot find a place to stay where they can afford the rent. The few places that are left that are really nice have been converted to condos or they're not on the rental market any more, so that's it.

You take Woodlawn on Chicago's South Side. That's an area that's dying. Sixty-third Street is dead. Almost all city services have been withdrawn, except you get minor police protection and things like that. And there's very little up there now, other than a few food stores that are viable and some drugstores which are still alive on 63rd. And these places stay alive because they are catering to illicit drug trade. They're being paid through green cards and whatever, that's just what's going on. These addicts are able to get legitimately-made drugs that are easily converted to illicit purposes using a green card.

There are a lot of pills on the market that produce various forms of highs that kids and others take. Some of these pills sell for $1 to $2 each, and they're very toxic; they can cause serious problems—they can cause death. And these kids get these pills and sell them to each other. For instance, there's a substitute for heroin that can be made from a prescription drug that's purchased with a prescription. They take it and convert it, and they make a heroin substitute, which gives the same high as heroin. Now, the police know that—and the druggers know that—and so what? It's just something that goes on.

Well, see, that kind of stuff is allowed to go on when a community is being taken apart, when it's allowed to disintegrate. You may find some of these activities in viable communities, but they're controlled, restricted. Not in Woodlawn. I mean, Woodlawn is just up for grabs. They're letting it go down to the point where it will be cheap and easy to move in on it. And they have to get more people out of there first. People are fleeing to South Shore. South Shore almost went under because there was such an influx of people moving out of Woodlawn, but South Shore's trying to stabilize now. Where else are people going to go?

There's no place to go.

Some could qualify for the Chicago Housing Authority. The problem is that CHA is full. You've always got a few vacancy turnovers every month, but we've got 25,000 people on a waiting list. There used to be more vacancies in certain developments, and those were quote "the most undesirable places." Robert Taylor was one of those places; so was Cabrini-Green, and so were a few others.

Now you've got about 100 vacant units in Cabrini, maybe 120. There are 4,000 apartments in Cabrini. The vacant apartments will be rented as soon as they're painted and they're put back in some kind of shape.

People tear those places up when they leave—kick holes in the walls. You know, you can't rent them. They take the refrigerators out, knock the windows out, and they write up the walls. So, by the time you go in, the tile is broken up and you have to put down fresh tile. You have to do so much to get these places back in order. Sometimes tenants kill a whole floor of apartments, just starting at one end, knocking the walls out all the way down.

Now, they did that in Cabrini a couple of years ago. And they had to close off, in some instances, as many as three floors, because they were just totally unsafe. In fact, they had closed off three floors in about three or four of the big buildings, and a girl, a young girl about 17 years old, was taken up to one of those floors. She was raped and then thrown out of the window of the 17th floor or the 16th floor or something. You know, murdered. Her parents sued CHA, and CHA disclaimed any responsibility because that was off limits. But the case now has been sent back, and CHA does have responsibility. So maybe this child's parents and maybe many other parents will be able to now sue the CHA for not providing them with security.

The vacancy rate has fallen tremendously. You remember several years ago the interest rates were still 10 per cent. And now, there is no more 10 per cent, so people can't buy a house any more. So they have to stay.

Tell me, how did the fight for the Afro-American Patrolmen's League start? What was your objective? Tell me how you got into it.

It started off in 1967 principally as a way of stopping the police department from being so inhumane and brutal to Blacks, and also to improve the service. The police were beating the hell out of everybody, but not providing any service.

You were as afraid of the police as you were of the burglar, the thief or the robber. Because if you did run into a police officer, he was kicking you in the teeth, rather than helping you. So we wanted to provide good service and stop the abuse. In order to do that, we found that you couldn't convert white folks to liking Blacks. We figured we needed more black law enforcement people, that blood was thicker than water, and that maybe a black person would react to a black person better than a lot of white people would. Now that rule didn't hold up all the way across the board, because we had a lot of foolish black cops who were antiquated in their thinking and who still thought that the way you resolved a problem was to kick everybody in the teeth and lock everybody up, because that's how they had been taught to treat black people by their white counterparts.

Although, if you worked in the white community, you couldn't do that. When I got on the police department, I worked in the white community. It was altogether different. That was on the West Side. It was altogether different than anything else. Right next to where all the white people were, they had all the black people and they had bombings right between them. The boundaries, let's see. The other side of 18th Street was generally white, going the other way, north, was black. The police department was on Damen at 22nd Street. All around the station were Whites at that time; 22nd Street was all white all the way down until it ran out, from Damen—there were no Blacks at all. From Pulaski west was mostly white too—so the Blacks were in a little pocket, and Roosevelt Road was the dividing line, because another district took it from there. So Blacks were on the other side of Roosevelt Road going to the expressway. This was in the early '60's.

In that area, it was like two police stations, because all of the white folks from 18th Street all the way to 31st Street from Damen, and all the way over to Cicero got treated one way, and all the Blacks got treated an entirely different way. The same way with the treatment of the liquor stores, taverns, restaurants, places where the kids hung out, the schools. Everything was just like night and day. And at that time there were a couple of big gangs of Blacks over on the West Side. There was no Rangers and all that, they hadn't come quite that far yet, it was the Cobras—they had different names, but they were just as bad.

During those days they had people like Gloves Davis, you may remember, one of our notorious black officers, who beat people up pretty good. You had a lot of folks who agreed that you treat white folks one way and black folks another way—and I just thought that it was ridiculous. A lot of other officers thought it was too. We said, "Now you know, everybody is supposed to get the same kind of treatment." They'd bring a Black into the station, beat him, and then throw him into a cell, and that was just normal everyday stuff. They'd bring a white woman into the station for a traffic violation, they'd let her use the commander's washroom, they'd sit her down and they'd call her counsel, they'd do whatever. They'd bring a black woman in and make her sit on the floor, urinate on herself. It was altogether really different, and it just took a short time for just a group of us to say, "Something's got to be done to stop the abuse and improve service."

So that's what got us started talking about starting some organization. There was an organization called the Guardians at the time, and at first we thought about trying to get the Guardians to do something. Then we realized that their purpose for being was more or less of a social organization. They weren't interested in doing anything that imperiled their jobs. If they thought that they had their jobs and they had come through harder times than these, they weren't interested in rocking a boat. I can remember the officers telling me, "Renault, you don't remember, by the time you came on the job they were letting us get into squad cars with white officers."

A few years before, if there were only black officers available for work, they wouldn't let them drive the squad cars. They'd leave them parked.

There were no integrated teams. These guys were saying to me, "Renault, we just got out of real slavery, and things are a lot better than they used to be. So, you know, you ought to be happy with things the way they are." So we could see that we couldn't get any help from them. Besides most of them had been on the job for a long time and didn't want to cause any problems—they didn't speak out about injustice, they didn't speak out about anything.

And I remember in those days too, policeman were on the take pretty heavy. Everybody was taking $2 for traffic violations, and whatever . . . and so nobody really wanted to raise any issue. So it was the younger guys who said, number one, we didn't want to get all involved in the stealing aspect of it, because we thought we were going to go to jail. The others thought that's how they paid for their houses. They'd say we were young and foolish.

But, in any event, we started this group underground—because we knew once we surfaced, somebody's head was going to be wiped out. We couldn't even trust our own guys, because our guys were known for going to a white man saying what another Black was getting ready to do. So we met clandestinely in my basement or somebody else's basement for seven or eight months before we finally developed a name.

It took us two weeks to come up with a name. All that time we had been meeting and didn't even think about any name; we were just black officers getting together. So finally, now we're ready to go, we're ready to come out of the closet, and we met one day at Crane Junior College. That later became Malcolm X, but it was Crane High School then, and they had a little junior college section. We met over there, and we said, "Let's come up with a name so that we can go public." There was one group that said, "OK., let's call it the American Negro Police Association." Well, that horrified two-thirds of the people. Then there was another group that said, "Let's name it the Black Police Association," and that horrified everybody. Then there was another group that said, "Let's call it the Afro-American Patrolman's League." And that was the group that I was with. I was scared of the black police thing because I knew what was going to happen. I was also horrified with the thought of, in the 20th Century, calling yourself the American Negro, we thought it was time-out for that. So we settled on Afro- as a mix between the more militant guys in the group and more fearful guys in the group. We all settled on Afro-American, but only after many, many hours of long debate.

Then we were still afraid, so we went and got a couple of lawyers, and a State Senator. We went and got State Sen. Richard Newhouse and attorneys Eric Graham and Kermit Coleman to help us pull this thing together. Eric was very helpful in the early days. He helped us put together our charter. Newhouse helped us with it in Springfield, and we finally got a charter. And then all hell broke loose. In fact, it was so bad that when we finally announced our existence, the police department intelligence unit and the FBI, by that time, had us under surveillance, we now know. Because we had been classified as subversive, they thought we were going to do something dangerous. That's a big joke, but one of our guys was reporting everything that we were doing, all of our secret meetings, he was reporting everything. And, later, he became an undercover policeman, and some people were charged with treason as a result of his testimony. It became a big celebrated case, and this guy got big promotions and went on to do other things, but you know, all that time he had been telling on us. He's still with the police department.

But again, we realized that there had to be a snake somewhere, and that we weren't going to go unnoticed and that we just had to take our knocks, and we ended up doing just that. I mean, they came right out and told us right out front that they didn't like what we were doing, didn't like the name of the group and didn't like what it stood for. We started handling police brutality complaints because we felt that that was one of the reasons for our organization. And people started to like us and to trust us, because they said, "Well, somebody is concerned about our mistreatment at the hands of the police." But most people didn't realize that they treated black policemen the same way. I mean, there was case after case of black policemen being stopped by white policemen and getting beat up. I mean they just didn't care about black police officers or black nothing. I saw black sergeants and others being abused by white patrolmen, and nobody cared. It was really bad.

Now, Blacks can go out on 87th Street and all that, because it's Blacks all the way around there, the Dan Ryan Woods. But at that time all that was still white. And one black officer went out there with his family. He was having a picnic out there. A bunch of white guys jumped on him and his kids, and a big fight started. Someone called the police— and the police came. He had his gun on through all of this, but he never took it out, he never fired it, never did anything. You know, they beat the hell out of him and his family. Anyway, the police came and saw him and his gun and jumped on him and beat him up pretty badly and beat up his wife. I think they broke her arm, beat up his oldest son, and the officer's yelling, "I'm a policeman."

And they said, "You are a nigger out here molesting these white kids." It was just an incredible situation. We finally tried to get something straightened out, and we had gotten a lawyer and we were going to sue on the officer's behalf. Those white folks had convinced that officer that they made a mistake and they were sorry they had beat the black officer up and his family and all the rest of that. And he didn't want to do anything. He was scared to do anything.

We had another case, where a police officer was married to a white lady, and he was working in a district which was almost all white, South Side again. He was driving down the street in the district where he worked and he had just left a restaurant celebrating his wife's birthday or something—and he had his wife in the car and he was on his way home. There weren't but a handful of black officers in the station, and he was one of them, so everybody knew all the black officers.

So, he's on his way home, and he gets pulled over by a squad car, and the first thing they say is, "Hey, nigger, what are you doing with that white woman in your car."

And the other guy says, "You know she must be a whore or else she wouldn't be in there with no nigger."

They told him. "Get out." They began talking to him real bad and all that, and he said, "Hey, this is my wife."

And they went through a lot of negative stuff, a lot of pushing him around, a lot of pushing her, calling her a lot of derogatory names and stuff like that. One thing led to another, and he kept telling him he was a policeman. They didn't care about that, his being a policeman, and a nigger shouldn't be a policeman anyway and this is why—'cause they marry white women. So, anyway, they beat him up.

We went to his aid—he decided in the end that since he was married to the white woman, he would let the white police association help him instead of us. So we said, fine, if that's what you think is the best thing for you.

And the police association got him strung out and let him get fired. So he got fired as a result of this particular incident.

We had another incident where a police officer's son got beat up by a couple of policemen. He went to the station to inquire about what happened to his son, and was looking for the policemen involved. So the police involved surrounded him in the station and they all jumped on him, like about fifteen of them, beat him up in the station. They fired him.

I mean these things were happening, they were commonplace. Blacks would get stopped and get tickets all the time. I mean you'd just get a ticket. They didn't care if you showed a badge, they'd say, "Now, nigger, that don't mean nothing to me." They'd write you out a ticket—you could be a sergeant, lieutenant, whatever, I know a black sergeant, and this guy liked Cadillacs. He was on his way home from work in a Cadillac, and this was during the daytime, this wasn't night, this was in the afternoon. He's a guy 55 years old, you know, 'cause you didn't get to be a sergeant unitl you were 55 years old or ready to retire anyway. He was driving down the street, and two white officers stopped him and they said, "Nigger, what are you doing in that Cadillac?"

He said, "None of your damn business."

So they said, "Aww, we got a smart one."

Two young guys who just got on the job, right? This guy has been on the job all his life, right, so he said, "You punks, call your sergeant, I'm a police officer.

"We don't give a damn about your being a police officer, you better get out of that car and open the trunk and the rest of it before we kick your ass."

He said, "Call your sergeant."

And they said, "You ain't in charge here, we are."

And so, he then pulls out his sergeant's badge, and they said, "I don't care what you got on here, it can say Mickey Mouse, we run this. Get out of your car, raise your trunk and open your glove compartment."

He said, "I ain't doing none of that, you'd better call a supervisor."

They said, "We ain't calling nobody, we'll call the wagon. We'll drag you out of the car, now, and you're either gonna open it up or we're gonna open it up."

Well, so he got out, and he opens up his stuff and all of that and they search through all his stuff, search him and all of that, and then they go back to their car and called a sergeant or somebody because he's a sergeant and they can't deal with that anyway, I mean the rules say that. So they go ahead on and call, and the white sergeant comes, and they and the white sergeant get together and say, "Well, let me talk to you a minute, Sarge." And he said, "Well, I'll talk to you in a minute. You just go sit in your car."

The black officer says, "Yeah, well I'm a sergeant." And the other officer says, "Yeah, I know you are."

Now this guy has never been militant, he never did nothing, he worked in headquarters, so you know he wasn't doing anything. So the white guy said to issue him a summons, and they took him into the station and they made a complaint against him for being abusive to them. Wrote him up, suspended him for thirty days, and that just crushed him, because he just felt he had gone along so long, had done everything, bowed and scraped. He just didn't have to take that, he felt. And it was that way for everybody.

I'm telling you, we had some black officers who became commanders. One of their mothers got abused, and there was nothing that he could do, because he was afraid that if he said something or did anything they'd snatch his little commander's badge away from him, so he would just take the abuse. I could go on and on telling some of the horrible stories about the different things that they've done to black officers and their families in the '60's that were worse then than they are now.

So we said, "All that's going to stop. We're going to treat these white officers like they treat us."

Well, it was difficult, because if you grabbed a white officer, by the time you got into the station you were the criminal. I mean it was just that they didn't want to hear that. So we knew then that we had to file a discimination suit to get more Blacks into the department, because that was the only way we were going to offset the past. Black cats were too afraid, their number was small, too small, and nobody gave us any chance of ever really changing.

We just hung in there and filed the lawsuit and it went through. The first judge that got our lawsuit was a black judge, James B. Parsons. He is now a chief judge of the Federal Court in Chicago. He would not hear the case. He said he didn't want to hear the case because he didn't know if he could be impartial.

His son had gotten beaten up by the police. They beat his son and his son called us, but his son never followed through. I think his son got a $100,000 out-of-court settlement from the police department about the same time that Parsons dropped our case.

Then it was given to a white judge who was Jewish, Abraham Lincoln Marowitz. He didn't want the case either. It then went to a Republican judge and he didn't want it. Finally it went to the guy who is the one who actually heard the case, Prentice Marshall, who hadn't even been a judge when the case started. And he heard the case and—it's all history: we won.

But the case is not actually over yet. It's been going on now since 1970, and parts of it are still pending in court. So it's still a battle.

If we had known it was going to take this long, I'm sure most of us would have done something else. But I am glad that we did do it, because the case has sufficiently changed law enforcement hiring practices nationwide, which was one benefit we never expected this case to have. Because (former Mayor Richard J.) Daley was so hard-nosed, he appealed this case to the U.S. Supreme Court. By doing that, we won and it now applies to everywhere. See, if we win a verdict here and it doesn't appeal, it only applies to Chicago; but if it goes to the Supreme Court, then it applies to the whole nation. By taking our case to the Supreme Court, Daley did us a favor and did black people all over the United States a favor. Because people are using our case now to force police departments to integrate. So the case in the end turned out to be something that was very helpful to Blacks, because it increased the number of Blacks all around, changed all the practices, changed a lot of stuff that would have never have been changed in 100 years, including Whites' attitude about police brutality against Blacks, which has changed.

Brutality, first of all, still takes place. There are no ifs, ands or buts about that. There is still a bunch of foolish, ridiculous, sadistic white police and just a few Blacks now, who still engage in that kind of treatment. But for the most part it's not as wholesale as it used to be, when they just ran roughshod over you. Now they have to worry a little bit about who they're grabbing, and who they're pushing around. They still do it, but not nearly as much as they used to. You gotta stay on them, otherwise there is still no change in that area. Also, the union now is playing a role that the public is not aware of. See, the union is trying to turn the clock back on Blacks. They're put together a contract which is something out of Mississippi, out of the Dark Ages. All of the gains that we've made over the years will be reversed if this is allowed to go through. Now, of course, our lawyers are studying the contract. What it does, it institutionalizes white folks being in power forever. It provides that seniority becomes the basis for all promotions. Whites have been on longer than the Blacks, so they get the promotions. It provides subjective evaluations, which will allow a White who doesn't have much service to still beat a Black out because somebody rates him higher than you. They've got a lot of tricks. (In 1981, the City of Chicago agreed to grant policemen a contract recognizing the Confederation of Police as bargaining agent.)

When we started off, 60 per cent of the composite exam score was written, a pencil and paper test. The other 40 per cent was subjective. Now 40 per cent is written—that's after we've won the lawsuit--and 60 per cent of the test is subjective, which means that they can still pick and choose who they want. Sixty per cent of your score, there's nothing written. It's just what they say.

Renault, let me ask another question that might be a little hard. In many instances even young black officers who didn't have a chance before are moving on up the line now, yet they don't seem to want to see you get recognition in the Afro-American Police League. Why?

We have social leaders in town who have helped get Blacks into certain white companies. Blacks get promoted, and nobody wants to give them credit for helping. There are Blacks who picket, march and demand black products be put on people's shelves. And after the black products get put on the shelves, the same black guy whose product is on there is now a millionaire and doesn't want to contribute any money for the people who march. I think there's something about black people that they have not yet come out from under an inferiority complex which makes them feel that if they give credit to their own for something significant, then Whites will look down on them. So when a white officer says to them, "You don't want to be made sergeant because you're on this quota thing, now that wouldn't be fair, would it?" there have been young black officers who say, "That's right. If I can't get to be a sergeant fair and square, I don't want to be one, I don't want to be one just because of this court ruling."

Can you believe that? Yeah, there are some fools out there like that. And here we have proven that the exam processes are biased for Whites. Not that everybody didn't know that, but we proved it in a court of law with a white judge. During the course of that trial, I had a black guy come up to me and tell me that he had had a chance to be made a sergeant if we would just drop our thing. Why couldn't we sue later? he said. As a result of that lawsuit we got a couple of hundred guys made sergeant, but he didn't care about that. All he wanted was for him to be a sergeant. I think that it boils down to this: we do not yet have faith and confidence in our own.

You're a college man with bachelor's and master's degrees, and probably would have gone on to be a commander or whatever in the police department. Can you describe the price?

The worst part of it was from 1967 to 1973. I was suspended more times in that period than any other policeman in the history of the department. That's the first thing, more than 100 times. One of the suspensions alone lasted a year. All of that, they have to give me all of that money back. I haven't gotten it yet, but they have to give it to me at some point as a result of winning the suit.

I had every kind of assignment from working in an office to "guarding" an alley behind police headquarters, to working in a parking lot between two posts. Under normal circumstances, some guys would have given right arms because they were do-nothing jobs. Sitting in an alley—nobody cares; some love to sit in an alley. But they put me in the alley to ridicule me. They put me in the alley with nothing to do but stand in the alley so that they could laugh.

They said, "Well, we'll fix you." And it backfired on them, mainly because people were going along with all other kinds of things. But when they heard they had put me in an alley, they said, "Now, this is ridiculous. This is stupid."

In order to prove that they weren't discriminating against me by putting me in the alley, "my" alley behind police headquarters was made a street. They named it a street, and today if you go to 11th and State Street, between 11th Street and Roosevelt Road, that alley with no way to go out is a street. Holder Court, it's called. And there's an actual street sign up there that says it.

Now, see, the press and everybody came around. There's garbage cans, loose garbage, rats running around, you know it's an alley—wine bottles and everything else out there. And there I am standing in the alley. This is where all the police bosses park their cars and stuff. And as I'm walking up and down, I got the bright idea, the day they made it a street. They said to the press, "We got him on a street like any other police officer; it ain't no alley. It's a street, a city street," that's what my commander said.

So I said, "Well, good, if it's a city street," and the press said, "If you're on a city street, what's your feelings now?"

I said, "No problem. If this is a city street, I'm glad to know that. Look at all these illegally parked cars." So I went inside the station and I said, "Give me six ticket books."

They said, "What?"

I said, "Yeah, I want six ticket books."

They said, "Wait a minute." So they went into the commander's office and said, "This guy wants six ticket books, and we don't know what this is all about."

So the commander came out and said, "What do you want ticket books for?"

I said because I want ticket books.

So he walked away. He just looked at me and walked away.

So, I stood there for awhile, stood there and stood there and stood there. Finally they got busy and tried to forget about me. So the ticket books are stacked up nearby, so I took two or three of them and I filled out the officers' copy and tore them off and left them on the desk. But nobody's paying any attention. So I went out in the alley, and I started writing tickets on the bosses' cars. I mean the superintendent's car is out there, everybody's car is out there. I started writing tickets. I put down the address. I didn't get but about a couple of dozen tickets written before somebody realized what was going on, and they ran out there, grabbed me and took me inside. They said, "Look, this is ridiculous, what are you doing?"

I said, "I'm writing tickets—this is a street—this is my job."

They said, "Nobody told you to write tickets."

"Yeah," I said, "but I'm a good police officer and I saw a crime and I took action."

So they said, "OK, we'll fix you."

So they had me sit around for awhile while they tried to figure out what to do. They finally took me to the mouth of the parking lot, which is about ten feet between where the cars drive in and park, and this is the alley here, and this is the police parking lot (next to the station) right?

So I said "Well, I can't walk back and forth across these two posts."

And they said, "You can work it out."

And they said, "By the way, right upstairs there's the IAD office so they can watch you and we're gonna have a sergeant back here watching you."

I said very good and I went and got in my car which was a station wagon, and I parked it in the alley—I opened up my car door, my back wagon door, and sat there and got a newpaper to read. And these places where police officers turn to go in the lot were right here. So I had my car right there and they would turn and go in, and I was sitting with my legs crossed drinking some coffee, reading a paper. So the police superintendent came in one morning, and he looked at me, and I waved and then a series of all of the brass came. You know, it was a joke I was sitting there. I turned my back on them and got some coffee, and a newspaper. And I sat down and my sergeant came running out.

"What are you doing sitting out here with coffee, sitting, you're supposed to be walking your posts."

I said, "What posts? You're not going to ask me to get killed, are you? Everybody in that building is drinking coffee right now and reading a newspaper, and if you're going to get me, you better get them. So what are you hollering at me for?"

So he said, "Well, come on."

So they took me inside to the police brass, and they said, "Well, what are we going to do with him now?"

So, by this time, they said, "Well, look, you'll stay there anyway."

I said, "Well, I'm going to sit in my car. You haven't got anything for me to do. It's not a police assignment. I'm not guarding anything, watching anything, securing anything. So, I'm going to sit in my car."

And he threatened to write me up. I said go ahead and, so, the case got started in court. We started with preliminary stuff, and they asked police officials if they had ever spied on the Patrolmen's League or any of its members or Renault Robinson, or tapped their phones.

They said, "Oh, no, we wouldn't do a thing like that."

But a friend of mine worked in the intelligence division, and he said, "Renault, I'm telling you they got a file that (he holds his hands about a foot apart)—big—they got a whole crew of guys who don't do anything but spy on you all."

He said one day they sent him into a room to get something, and he saw a whole bank of files on us. So he took a report which he sent to me, which we took to the judges as an intelligence report, a current one, and documented that they had been watching us do this and do that.

Then my attorney said to the judge "Judge, are they swearing that they have no documents, no surveillance, nobody working? They swore they had nothing."

And we showed this report to the judge and the report showed that the Chicago Police Department Intelligence Division had a code for a special file. The judge hit the ceiling, and then said, "I want all the files you have brought into the court this afternoon."

Well, I didn't want to tell the judge that they had to get a truck to move all those files.

He said, "It's in your files, get it today."

My lawyer said, "Well, look, let us go over there right now, judge, and we can get the stuff and bring it right back over here. I'm sure we can just walk to the file and get it."

So the lawyer for the city was unaware what was going on and he said, "Well I have no objection. I thought they didn't have anything. But they found something and they had numbers all over it; maybe there's more."

He seemed embarrassed, because the city had told him that they had burned all the stuff, but they don't burn all that stuff—they always keep it. They got stuff right now they aren't supposed to have. So we went over there and went up to the intelligence division. And I knew where all the stuff was when we got inside. The commander was at lunch, the superintendent was at lunch, all of the brass was at lunch. At lunchtime, nobody's running the ship, you know? We didn't know, we just got there at that time, and there's a sergeant sitting at the desk. And here we are with lawyers and all that, so he don't know, so he asked us what we wanted. We wanted to get a couple of files, but he didn't know anything, so we got in there. When I started going through the files, not only did they have files on me, they had files on Rev. Jesse Jackson (of Operation PUSH). They had files on newspapers like the *Chicago Daily Defender.*

That's when the big spy thing came about. When I saw all that stuff, I wrote down all the numbers of everybody else's file and that's how they found out that they had a spy in Jesse's group, and a spy in this and that group—it came out of me going up there with my lawyer and seeing all the files.

So we were in there for about an hour, just copying stuff, you know, numbers. We could see it was too massive to try and take one or two files at a time, because the files on me alone were massive. So we wrote down all the reference numbers so nobody could say they didn't exist. All of a sudden lunch was over and almost everybody got back to the building. And when they found out that we had been in that building, they could have died because we were up in the section that nobody was supposed to be in. I don't know what they did to that sergeant on duty. But in any event, we had let the cat out of the bag then, but by the time we finally did manage to subpoena the documents we had requested, they still threw away a lot of stuff.

It has been a very, very horrible situation over the years. Let me say this: I wouldn't do it again if I had the same choice to make today as I made twelve years ago. I wouldn't do it. I just wouldn't do it, because now I know what I would be facing. When I did it then, it was not as though it was a crusade.

All I was trying to do was gather up a group of guys and see if we could make the police department change a few things. They just treated us like we didn't exist and they made it worse—instead of killing the fly with a fly-swatter, they'd get a fifty-pound cannon and shoot at you. And you didn't have any choice but to fight back. They were so overwhelming that I had to get overwhelming odds to help me fight. We got a law firm that spent over a million dollars defending us, and when the case was over and they won, the judge awarded them legal fees and they turned them down.

The firm was Kirkland and Ellis, one of the major law firms in Chicago, in the United States. So they could afford it. But, in addition to that, this firm must have wanted to prove a point. They took a lot of abuse from a lot of people who'd say, "What are you doing protecting those niggers?" Now, this was a very prestigious law firm and they didn't have no niggers working there at the time. None. And it's a big firm. They've got five floors in the Standard Oil building, so it's not a small firm. But they took the case on, and they said they were going to do it as a public service, that what we were after was something that would benefit black people nationwide and that to them that was a significant enough reason. They wrote a nice letter to the judge and refused the fees—and that was something.

But, in any event, I say all that to say I had help from a lot of people along the line who have made the fight a little more tolerable.

An example: Without Father George Clements there wouldn't have been a League. He was more than just a helper. I wouldn't put him, pastor of Holy Angels Parish in Chicago's South Side, in the category of the law firm or anything like that, because he was more like blood. Without him we'd have died. He was really very instrumental in keeping the League alive. I mean, when people wouldn't help us at all, wouldn't give us any money, wouldn't support us, wouldn't help pay our rent, he would do it. When I wanted to give up, and I must have wanted to give up at least a thousand times, he would encourage me not to. So I think there is no way to measure his impact, except to say that without him I'm sure that this would have ended a long time ago. We've had a lot of others who have helped in various and very significant ways. But all in all, I would absolutely not do it again.

Okay. We're going to look at the year 2000, roughly twenty years from now. At that point you'll be approaching the year of your 60th birthday. What would you think the Chicago Police Department's future?

Well, first of all, we'll probably have a police department that will be 85 per cent Blacks in the officers' ranks and everywhere else. That's because of the population trend which is shifting incredibly in the City of Chicago. You see, there's a political thing there too. There's no political stability in Chicago right now, and so that works to Blacks' advantage. They'll be topsy-turviness in the election situation for a few years or a few elections, and that's going to work to the advantage of Blacks.

As long as the white establishment doesn't get a stranglehold on us the fact that Whites move back won't mean anything, because they'll still be patrolled by Blacks. The city's workforce will be largely black. That doesn't mean that the downtown department stores or the insurance companies or banks are going to turn black, although more than lower level personnel will be Blacks, just because they're here. But most civil servants will be Blacks. I don't say that the same things would hold true for the fire department until we have Blacks at the top.

But I would say in 20 years you would see a police department that will largely reflect the population—of the city, not the people who work here and go home, but the people who live here. There is a recycling in this city and others; there are more Whites coming back into the city, but that is not going to overwhelm the situation that we have. Whenever a school system is 70 per cent minority, that tells the story right there.

Reggie Theus

Reggie Theus, entering his fourth season with the Chicago Bulls basketball team, was drafted by the Bulls after his junior year at the University of Nevada, Las Vegas, thus passing up his final year of eligibility to go into the National Basketball Associations's (NBA) hardship draft. In 1980, Theus made the NBA All-Star team for the first time in his career as starting guard. The 6'7" athelete grew up in Los Angeles and still makes his home there.

"It used to be an old stigma that when a black athlete gets a contract, he goes and buys a Cadillac car. It's a Mercedes now. Because when the kid was growing up his father drove around in a 1938 Buick or whatever."

Reggie Theus

I grew up in Englewood, California, near Los Angeles. Fortunately I was so involved with athletics that I didn't have a chance to get involved with gangs like other teenagers. I was involved in four baseball teams in one summer, and I enjoyed myself.

I was into sports and girls. Sports, girls and drugs don't mix. If you keep yourself occupied you develop different types of morals. I haven't developed a taste for alcohol. I have been around drugs all my life, but I really never had the desire to deal with it.

I talked to some people some time ago about drugs. I think it's blown out of proportion, because basketball is primarily black. Every time you hear something blown out of proportion about sports, it's always basketball. I don't understand that, and I hope it is not a race thing, because basketball is 75 per cent black. But half the people in certain income brackets or social backgrounds deal in drugs. People that you wouldn't **believe** deal in drugs.

It's an outlet. Some guys I heard do it to relieve tension, because of the constant go go, and to relax. They have the money to spend on it, and it's fun. While I was in California recently at a disco, some people were on the floor dancing and blowing coke. When athletes do it, I think it destroys the children's image of athletes. I had a kid ask me for some drugs. It bothered me, and I sat him down and talked to him. He was 12 years old, and he asked me did I have some blow? That's cocaine. For a kid to come up to me and assume I had it because I was an athlete—this is an image we must destroy.

I have had times in my life when if I was weak-minded and not properly motivated, I could have used drugs. My father passed when I was going into my senior year in high school. A couple of years ago things weren't going well during the season, and we were losing constantly, and people were on your back. People use drugs to escape. But when you come down, the problem is still there, and it's grown bigger while you were asleep.

As a young man, how do you deal with the money, the opportunity to make a half million dollars a year?

There are tremendous problems. Basically, after the first two years, I am able to sit back and see where my mistakes were made. A lot of guys don't do this until it's too late. The money that you make—if you don't do something with it early in your career, you have a chance of coming away broke. That's what happened to a lot of athletes ten years ago. I think half the problem lies where you can't trust anyone. You give a person power of attorney, and that gives them certain opportunities, and they end up taking your money. They take it because we athletes are basically kids. I don't think you have really grown up until you reach 30 years of age. You are as old as your experience.

I am 23 years old, and I have grown up in the last two years. I am now taking a strong look at everything. I remember when I came into the league I decided to turn everything over to someone and let them deal with it. That was a mistake. When a kid comes out of college, they have all these ideas about success. The drive to get out of the ghetto. Growing up basically poor or in the lower middle class and not being exposed to certain types of things, you have a lot of people with lots of money and no sense. All of a sudden they've got 300, 400, 500 or 600 thousand dollars a year.

I was in Acapulco, Mexico with a friend, and I told her to look around. She said, "I don't see anything but some people." Then I told her to look again. We didn't see anybody but Mexicans and white kids.

There is more to life than the next country or moving out of a black neighborhood into a white neighborhood. It used to be an old stigma that when a black athelete gets a contract, he goes and buys a Cadillac car. It's a Mercedes now. Because when the kid was growing up his father drove around in a 1938 Buick or whatever.

My father was a janitor. He never had a decent car. He put all his equipment in the car. When you get a chance to buy something you go buy a very big expensive car. If you are into drugs, you buy your drugs and new clothes, and that is a large step from where you were, and a large step from where you should be.

It is very difficult to deal with the money at first. I think of myself as a stepping stone for somebody else. I believe that when someone from a family does well, he in turn should give support to his family to make them grow up to be doctors, lawyers and somebody that has a certain type of value attitude.

Without money you limit yourself to certain types of things. Get rich first, and work on being happy afterward. That's how I feel. I am the only one in my family that's making a certain amount of money. My family is not an extremely educated family. I may be the first in my immediate family to get a degree. I left school a year early. I am going back to get a degree. I am the youngest of seven. A couple of them are half brothers and sisters.

My father was 59 years old when he died. My father practically worked himself to death. He had a heart attack. I learned a lesson, because I could have helped him more. This was a tremendous price to pay. The lesson is kids don't appreciate their parents. I get on my nephew about appreciating his mother, grandmother and father more. They take them for granted. I have been in situations where friends of mine have argued or fought with their parents, and it really bothered me, because I know how that person is going to feel when the parents are no longer around. It is going to happen—just a matter of time.

I watched my mother make it on less than $20,000 per year, and I've got problems making over $100,000 per year. She fed five or six kids. Kids should step back and take a look, see what life is all about, and love your parents while you can.

Athletes make a tremendous amount of money, but it takes them so long to develop into something with the money, in the dozen or so years they are playing. It takes them a long time to learn what to do with it, and by the time they learn what really to do with it, half of it has gone. They are half gone, too, because of the grind and wear on your body. Your knees are aching, and you have arthritis in you back.

I asked a rich black man not long ago for advice. I told him that I make a certain amount of money, I am a social service major, and trying desperately to find out how to turn this money into something else.

He said, "First you get somebody smart."

I thought I was talking to somebody smart! Why can't a guy—if he is thinking about your black brother and thinking of the situation of Black—why can't he say, "This is the way I did it?" Most of the lawyers, agents and accountants for black atheletes are white businessmen. I think the black businessmen should come together and reach out and help the black athlete. Doctors, lawyers and athletes are the only ones making big dollars, and black businessmen should give them a chance to invest.

Athletes and entertainers are set aside from color barriers. There is no color barrier in music. People like to be entertained. A lot of time I am accepted because I am an athlete.

I have seen changes in people. I was at some friends' house who were very wealthy. I was coming out of the house by some doors that were very beautiful; they were Gucci doors. I told the man, "I love your doors." He said. "Would you like to wash them?" I said no I would like to buy them. Had he known I was a ball player and made a certain amount of money, he wouldn't have said that. His remark was certainly racist.

Another form of racisim can be seen in T.V. commericals. For example, Ken Brett from the Kansas City Royals is on big billboards all over Chicago for 7-Up. I don't see why a white athlete should be doing this when a Chicago black athlete could sell the product just as well. Percentage wise more Blacks drink 7-Up than Whites.

Thomas N. Todd

Thomas N. Todd, 42, is a civil rights activist and attorney now in private practice in Chicago. He originally came from Alabama but has lived in Chicago since 1965. Todd received his law degree from Southern Law School in Baton Rouge, Louisiana. As an assistant U.S. attorney in the 1960s, he handled a number of major civil rights cases. He went on to become the first black law professor at Northwestern University in 113 years. In 1970, Todd became attorney for Operation Breadbasket and in 1971 was named deputy director. He went on to serve as vice president of Operation PUSH, working as second in command to the Rev. Jesse Jackson.

"I am a black lawyer. But no matter how much we have access to private clubs or a lot of other kinds of things, you can never, never forget the fact that you're walking in there as a black man. Because the crackers never see you as anything else but a black person. You know, that's the truth.

Thomas N. Todd

I came to Chicago in 1965 in the military when I was 23 years old. I was in the judge adjutant general corps at that time, one of fifteen black lawyers in the Army, and I was stationed in Fort Sheridan. It was my first time coming to Chicago and I guess what one of the interesting things was at that time, was that all of my friends told me Chicago had open housing. And I had to go to Fort Sheridan, thirty miles north of Chicago, and I stayed at Prairie Shores at 29th and King Drive a couple of nights and then I had to take that drive up to Fort Sheridan and I just couldn't do it. And so that was 1965, and I had just come from Alabama where I graduated law school at Southern Law School in Baton Rouge, Louisiana, in 1963. I had gone to Washington to work in the solicitors' staff of the Department of Labor in September of 1963 and then had gone in the military in 1964 and had completed training for judge adjutant general, but I had never been in Chicago.

I read about Chicago and all that, so when I got here in 1965, February of 1965, I started looking for an apartment. You know, I figured, hell, I can look anywhere I want, this is Chicago—since I didn't want to live in Lake Meadows or Prairie Shores. So I took the *Chicago Tribune,* to show you how naive I was, and I started looking at real estate ads and trying to get an apartment up north so I could get out to Fort Sheridan within a reasonable period of time. Someone told me about Carl Sandburg Village and so in May of 1965, I moved into Carl Sandburg Village on the Near North Side. I think at that time they had less than 1 per cent of the population who were Blacks, and so I lived on the Near North Side of Chicago since 1965. I left the military in 1966 and became an assistant United States Attorney.

It's really at that time that I count my time in Chicago, because while I was living there, I was commuting to Fort Sheridan every day, so I really was not a part of any community in Chicago. But in 1967, I went into the United States Attorney's office as an assistant attorney, the criminal division, remembering from my black law school at Southern that the U. S. Attorney's office had jurisdiction for certain civil rights statutes that were enacted during the Reconstruction Era, specifically, in 1866. So after about six months in the office—that was a period of a great deal of turmoil in Chicago—I began to push the office toward the enforcement of civil rights, particularly the police brutality problem in Chicago, which at that time was looming tremendously. The U.S. Attorney's office in Chicago had never indicted a Chicago policeman for a deprivation of civil rights. So, after the Democratic National Convention, you remember in 1968, we had several things happen while I was in that office. First, of course, Dr. Martin Luther King, Jr., was assassinated in April of 1968, and I became very involved with the office, in pushing it toward the black community.

My attitude has always been that wherever you are, whether it's in a government office or whether you are a law professor, you should use the facilities you have to make them work for the black community. I don't care where you are and if you're a Black, that's a part of the responsibility. I just can't be a lawyer, I've also got to use my legal skills and everything to work for black people.

So, after Dr. King's assassination, the whole community was radicalized. And, lest we forget, at the Democratic Convention here, if you remember, long-haired, white students were whipped by Chicago policemen. I used that incident where the concern of White America was directed toward policemen in Chicago beating white children. Remember Mayor Daley's shoot to kill arsonists, aim to maim looters order after the assassination of Dr. King? It didn't create a lot of furor in the white community, but in 1968, with these policemen beating white kids the way they've always beaten black people in Chicago, White America became concerned. Well, Ramsey Clark sent a task force out here to investigate the deprivation of civil rights of the white students. I said to them, "Chicago has a history of black people being beaten by police. How the hell can you bring the first indictments against policemen for beating white kids?" So I used that incident to force the federal government to indict the first Chicago policemen for deprivation of civil rights in 1968.

Joseph Fine was the first policeman indicted for the deprivation of civil rights in the history of Chicago. Eldridge Gaston, a black man, had stopped in front of Queen of the Sea restaurant and these two policemen got out, and within a few minutes he was lying on the pavement, blood trickling from his nose. They threw him into the squad room, and then took him to the drunk tank, where they said he was drunk. But some policemen noticed that he was trickling blood and they took him to Jackson Park Hospital. But they couldn't half help him, and then they took him to Cook County Hospital and he died. So, in effect, the policeman took his life. But before that there had been no indictment. So we got the indictment against the policeman, Joseph Fine, and once he was indicted, of course, he was elected vice-president of the Confederation of Police—that was the white response to it. I got the indictment, I did the investigation, but because it was the first case and because I was a Black, we allowed the white U.S. Attorney, Thomas Foran, and the white assistant, Bob Weber, to try him and it was tried before an all-white jury right here in Illinois in 1969 in federal court in the northern district of Illinois. An all-white jury acquitted the policeman in forty-five minutes. But we had broken the ice. We had gotten the first indictment and we had gotten the government to move for the first time in Chicago on a statute that had been enacted in 1866.

I never handled a civil rights case that dealt with white peoples' civil rights. My attitude was that we had to establish some protection in the black community. My next case was in the early '70's, when the Tilden High School erupted in racial violence. Black kids were being stoned and beaten along the Rock Island railroad track that separates the black and white community in that Southwest Side area. And this young woman, a 16-year-old black high school kid, Roxanne Northerly, was beaten unmercifully by a policeman. A photographer caught the policeman in the act and published the newpaper pictures. So I took the newspaper pictures, conducted the investigation and presented it to the grand jury and got the indictment of the policeman, J. J. Gorman. I tried the case and the jury was hung eleven to one for conviction. In 1970, there had been no convictions of policemen at all. So that was my entrance into the civil rights movements from a legal standpoint. In Chicago, I went on to deal with some other landmark cases involving real estate. The West Suburban Board of Real Estate case, against which the first civil rights lawsuit was brought by the federal government in the 1968 Housing Act, involved a multiple listing. The suit charged the West Suburban Real Estate Board with racial steering, and we sued them and broke it up. I used the U.S. Attorney's office, the law, as a vehicle to make an entrance into the black community.

As a matter of fact, in 1967, when I was appointed to the U.S. Attorney's office, nobody knew Tom Todd in Chicago. Nobody—none of the established black political leaders or anybody else, because I was sponsored by a white politician, George Dunne, of the 42nd Ward, and put into the U.S. Attorney's office in preparation for some future political run in the 42nd Ward. You know they pick Blacks, they hand-picked them, rewarded them and then they brought them in to use them. That was the whole scheme with me. Of course, George Dunne didn't know me either. (Laughs.)

It was an unusual kind of phenomenon. It was from the U. S. Attorney's office that I met Rev. Jesse Jackson, now of Operation PUSH, during the construction workers' demonstration—white construction workers in 1969. When they took over the hearing from Art Fletcher, then the Under Secretary of Labor and I was an assistant U. S. Attorney, I was put in charge of running the hearings for Art Fletcher and Jesse was one of the people who testified.

You know, after a lot of publicity and trying to deal with faculty segregation in Chicago, the West Suburban Board of Realtors and policemen, occasionally I would have black people who would come to the U. S. Attorney's office and say, "We just want to see this man. Who is he?"

There was this little lady who had on her Sunday best, who came up with a hat on and the receptionist said, "Mr. Todd, you have someone to see you."

I didn't know who it was but I went out and she said, "God bless you, I just want to shake your hand," and she went on about her business.

But the whole attitude was, the U. S. Attorney's office belongs to everybody, it's not just the Irish mafia and everybody else, so I moved that office into the community.

So when Fred Hampton and Mark Clark were killed in December, 1969, the Black Panthers, because of the reputation I had developed, selected me as a prosecutor that they could trust—they said if the federal government was prepared to appoint me as the chief prosecutor, the Panthers would cooperate.

So as an assistant U. S. Attorney, the night the autopsy was performed on Fred Hampton, I was in a meeting with the Panthers and with the Panthers' lawyers, as the only government official who was trusted in that area.

Then the Federal Government decided that they did not want to use me, and they imported two black U. S. assistant attorneys and put them on the team, and consequently they did not, in their investigation, get the cooperation of the Panthers. So those are the kinds of moves that helped me to establish a community base.

The Contract Buyers League was another case I was a part of. By using that, I developed a community base and developed a reputation as an individual who cared about what was going on and who was willing to use whatever power or talents that were available to try to make a difference.

When I was at Southern Law School in 1960 in Louisiana, where they had the sit-in demonstrations and freedom rides, I was in the middle of turmoil. But I was in law school trying to get a law degree. I had to make some tough decisions early in life. It wasn't easy, because my mother died in 1958 and I graduated from college in 1959, didn't have a job and went back to law school. It was my last chance. I was always considered articulate and crazy to some extent. I'd tell white people to kiss my ass—that's what takes a good leader—but you know I went back to law school when Southern got involved in the demonstrations in 1960. The demonstrating leaders came to me and asked me to lead them, to participate in their leadership. I had to make a decision—I was 20 years old—whether or not I would lead the demonstration or participate in leadership of the demonstration to try to make a difference immediately, or whether I would stay in law school three years (and I had just started law school) and try to make a difference over the long haul. It took me two weeks of agony. While I was in law school, in the comfortable confines of a law school, every afternoon students would come back, tear gas reeking on the campus and young women with their clothes torn by dogs, and the campus would literally reverberate with strains of "We Shall Overcome."

I wept, I wept, because I knew that I wanted to be in that fight. But I knew if I got in that fight then, right there I would never finish law school. I knew that I might totally waste my life, so I made the hard decision not to join the demonstration, but to stay in law school. In making that decision I contracted with myself. I said to myself that when I finish law school and have a license and am in a position to help or make a difference that somewhere, somehow no matter what I'm doing for the rest of my life, I will have some involvement trying to alleviate some of these pains.

And I said all that, it's a long story to say that. But guys who are going into the board rooms now, many of them never saw a board room before except on the side of a house. They are dealing now not with

282/ *Thomas N. Todd*

that kind of commitment. They go in, and then they become a part of the whole system which itself, the system itself, is oppressive and racist. And they begin to play the game in accordance to the rules made by the system. Well, you don't confront the system and then go confront the corporation about what they're doing—if it's designed to oppress women, to oppress black folks, minorities and oppress small people. So the Vernon Jordans—Vernon I guess earns more money on corporate boards than he does from the Urban League—I see it as a conflict, but he doesn't. But it makes a Vernon have to defend Xerox's presence in South Africa, which to me is indefensible. You cannot defend it. So I think what has happened to us in terms of this new access to the trappings of power, still not real power—thirty million black folks in the country spending $125 billion dollars a year, but we don't have any power.

As a matter of fact, one of the most devastating facts about it is that we spend $125 billion dollars a year and every penny will eventually end up in some white person's pocket. We can't even provide the basic fundamentals for our family. I can't even provide milk for my little girl without going to some white person. We're consumers and we consume. We spend every penny that we have. So that is what has made a difference for us. Because many of the people who go in, go in and become a part of it. My attitude is, the only way we've ever gained any modicum of movement toward any semblance of equality in this country, whether we were confronting in the courtroom like Earl Dickerson and Thurgood Marshall and Constance Baker Motley and Charlie Houston, or whether we were confronting in the streets like Martin Luther King Jr. and that sort of thing. Wherever we have gotten a modicum of gain in this country, it has been through confrontation. There's a lawful confrontation in the streets or legal confrontation in the courtrooms, and now black folks have moved from the streets to the suites. And we now think that we can have conferences to freedom, we now think that we can have workshops to freedom.

We're the only people in the '70's and in the '80's who left the streets. White people never left the streets, whether it was Three-mile Island, whether it was ERA, whether it was the protest against the draft, whether it was any of that, the people who were marching and demonstrating in the latter part of the '70's and beginning in the '80's were white people. Now, there are a few marches around the Voters Rights Act, but they're very small but the big marches are only managed by white people. So that white people seeing what marching and demonstrating and confrontation did for Blacks in the '50's and in the '60's in the streets have done the same thing with protests as they did with music, as they did with literature, as they did with everything else black folks had. They have taken it, and we have abandoned it. I think that's one of the problems that we're having now.

I guess I had a lot of firsts in Chicago, because Chicago's way behind. For instance, I went into Northwestern University as the first black law professor in 113 years. Well, it was so incredible. I think I was the only black law professor in the city, because Bob Ming was no longer teaching at the University of Chicago. It's incredible that with thirty million Blacks at that time, with all the black people, there there were no black people teaching law. Well, anyway, I went into Northwestern as the first black law professor, and then I got the opportunity to join Rev. Jesse

Jackson to round off the experience. In other words I had had the official experience in the U.S. government. I had become a professor where I was teaching law, I was now a living part of the civil rights movement because now I was breaking barriers.

When Operation Breadbasket was in its heyday in the late part of '68 and '69, I met Jesse, and in 1970 Jesse asked me to work with him. I became his lawyer with Bob Tucker, and we represented him in several cases including one lawsuit in 1971 which helped to open up the political process. But then in September of 1971 I joined Breadbasket physically, as a deputy director and later as the President of the Southern Christian Leadership Conference, Chicago Chapter. So I am now beginning to get front-line experience so that I am now catching up to myself with the direct experience which I missed in Louisiana. I have now gotten a law degree, some credentials, and now I'm going back to get the direct experience. I went in as the executive vice-president of Operation PUSH, working directly with Jesse, and named Operation PUSH in fact. Some people may never forgive me for it, but that's all right. People United to Save Humanity is the acronym PUSH. It came directly from me, walking down Dearborn on a rainy, rainy afternoon. I walk in the early mornings sometimes, and these ideas hit you and you don't know where they come from. People United To Save Humanity is mine.

I did it for several reasons. I kept my professorship at Northwestern, but I did it for another reason. All called experience.

First of all, if I asked you right now who is the deputy director of the Urban League and who Vernon's number two man is, you couldn't tell me his name. If I asked you who Joe Lowery's deputy man was, you couldn't tell me his name. The same thing is true of Ben Hooks. What I had found in our civil rights movements from Dr. Martin Luther King, Jr. on—because Abernathy was not a strong person, Martin was the strong personality—what I found was that we had a tendency to go along the lines of the black church. The strong figure at the top, and everything else kind of pales by comparison. The assistant pastor may get a chance to preach every three or four months, but it's that big symbol. I said that first of all I'm a very strong personality. I thought I had some talents. I was professor of law. I had a lot, in terms of credentials. But I chose to be a deputy. I chose to be a number two person because my attitude was we need to get away from the ego conflicts where the strong personalities—black—cannot work together, where you've got to have a strong number one personality and a strong number two personality, but the gap is so great it's like no person at all.

My attitude was that my ego was healthy enough, and I was healthy enough, to become the number two man at Operation PUSH. But I also knew that because of some God-given talents of which I had no control that I would be a powerful number two man, and that Jesse and I could harness all of this—and that there would be nothing that could stop us. I felt also with my professorship at Northwestern, again, my theory of wherever you are, whatever you do, you take the facilities, especially if they're white, and deliver them to the black community. I don't care where it is. I never wanted to be a law professor. I mean my attitude was, "How can I use the professorship to provide for my family, and to provide for the black community?" So I used the prestige of Northwestern, and they used me. Northwestern's conservative Whites would say "We got Tom Todd, he's with Jesse Jackson." And I used them, because

I delivered all the facilities I could in terms of brain power and everything else from Northwestern to the black community. It did something else, it provided the symbol of a civil rights person holding a professorship on a prestigious faculty from a prestigious university that attracted folks who would not have come otherwise. We attracted a whole council of economic advisors. Jesse had the ability to attract athletes, ministers, entertainers, business leaders and civil rights people, but I said we are leaving totally untapped the resources of the university. We have a lot of black minds. There were a lot of so-called middle class people who didn't want to be associated with PUSH because it was considered ragtag and not organized. But with a law professor there from Northwestern University, it was their cover. They wanted to come all the time. We brought in some folks to PUSH in 1971 and 1972 who never would have spoken to Jesse before.

So what we were doing, I thought, is that we had what I consider two very strong persons in the leadership. I ran the day-to-day operation. We used to talk in terms of the charismatic and the systematic. And the broadcast was mine, and I ran it—and built the organization. But that gave me the rounding off and experience that I needed to continue to keep a commitment I made to myself in 1960. As long as PUSH and as long as Northwestern were in a position to allow me to deliver to the black community, I stayed. And then when I got to the position where I thought neither one of them was delivering anymore, I left.

I did not go to Northwestern to stay twenty years. Northwestern said to me, "It's time for you to pursue tenure, and we want you to come out of the streets, leave the directives of the community and write about it, but don't participate in it. We want you to write law review articles about this shit that's going on." I said, "That's not why I came here. I came here as an activist to teach, not as a teaching activist." So when we got to that point, I told them I wasn't interested in pursuing a tenure trek. All I wanted was to make sure that when I left Northwestern my professional record was protected so that ten or fifteen years from now if I came back and decided to be a full professor, I could. That's the way we agreed to that.

When I got to the point that I felt PUSH's programs were no longer genuine, no longer providing what I thought they should or could have for the black community, I made a decision to leave. And then, of course, the more I grew, the more the potential for conflict developed between Jesse and me. It just so happened that at that time, with Watergate, there were a lot of constitutional issues, if you recall. I was teaching constitutional law on my broadcast. People were filing into that auditorium 2,000 or 3,000 every Saturday at Operation PUSH. And there were some problems that developed, so I made the decision there was no longer any reason to stay there. So I left.

I'll be quite honest with you, Dempsey, I had withdrawal symptoms. When you go through the five years and almost your every utterance is picked up by press, or you're sitting at home at two o'clock in the morning asleep and some reporter calls from New York and needs a story and needs a quote, your name is in the paper, your name is out there, you're on television, you're on radio, you're everywhere. When all of a sudden that leaves you, you really have withdrawal symptoms. People told me I was crazy to leave PUSH at the highest point of my popularity and exposure, and that I'd no longer have the association. And when

I left Northwestern, they said, "You can't do it by yourself, you need that institution." You know, I went through some periods of self-doubt and concern also about evaluating and what have you. But my attitude was, "I now have the experience. I have now rounded off my experience. I've been a lawyer, I've been a law professor, I've taught law, I've litigated, I've gone to the Supreme Court of the United States, I've been on the front lines, I've been in demonstrations, I've confronted crackers, and I have done it all now." Now if I can't, with all of that experience and a license to practice law and all that now, if I cannot survive out here as an individual, then Tom Todd is far less than what I thought he was.

I worked and worked and worked and the thing that sustained me in that area was speaking and the ability to move people. And people began to invite me as an individual, not as a person who was close to Jesse, and not as a law professor at Northwestern, but as an individual who had something to say. And so now I have freed up, in one sense, my thoughts because I was no longer selling a banquet, no longer selling this activity or that activity, I was no longer harnessed within the framework of somebody else's thoughts. I was ready now for the world to take Tom Todd as he is for whatever he is, good, bad or indifferent. It took me five years before I began to come back to the measure of stature that I had when I was at Operation PUSH, but it is back now. As a matter of fact, it has even grown as an individual not as an organization—people will now listen to my views because they think I am a thoughtful person. Because I'm not selling anything anymore. You can't buy me and that sort of thing. It's been a struggle financially—it still is—but I don't regret having gone to PUSH and I don't regret having left.

I have gone through a series of platforms. My major platform in this nation stems from my God-given oratory. I am invited to speak somewhere in this country almost every week in the year, whether I accept or not. I have just completed, for instance, five commencements. At Fayetteville State, in Fayetteville N.C., there were 5,000 people there. At Forest Brook High School in Houston, Texas, there were 8,000 people. And then I came back to Chicago and at Carver there were 1,500 people and at Percy Julian's commencement there were almost 4,000 people. My platform is the oratory status I still have. I have been fortunate to have been offered periodic platforms—the article in Dollars & Sense magazine, "From Dred Scott to Bakke and Beyond—The Evolution of a Circle," added another dimension I had never had before. I had had small pieces published and that kind of thing, but this was a major thing, and that helped to legitimatize and to generate its own platform, of course. Out of that grew the commercials for *Dollars & Sense* and then as you know a radio show that lasted a year and a month. It was cancelled because it was considered too black on WLS. But again, when the radio show could no longer be a forum to educate black people, and when they asked me to change that format, I wouldn't. I have never found that thing which will allow me to compromise the principles I believe in and make me break the contract I made with myself in 1960.

I don't consider myself a leader.

I have studied the movement in the past dozen years. The combination is the thing, my law practice keeps me going. I'm a licensed attorney, I'm a professional, that's where I want to earn my living. I want to keep that because that's what helps me become independent. I won't be wealthy, but at least that keeps me independent. I don't want to lead a civil rights organization. I want to offer my talent, I want to be involved, and I want people to listen and to believe in what I say. What I try to do is to become involved wherever they want me to become involved, but I can't conceive where they will ever become involved in an organization led by Tom Todd.

I think that's the trap that Jesse's in, as well as Vernon and other civil rights organizations that have become big business. They talk about a six million dollar operating budget for a year, and that's big business. I don't know what the total budget for the Urban League is, but it's big; you're talking about millions of dollars.

Now, if you're going to get millions of dollars to just open your doors, and you're in a depressed black economy—I mean this recession is deep—the money's got to come from some other sources. And I ain't never seen nobody who's willing to pay you for beating them upside the head. I mean the Urban League's operating budget comes from private foundations, from the federal government. It comes from corporations and it comes from small contributions from individuals that—and listen to this—a couple of years ago I think $225,000 and 60 per cent of that came from the Jewish community. Well, obviously, Vernon can't be free. So Vernon has to make some concessions.

But the money is coming in from the federal government now. The Reagan administration just released $825,000 to Jesse. You tell me what that means. I don't care how good a friend Dempsey Travis and Tom Todd happen to be, Dempsey ain't gonna be my friend too long if I'm gonna knock Travis Realty. And if I'm going to knock Travis Realty and I'm gonna cause you some problems, then you ain't gonna give me no money, or no business. I mean it just makes sense. So that if I want to get along with you, I may go to you and say, "Now Dempsey, I'm gonna have to say a little something and you know it's sincere." How can you take on the very people who are supporting you? You can't and that what bothers me.

Now, I don't see the ability in the community to finance major organizations. So as a result of it, I think what we've got to do is go back to the pre-King era. See, the two things that came out of the civil rights movement that we're still suffering from in the '70's and in the '80's, and I guess we'll continue to suffer from one of them, is the unfortunate side effect of the civil rights movement. We helped to create an atmosphere where our children developed an attitude that they were automatically entitled to everything that they got. I mean I know your life story, I know how you worked and how you put things together, and what you did, but our kids aren't gonna do that. The movement helped to create in them what I call a kind of "automatic entitlement syndrome." I called it "grantitis" on the college campuses, but even when the kids get a college degree or law degree they don't want to work—they think that they can just show up and that the circumstances are going to sweep them along to success. They think they don't have to work four times as hard as a white counterpart. We never had that kind of problem. And I think that one of the reasons we got into that is because we helped to create that kind of atmosphere.

The other kind of thing is too many leaders who declare leadership and then go looking for people.

The Montgomery boycott was the most successful single black movement in this country. It was more successful than Marcus Garvey's movement, although they all had their place, and more successful than mass revolt. But in the Montgomery boycott the lesson of history was that Rosa Parks refused to get up and let a white man sit down. She didn't have to apply for any grant. If she had to apply for a grant she would still be somewhere in jail. And then Mr. Nixon and the Montgomery Improvement Association organized around her, and then they went looking for a leader. And Dr. Martin Luther King Jr. was the last person they went to. Lerone Bennett says that the genius with Martin was that when they found him, he was willing, ready and able to take it. But the lesson in Montgomery is that people went looking for a leader, not the leader going to look for people. And now we have leaders popping up all over. That's why I reject the notion of being a leader.

I don't believe White America has ever changed. It's always remained constant, in this country. When we look at businesses we look in terms of progress or no progress in peaks and balances. If you're at the top of the peak, things are going well, if you're at the bottom you're losing. I have a little prayer that says, "Oh God, I will make a stand in my interpretation of law; I will make mistakes when I speak; and I will ask that you forgive me; but, Oh God, don't let me make mistakes when it comes to interpreting history." We have the need, I guess, to feel as if we're making progress, so we begin to articulate that we are making progress. But it's an illusion.

First, we have a tendency to allow people to judge the progress of an entire race of people by the illusion of progress by a few of its members. Between 1870 and 1901 we had twenty-two Blacks in the U. S. Congress. Two of them were Senators. They were both Republican and both from Mississippi. We have eighteen now, and one is a non-voting delegate. That means seventeen, and there are no U. S. Senators. When we elect another black Senator, and we will—Edward Brooke was the first black Senator since Reconstruction—when we elect another one, we'll hail it as progress, but we're really going around in a circle. We get, we lose, we regain what we lost, and we call it progress. That has been the history of Blacks in the country.

In the early history of the country, when Blacks were here, it was against law to teach a slave to read. Frederick Douglass talks about it in his book, *My Bondage and My Freedom,* and when his master found out that he was being taught to read, he said, "If you teach a nigger to read, the next thing you know he'll want to be free. Give him an inch and he'll want to take a mile." We're facing a situation now that existed in the 1840's.

Let me just add another fact: in 1825 when Wilberforce was founded, black schools were established basically with white missions. And that was to keep black students away from white students. Nobody ever thought that Wilberforce would last 125 years, or Southern at Baton Rouge would last 100 years. Those schools were given missions not to educate black minds, but to really to keep black students away from white students. But they, the white educators and black educators involved, saw the opportunity and took what they had and made a contribution in spite of White America.

So I say to kids now as they begin to come up for commencements, first of all education makes a difference for us as a people. I don't care,

I know what the figures are. I know that the unemployment rate for black college graduates is seventeen per cent and the unemployed rate for white high school drop-outs is eight per cent. I know that being a White in America is an advantage that's automatic from birth that Blacks don't have. But I say to them that education has always made the difference for us. Whether we can understand it or not depends on how much of a context we can put in there.

Lerone Bennett talks of education being a matter of life and death. My father can't read and write in Alabama today; he never could. He had to be able to read "white" and "colored," because if he went to the white waiting room or to the white washroom or drink at a white water fountain, his life could be taken. So even that fundamental education was a matter of life and death.

So I tell our kids that even right now, more than ever, education is our life and death. Education is the key to liberation and the passport to freedom. It doesn't mean that if you get the education it's going to be automatic, but you've got to get the education first. Then you've got to work. So I say to them—it's almost an old-fashioned kind of philosophy I guess—not to be confused by what's going on now. White people have never changed. You know people are saying, "Well, the country's moved to the right," well, the country's always been to the right. You know in 1619, when they dragged niggers here in chains, that wasn't no flaming liberalism. I mean white folks have always been. I describe America as being the same old house, same old paint, painted with the same old brush. I don't care what you do to this house, it's the same one. You can paint this paint on it or that paint, but when that shit comes down, America ends up being just where it is. The only difference is that they let Blacks, some Blacks—a handful of Blacks—out of the yard into the kitchen. You've never gone into the front room, the living room and what have you. So what has changed in America, what has caused the situation to look so bleak and to look so devastating, is that we have changed—not White America. The Ku Klux Klan has never changed, the White Citizens' Councils have never changed, the rednecks have never changed; we have changed. We have really sincerely bought the idea that America would be willing at any time in its life or in its existence to treat us equally. I don't believe that.

It is hard to be a Black in America. It is hard to say that I'm going to live to be seventy or live to be eighty years old and live and be black and I will never be able to be comfortable, to be off-guard or to be out from under pressure. That I can make fifty million dollars and the fact is that I am a nigger in America will continue to keep pressure on me— that's hard to face. It's hard to face, but it's real. I know there's a desire to cast it aside, to put it in the background to say color doesn't matter, to say you know, now that I have the trappings, I own a condominium on the Gold Coast or I'm a lawyer on LaSalle Street, that somehow this is going to make a difference. But it will not transform the fundamental fact that you're black in America, and that America is white.

How do your white nieghbors react to you and your family here on the Gold Coast?

They don't bother me and I don't bother them. When I first came in they wanted to be friends and all that. I'm very private. They're courteous, they're courteous to my children and to my wife. On this floor, we have two apartments. As a matter of fact there's only two people, two cats that live next door, and it's to our mutual benefit that we have a good relationship because we depend upon each other. That's it. There are about fifty families. So there's no big problem at all. We're the only black family here. I'll be the token, the symbol or whatever they want.

But even with all of this, whenever I walk out of this apartment, not only out but anywhere, whether it's here or whether it's on the airplane, they ask me if I'm Rosie Greer or like they did in the elevator the other day, ask me did I sing at some plaza. It's a hard reality to face, but as long as you are black in America, you got to carry an extra burden. The mistake is when we think that money or prestige or membership in some club somehow will relieve that burden; it just won't do it. And it's because of that fact that I'm beginning to understand now why segregation was so important to us and why slavery was so important to us. Because segregation never allowed us to even pretend for one moment that we weren't black. As a result of that, we took the burden and turned it into glory. We took the burden and used it as a motivating rather than as a depressing kind of element.

But I guess with some access to some of the other parts of the white world we become confused, because the natural tendency is to want to throw the yoke off. You can't throw it off. Now, what has happened with our kids, is that they have in many instances never had the yoke, so they're confused. We raised a generation of neurotics. Even when they get an education they become confused and they find out that even with a BA, MA or PHD., or JD, or an MBA, that none of those things mean the same things for you as a black person as it does for the white person. Because the systems are designed to protect the white community. What we must understand is that we must learn the system and understand it and make it work for us, but never overlook the fact that you are a black real estate dealer and I am a black lawyer. But no matter how much we have access to private clubs or a lot of other kinds of things, we can never, never forget the fact that we're walking in there as a black man. Because the crackers never see us as anything else but a black person. And that's the truth.

I never walked out of this apartment without credentials, I never walked out of here without identification, I've never walked out of here without being alert to the fact that I was black and that I am walking into a predominantly white neighborhood. That's true when I walk in a first-class cabin on an airplane, it's true when I walk into a suite in a hotel. I never, never, never allow myself to slip for one moment and think that I am just a lawyer sitting up in first-class, even if I got on a dashiki, and sometimes I wear dashikis. It drives those crackers crazy. I had on a safari suit and a hat the other day in an airport in Atlanta, and a white dude walked up to me and said, "What country is that uniform from?" I said, "I don't know."

I got on the elevator in my building on LaSalle Street and I was dressed nice. One North LaSalle. LaSalle and Madison, American National Bank Building. A cracker got on the elevator, looked up at me and said, "My God, how tall are you?"

I said, "Well, I'm six foot five. How tall are you?"

He said, "I'm five foot two."

I said, "I haven't been that short since I was nine." I say to my kids that we have to understand that color is a pervasive thing in this country, and that we have to take the extra burden, we just have to share the extra burden.

I think the dynamics will change and shift just like the earth moves and shakes. I think fundamentally this country will always be racist. I think we have to understand that and deal with the country to come to an accord with us. Not to think that the country will ever accept us, not as equals or anything else, but I think they will reach accord out of convenience. As Whites have.

We are the only black family in this building. The white family on this floor have reached an accord, because our circumstances are inextricably intertwined. We don't drink together, they don't come to my house, I don't go over to their house; they leave me in charge or I leave them in charge because our well-being, you see, is tied up together. And I think that is the kind of accord we may reach and that's all I ask.

All the people who come to my house are Blacks. Now somebody in the building who's working on the board maybe may come in, or somebody may come in from next door, what have you, but to invite people in, to socialize into my home, they're black people.

I'm involved with white people; the law profession is a legal profession, I mean a profession that's dominated by whites basically. At this stage of my life, I don't socialize.

One of the things I have to say about my profession and that's that I practice law like I've done everything else. I do it in accordance to the rules which I set for myself. Which means that most of my clients are small businesses and small individuals. Incidentally, two or three of them are white. I don't socialize in business. But I have a difficult practice because I won't get the big fat companies, because my politics and my attitude and my philosophy all are contrary to that. So I eke out a living from small clients and from individuals who are concerned more about what I can do for them legally than what I may say or do philosophically or politically. So that means, of course, that even with a law degree and with some experience I have a tough practice. It's a struggle. That's another realization which I have come to is that no matter how long I live, I'm going to struggle as long as I am in this country.

The educational process in Chicago is political. The Board of Education in Chicago is so highly politicized that it doesn't deal with education at all. It's one of the things which I've had conversations with Dr. Ruth Love (newly-appointed Chicago Superintendent of Schools in 1981) about. And her concern is, "Can I get through the layers and layers of politics to educate our children?" Our children can be taught. But the Board of Education, with a $400 million dollar budget, is the biggest business in Chicago, bigger than the City of Chicago. It exists to some extent to perpetuate the Democratic machine, the contracts that are let. The Board of Education is the biggest client of Commonwealth Edison, it uses more electricity than any single client in Chicago, it uses more natural gas than any other single client in Chicago. So that it is basically designed to sustain the big business community and not to educate. If there's any way to break through the layers of politics in Chicago so that the educational system can be dealt with, I think that our children can be taught. But unless we deal with the politics of Chicago the system will never serve our children.

There are some schools in Chicago—my little girl goes to Ogden which is on Oak and State. It's one of the finest schools in the country.

It's a public school. There are some fine public schools in Chicago. Why is it that Ogden can educate so well and other schools can't? Well, Ogden is seventy per cent white and seventeen per cent black. They manage the racial numbers, they manage the number of wealthy and poor people, they manage the number of everybody who goes in—and it's an excellent school. So it can be done, and it is being done in Chicago. It's not being done in the predominantly black schools. There are one or two all-black or overwhelmingly black schools that are educating very well. Beasley is educating very well, for example. That's the school that Dr. Alice Blair helped to put together over in District 13. So it can be done, but I've said to teachers over and over again, "Teachers must educate." That the teachers must teach whatever the facilities are. Now, I use the story of Booker T. Washington and George Washington Carver—when George Washington Carver finished in Iowa and got his doctorate—he was working in research in Iowa and Booker T. Washington wrote him and said, "I need you. Your people need you here in Alabama. Come on over and teach at Tuskegee." And he got ready to leave Iowa, where he had been working in the confines of their very fine laboratory and fine circumstances. His colleagues gave him a microscope and he took it to Tuskegee. That was all he had. And so when he got off the wagon at Tuskegee and was met by Washington, they exchanged pleasantries. And so he asked Booker T. Washington, "Say, well, where is my laboratory?

Booker T. Washington walked into the inside of an old rickety building and opened the door to an empty room and said, "Dr. Carver, here is your laboratory."

George Washington Carver went to the middle of the room, put the microscope down and said, "It is a laboratory." And then he took thirteen black students and went out and scoured the country for everything—number two tub, old kerosene lamps. Within two or three weeks he had developed a laboratory from nothing, and from that laboratory developed 300 products from the peanut, 118 products from the sweet potato. So whatever you do, my attitude about teachers is, you must teach. I use this whole thing to try to deal with our teachers and our students. Long before a Jesse Jackson or a Julian Bond, some black teacher touched their lives. I still remember my first grade teacher. I was in one of those one-room schools in Mobile, where we had two or three classes, in the same room, around that pot-bellied stove. But my first grade teacher taught. So, I run the whole gamut: let the lawyers lawyer; let the doctors doctor; let the judges judge; and teachers, you must teach. And that's what we've got to do. Schools have become too complicated to educate and too complex to teach.

My mother could hardly read and write. She was a maid, she worked in white people's kitchens all her life. My father was a longshoreman, and he cannot read and write; he's still living in Mobile, but again, education was the difference. Their interest in my education coupled with the extended community—I mean, how did I go to law school? I went to law school because the dean of Southern's law school thought that he saw something in me, a part of my extended community. It wasn't that when I was born my mother and father sat down and said, "He's gonna be a lawyer, like his daddy or like his uncle." Because I was the only lawyer in the family. We don't have these traditions of the symbols going on. I hope that my daughters will at least know that the legal profession exists by seeing me.

My parents didn't have a lot. My mother worked every day for two dollars a day, washing and ironing for white folks, but she worked, so I grew up seeing her go to work. My father was a longshoreman. He went to work every day. I grew up knowing that you've got to work. Whether you're working as a longshoreman, lifting that mustard gas in World War II on the docks or whether you work in a white person's kitchen, I knew the idea was that you had to work.

That's what we have to understand also. If children grow up seeing fathers unemployed and seeing them lying around the house and seeing them loitering and loafing and seeing mamas doing what they do, the children are going to do that. They're gonna do just that. We need to deal with how to break that. We're not involved with breaking that kind of cycle, so we have an awful lot of work to do.

I think that one of the most devastating things on us has been the urbanization of black people. The urban scene has just devastated our natural instinct. For instance, Dempsey, we've been friends for about ten years, but this is the first time you've ever been to my house and I've never been to your house. Now Manford Byrd and I have been friends for ten years, and he's been to my house once and I've been to his house once. Now you know, that's ridiculous. Lerone Bennett and I are close friends. He's been to my house once and I've never been to his house. What I'm saying is that that is unnatural for us. I live ten miles from you, and I live in Chicago, and I can't walk down the street to your house and you can't walk to mine. That's the way it is. We come from a very, very close kind of community, a community where it's not talked about now, where my mother would leave me on the porch to go to work and every adult in that whole neighborhood had the authority to discipline me. I belonged to that whole neighborhood, to that whole community. We don't have that sense anymore. Urbanization has broken it up. I laugh and I chuckle all the time when they talk about scattered low-income housing on the Southwest Side or Northwest Side but, shit, when it goes into Chatham, you ain't seen no protest. When I lived in Mobile, I went to school with the son of Mr. Ty, who was a successful insurance man. I went to school with Dr. Franklin's son, who was the doctor in the neighborhood, because we had amidst all the poor black folks, middle income. We were all black. Now the kids in Cabrini Green, they go to school only with the people from Cabrini-Green, only with people from that very area. So there is no economic mixture of black folks, let alone talking about desegregation with white folks. That's one reason a school like Ogden is successful. Because they have a mix of poor kids, middle income kids, black kids, Oriental kids, Hispanic kids. You know, its a melting pot kind of thing, and my daughter is responding very, very well to it.

Donald C. Walker

Donald C. Walker, 40, is publisher and editor of *Dollars and Sense* magazine, a monthly publication concerned with financial issues facing Blacks. Walker is a native Chicagoan and an admirer of the positive approach to business success advocated by Chicago insurance magnate W. Clement Stone.

"Chicago has been a very viable city for Blacks, historically. But we haven't even capitalized on what Jesse Binga, Anthony Overton, Madame C. J. Walker, Earl B. Dickerson and T. K. Gibson and others started . . . We are no further today, in my opinion, than we were in the '20's, when Jesse Binga started a bank."

Donald C. Walker

Are affirmative action programs formulated in the streets or board rooms, or both?

I never like to advocate violence. But once we left the streets—I said "we" because I was on the streets—and started negotiating, we (Blacks) couldn't beat them (white people) at that game. We have never been able to negotiate effectively without something happening out in the streets. It takes both of those elements: marching, protesting and boycotting while others are sitting down negotiating.

Some black businesses have grown since those days. But an effective program of selective buying and/or boycotting—whatever you want to call it—has to help the masses. It not only helps the persons sitting down negotiating, but also the persons who are boycotting and throwing rocks and bricks. Those persons—the street brigade—have to be helped, also. They didn't get their fair share, I don't care what anybody says. They're not going back out to march in masses. You'll get little spotty demonstrations, but not like in the '60's. Now, everybody is so sophisticated. Blacks have helped bring about this conservative era. Black professionals, black business people—we got our little piece of cake, and now we think we are in the mainstream. We don't realize that there are millions who never got their fair share. The black masses are very resentful of that. They are not teens now—they are in the '30's and '40's. Teens don't even know who Dr. King was.

Speaking of Dr. Martin Luther King, Jr., where is our Dr. Martin Luther King, Jr. of today? And the other leaders? Where are our Stokeley Carmichaels, Malcolm X's and Julian Bonds?

They are sleeping giants, in business and the various professions and civil rights organizations. They may even be elected officials. They have reached their positions as a result of the activities of the '60's. They have reached the middle class "comfort zone," as I call it. They are not asserting themselves to take more leadership, because they don't want to rock the boat. They are afraid they may lose ground themselves. They know that when the wrath of the major corporations comes down on you, they can do a job on you. The major media in this country can do such a job on you that you will be nothing in the end.

Black college graduates, MBAs and so forth, particularly MBAs, have to understand that when they enter the white corporate world they lose all identity. We need some of them to remain in the corporate world; but we also need some of them to learn and get the expertise and bring it on back home. Enough of that has not been taking place. We start to make $25,000 to $30,000 a year and we get to the comfort zone, and we forget who we are. That's a major problem.

Chicago has been a very viable city for Blacks, historically. But we haven't even capitalized on what Jesse Binga, Anthony Overton, Madame C. J. Walker, Earl B. Dickerson and T. K. Gibson and others started. We have never taken it farther. We are no further today, in my opinion, than we were in the '20's, when Jesse Binga started a bank. There was a time recently when we had seven black banks, but all of them were not sound. Many of our institutions, unfortunately, are not sound.

That's why some of these key politicians keep getting elected. They service people. The same is true in terms of civil rights or economic matters. You must give people service.

Just take a very close look at the following Rev. Jesse Jackson once enjoyed. He filled the Capitol Theatre, and it was much larger than the present Operation PUSH auditorium. He can't fill up the PUSH auditorium on a regular basis now. I'm not saying this is because he is a poor leader—that's not the case. But his organization has not been able to give service. The people in business who he helped don't support him in the manner in which they should. The people who benefit from organizations like PUSH, the NAACP and the Urban League need to support those organizations so they can continue to service people. The struggle is continuous. As we want the progress to be continuous. This is where we missed the boat.

We struggled to get what we wanted, and we haven't reached back to help anybody else. Sure, we may make a contribution to the United Negro College Fund. But we haven't helped the service-type organizations like PUSH, the grass roots organizations that give service to the masses. If we did, we could still have the protesting, boycotting and marching in the streets while we are at the negotiating table. It's a two-way street.

What kind of responsibility do you think political people have?

When you are elected to a political office, whether state, local or federal, you have a mandate from the residents of your district or ward to protect their interests.

Let's talk about an ethnic group that I know a little about: the Jewish people in America. It seems there is a thirst for scholarship and a thirst for excellence. Why can't that same kind of thing be true of the black community?

Because we haven't had enough generations in the middle class, unfortunately. We are just now getting into a middle class situation. We have not had a continuous business experience from one generation to another. You know yourself it was hard for the Blacks at the turn of the century who made it and hard for the Blacks in the '20's who made it. When they passed on, they didn't have anybody to pass it on to. When they did have someone to pass it on to, those following could not carry the business up scale. It either died or leveled off.

Take the Chicago Defender. When (Robert) Abbott was alive, it had a circulation of 500,000. It has a much smaller circulation now. The Defender has a lot of newspapers across the country. But the Chicago Defender, the baby of the founding company, has not grown. There is a reason for all of this. We don't have the trains with the porters taking papers up and down the railroad, to the South and the Midwest. There are more black newspapers today. I think it's interesting that so many black-owned companies are first generation companies.

We are still being held back by the so-called free enterprise system. I am not free to market our magazine *(Dollars and Sense)* all over the country or in any community. We are primarily limited to the downtown area, the inner city of Chicago and suburban areas where you find a large number of Blacks. The same situation exists in other cities. We know we have people who like to read *Dollars and Sense* in other communities. Of course, our prime market is black professionals. The success of the magazine is based on self-determination and a well rounded staff that believes in putting out a quality product. We do more, I would say, than the average black or white magazine in promoting the magazine. We do extensive radio advertising here in Chicago and ten other major markets, including New York, Atlanta and Washington, D.C.

Unfortunately, there seems to be a real problem among black business folks in terms of really helping each other. We all talk about black economics and black liberation. We talk about the economic condition of the black consumer and what he ought to be doing. But we should be doing more among ourselves.

It is not true, unfortunately, in the publishing industry, that we work together. There have been some attempts to form different associations and alliances, basically out of New York. I don't know why it should come out of New York, the largest amount of black publishing takes place in Chicago. I think the Black-Owned Communication Alliance (BOCA) is making serious attempts to get black publications to promote each other. They plan to go to major concerns to ask for more advertising revenue for black publications.

The problem is not the black publisher. We are all able to sustain our businesses. The problem is that the major corporations of this country still practice institutional racism. The fact is that they don't appropriate enough money to support seven, eight, nine or ten viable black magazines in this country. I don't think they can reach the black people by any other means. The point is that *Ebony* magazine is not the epitome of the black publishing industry. *Ebony* has been here the longest; but we think there is room for other types of black magazines.

I think it is unrealistic to say that Blacks are not being competitive. They (white folks) are competing in a much broader market. Blacks are competing in a very limited market. For instance, major corporations appropriate just so much money for advertising in black media. So, virtually, we are all fighting for the same dollar. For example, if X Corporation appropriates $250,000 for black print media, that means all your newspapers and magazines are competing for that $250,000. I think it would be helpful to sit down and compare notes to try to get more money for advertising.

White businessmen have all kinds of clubs where people who are competitive sit down and discuss common problems. Do you know of any instance where black heads of organizations sit down and talk about serious problems, other than at a convention?

Except for Chicago United, I can't think of any meeting called on a regular basis, unless there's a crisis. In terms of a club where you can have a drink or eat dinner, that type of association or club does not exist for Blacks. I am concerned but, frankly, I don't want to meet everybody. I don't have the time to talk to everybody.

I would like to see a closer alliance among black media, be it print, electronic or whatever. I think black media people should get together more often. I don't have a problem with anyone. I am out here trying to put out a quality publication. I think there's room in the marketplace for our magazine or for *Black Enterprise* or *Ebony*—you name them, they ought to have room. I think we ought to come together, especially the heads of these publishing companies, to find a way to get more dollars appropriated for black print media.

And let's talk about black businesses in Chicago. You have over 8,000 black-owned businesses in the Chicago metropolitan area. They only receive about 5 per cent of the $10 billion disposable income of the black population. Approximately 50 per cent of that figure is spent downtown, and 45 per cent or more goes to the suburban area. That tells you the future of black businesses. I think retail black businesses are in trouble, with the exception of gas stations and/or other types of service businesses. Grocery stores are in trouble, especially the little "ma and pa" type stores. I don't think there is a future for these types of businesses. Some of them will be around, but in terms of growth potential, I don't see it. The black consumer—and we can't blame everything on the black consumer—spends only 5 per cent of his disposable income in his own community.

We need to have community economics taught at the grade school level. That is the challenge that black businessmen in Chicago should issue to the president of the Chicago Board of Education and the new superintendent of schools. We need to have community economics, not just in the black community, but whatever community you live in. You need to stress spending some of your disposable income in that community if you are going to maintain the tax base of a particular community.

We have black businesses that are failing at about the rate of 45 per cent per year in Chicago. Eighteen to 20 per cent of black businesses have been in business less than a year. New businesses across the country are failing at a very high rate.

In Chicago we can be more specific. You are looking at $10 billion dollars in black disposable income. Blacks are a power force in Chicago. We have $140 billion of disposable income across the country. We are the margin of profit for many major companies. No one, unfortunately, not any national organization, has been able to effect a program of selective buying that will bring more dollars, jobs and other economic benefits back to the community.

Let's go back to when I was a child. The black business streets, such as 47th and 63rd in Chicago, contained viable businesses. Who owned those businesses? The Caucasians and the Jews. The community was thriving. People shopped within this community. Now most of the stores are owned by Arabs, and we will shop at their store instead of a black-owned store.

The point I am trying to make is that on streets such as 47th and 63rd, the few black businesses that were along the strips did better in the past than they are doing now. It says something about the black mentality, in terms of where they want to spend their dollars. It is a serious psychological problem. The people are still there. The folks who live in the immediate vicinity of those business locations do not shop there. They'd rather take their money elsewhere. If they continue to take money from the area, local black businessmen cannot survive.

What I think is going to happen is either one of two things: white people will come back in and create shopping malls, or they will take over these establishments. I know they are satisfied with what they are getting in the suburbs, as long as they can be twenty miles or so away from the city and still get 45 per cent of the $10 billion of black Chicago's disposable income. But it is a fact that white people will return to the city and buy homes in the city because of the high cost of things like gas and transportation. My theory is that you are going to see more white-owned enterprises back in the inner city and they are not going to support black businesses.

It has a lot to do with the black consumer. Black businesses, in general, have a hard time trying to meet the demands of the consumer. If the black consumer goes downtown, he may not get the service he wants, but he will go back again. When I talk to black business people, especially community people, I tell them they only have one shot. Let the employees know.

Why can't black consumers and black businesses get along? Instead of walking away from the establishment, make a complaint to the owner or the manager, or write him a letter. Take that type of initiative--don't just turn your back. Give that black business the second or third opportunity to serve.

Some people say if we spend the money in our neighborhoods, there is no guarantee the tax money will get to our schools. We've got to use our economic muscle and political muscle. They go hand in hand to make certain those dollars are channeled back into our neighborhoods. Why don't we have a black-owned shopping center on Chicago's South Side? Or on Chicago's West Side? I'm talking about a major shopping center, where you might have a theater and an entertainment center. If you want to see some good black entertainment, you have to go to Mill Run Theatre in Niles, Illinois, or to Merrillville, Indiana.

Since the *Blackbook Business and Reference Guide* first appeared in 1970, we have steadily advocated the economic improvement of our communities and black business. We have done this in two ways: first, by encouraging black people to shop in their own communities at black business establishments and urging black businesses to upgrade their services and facilities, and second, by bringing black businesses to the attention of major corporations seeking minority vendors. We continued this tradition with publication of *Dollars and Sense* in 1974.

In addition, we are dedicated to presenting positive images for others to emulate, especially young Junior Achievers, by highlighting business and professional people at our annual Blackbook Awards Dinner. We believe that we have been consistent in our efforts to become a symbol of economic determination and to help others to do the same.

I firmly believe that any time you can provide a service to the community and make a profit doing so, that's the best of the capitalistic system.

Part Three:

*PICTURES FROM CHICAGO
ALBUMS OF THE PAST*

A Selective List of Interviews
Conducted by Dempsey J. Travis
between June 10, 1969 and July 30, 1981.

Ripley B. Mead, Sr., age 79, June 10, 1969
Ripley B. Mead, Jr., age 56, June 10, 1969
Dr. Reginald Smith, age 86, June 15, 1969
Dr. Bishop Smith, age 70, June 15, 1969
T. K. Gibson, age 87, September 10, 1969
Frank Alexander, age 80, August 12, 1972
Elmore Baker, age 92, June 12, 1977
Mae Robinson, age 71, June 12, 1977
Mittie Travis, age 80, June 12, 1977
Oscar Freeman, age 80, June 15, 1977
Alfreda M. Barnett Duster, age 73, July 10, 1977
William Y. Browne admitted to being over age 74, July 26, 1977
Anna Mary Grinnell, age 94, July 29, 1977 and August 21, 1977
Lovelyn J. Evans, age 82, August 4, 1977
Oneida Daniels Woodard, about 80 years old, August 4, 1977
Ira W. Williams, age 92, August 10, 1977
Lloyd Wheeler, III, August 14, 1977
Earl B. Dickerson, age 90, August 21, 1977 and various dates in 1978,
    '79, '80, and '81.
George S. Harris, age 79, September 17, 1977
Mary Herrick, age 84, and various dates in 1979, '80 and '81
John Ragland, age 96, April 13, 1980
Joe Crawford, age 71, December 27, 1980
Thomas N. Todd, age 42, July 5, 1981
Renault Robinson, age 40, July 6, 1981
Robert Lucas, age 56, July 9, 1981
Paul King, age 42, July 10, 1981
Johnny Brown, age 33, July 15, 1981
Donald C. Walker, age 40, July 15, 1981
Reggie Theus, age 23, July 20, 1981
Jewel Lafontant, age 58, July 23, 1981
Alice Blair, age 57, July 27, 1981
Alvin Boutte, age 52, July 30, 1981

- NOTES AND DOCUMENTATION -
PROLOGUE:
SOURCES

BOOKS
Anderson, Jervis. *A. Philip Randolph: A Biographic Portrait.* Harcourt, Brace, Jovanovich, Inc., New York, 1972.
Angle, Paul M. *The Chicago Historical Society: 1856 to 1956, An Unconventional Chronicle.* Rand McNally & Company, Chicago, 1956.
Andreas, A.T. *History of Chicago, Volume 1. A.T. Andreas Company* 1885.
Car Service Rules of Pullman's Palace Car Company. W.R. Pottinger, Printer, Chicago, 1893.
Dubin, Arthur D. *Some Classic Trains.* Kalmbach Publication, Milwaukee Wisconsin, 1964.
Historic City: The Settlement of Chicago. City of Chicago, Department of Development and Planning, 1976.
Instruction Manual for Employees on Cars of the Pullman Company. The Pullman Company, Chicago, 1897.
Lowe, David. *Lost Chicago.* Houghton Mifflin Company, Boston, Massachusetts, 1975.
Mayer, Harold M. and Richard C. Wade. *Chicago: Growth of a Metropolis.* The University of Chicago Press, Chicago, 1969.
Pierce, Bessie Louise. *The History of Chicago: 1673-1848.* Alfred A. Knopf, New York, 1937.
Ransom, Reverdy C. *The Negro.* Ruth Hill, Publisher; Boston, Massachusetts, 1935.
Ransom, Reverdy C. *The Pilgrimage of Harriett Ransom's Son.* A.M.E. Sunday School Union, Nashville, Tennessee, 1946.
Sinclair, Upton, *The Jungle.* Upton Sinclair, Publisher, 1905.
Work, Monroe Nathan. *Negro Real Estate Holders of Chicago.* Unpublished M.A. Thesis; University of Chicago, 1903.
OFFICIAL STATISTICS
Census Data for the City of Chicago, 1900.
Illinois Central Train Schedule, 1900.
DIRECTORIES AND REFERENCE
Chicago City Directory for years 1860-61 and 1870-71.
Tillotson's Pocket Map and Street Guide of Chicago and Suburbs, 1904.
PERIODICALS
"A 100-Year Odyssey On Black Housing: Chicago, 1900-2000," *Dollars and Sense Magazine,* 3rd Quarter, 1977.

CHAPTER ONE:
SOURCES

BOOKS
Angle, Paul M. *The Chicago Historical Society: 1856-1956, An Unconventional Chronicle.* Rand McNally & Company, Chicago, 1956.
Duster, Alfreda M., Editor. *Crusade for Justice: The Autobiography of Ida B. Wells.* University of Chicago Press, 1970.
Gosnell, Harold F. *Negro Politicians: The Rise of Negro Politics in*

Chicago. University of Chicago Press, 1935.

Hammurabis, F.H. *The Negro In Chicago: 1779 to 1929. Vol. 1 & 2.* Washington Intercollegiate Club of Chicago, Inc.

Historic City: The Settlement of Chicago. City of Chicago, Department of Development & Planning, 1976.

Lowe, David. *Lost Chicago.* Houghton Mifflin Company, Boston, Massachusetts, 1975.

Mayer, Harold M. and Richard C. Wade. *Chicago: Growth of A Metropolis.* The University of Chicago Press, Chicago, 1969.

Ransom, Reverdy C. *The Negro.* Ruth Hill, Publisher; Boston, Massachusetts, 1935.

Work, Monroe Nathan. *Negro Real Estate Holders of Chicago.* Unpublished M.A. Thesis; University of Chicago, 1903.

PERIODICALS

"The South Loop Legacy," *Chicago Magazine.* September, 1978.

DIRECTORIES AND REFERENCES

The Colored Men's Professional and Business Directory of Chicago. I.C. Harris, Publisher, Chicago, 1885.

CHAPTER TWO:
SOURCES

BOOKS

Ashbaugh, Carolyn. *Lucy Parsons: American Revolutionary.* Charles H. Kerr Publishing Company, Chicago, 1976.

Cayton, Horace R. and George S. Mitchell. *Black Workers and the New Unions.* Negro University Press, Westport, Conn., Reprinted, 1970.

DuBois, W.E.B. *Black Reconstruction.* Albert Saifer, Publisher, Philadelphia, Pa., 1935 (Reprint).

Duster, Alfreda M., ed. *Crusade for Justice: The Autobiography of Ida B. Wells.* University of Chicago Press, 1970.

Gosnell, Harold F. *Negro Politicians. The Rise of Negro Politics in Chicago.* University of Chicago Press, 1935.

Hammurabis, F.H. *The Negro in Chicago: 1779-1929. Vol. 1 & 2.* Washington Intercollegiate Club of Chicago, Incorporate, 1929.

Hanna, Hilton E. and Joseph Belsky. *The 'Pat' Garman Story: Picket and the Pen.* American Institute of Social Science, Inc., Yonkers, New York, 1960.

Harlan, Louis R. *Booker T. Washington: The Making of A Black Leader, 1856-1901.* Oxford University Press, New York, 1972.

Historic City: The Settlement of Chicago. City of Chicago, Department of Development & Planning, 1976.

Holli, Melvin G. and Peter 'd A. Jones, ed. *The Ethnic Frontier.* William B. Eerdmans Publishing Company, 1977.

Hoyt, Hommer. *One Hundred Years of Land Values in Chicago: 1830-1933.* The University of Chicago Press, Chicago, 1933.

Lewis, Lloyd and Henry Justin Smith. *Chicago: The History of Its Reputation.* Harcourt, Brace & Company, New York, 1929.

Lowe, David. *Lost Chicago.* Houghton Mifflin Company, Boston, Massachusetts, 1975.

Mayer, Harold M. & Richard C. Wade. *Chicago: Growth of A Metropolis.* The University of Chicago Press, Chicago, 1969.

Ottley, Roi. *The Lonely Warrior: The Life and Times of Robert S. Abbott.* Henry Regnery & Company, 1955.

Pecks, Edward. *The Long Struggle for Black Power.* Charles Scribner Sons, New York, 1971.

Sandburg, Carl. *The Chicago Race Riots.* Harcourt, Brace & Howe, 1919.

Scott, Emmet J. *Negro Migration During the War.* Arno Press and The New York Times, New York, 1969.

Spears, Allan H. *Black Chicago: 1900-1920.* The University of Chicago Press, 1967.

Stuart, M.S. *An Economic Detour: A History of Insurance in the Lives of American Negroes.* Wendell Mallett and Company, New York, 1940.

Strickland, Arvah E. *History of the Chicago Urban League.* University of Illinois Press, Urbana and London, 1966.

Taitt, John, ed. *The Souvenir of Negro Progress: Chicago, 1779-1925.* The De Saible Association, 1925.

The Negro In Chicago. The Chicago Commission on Race Relations. The University of Chicago Press, 1922.

Tuttle, William M., Jr. *Race Riot.* Atheneum Press, New York, 1977.

Washington, Booker T. *Up From Slavery.* Double Day Press, New York, 1901.

Washington, Booker T. and W.E.B. DuBois et al. *The Negro Problem.* Arno Press, New York, 1969.

Woodson, Carter G. *The Rural Negro.* The Association for the Study of Negro Life and History, Inc., Washington, D.C., 1930.

PERIODICALS

"Some Chicagoans of Note," *The Crisis,* November, 1915.

"Race Riots and The Press," *The Half-Century Magazine,* August, 1919.

"Negro Life in Chicago," *The Half-Century Magazine,* May, 1919.

NEWSPAPERS

Chicago Defender. "Binga-Johnson Wedding The Most Brilliant Ever Held In Chicago," Feburary 24, 1912.

Chicago Defender. "Welcome To Our Carnival Delegates And Friends," August 17, 1912.

Chicago Defender. "Miss Hattie Holliday Crowned Queen of State Street Carnival," August 31, 1912.

Chicago Defender. "Mrs. J.C. Binga Hostess," August 2, 1913.

The Chicago Daily News. "One Chicago Bank Is Entirely 'Colored'," December 14, 1916.

The Chicago Tribune. "The Coliseum: Historically, An Incredible Hulk," March 27, 1980.

OFFICIAL STATISTICS

Census Data for the City of Chicago, 1900.

LETTERS

Letter from Oneida Daniels Woodard, dated August 12, 1977 states that Roy Frence, Sr. and his family moved into a two-flat building next to her family in the 4000 block of Winthrop Avenue in 1908. She also discussed another black family by the name of Frinches who opened an integrated fashionable restaurant that same year called "Frinches Pantry" on Evanston Avenue, which was later re-named Broadway. The "Pantry" was located on Broadway near Lawrence.

CHAPTER THREE:
SOURCES

BOOKS

Bruder, Stanley. *Pullman: An Experiment In Industrial Order and Community Planning.* Oxford University Press, New York, 1967.

Cayton, Horace R. and George S. Mitchell. *Black Workers and the New Unions.* Negro University Press, Westport, Conn., Reprinted, 1970.

Duster, Alfreda M., ed. *Crusade for Justice: The Autobiography of Ida B. Wells.* University of Chicago Press, 1970.

Gosnell, Harold F. *Negro Politicians: The Rise of Negro Politics in Chicago.* University of Chicago Press, 1935.

Hanna, Hilton E. and Joseph Belsky. *The 'Pat' Garman Story: Picket and the Pen.* American Institute of Social Science, Inc., Yonkers, New York, 1960.

Herrick, Mary J. *The Chicago Schools: A Social and Political History.* Sage Publications, Beverly Hills/London, 1971.

Historic City; The Settlement of Chicago. City of Chicago, Department of Development and Planning, 1976.

Hoyt, Hommer, *One Hundred Years of Land Values In Chicago: 1830-1933.* University of Chicago Press, 1933.

Lewis, Lloyd and Henry Justin Smith. *Chicago: The History of Its Reputation.* Harcourt, Brace and Company, New York, 1929.

Lowe, David. *Lost Chicago.* Houghton Mifflin Company, Boston Massachusetts, 1975.

Mayer, Harold M. and Richard G. Wade. *Chicago: Growth of A Metropolis.* The University of Chicago Press, Chicago, 1969.

Ottley, Roi. *The Lonely Warrior: The Life and Times of Robert S. Abbott.* Henry Regnery and Company, Chicago, 1955.

Sandburg, Carl. *The Chicago Race Riots.* Harcourt, Brace & Howe, 1919.

Scott, Emmett J. *Negro Migration During the War.* Arno Press and The New York Times, New York, 1969.

Spears, Allan H. *Black Chicago: 1900-1920.* The University of Chicago Press, 1967.

Strickland, Arvah E. *History of the Chicago Urban League.* University of Illinois Press, Urbana and London, 1966.

Stuart, M.S. *An Economic Detour; A History of Insurance In the Lives of American Negroes.* Wendell Mallett and Company, New York, 1940.

Taitt, John, ed. *The Souvenir of Negro Progress: 1779-1925.* The De Saible Association, 1925.

The Negro In Chicago. The Chicago Commission on Race Relations. University of Chicago Press, 1922.

Tuttle, William M., Jr. *Race Riot.* Atheuneum Press, New York, 1977.

Woodson, Carter G. *The Rural Negro.* The Association for the Study of Negro life and History, Inc., Washington, D.C. 1930.

Woodson, Carter G. Association for the Study of Negro Life and History, Inc., Washington, D.C. 1930.

CHAPTER FOUR:
SOURCES

BOOKS

Gosnell, Harold F. *Negro Politicians; The Rise of Negro Politics In Chicago*. University of Chicago Press, 1935.

Hammurabis, F.H. *The Negro In Chicago; 1779 to 1929. Vol. 1 & 2.* Washington Intercollegiate Club of Chicago, Inc., 1929.

Harris, Abrams L. *The Negro As Capitalist: A Study of Banking and Business Among American Negroes*. The American Academy of Political and Social Science, Philadelphia, Pa., 1936.

Hickok, Lorena. *One Third of a Nation*. University of Illinois Press, Chicago, 1981.

Historic City; The Settlement of Chicago. City of Chicago, Department of Development and Planning, 1976.

Lowe, David. *Lost Chicago*. Houghton Mifflin Company, Boston, Massachusetts, 1975.

Mayer, Harold M. and Richard C. Wade. *Chicago: Growth of A Metropolis*. University of Chicago Press, 1969.

Myrdal, Gunnar. *An American Dilemma*. Harper and Brothers, New York, 1944.

Pells, Richard H. *Radical Visions and American Dreams*. Harper & Row, 1973.

Quarles, Benjamin. *The Negro In The Making of America*. Collier-MacMillan Ltd., London, 1970.

The Fabulous Century: 1930-1940. The Editors of Time-Life Books, Time Inc., New York, 1969.

Stuart, M.S. *An Economic Detour: A History of Insurance In The Lives of American Negroes*. Wendell Mallett and Company, New York, 1940.

PERIODICALS

"Jesse Binga," *The Crisis,* December, 1927.

"The Poignant Relevant Backward Look At Artist of The Great Depression," *Smithsonian,* October, 1979.

NEWSPAPERS

Chicago Daily Defender. "Saga Of Two Banks Brings Up An Old Tune," July 17, 1979.

Chicago Daily Defender. "South Park National Bank Will Soon Open," January 7, 1930.

Chicago Daily Defender. "To Re-Open," March 7, 1930.

Chicago Daily Defender. "Banks Closed Temporarily,"

Chicago Daily Defender. "MT. Glenwood Plans Loans For Victims Of Bank Crisis," August 9, 1930.

Chicago Daily Defender. "Given Plans Whereby Institution Can Open," September 6, 1930.

Chicago Daily Defender. "Jesse Binga's Wife Asks That Estate Be Conserved," October 11, 1930.

Chicago Daily Defender. "To Open Binga Bank," February 14, 1931.

Chicago Daily Defender. "Binga Arrested," March 7, 1931.

Chicago Daily Defender. "Binga Still In Jail On Soup Diet," March 14, 1931.

Chicago Daily Defender. "J. Binga Is Released From Jail On Bond," April 18, 1931.

Chicago Daily Defender. "Binga Bank To Pay Some Money Soon," May 16, 1931.

Chicago Daily Defender. "High Cost of Settling Bank's Affairs Is Under Court Probe," November 7, 1931.

Chicago Tribune. "State Street Yesterday And Today," October 28, 1979.

DIRECTORIES AND REFERENCES

Black Whose Who In Chicago, 1927, from F. H. Hammurabis, *The Negro In Chicago: 1779 to 1929, Volume 1.* Washington Intercollegiate Club of Chicago, Inc., 1929

Simms' Blue Book and National Negro Business and Professional Directory, James M. Simms, Publisher, Chicago, 1923

Chicago Tribune. "State Street Yesterday And Today," October 28, 1979.

DIRECTORIES AND REFERENCES

Black Whose Who In Chicago, 1927, from F. H. Hammurabis, *The Negro In Chicago: 1779 to 1929, Volume 1.* Washington Intercollegiate Club of Chicago, Inc., 1929

Simms' Blue Book and National Negro Business and Professional Directory, James M. Simms, Publisher, Chicago, 1923

CHAPTER FIVE:
SOURCES

BOOKS

Brashler, William. *The Don: The Life and Death of Sam Giancana.* Harper & Row Publishers, New York, 1977.

Calloway, Cab. *Of Minnie the Moucher and Me.* Thomas Y. Crowdly, 1976.

Cronon, Edmund David. *Black Moses: The Story of Marcus Garvey and the Universal Negro Improvement Association.* The University of Wisconsin Press, Madison, 1955.

Dance, Stanley. *The World of Earl Hines.* Thomas Y. Crowdly & Company, New York, 1977.

Drake, St. Clair and Horace Cayton. *Black Metropolis: A Study of Life In a Northern City. Volume I & II.* Harper & Row Publishers, New York, 1945.

Garvey, Amy Jacques. *Philosophy and Opinion of Marcus Garvey.* Frank Cass & Company, Ltd., London, 1967.

Gilmore, Al-Tony. *Bad Nigger!: The National Impact of Jack Johnson.* Kennikat Press, Port Washington, New York, 1975.

Gottfried, Alex. *Boss Cermak of Chicago.* University of Washington Press, Seattle, 1962.

Hammurabis, F.H. *The Negro In Chicago: 1779 to 1929. Volume I & II.* Washington Intercollegiate Club of Chicago, Inc., 1929.

Henderson, Bancroft Edwin. *The Negro In Sports.* The Associated Publishers, Inc., Washington, D.C., 1949.

Holt, Glen E. and Dominic Pacyga. *Chicago: A Historical Guide To The Neighborhoods - The Loop and Southside.* Chicago Historical Foundation, 1979.

Hoyt, Hommer. *One Hundred Years Of Land Values In Chicago: 1830-1933.* University of Chicago Press, Chicago, 1933.

Johnson, Jack. *Jack Johnson Is A Dandy: An Autobiography.* The New

American Library, New York, 1969.

Kobler, John. *Capone*. G.P. Putnam's Sons, New York, 1971.

Lait, Jack and Lee Mortimer. *Chicago Confidential*. Crown Press, New York, 1950.

Lomay, Allan. *Mister Jelly Roll*. University of California Press, Berkley, 1950.

Lucas, Robert. *Black Gladiator*. Dell Publishing Company, Inc., New York, 1970.

Mayer, Harold M. and Richard C. Wade. *Chicago: Growth of A Metropolis*. University of Chicago Press, 1969.

Myrdal, Gunnar. *An American Dilemma*. Harper and Brothers, New York, 1944.

Ottley, Roi. *The Lonely Warrior: The Life and Times of Robert S. Abbott*. Henry Regnery & Company, Chicago, 1955.

Philpott, Thomas Lee. *The Slum and The Ghetto: Chicago 1880-1930*. Oxford Press, New York, 1978.

Twombly, Robert C. *Blacks In White America Since 1865*. David McKay Company, Inc., New York, 1971.

NEWSPAPERS

Chicago Daily Defender. "Johnson In The Lime Light," February 12, 1910.

Chicago Daily Defender. "We Have Them All To Beat," February 5, 1910.

Chicago Daily Defender. "Champions Take Long Road Jog," April 6, 1910.

Chicago Daily Defender. "Champion Jack Johnson: The Undefeated Hero," April 23, 1910.

Chicago Daily Defender. "Champion Jack Johnson In Town Tomorrow," March 12, 1910.

Chicago Daily Defender. "Jack Johnson And James Jeffries," July 2, 1910.

Chicago Daily Defender. "$1,000.00 Punch Bowl To Champion Jack Johnson," August 6, 1910.

Chicago Daily Defender. "Johnson Is After $60,000 Property," December 3, 1910.

Chicago Daily Defender. "Jack Johnson In London," June 17, 1911.

Chicago Daily Defender. "Jack Johnson Forms Land Co. In Mexico City, Mexico," June 7, 1919.

Chicago Daily Defender. "Johnson Refused Service, Druggist License Revoked In Mexico City, Mexico," June 12, 1919.

DIRECTORIES AND REFERENCES

Black Who's Who In Chicago, 1927 from F.H. Hammurabis, *The Negro In Chicago: 1779 to 1929, Volume 1*. Washington Intercollegiate Club of Chicago, Inc., 1929.

CHAPTER SIX:
SOURCES

BOOKS

Cronon, Edmund David. *Black Moses: The Story of Marcus Garvey and the Universal Negro Improvement Association*. University of Wisconsin Press, Madison, Wisconsin, 1955.

Garvey, Amy Jacques. *Philosophy and Opinion of Marcus Garvey*.

Frank Cass & Company, Ltd., London, 1967.
Hammurabis, F.H. *The Negro In Chicago: 1779 to 1929 Volumes I & II.* Washington Intercollegiate Club of Chicago, 1929.
Herrick, Mary J. *The Chicago Schools: A Social and Political History.* Sage Publications, Beverly Hills/London, 1971.
Hoyt, Hommer. *One Hundred Years Of Land Values In Chicago: 1830-1933.* University of Chicago Press, 1933.
Kobler, John. *Capone.* G. P. Putnam's Sons, New York, 1971.
Lucas, Robert. *Black Gladiator.* Dell Publishing Company, Inc., New York, 1970.
Travis, Dempsey J. *Don't Stop Me Now.* Children's Press, 1970
NEWSPAPERS
Chicago Daily News. "The Bloody Reign of Tony Capone," January 4, 1976.

CHAPTER SEVEN:
SOURCES

BOOKS
Allen, Jack and John L. Betts. *History: U.S.A.* American Book Company, New York, 1969.
Barnett, Ida Wells. *On Lynching.* Arno Press and New York Times, 1969.
Beldon, F.E. *Christ In Song.* Review & Herald Publishing Association. Washington, D.C., 1908.
Carter, Dan T. *A Tragedy of the American South.* Louisianna State University Press, 1960.
Drake, St. Clair and Horace Cayton. *Black Metropolis: A Study of Life In a Northern City, Volumes I & II.* Harper & Row Publishers, New York, 1945.
Franklin, John Hope. *From Slavery To Freedom.* Alfred A. Knopf, New York, 1947.
Haskell, S.N. *Bible Handbook.* Review & Herald Publishing Association, Washington, D.C., 1919.
Myrdal, Gunnar. *An American Dilemma.* Harper and Brothers, New York, 1944.
Patterson, Haywood and Earl Conrad. *Scottsboro Boy.* Double Day, New York, 1950.
Strickland, Arvah E. *History of the Chicago Urban League.* University of Illinois Press, Urbana and London, 1966.
The Fabulous Century: 1930-1940. The Editors of Time Life Books, Time Inc., New York, 1969.
White, Walter *Rope and Fagot.* Arno Press and New York Times, 1969.
Wright, Richard. *Black Boy.* Harper & Brothers Publishers, New York, 1937.
NEWSPAPERS
Chicago Daily News. "Welcome to the '30's," March 10, 1975.
Chicago Daily News. "Chicago Flocked to Big 1933 Fair," December 6-7, 1975.

CHAPTER EIGHT:
SOURCES

BOOKS

Allen, Jack and John L. Betts. *History: U.S.A.* American Book Company, New York, 1969.

Barnum, Donald T. *The Negro In the Bituminous Coal Mining Industry.* The Wharton School of Finance & Commerce, Department of Industry, Industrial Research Unit, 1970.

Bennett, Lerone, Jr. *Before The Mayflower.* Johnson Publishing Company, Chicago, 1964.

Cayton, Horace R. and George S. Mitchell. *Black Workers and the New Unions.* Negro University Press, Westport, Conn., Reprinted, 1970.

Dubin, Arthur D. *Some Classic Trains.* Kalmbach Publication, Milwaukee, Wisconsin, 1964.

Haggard, Howard W. *The Science of Health and Disease.* Harper and Brothers Publishers, New York, 1938.

Kardiner, Abram. *The Mark of Oppression.* The World Publishing Company, 1962.

King, Martin Luther, Jr. *Stride Toward Freedom.* Harper & Brothers Publishers, 1958.

McKissick, Floyd. *3/5 of a Man.* The MacMillan Company, London, 1969.

Mays, Benjamin E. *Born To Rebel.* Charles Schribner's Sons, New York, 1971.

Myrdal, Gunnar. *An American Dilemma.* Harper and Brothers, New York, 1944

Scheener, Allen, ed. *Harlem On My Mind: 1900-1968.* Random House, New York, 1968.

Woodson, Carter G. and Lorenzo Greene. *The Negro Wage Earner.* The Association for the Study of Negro Life and History, Inc., Washington, D.C. 1930.

Woodward, C. Vann. *The Strange Career of Jim Crow.* Oxford University Press, 1957.

PAMPHLETS

The Power of Coal. National Coal Association, Division of Education, Washington, D.C.

PERIODICALS

The Message. "Soul Food and Survival," November - December, 1978.

NOTES FROM INTERVIEWS

Notes from interviews with Dr. Robert L. Kimbrough of Chicago, an ex-Alabama coal miner; my cousin, Joseph Story, of Cleveland, Ohio, an ex-Kentucky coal miner; and my cousin, Strickland Davis, of Newark, New Jersey, an ex-Pennsylvania coal miner. Both first cousins were present at our grandmother's funeral.

CHAPTER NINE:
SOURCES

BOOKS

Bogle, Donald. *Toms, Coons, Mulattoes, Mammies and Bucks.* Viking Press, New York, 1973.

Chilton, John. *Who's Who of Jazz. Storyville to Swing Street.* Time-Life Records, Special Edition, New York, 1978.

Drake, St. Clair and Horace Cayton. *Black Metropolis: A Study of Life In a Northern City, Volumes I & II.* Harper & Row Publishers, New York, 1945.

Dykeman, William and James Stokely. *Neither Black nor White.* Rhinehart & Company, Inc., 1957.

Frazier, E. Franklin. *Black Bourgeoisie: The Rise of a New Middle Class In the United States.* The Free Press, Glencoe, Illinois, 1957.

Garvey, Amy Jacques. *Philosophy and Opinion of Marcus Garvey.* Frank Cass & Company, Ltd., London, 1967.

Grier, William H. and Price M. Cobbs. *Black Rage.* Basic Books, Inc. New York, 1968.

Hammonds, John with Irving Townsend. *John Hammond on Record.* Ridge Press, New York, 1977.

Herrick, Mary J. *The Chicago Schools: A Social and Political History.* Sage Publications, Beverly Hills/London, 1971.

Louis, Joe with Edna and Art Rust, Jr. *Joe Louis: My Life.* Harcourt, Brace, Jovanovich, Inc. New York, 1978.

Major, Gerri and Doris E. Saunders. *Black Society.* Johnson Publishing Company, Inc., Chicago, 1976.

McCarthy, Albert. *Big Band Jazz.* Berkley Publishing Corp., New York, 1977

Patterson, Lindsay, ed. *The Negro In Music and Art.* Publishers Company, Inc., New York, 1967.

NEWSPAPERS

Chicago Daily News. "Blacks' Distrust Leaders," May 15, 1968.

Chicago Sun Times. "Black Singles Mingle But Not In Loneliness - Industry Activity," November 28, 1972.

Chicago Sun Times/Parade. "Black Is Beautiful But Not In South Africa," April 8, 1973.

Chicago Tribune Magazine. "In Defense Of Being Black And Successful," August 18, 1974.

New York Times Magazine. "The Negro Is Prejudiced Against Himself." November 29, 1964.

New York Times Magazine. "The Negro's Self Image - The Reader React," December 13, 1964.

New York Times Magazine. "The Negro's Middle-Class," October 24, 1964.

PAMPHLETS

Goodman, Benny. *Giants of Jazz* Time-Life Books - Inc., 1979.

DIRECTORIES & REFERENCES

DuSable High School's First Four June Class Year Book, 1935-39, Chicago Illinois.

Reviewed both the 1933 and revised 1961 blue prints and plot plans for DuSable High School.

Music Master - Official monthly Journal of the American Federation of Musicians, local 208, Chicago, Illinois, March, 1941.

Savoy Chatterbox. November 28, 1938, Chicago, Illinois. Music contract between Jack Travis and Club Deluxe, dated November 1, 1939.

LETTERS

Letter dated August 15, 1939 from Colored Associated Orchestras to Jack Travis confirming date at Warwick Hall on September 1, 1939.

Letter dated August 6, 1938 from Musician Protection Union Local #208, A.F. & M., Inc. to Jack Travis giving official notice that my band was to appear at the Musicians Annual Picnic, August 8, 1938, Birutes Grove, 79th at Archer, at 2 p.m.

Letter dated September 23, 1941 from Madelle B. Boosfield, Principal of Phillips High School and C.C. Willard, Principal of DuSable High School inviting me to be their guest at a luncheon to be given on October 2, 1941, at Morris' Eat Shop, 410 East 47th Street, Chicago, Illinois.

CHAPTER TEN:
SOURCES

BOOKS

Allen, Jack & John L. Betts. *History: U.S.A.* American Book Company, New York, 1969.

Anderson, Jervis. *A. Philip Randolph: A Biographic Portrait*. Harcourt, Brace, Jovanovich, Inc., New York. 1972.

Brooks, Gwendolyn. *A Street In Bronzeville*. Harper & Brothers Publishers, New York, 1945.

Dobson, Andrew. *Uncle Joe's Journal*. Minsip Publishing Company, Indianapolis, Indiana, 1937.

Drake, St. Clair and Horace Cayton. *Black Metropolis: A Study of Life In a Northern City, Volumes I & II*. Harper & Row Publishers, New York, 1945.

Franklin, John Hope. *From Slavery To Freedom*. Alfred A. Knopf, New York, 1947.

Herrick, Mary J. *The Chicago Schools: A Social and Political History*. Sage Publications, Beverly Hills/London, 1971.

Hickok, Lorena. *One-Third of A Nation*. University of Illinois Press, Chicago, Illinois, 1981.

Myrdal, Gunnar. *An American Dilemma*. Harper and Brothers, New York, 1944.

Pells, Richard H. *Radical Visions and American Dreams*. Harper & Row, 1973.

Strickland, Arvah E. *History of the Chicago Urban League*. University of Illinois Press, Urbana & London, 1966.

LETTERS

Letters dated from September, 1939 through December, 1941, to Mrs. Mary Herrick from DuSable graduates who were unsuccessful in finding employment.

NEWSPAPERS

Chicago Defender. "Satchumo Armstrong Opens At State-Lake Theatre," July 1, 1939.

Chicago Defender. "Another Delay For Speedy Erection Of Ida B. Wells, Low-Cost Housing Project," July 29, 1939.

Chicago Defender. "Bunny Berigan Opens At Savoy August 12," August 5, 1939.

Chicago Defender. "Preliminary Ground Work on $8,000,000 Ida B. Wells Began Wednesday," August 5, 1939.

Chicago Defender. "W.P.A. To Drop 2 Million From Rolls By August," July 22, 1939.

Chicago Defender. "Family's Window Stoned At Jane Adams Homes," August 12, 1939.

Chicago Defender. "Pay Binga Depositor $55,536.96," August 19, 1939.

Chicago Defender. "New Scale Boosts W.P.A. Salaries $60,000,000," August 19, 1939.

Chicago Defender. "78,750 people in Chicago Will Be Effected By W.P.A. Shut Down," September 2, 1939.

Chicago Defender. "Committee Asked To Act In Delay Of Ida B. Wells Homes; Seek U.S. Probe," September 30, 1939.

Chicago Defender. "Women Cry And Laugh As Joe Louis Wins," September 30, 1939.

Chicago Defender. "Hansberry Loses In A Restrictive Covenants Case," October 21, 1939.

Chicago Defender. "1,000 To Get Jobs On Ida B. Wells Homes Within 3 Weeks," October 28, 1939.

Chicago Defender. Reliefers To Be given W.P.A. Jobs," November 11, 1939.

Chicago Defender. "Freedom for Scottsboro Boys in Sight," November 18, 1939.

CHAPTER ELEVEN :
SOURCES

BOOKS

Allen, Jack and John L. Betts. *History: U.S.A.* American Book Company, New York, 1969.

Brooks, Gwendolyn. *A Street In Bronzeville.* Harper and Brothers Publishers, New York, 1945.

Burrell, Berkley. *Getting It Together.* Harcourt; Brace and Jovanovich, New York, 1971.

Chilton, John. *Who's Who of Jazz: Storyville to Swing Street.* Time-Life Records, (Special Edition), New York, 1978.

Drake, St. Clair and Horace Cayton. *Black Metropolis: A Study of Life In A Northern City, Volumes I & II.* Harper & Row Publishers, New York, 1945.

Killens, John Oliver. *And Then We Heard The Thunder.* Alfred A. Knoph, Inc., New York, 1963.

Lee, Ulysses. *United States Army In World War II - Special Studies: The Employment of Negro Troops.* Office of the Chief of Military History, United States Army, Washington, D.C., 1966.

McCarthy, Albert. *Big Band Jazz.* Berkley Publishing Corporation, New York, 1977.

Motley, Mary P., Editor. *The Invisible Soldier: The Experience of the Black Soldier in World War II.* Wayne State University Press, Detroit, Michigan, 1975.

Quarles, Benjamin. *The Negro In the Making of America.* Collier-Mac-Millan Ltd., London, 1970.

Schoefeld, Seymour J. *The Negro In The Armed Forces: His Values and Status Past, Presently, and Potential.* The Associated Publisher,

Washington, D.C., 1945.

Stuckey, Elma. *The Big Gate.* Precendent Publishing, Inc., Chicago

This Fabulous Century: 1940-1950. Editors of Time-Life Books, Time, Inc., New York, 1967.

Travis, Dempsey J. *Don't Stop Me Now.* Children's Press, 1970.

PERIODICALS

"Black Chicago: Three Score Plus One, Part VII," by Dempsey J. Travis, *Dollars & Sense* Magazine, June/July, 1980.

"This Is The Army," *Negro Digest,* February, 1944.

NEWSPAPERS

The Chicago Defender. "Mourn City Victim of Georgia MP," December 12, 1942.

The Chicago Defender. "War Workers Rallying As Good Fellows," December 12, 1942.

The Chicago Defender. "Chicago Given Status Of Acting Civilian Aide By Stimson," February 13, 1943.

The Chicago Defender. "Library Life Assets Show Gain of $400,000," April 3, 1943.

The Chicago Defender. "Negro Sailors At Great Lakes Lead Bond Sales," April 3, 1943.

The Chicago Defender. "To Fight 'Jim Crow' In Local Bar Association," May 29, 1943.

The Chicago Defender. "Kill M.P. In Race Clash At Ga. Camp," June 12, 1943.

The Chicago Defender. "Weaver Heads Mayor Kelly's Race Committee," January 8, 1944.

The Chicago Defender. "Mayor Seeks Data On Employment Of War Veterans," January 29, 1944.

The Chicago Defender. "Protest Slum Project Site On Southside," February 19,1944.

The Chicago Defender. "Shoe Stamp 18 Not Good After April 30," April 8, 1944.

The Chicago Defender. "Covenant Suit Would Evict 1000 Families," February 5,1944.

The Chicago Defender. "Randolph Maps Plan For Nation Wide Conference," May 13, 1944.

The Chicago Defender. "Keep Hands Off West Chesterfield Project-- NAACP," April 8, 1944.

The Chicago Defender. "FDR Names 3-Man Board In FEP-Railroad Dispute," January 8, 1944.

The Chicago Defender. "Housing Has Not Failed, Declares CHA Chairman," January 8, 1944.

The Chicago Defender. "Spur Bond Drive For S.S. Robert S. Abbott," March 18, 1944.

The Chicago Defender. "OPA Starts Big South Side Drive On High Rentals," March 18, 1944

The Chicago Defender. "Overcrowding Tenants More Serious Than Ever," March 18, 1944.

The Chicago Defender. "Service Guild To Aid Abbott Ship Bond Drive," April 22, 1944.

CHAPTER TWELVE:
SOURCES

BOOKS

Burrell, Berkley. *Getting It Together: Black Businessmen In America.* Harcourt, Brace and Jovanovich, Inc., New York, 1971.Jones, Henry Williams. *The Housing of Negroes In Washington, D.C.* Howard University Press, Washington, D.C., 1929.

Killens, John Oliver. *And Then We Heard The Thunder.* Alfred A. Knopf, New York, 1962.

Lee, Ulysses. *United States Army In World War II - Special Studies: The Employment of Negro Troops.* Office of the Chief of Military History, United States Army, Washington, D.C., 1966.

Motley, Mary P. *The Invisible Soldier: The Experience of the Black Soldier In World War II.* Wayne State University Press, Detroit, Michigan, 1975.

Schoenfeld, Seymour J. *The Negro In the Armed Forces: His Value and Status Past, Presently, and Potential.* The Associated Publishers, Washington, D.C., 1945.

Travis, Dempsey J. *Don't Stop Me Now.* Children's Press, 1970.

PERIODICALS

"Black Chicago: Three Score Plus One, Part VIII," by Dempsey J. Travis, *Dollars & Sense Magazine,* August/September, 1980.

"White Folks Do The Funniest Things," by Langston Hughes, *Common Ground,* Winter, 1944.

"For Germans Only," by Donald Jones, *Common Sense,* December, 1943.

"These Are Our Heroes," by Louis E. Burnham, *Spotlight,* December, 1943.

NEWSPAPERS

Chicago Daily Defender. "Blast Detroit Mayor In Cop Whitewash," July 17, 1943.

Chicago Daily Defender. "Van Dorn Soldiers Keep Arms," July 17, 1943.

Chicago Daily Defender. "Riots At A Glance," June 26, 1943.

Chicago Daily Defender. "Blame Prejudice Police For Detroit Fatalities," June 26, 1943.

Chicago Daily Defender. "Riots In Los Angeles," June 26, 1943.

Chicago Daily Defender. "Segregation Rules WAAC Race Volunteers Lag," by Enoch P. Waters, Jr., January 16, 1943.

Chicago Daily Defender. "Savoy Ballroom Closed; Mixed Dancers Seen Cause," by Alfred Duckett, May 1, 1943.

Chicago Daily Defender. "Covenant Ban Loses Test In Legislature," June 12, 1943.

Chicago Daily Defender. "Seven Die, 150 Hurt In Ten Outbreaks," June 19, 1943.

Chicago Daily Defender. "Pennsylvania Railroad Ends Jim Crow Trains In State of Illinois," January 16, 1943.

Chicago Daily Defender. "Reign of Terror Against Black Soldiers In Valle Jo, California," January 2, 1943.

Chicago Daily Defender. "Ask Street Car Jobs For Negroes," January 16, 1943.

The New York Age. "Dancer Joins Negro USO Camp Shows Unit," June 3, 1944.

The New York Age. "Negro And White Wainwright WAC's Separated In Iowa, Paper Charges," November, 1944.

The New York Age. "President Roosevelt Declares For Permanent FEPC; Wants Post-War Period Free From Discrimination," November 4, 1944.

The New York Age. "President Roosevelt Approves Navy's Plan To Enlist Negro Women As Waves and SPARS," October 28, 1944.

The New York Age. "57 Negro Soldiers Jailed In Arizona When They Strike Against Prolonged K.P. Duty," September 23, 1944.

The New York Age. "War Department Order Forbidding Discrimination At Army Posts Is Protested by Governor of Alabama," September 21, 1944.

The New York Age. "Philadelphia Strike Ended; Four Strike Leaders Arrested, Fired From Jobs; Army Still On The Job," August 12, 1944

The New York Age. "Philadelphia Scene Of Riot In Protest Against Negro Motormen," August 5, 1944.

Afro-American. "D. C. Rooms Advertised For 'Light Colored' Tenants," August 15, 1944.

Afro-American. "General Davis Denies Saying Army Free of Bias," by J. Robert Smith, April 15, 1944.

Afro-American. "Dr. Charles Drew Wins 29th Spingarn Medal," April 1, 1944.

Afro-American. "30 Get Wings At Tuskegee," May 27, 1944

Afro-American. "CIAA Hits Army, Navy For Ignoring Colored Athletes," April 29, 1944.

Afro-American. "Hitler Preaches Ghetto System, U.S. Practices It," April 29, 1944.

Afro-American. "Robeson Weeps As 8,000 Cheer At Birthday Party," April 22, 1944.

Afro-American. "Increased Racial Tension Looms In San Francisco," April 15, 1944.

Afro-American. "Ask Volunteers For Ethiopia," April 15, 1944.

Afro-American. "Racial Progress Cited At Tuskegee," April 15, 1944.

CHAPTER THIRTEEN:
SOURCES

BOOKS

Abrams, Charles. *The City Is The Frontier.* Harper & Row Publishers, New York, 1965.

Clark, Dennis. *The Ghetto Game: Conflicts In The City.* Sheed and Ward, New York, 1962.

Ebony Pictorial History of Black America, Volume II, Editors of Ebony Magazine, Johnson Publishing Company, Chicago, 1970.

Glazer, Nathan and Davis McEntire. *Housing and Minority Groups.* University of California Press, Berkley, 1960.

Myerson, Martin and Edward C. Banfield. *Politics, Planning and the Public Interest.* The Fress Press, New York, 1955.

Myerson, Martin and Barbara Terrett and William L. C. Wheaton.

Housing, People, and Cities. McGraw-Hill Book Company, Inc., New York, 1962.

McEntire, Davis. *Residence and Race.* University of California Press, 1960.

Rapkin, Chester and William G. Grigsby. *The Demand for Housing In Racially Mixed Areas.* University of California Press, Berkley, 1960.

Steiner, Oscar H. *Our Housing Jungle and Your Pocketbook.* University Publishers, Inc., New York, 1960.

Weaver, Robert C. *The Negro Ghetto.* Harcourt, Brace and Company, New York, 1948.

NEWSPAPERS

Chicago Daily Defender. "Loop Hotels Ban: Won't Serve Both Races Together," January 26, 1946.

Chicago Daily Defender. "Crack Down On Jim Crow Rink At White City," January 26, 1946.

Chicago Daily Defender. "Pressure On Congress Key To More Homes, Expert Say," by Robert Lucas, June 8, 1946.

Chicago Daily Defender. "U.S. Supreme Court Aids Race Restrictive Pacts, NBA Charges," May 4, 1946.

Chicago Daily Defender. "New Dormitories 'For White Only,' " by Richard E. Goldsberry, April 27, 1946.

Chicago Daily Defender. "Northwestern Gets O.K. On Jim Crow Dorm," May 4, 1946.

Chicago Daily Defender. "Hunt White Vandals Who Bomb Negroes," February 2, 1946.

Chicago Daily Defender. "NAACP Brings Columbia Riot Victims To Chicago," April 27, 1946.

Chicago Daily Defender. (Advertisement) "Anna Lucasta," a play by Philip Yordan with original New York cast.

Chicago Daily Defender. "Open Fire On Jim Crow In U. Of C. Hospitals," February 9, 1946.

Chicago Daily Defender. "Ask Probe of Bus Firm's Anti-Negro Policy," February 2, 1946.

Chicago Daily Defender. "Police Arrest 10 Pickets In Strike At Stockyards," January 12, 1946.

Chicago Daily Defender. "Restrictions On Labor Are No Path To Progress," June 8, 1946.

Chicago Daily Defender. "Says Return To Africa Negroes' Only Salvation," June 1, 1946.

Chicago Daily Defender. "Huge Housing Meet Sunday: OPA, Low-Rent Chief Topics," April 27, 1946.

Chicago Daily Defender. "A Glimpse Of Beauty," by W. E. B. DuBois, April 27, 1946.

Chicago Daily Defender. "Americans Set Roots Of Racism In Panama," by U. G. Dailey, M.D., May 4, 1946.

Chicago Daily Defender. "Widows Fight Over Body of Marcus Garvey," by George Padmore, London Correspondent, 1946.

Chicago Daily Defender. "Rip White City Roller Rink," February 2, 1946.

Chicago Daily Defender. "Tenants To File Feb. 1 For Wentworth Gardens," January 26, 1946.

Chicago Daily Defender. "Clear Officer In Loading Of Negro Troops," by Venice Spraggs, January 7, 1946.

Chicago Daily Defender. "Judges Refuses To Drop Jim Crow Covenant Case," January, 1947.

Chicago Daily Defender. "Evanston Veterans Sue City For Housing Equality," January 11, 1947.

Chicago Daily Defender. "The Need For Interracial Solidarity In Unions," January, 1947.

Chicago Daily Defender. "Educator Tells U.S., End Bias," January, 1947.

Chicago Daily Defender. "American Race Prejudice Must Be Destroyed," by Robert Abbott, April 5, 1947.

Chicago Daily Defender. "Probe Attack By Whites In Tension Area," January, 1947.

Chicago Daily Defender. "Jackie Robinson Signs To Play For Brooklyn," January, 1947.

Chicago Daily Defender. "1946 Lynching Record," January, 1947.

Chicago Daily Defender. "Survey Shows White Only Ads Gain Job Market," April, 1947.

Chicago Daily Defender. "Governors Rename Racist To Own Vacancy," January, 1947.

Chicago Daily Defender. "4 Testify To Jim Crow On I.C. Crack Train," March 13, 1948.

Chicago Daily Defender. "Thousands Vow To Keep Park Manor White," by Stephan Lewis, March 6, 1948.

Chicago Daily Defender. "Bar GI's From Nurse Training," by Charles A. Davis, March 13, 1948.

Chicago Daily Defender. "Negroes Play Big Role In Meat Strike," March 13, 1948.

Chicago Daily Defender. "Fear Mounts At Rumor Anti-Slum Program Means Negro Clearance," March 13, 1948.

Chicago Daily Defender. "Railway Workers Win Injunction To Halt Replacement By Whites," February 14, 1948.

Chicago Daily Defender. "Charges Mail Order House With Job Bias," January 31, 1948.

Chicago Daily Defender. "Order Ends Segregated National Guard," February 14, 1948.

Chicago Daily Defender. "Neisner Dime Store, Hit By Job Bias Charge, Closes Its Door," March 6, 1948.

Chicago Daily Defender. "Vets Appeal Cab Bias Verdict of U.S. Court," March 13, 1948.

Chicago Daily Defender. "Randolph Asks Civil Disobedience Unless Military Forces End Bias," April 13, 1948.

Chicago Daily Defender. "Ask Anti-Trust Probe Of Bias In Home Loans," April 3, 1948.

Chicago Daily Defender. "Buttons To Boost War On Segregated Army," April 24, 1948.

Chicago Daily Defender. "Neisner Bros. Tells Service To Community," April 24, 1948.

Chicago Daily Defender. "Hurl Stones, Lawsuit At Woodlawn, Residents," April 24, 1948.

Chicago Daily Defender. "25 Families Escape Ouster From Englewood," by Charles A. Davis, April 24, 1948.

Chicago Daily Defender. "Hoodlums Mob Man On Street," January 3,

1948.

Chicago Daily Defender. "Prejudice Blocks Nurse Training," by Lillian Scott, January 24, 1948.

Chicago Daily Defender. "White Mother Charges New Son-In-Law Has Negro Blood," 1948.

Chicago Daily Defender. "Train Bypasses Jim Crow Fans," by Lillian Scott, July 3, 1948.

Chicago Daily Defender. "New VA Chief Pledges Equality Of All Vets," January 10, 1948.

Chicago Daily Defender. "Segregated Travel Law Under Fire; High Court To Study Biased Policy," by Venice Spraggs, October 15, 1949.

Chicago Daily Defender. "Truman Pat on Ending Army Bias," October 8, 1949.

Chicago Daily Defender. "No Civil Rights Compromise - Truman," January, 1949.

Chicago Daily Defender. "Segregtion In County Jail Ends," by R. B. Goldsberry, 1949.

Chicago Daily Defender. "Action on FEPC Slated Next Week," 1949.

Chicago Daily Defender. "Green, AFL Chief, Warns Congress: Wants Action On Civil Rights Bill," by Louis Martin, 1949.

Chicago Daily Defender. "Seeks Missouri Law To Oust Railroad Porters From Jobs," 1949.

Chicago Daily Defender. "Negro Wins Plea To Enter Kentucky U.," April, 1949.

Chicago Daily Defender. "Convenant Leaders State Opposition At City Council Hearing," by Richard Goldsberry, February 5, 1949.

Chicago Daily Defender. "Hospital Bias Bill Again In Legislature," 1949.

Chicago Daily Defender. "NAACP Youth Gets Offer Of Compromise In Theatre Row," 1949.

Chicago Daily Defender. "Brokers Charge FHA, VA Deny Mortgage Insurance To Negroes," by Chuck Davis, 1949.

Chicago Daily Defender. "Truman Stands Firm On Rights, Demands A 'Square Deal' For All," 1949.

Chicago Daily Defender. "Hoodlums Try Again To Burn Park Manor Home," April, 1949.

CHAPTER FOURTEEN:
SOURCES

BOOKS

Anderson, Martin. *The Federal Bulldozer: A Critical Analysis of Urban Renewal, 1949-1962.* The M. I. T. Press, Cambridge, Mass., 1964.

Banfield, Edward C. and Morton Grodzins. *Government and Housing.* McGraw-Hill Book Company, Inc., New York, 1958.

Bowly, Devereux Jr. *The Poorhouse Subsidized Housing In Chicago: 1895-1976.* Southern Illinois University Press, Carbondale, Illinois, 1978.

Brown, Frank London. *Trumbull Park.* Regnery, Chicago, 1959.

Haar, Charles M. *Federal Credit and Private Housing.* McGraw-Hill Book Company, Inc., New York, 1960.

Mayer, Harold M. and Richard C. Wade. *Chicago: Growth Of A Metropolis.* University of Chicago Press, 1969.

Meyerson, Martin and Edward C. Banfield. *Politics, Planning and The Public Interest.* The Fress Press, New York, 1955.

Ross, Peter H. and Robert A. Dentler. *The Politics of Urban Renewal.* The Fress Press, Glencoe, Illinois, 1961.

Weaver, Robert C. *The Negro Ghetto.* Harcourt, Brace & Company, New York, 1948.

Wilson, James Q., Editor. *Urban Renewal: The Record and The Controversy.* The M. I. T. Press, Cambridge, Mass., 1966.

Wolman, Harold. *Politics of Federal Housing.* Dodd, Mead & Company, New York, 1971.

OFFICIAL DOCUMENTS

Housing Hearings Before The United States Commission On Civil Rights: May 5 and 6, 1959. U. S. Government Printing Office, Washington, D. C., 1959.

NEWSPAPERS

Chicago Daily Defender. "Dr. Julian Raps Housing Farce," January, 1950.

Chicago Daily Defender. "Rap Judge, Prosecutor In Chicago Riot Trials," January, 1950.

Chicago Daily Defender. "Police Lift Ban On 'No Way Out' Film," January, 1950.

Chicago Daily Defender. "Puts O.K. On Jim Crow Travel," February 25, 1950.

Chicago Daily Defender. "Governor Acts As Cicero Cops Flop," July 14, 1951.

Chicago Sun Times. "Frank London Brown, Labor Teacher, Dead At 34," 1962.

CHAPTER FIFTEEN:
SOURCES

BOOKS

Bogle, Donald. *Toms, Coons, Mulattoes, and Bucks.* Viking Press, New York, 1973.

Conant, James B. *Slums and Suburbs: A Commentary On Schools In Metropolitan Areas.* McGraw-Hill Book Company, New York, 1961.

Cripps, Thomas. *Slow Fade To Black: The Negro In American Film, 1900-1942.* Oxford University Press, London, 1971.

Doob, Leonard W. *Public Opinion and Propaganda.* Archon Books, Hamden, Connecticut, 1966.

Griffith, Richard and Arthur Mayer. *The Movies.* Simon and Schuster, New York, 1957.

Hughes, Langston and Arna Bontemps, ed. *The Poetry of The Negro: 1746-1949.* Double Day and Company, Inc., New York, 1951.

King, Martin Luther, Jr. *Strides Toward Freedom.* Harper and Brothers, 1958.

Wilson, James Q. *Negro Politics: The Search For Leadership.* The Free Press, Glencoe, Illinois, 1960.

OFFICIAL DOCUMENTS

Housing Hearings Before The United States Commission On Civil Rights: May 5 and 6, 1959. U.S. Government Printing Office, Washington, D.C.

LETTERSLetter from Enoc P. Waters, Jr., Executive Editor, The Chicago Daily Defender, to Jack Travis, dated July 21, 1953.
Letter from Edward J. Sparling, President, Roosevelt University to Dempsey J. Travis, dated March 30, 1955.

PERIODICALS
Ebony. "The Till Case People One Year Later: Tragedy Alter Lives of Whites, Witnesses."
Ebony. "Land of The Till Murder: the Delta Is Blazing Today With Fierce Racial Tensions," by Clotye Murdock.
The Crisis, "Mississippi Barbarism," October, 1955.
The Crisis. "Fate of the World," October, 1955.
Parade. "Americans Who Can't Speak Their Own Language," by Lloyd Shearer, June 11, 1967.

NEWSPAPERS*Chicago Daily Defender.* "Urges Halt To South Side Minority Ghetto," April 3, 1954.
Chicago Daily Defender. "Mob Victim Faces Trial April 27," April 17, 1954.
Chicago Daily Defender. "Howard Hits City, Leaves Trumbull," May 8, 1954.
Chicago Daily Defender. "Marshall Receives Abbott Award; Says Jim Crow Will End By 1963," by Lee Blackwell, May 15, 1954.
Chicago Daily Defender. "Sees Danger Of Bias In 'Private' High School Proposal For Kenwood," January 9, 1954.
Chicago Daily Defender. "Interracial Schools Works In Atlanta: University System Shows It Can Be Done In Dixie," January 9, 1954.
Chicago Daily Defender. "Five Held In Trumbull Disturbance," January 9, 1954.
Chicago Daily Defender. "CHA Reaffirms Anti-Bias Policy, Asks Panel To Help Work It Out," January 16, 1954.
Chicago Daily Defender. "Ban School Jim Crow On Army Post," February 6, 1954.
Chicago Daily Defender. "Business League Studies Proposal To Drop 'Negro' From Its Name," October 23, 1954.
Chicago Daily Defender. "Racist Attacks Hit Englewood," May 1, 1954.
Chicago Daily Defender. "Violence Shocks W. Chesterfield," April 24, 1954.
Chicago Daily Defender. "Housing Industry Takes Wait, See Attitude On President's Proposal," January 30, 1954.
Chicago Daily Defender. "UNCF Hails School Decision As Major Step To Racist Equality," May 22, 1954.
Chicago Daily Defender. "10,000 Jam Till Mass Meet Here," by Robert L. Birchman.
Chicago Daily Defender. "Defender Puts Up $5,000 Reward For Till Killers," November 5, 1955.
Chicago Daily Defender. "U.S. Gets 3,000 Till Letters, But Can't Act," November 26, 1955.
Chicago Daily Defender. "World Awaits Verdict Of Till Kidnap Jury," by Lee Blackwell.
Chicago Daily Defender. "Senate May Hear Till Lynch Story," October 29, 1955.
Chicago Tribune. "Poitier's Legacy To His Family Breathes Life Into

The Past," May 28, 1980.

Chicago Tribune. "School Count Shows Racial Picture and Class Size," by Clay Gowran, November 3, 1963.

Chicago Tribune. "Principals Bare Problems, Needs of City Schools," by Casey Banas, July 26, 1964.

Chicago Sun Times. "Conant Reverses Stand, Backs Integrated Schools," by Terry Ferrer, November 15, 1964.

Chicago Tribune. "Suburb School Pay Is Higher: Teachers Start Better, Gain Faster," by Casey Banas, October 25, 1964.

Chicago Daily News. "Slum Pupils: Accent On the Positive," by Lois Wille, November 4, 1964.

Chicago Daily News. "Study Reveals Some Shocking School Flaws," by Sylvia Porter, April 15, 1965.

Chicago Sun Times. "Blame Schools For Few Negroes In Medicine," by Frank Sullivan, October 5, 1965.

Chicago Sun Times. "Academic Lag Indicated At Negro High Schools," by Christopher Chandler, June 8, 1966.

Chicago Sun Times. "List Most-Crowded High Schools," by Christopher Chandler, March 15, 1966.

Chicago Sun Times. "What Hurts DuSable Pupils," October 22, 1966.

The New York Times. "Substitutes for Ph. D.," June 26, 1966.

The New York Times. "Noe 'Educational Parks,' " June 26, 1966.

Chicago Sun Times. "Increased Segregation Reported In City's Public Schools," September 27, 1966.

Chicago Daily Defender. "Charges HEW Is Abetting 'New Kind' of Racial Bias," March 6, 1972.

CHAPTER SIXTEEN:
SOURCES

BOOKS

Anderson, Jervis. *A. Philip Randolph: A Biographic Portrait.* Hartcourt, Brace, Jovanovich, Inc., New York, 1972.

Brown, Frank London. *Trumbull Park.* Regnery, Chicago, 1959

McEntire, Davis. *Residence and Race.* University of California Press, 1960.

Rapkin, Chester and William G. Grigsby. *The Demand for Housing In Racially Mixed Areas.* University of California Press, Berkley, 1960.

Reddick, L.D. *Crusader Without Violence: Biography of Martin Luther King Jr.* Harper & Bros., New York, 1959.

Robeson, Paul. *Here I Stand.* Beacon Press, Boston, Mass., 1958.

Wilson, James Q. *Negro Politics: The Search For Leadership.* The Free Press, Glencoe, Illinois, 1960.

Wilson, James Q. (Editor). *Urban Renewal: The Record and The Controversy.* The M.I.T. Press, Cambridge, Mass., 1966.

NEWSPAPERS

Chicago Sun Times. "Catholic Weekly Hits Martin Luther King Ban," February 16, 1957.

Chicago Sun Times. "Desegregation Strife Boosts NAACP Fund Over $1Million," January 8, 1957.

Chicago Sun Times. "WGN-TV Keeps Martin Luther King Film Ban,"

January 9, 1957.

Chicago Sun Times. "Warn Of A Trend To Negro 'Ghetto,'" by Ruth Moore, January 24, 1957.

Chicago Defender. "General Gruenther Says 'No' To Restrictive Covenant," by Ruth Montgomery, February 3, 1957.

Chicago Defender. "Ark. Guards Show Mettle Enforcing Integration," by Shelby Scates, October 3, 1957.

Chicago Defender. "Suspend 3 At Central High After Kicking Incident," October 5, 1957.

Chicago Defender. "All Quiet, Guards Gunless At Little Rock School," by John Barrow, October 22, 1957.

Chicago Defender. "Nab Adult Coed; Pupils Hang Effigy," by Shelby Scates, October 5, 1957.

Chicago Defender. "Travel Bias Foe Runs Into Some," October 5, 1957.

Chicago Defender. "Says U.C. Aim: Thin Out Negroes," January 19, 1957.

Chicago Defender. "N.Y. Ask AAA to Oust Chicago Auto Club For Bias," February 23, 1957.

Chicago Defender. "New Book Probes Status of Chicago's Negro Life," April 13, 1957.

Chicago Defender. "Housing Integration Issue Splits Hyde Park," by Mansfield Peters, January 26, 1957.

Chicago Defender. "Reveal Move To Segregate Vets," April 13, 1957.

Chicago Defender. "State Troops Guard 9 Pupils," October 1, 1957.

Chicago Defender. "Fear Exclusion Scheme In Rebuilding Of Hyde Park," October 19, 1957.

Chicago Defender. "Real Estate Insurance Good Career To Follow: Ability To Mix Plus Training Equals Goal," by Dempsey J. Travis, December 14, 1957.

Chicago American. "NAACP Sees Ike, Hits School Ruling," June 23, 1958.

Chicago American. "Negro Student Says They Want To Go Back," June 23, 1958.

Chicago American. "NAACP's 9-Point Rights Plan," June 23, 1958.

Chicago American. "Nations Eyes On Hyde Park Plan. Protests May Reshape Big Housing Program," June 24, 1958.

Chicago American. "NAACP Objects," June 24, 1958.

Chicago American. "Smooth Integration," June 24, 1958.

Chicago American. "College Integration 8 to 25 Years Away," June 19, 1958.

Chicago American. "U.S. Judge Puts Off Action For 2½ Years," June 21, 1958.

Chicago American. "Negro Hits Race Bias In Chicago," by Les Brownlee, June 12, 1958.

Chicago American. "Minorities Urged To Unite," by Wesley South, June 19, 1958.

Chicago American. "More Fire Insurance For S. Side Urged," April 17, 1958.

Chicago Defender. "Threaten To Bomb Home Of Englewood Clergyman," October 21, 1958.

Chicago Daily Tribune. "Refuse to O.K. Insurance In Disputed Area," March 1, 1958.

Chicago Defender. "Friend's Suggestion Paid Off For Travis," February

22, 1958.

New Crusader. "Realtist Back Mayor's Slum Drive," February 22, 1958.

Chicago Defender. "Push Plan To Get Fire Insurance," July 26, 1958.

Chicago Defender. "Civic Leaders Seek Daley's Aid In Fight On Arsonists," July 30, 1958.

Chicago Defender. "Group Of Officers From Chicago Insurance Brokers Association Calls On Illinois Insurance Directors Joseph S. Gerber, February 8, 1958.

Daily Defender. "Dearborn Real Estate Board Members Meeting With State Insurance Director Joseph S. Gerber," April 23, 1958.

Daily Defender. "Install Travis As Realty Head," February 22, 1958.

Chicago American. "South Side Plans Slum War Huddle," By Les Brownlee, February 7, 1958.

Chicago Defender. "Mass Meeting On Bias In Englewood," February 22, 1958.

Chicago American. "Mayor Daley Seeks Aid in War On Firetrap," January 31, 1958.

Chicago American. "Find Dixie-Style Terror In Englewood," May 23, 1958.

The New Crusader. "Dearborn Real Estate Board Refutes Charge," October 31, 1959.

Chicago Daily News. "Charges Race Bias In Fire Insurance," by Henry Hanson, March 25, 1959.

Chicago Defender. "In Chicago Racism Does Follow You To The Grave," by R. C. Keller, May 16, 1959.

Chicago Defender. "Insurance Conspiracy Against Negro Bared," by Simeon Osby, March 30, 1959.

Chicago Sun Times. "Sivart Corp. Become The First Negro-Owned Mortgage Comp," *Real Estate News,* June 30, 1961.

Chicago Daily News. "Realtist To Hear Author Frank London Brown," May 21, 1959. *Real Estate News,* May 15, 1959.

OFFICIAL DOCUMENTS

Statement of Dempsey J. Travis, President of the Dearborn Real Estate Board, Inc., before the President's Commission On Civil Rights, May 1959.

LETTERS

Letter From: A.L. Foster, Executive Director, Cosmopolitan Chamber of Commerce, To: Dempsey J. Travis, February 24, 1957.

Letter From: Edward J. Sparling, President, Roosevelt University, To: Dempsey J. Travis, February 25, 1957.

Letter From: Richard J. Daley To Dempsey J. Travis, May 1, 1957.

Letter From: Joseph L. O'Neal, President, Adams Oakley Property Improvement Association. To: Dempsey J. Travis—July 25, 1958 Re: Mass Meeting.

Letter From: Charles L. Warden, Secretary, National Society of Real Estate Appraiser's, Inc. To: Dempsey J. Travis July 25, 1958—Re: "Very Important Meeting"

Letter From: Dempsey J. Travis To: Richard J. Daley, July 26, 1958. — Re: Black Displacement as a Result of Highway Programs.

Letter From: Fred J. Smith, State Senator 11th District, General Assembly To: Dempsey J. Travis, March 25, 1959.

Letter To: Dempsey J. Travis, From: Commission on Civil Rights, Washington 25th, April 21, 1959.

Letter To: Dempsey J. Travis, From: James Q. Wilson, Instructor, The University of Chicago, September 24, 1959.

Telegram To Dempsey J. Travis From: Roy Wilkins NAACP, Executive Secretary, December 20, 1959.

CHAPTER SEVENTEEN
SOURCES

BOOKS

Bowly, Devereux, Jr. *The Poorhouse Subsidized Housing In Chicago: 1895-1976*. Southern Illinois University Press, Carbondale, Illinois, 1978.

Handlin, Oscar. *Race and Nationality In American Life*. Little, Brown & Company, Toronto, 1957.

Lowe, Jeanne R. *Cities In A Race With Time*. Random House, New York, 1967.

McKay, David H. *Housing and Race In Industrial Society*. Croom Helm, London, 1977,

Meyerson, Martin and Edward C. Banfield. *Politics, Planning and the Public Interest*. The Free Press, New York, 1955.

Steiner, Oscar H. *Our Housing Jungle and Your Pocketbook*. University Publishers, Inc., New York, 1960.

Tebbel, Robert. *The Slum Makers*. The Dial Press, New York, 1963.

Young, Whitney M., Jr. *Beyond Racism*. McGraw-Hill Book Company, New York, 1969.

JOURNALS

"The Urban-Suburban Investment—Disinvestment Process: Consequences for Older Neighborhoods," by Calvin P. Bradford and Leonard S. Rubinowitz. *The Annals of the American Academy of Political and Social Sciences,* Volume 422, (November, 1975), 77-96.

NEWSPAPERS

Chicago Sun Times. "Group To Fight Negroes Going To Park Forest," January 21, 1960.

Chicago Defender. "Pledges Fight For 'Fair Shake'," April 9, 1960.

Chicago Defender. "Housing Authors NAACP Speakers," April 16, 1960.

Chicago Defender. "Delegates of The National Association of Real Estate Brokers Met With Norman P. Mason, United States Housing Administrator," April 30, 1960.

Chicago Defender. Defy Racists At Park Swim Pool," July 30, 1960.

Chicago Defender. "Negro Family First In U.S.A. To Get New FHA Help," August 27, 1960.

Chicago Defender. "Dempsey Travis Out To Win 'Rights' Gain," July 23, 1960.

Chicago Daily News. "Mortgage Credit Refusals Squeeze Minorities Here: Loan Practices Force Them To Buy Homes On Contract," by Nicholas Shuman, June 25, 1961.

Chicago Daily News. "Negroes First Graduates of Mortgage Banking Class," June 17, 1963.

Chicago Daily News. "Negro Mortgage Firm Here Gets Eastern Funds," by Ralph Gray, August 26, 1963.

Atlanta Daily World. "Mortgage Bankers Get $40 Million For Housing," March 31, 1963.

Chicago Sun Times. "Banker Urges More Home Mortgage Loans To Negroes," August 27, 1963.

Chicago Defender. "Southside Realty Firm In $3 Million 'First'," July 15, 1963.

Chicago Courier. "Integration 200 Years Away Without An Open Occupancy Law: Travis," August 10, 1963.

Chicago Sun Times. "Negroes Move Into 'Wealthiest' Suburb," by Ronald Berquist, December 7, 1963.

NEWS RELEASES

WBEE *Citizen Salute* to Dempsey J. Travis dated April 11, 1963, re: mortgage funds available to Negro home buyers.

OFFICIAL DOCUMENTS

Housing Hearings Before The United States Commission On Civil Rights: May 5 and 6, 1959. U.S. Government Printing Office, Washington, D.C., 1959

LETTERS/TELEGRAMS

Letter from E. J. Dee, Assistant Commissioner, Field Operations, Federal Housing Administration to Dempsey J. Travis, President, The Sivart Corporation.

Letter from Donald S. Frey of the United Citizens' Committee For Freedom of Residence In Illinois to Dempsey J. Travis, dated May 3, 1960, re: NAACP Conference.

Letter from Rogers, Rogers, Strayhorn & Harth, Attorneys at Law to Dempsey J. Travis, re. discriminatory practice/s of the 50th On The Lake Motel and The Thunderbird Motel.

Letter from (Rev.) Theodore M. Hesburgh, C.S.C., President, University of Notre Dame to Dempsey J. Travis, dated March 10, 1960, re: NAACP Installation.

Telegram from Roy Wilkins to Dempsey J. Travis dated February 5, 1960, re: lobby for passage of civil rights legislation

Telegram from President Richard M. Nixon to Dempsey J. Travis dated March 2, 1960, re: 1960 Freedom Fund Dinner

Telegram from Roy Wilkins to Dempsey J. Travis dated April 28, 1960, re: State Conference Presidents and key NAACP leaders

Letter from Mayor Richard J. Daley to Dempsey J. Travis dated February 29, 1960, re: Non-partisan police board

Letter from Jerome M. Sax, Executive Vice President, The Exchange National Bank of Chicago to Dempsey J. Travis dated July 14, 1960, re: Sivart Mortgage Corporation

CHAPTER EIGHTEEN:
SOURCES

BOOKS

Allen, Robert L. *Black Awakening In Capitalist America.* Doubleday & Co., Garden City, New York, 1969.

Chrisman, Robert and Nathan Hare. *Contemporary Black Thought: The*

Best From The Black Scholar. The Bobbs-Merrill Company, Inc., New York, 1973.

Haddad, William F. and G. Douglas Pugh, Editors. *Black Economic Development*. Prentice-Hall, Inc., Englewood Cliffs, New Jersey, 1969.

Lecky, Robert S. and H. Elliott Wright, Editors. *Black Manifesto: Religion, Racism, and Reparations*. Sheed and Ward, New York, 1969.

Ofari, Earl. *The Myth of Black Capitalism*. Monthly Review Press, New York, 1970.

Reynolds, Barbara A. *Jessie Jackson: The Man, The Movement, The Myth*. Nelson-Hall, Chicago, 1975.

Sternbieb, George and James W. Hughes. *America's Housing Prospects and Problems*. Rutgers University Center for Urban Policy Research, New Brunswick, New Jersey, 1980.

DIRECTORIES AND REFERENCES
Ebony Pictorial History of Black America, Volume III, Editors of Ebony, Johnson Publishing Company, Chicago, 1970.

NEWSPAPERS
Chicago Sun Times. "Rights Groups Build Up To Massive Action," by Basil Talbott, Jr., July 10, 1966.

Chicago Sun Times. "King, Daley to Meet Monday, Discuss Rights Demands," by Basil Talbott, Jr., July 9, 1966.

Chicago Sun Times. "Cicero Leaders Hail Guard Call-Up," by Cecil Neth, August 25, 1966.

Chicago Sun Times. "W. Side Erupts In New Violence," July 15, 1966.

Chicago Sun Times. "Human Relations Unit Begins Probe of Realty Companies," by Robert S. Kleckner, August 5, 1966.

Chicago Sun Times. "37 Hurt As Mob Attacks Gage Park Rights Marchers," August 1, 1966.

Chicago Sun Times. "Experts Predicts No Early End To Negro Ghettos," by Ruth Moore, August 21, 1966.

Chicago Sun Times. "Open Housing Proposals Ready," by Basil Talbott, Jr., August 26, 1966.

Chicago Sun Times. "Court Acts Against Tavern Refusing To Service Negro G.I.," August 19, 1966.

Chicago Sun Times. "Sue 10 Maywood Aides In Sale of Home To Negroes," July 9, 1966.

Chicago Sun Times. "King Schedules March Into South Deering Today," by Art Petacque, August 21, 1966.

Chicago Sun Times. "President Signs Bill; Fair Housing Law Of The Land," by Tom Littlewood, April 12, 1968.

Chicago Sun Times. "$100,000 In Mortgage Funds Available To Contract Buyers," June 19, 1970.

Chicago Defender. "Dempsey Travis And C.B.L. Officers Discuss Victory On 'For Blacks Only'," July 11-17, 1970.

Chicago Defender. "Travis to D.C.: C.B.L. Okays Mortgage Plan," April 14, 1970.

Chicago Tribune. "Story of One Man's Fight to Aid Contract Buyers," by Arthur Siddon, AAugust 16, 1970.

NEWSPAPERS
Chicago Daily News. "$100,000 Relief: CBL Getting Second Break In

Two Weeks," by Betty Washington, June 19, 1970.

Chatham Citizen. "Travis Seeks U.S. Mortgage Aid: New Plan May Save CBL From Questionable Pact," by Gus Savage, Week of April 15, 1970.

Sun Times. "Daley Tells Terms of Pact To End CBL Evictions," by Thomas M. Gray, April 11, 1970.

Sun Times. "Urge Blacks: Learn Finance Expertise," October 9, 1970.

American Banker. "Black Mortgage Banker Voices Pessimism About Institutionalized Racism," by William Zimmerman, July 21, 1970.

Chicago Defender. "Blacks Trapped In Housing Fight," by Robert McClory, March 7, 1972.

Chicago Defender. "Denounce Racism In HUD, FHA," February 16, 1972.

New York Times. "HUD Criticized On Housing Curbs In Minority Areas of Cities," by John Herbers, April 18, 1972.

Sun Times. "Black Urges 'Urban Homestead Act'," by Grayson Mitchell, April 8, 1972.

Boston Evening Globe. "Black Caucus At Harvard: Suburban Housing Not Answer," by John Abbott, April 7, 1972.

New York Times. "Black Mortgage Bankers Discuss Problems," by Robert D. Hershey, Jr., February 11, 1972.

Sun Times. "Site Rules Hit In Housing Poor," by Philip Greer, February 11, 1972.

Chicago Tribune. "HUD Site Criteria Assailed," by Joseph Egelhof, February 11, 1972.

Chicago Tribune. "Between the Lines of HUD's New Plan," by Vernon Jarrett; February 6, 1972.

American Banker. "HUD's New Site Selection Criteria Attacked by Leading Black Banker," by Harry F. Wille, February 18, 1972.

The Washington Post. "Subsidized Housing Rules Hit," by Philip Greer, February 13, 1972.

PERIODICALS

Jet. "New HUD Regulations Hurt Urban Blacks," March 2, 1972.

LETTERS

Letter from Dempsey J. Travis, President, United Mortgage Bankers of America, to Senator Charles H. Percy dated September 6, 1967, re: mortgage capital gap in the central cities.

Letter from Senator Charles H. Percy to Dempsey J. Travis dated September 1, 1967 re: proposals to advance the opportunities for home ownership.

**CHAPTER NINETEEN:
SOURCES**

BOOKS

Allen, Robert L., *Black Awakening In Capitalist America: An Analytic History.* Doubleday & Company, Inc., New York, 1969.

Baily, J. Edward III., *Living Legends In Black.* Baily Publishing Company, Detroit, 1976.

Brink, William and Louis Harris. *The Negro Revolution In America.* Simon and Schuster, New York, 1964.

Burrell, Berkley. *Getting It Together*. Harcourt, Brace and Jovanovich, New York, 1971.

Gloster, Jesse E. *Economics Of Minority Groups*. Premier Printing Company, Houston, Texas, 1973.

A Summary Report Of The Forum—What Our National Priorities Should Be, April 5, 6, 7, 1972. Harvard University, Cambridge, Mass., 1972.

Travis, Dempsey, J. *Don't Stop Me Now*. Children's Press, 1970.

DIRECTORIES AND REFERENCES

Rather, Ernest R. (Editor), *Chicago Negro Almanac And Reference Book*. Chicago Negro Almanac Publishing Company, Inc., Chicago, 1972.

The Ebony Success Library, Volume I: 1,000 Successful Blacks. Editors of Ebony Magazine, Johnson Publishing Company, Inc., Chicago, 1973.

The Ebony Success Library, Volume II: Famous Blacks Give Secrets Of Success. Editors of Ebony Magazine, Johnson Publishing Company, Inc., Chicago, 1973.

PERIODICALS

Chicago Reporter. "Black Enterprise List Reveals Chicago Top Black Business Gross Up $5.47 Million," August, 1976.

Dollars & Sense. "Black Chicago: Three Score Plus One," (Twelve consecutive installments) June, 1979 through May, 1981.

The Bankers Magazine. "Banks Business, and The Black Community," by Dempsey J. Travis, Spring, 1969.

Real Estate Review. "An Autopsy Of The Ghetto," by Dempsey J. Travis, Winter, 1972.

Savings Bank Journal. "Opportunity Or Detour," by Dempsey J. Travis, May, 1972.

Risk Management Magazine. "Ghetto Investment: A Good Investment," by Dempsey J. Travis, June-July, 1972.

The Black Scholar. "Black Businesses: Obstacles To Their Success," by Dempsey J. Travis, 1973.

The Black Scholar. "Barrier To Black Power In The American Economy," by Dempsey J. Travis, October, 1971.

The Black Scholar. "The 1980 Homestead Act," by Dempsey J. Travis, November-December, 1979.

Jet. "Need Not Be 'Tom' To Be Accepted, Says Realtor, April 7, 1966.

Business Week. "Negro Business Feels Stresses of Success," April 9, 1966.

Ebony. "Negro Pioneers In Mortgage Banking," July, 1967.

Ebony. "Don't Buy Other Peoples Paint," February, 1976.

NEWSPAPERS

Chicago Sun Times. "Why Two Rich Blacks Prefer South Side Life," by Quida Lindsey, May 15, 1977.

The Atlanta Constitution. "Chicago: U.S. Black Business Mecca," April 9, 1980.

Chicago Daily News. "Union to Lend $7.6 Million for Low-Cost Negro Homes," by Robert M. Lewin, July 30, 1965.

The New York Times. "Union allots aid for Negro homes: $7.6 Million being lent by garment workers here," July 30, 1965.

Chicago Defender. "Travis Realty to sell 70 Markham homes," Week of

August 28-September 3, 1965.
The Courier. "Exclusive Sales Agency Awarded to Travis Realty," August 28, 1965.

LETTERS

Letter from Gaylord A. Freeman, Jr. Vice Chairman of the Board, The First National Bank of Chicago to Dempsey J. Travis dated May 21, 1964. Re: Invitation to join Chicago Urban League Business Advisory Council.

Letter from Otto Kerner, Governor of Illinois to Dempsey J. Travis dated November 2, 1964. Re: Thank you for support.

Letter from Jacqueline Kennedy to Dempsey Travis dated September 4, 1964. Re: Contribution to John F. Kennedy Library.

Index

Abbott, Robert S. 16, 37, 296
Aberdeen Proving Ground 100, 109, 111
Adams, George 129
Addams, Jane (also see Hull House) 2
Adventistism (Sabbath on Saturday) 52, 53, 54
Afro-American Patrolmen's League 259,261, 263,267
Alcorn College 238
Alexander, Frank 20
Alexandria, Indiana 230
Allen, Charlie 80
Alix, Mae 96
Alpha Hotel 36
Alperin, Norman M. 160
Alpha Phi Alpha Fraternity 222
Alton, Illinois 9
American Bar Association 230
American Federation of Musicians 74
American Friends Service Comm. 146
American Institute of Real 138
   Estate Appraisers
American Negro Police Assoc. 261,263
American Negro Theatre 113
American Railway Union 19
American Railway Union Constitution 19
Amerian Revolution 168
American Savings & Loan Institute 241
American Savings & Loan League 236, 240
Americana Hotel (New York) 156
Ammons, Albert 78
Ammons, Bishop Edsel 79
Ammons, Gene 79
Anderson, Ivy 121
Anderson, Louie 206
Anderson, Robert 48
Anderson, M. J. 156
Anna Lucasta 113
Apex Box Company 85, 86
Armistice, 1918 25
Armour 84
Armour Employment Office 84, 90, 94
Armstrong, Louis 40, 79, 80, 96
Army Special Training Program 106
Aronin, Aaron 147
Art Institute 217
Assistant United States Attorney 278, 281
Atlanta, Georgia 180
Auditorium Hotel XIX
Army PX 103
Aunt Della's(dream book) 36
Aunt Sally's(dram book) 36
Austin, Willie (Aunt) 28,60,62,114

356/

Babcock, Richard (Lt. Colonel) 108, 110
Baldwin Ice Cream Co. 141
Baker, Elmore 18, 139, 141
Baldwin, James 200
Baldwin, Kit 141
Banach, Henry 129
Barge, Curtis (Rev) 147
Barnes, John P. (Federal Judge) 130
Barnett, Alfreda Duster 15
Barnett, Ferdinand 11,15
Barnett, Ida B. Wells 14, 15
   (See Also Ida B. Wells)
Bartlett, Frederick 15, 204, 208
   (See Chicago Conservator)
Barry, Marion 149
Basie, Count 110
Bates, Daisy 144
Bates, L.C. 144
Bates, Ruby 49, 52
Bearskin, Sybil 248
Beasley School 188, 189, 291
Bechet, Sidney 40
Bell, "Baby the Pimp" 94
Bendix Corporation 233
Ben Franklin Store 36
Bennett, Lerone 287,288
Bentley, Lemuel 147
Beavers, Louise 71
Bethel A.M.E. Church 2
Bible Class (see Rev. Reverdy 2
   Ransom)
Bickers, Joseph T. 156
Billings Hospital 135
Binga Arcade Building 39, 127
Binga, Jesse 39, 204, 205, 209, 219, 256, 258, 294, 295
Binga State Bank 33, 39, 258
Birmingham, Alabama 25
Bismarck Hotel 162
Brinks Service 258
Blackstone Hotel 146
Black Angel of the Violin 116
Black Belt .... XIX, 20, 25, 26, 36, 40
Blackbook Awards Dinner 299
Blackbook Business Reference & 298
   Guide
Black Codes 220, 215
Black Devils 16, 17
Black Enterprise 297
Black, Julian 219
Black, Julian (Mrs.) 150
Black Laws 10
Black Manifesto Against White 37, 168

Supremacy
Black Mariah 132
Black Mine Workers 65
Black Owned Communication Alliance 296
(BOCA)Black Panthers 280
Black Police Association 263
Black Scholar 167
Black Starline 42
Blackstone Hotel 162
Blackstone P. Rangers 222
Black Strikebreakers (stockyard) 14, 19, 210
1904
Black Thursday (Stock Market Failed) 33
Black, Timuel D. 148
Blair, Alice 184-190, 291
Blueprint for Democracy in Housing 146
Bluesheets XVI
Blue Stocking Candidate 144
Board of Directors-National Negro 136
Business League - 1954
Bond, Julian 168, 291, 294
Bousefield, Dr. M.D. (also see 16
Supreme Life Insurance Co.)
Boutte, Alvin 191-196
Braddock, James J. 80
Brazier, Arthur (Rev) 249
Brett, Ken 276
Bridges, Marion 100
Brooke, Edward (Sen) 287
Brocks, Wayland (Rep) 110
Brotherhood of Sleeping Car Porters 89, 230
Brown, Albert 165, 166
Brown, Clarence 137
Brown, Frank London 124, 132, 139
Brown, Frank 44
Brown, John 9
Brown, Johnny 197, 201
Brown, Oscar Jr. 124
Brown, Sidney 237, 238, 239
Brown, Willa 88, 89
Browne, William Y (also see Riley - 15, 13, 20, 202, 206
Brown Real Estate Company
Bryant, Roy 137
Buckner, James (Dr.) 162
Buckner, Musco C. 74
Buena Park 217
Burke School 186
Bullock, Gerald 144, 147
Burns, Tommy 37
Burnside School 199
Burrell, Curtis 254
Byrd, Manford, Jr. 292
Byrne, Jane M. 226, 259

Cabrini Green 103, 186, 261, 292
Cafe Montclare 78
Calloway, C.W. 156
Campbell Soup 216, 219, 220
Camp LeJeune, North Carolina 105
Camp, Reynold 110
Camp Shenango, Pennsylvania 103, 104, 105, 106, 107, 110
Camp Van Doren, Mississippi 105
Capitol Theatre 295
Capital Transit 110
Carey, Archibald, Jr................ 131, 218, 239
Carl Sandburg Village 278
Carmichael, Hoagy 70
Carroll, Cora (Mayor of Brownsville) .. 151
Carroll, Diahann 161
Carry, Scoops......................... 78, 80
Carson, Willis........................ 176
Carter, A. (Mrs.) 125
Carter, Jimmy, Administration 180, 240
Catherine (DuSable wife) 3
Central High School, Little Rock Ark. . 144
Central National Bank 160, 161
Central Railroad 40
Central YMCA Junior College 119, 160, 180
Central YMCA Mortgage Banking School ... 160
Century of Progress 52
Calloway, Cab 40, 77, 112, 120
Calloway, Dr. N.O...................... 140
Carver, George Washington 48, 291
Chatham 126, 194, 196, 292
Chesterfield Savings & Loan 194
Chicago Beach Drive 208
Chicago Bee Newspaper 16, 39
Chicago Bulls Basketball Team 273
Chicago Commons 2
Chicago Conservator 11
Chicago Convention Movement 145, 148, 151
Chicago Defender 16, 33, 37, 72, 73, 251, 270, 296
Chicago Economic Development Corp.(CEDCO)222
Chicago Fest.......................... 196
Chicago Everleigh Club................ 38
Chicago Historical Society 215
Chicago Housing Authority 227, 237, 259, 261
Chicago Insurance Brokers Assoc. 141
Chicago Junior College System 122
Chicago Kent College of Law 126, 180
Chicago Lakefront..................... 52, 103
Chicago March Committee.............. 148, 151
Chicago March on Convention Committee ... 145
Chicago Metropolitan Area 129
Chicago Metropolitan Mutual Ins. Co. ... 149, 150, 170
Chicago Mortgage Bankers.............. 160
Chicago Negro Chamber of Commerce 136

Chicago Postal Alliance 249, 250
Chicago Regal Theatre 112
Chief Sam-Black Kingdom of Africa 37
Chicago Teachers College 122
Chicago Title and Trust 174
Chicago Tribune 9, 10, 124, 253, 274
Chicago World's Fair 1933 52
Chicago Urban League 25, 52, 141, 146, 223
Christian Science Monitor 180
Churchill, Winston 108
Cicero 129, 130, 131, 250, 252, 253, 254, 262
Civil Rights Act of 1866 153
City Roller Rink 120
Clark, Harvey Jr. 129
Clark, Mark 166, 280, 281
Clark, Ramsey 279
Clark, Sidney 170
Clements- George, Fr. 271
Cleveland, Ohio 197, 199
Cleveland, Tennessee 125
Club Delisa 78
Coffey School of Aeronautics 88
Coffeyville, Kansas 229
Cogwell, Mickey 254
Cohn, Zinky 114, 116
Colbert, Claudette 71
Cole, Nat "King" Cole 70, 73, 76, 78, 81, 134
Cole, "Pretty Willie" Stockyard 93
Coleman, Kermit 263
Coles, Charlie 114
Coles, Eddie 78
Collins, Johnny 78
Collins, Samuel 71, 72, 73
Color Caste System 71
Colored Amateur Billiards Players Assoc. 230
Colored Post Exchange 111
Columbia Law School 230
Columbia University 238
Columbus, Georgia 16
Columbus, Indiana 16
Comiskey Park 80
Commonwealth Edison 290
Communist Party 107, 231
Communist Red Squad 48, 49, 52
Community Conservation Board 158
Confederation of Police (COP) 267
Congress Hotel . . . .
Congress of Racial Equality (C.O.R.E.) . . . 233, 235, 243, 248, 249, 250, 252
Congressional Black Caucus 221
Continental Illinois Bank 233
Contract Buyers League 165, 169, 170, 171, 172, 281
Cook County Bar Association 232
Cook County Commissioner (John Jones) 9, 11

Cook County Hospital 59, 113, 279
Cook County Sheriff 131, 170
Cook, Dustalear 121
Cook, Rufus (attorney) 147
Cosmopolitan Chamber of Commerce 136
Cosmopolitan Club 232
C.O.R.E. (See Congress of Racial Equality
Cotton Club Review 112
Crane High School 263
Crane Junior College 263
Crank, George W. 139, 156
Crawford, Bee (uncle) 20
Crawford, Claude (aunt) 20, 25, 47
Crawford, Cornelius (cousin) 20
Crawford, Frank (cousin) 28, 32, 61, 65, 112
Crawford, Joe (cousin) 20, 60
Crawford, Ralph Jr. 20, 47, 48, 49, 50
Crawford, Russell (uncle) 63
Crawleys 209
Crowder, V.C. 147
Daddy-O-Daylie 150
Daley, Richard T. (mayor) 167, 177, 250, 251, 259, 266,
Dallas, Texas 159
Dances-Trucking, Lindy Hop, Pecking 113
Daniels, Oneida 13
Dan Ryan Woods 264
Daugherty, Charles 123
Dave's Cafe 78
Davis, Ben (uncle) 61, 63, 65
Davis, Charles 171, 258
Davis, Eddie 69, 71, 72
Davis, Frank 71, 72
Davis, Gloves 262
Davis, Martha 73
Davis, Sammy Jr. 150
Davis, "Stinky" 90
Dawson, William L. (U.S. Rep.) 110
D & C. Lunchroom 71
Dearborn Park 226
Dearborn Real Estate Board 138, 139, 140, 141, 144, 149, 157, 181
Declaration of Independence 256
DeLaSalle High School 224, 226
Democracy in Housing 157, 146
Democratic National Convention 148
Democratic Party 145, 148
Demopolis, Alabama 198
Denver, Colorado 156
Department of Agriculture 232
Department of Commerce 222
Department of Housing & Urban Development 154, 155, 158, 167
Department of Public Works, Chicago 227
Department of Sanitation, Chicago 227
DePaul University 119

Depression 33, 39, 74, 185, 206, 214, 258
Depres, Leon (Alderman) 147
DePriest, Oscar (Illinois first black Congressman) 2, 205
Desegregation in Armed Forces 16
Diamond, Louis 170
Dickerson, Earl B. 147, 151, 140, 88, 89, 170, 207-210, 218
Disciples 222
District of Columbia 110
Dixon, Chester 139
Dodd, Baby 40
Dodd, Johnny 40, 79
Donegan, Dorothy .... 73, 81 ,112
Don's Pool Hall 69, 70
Dollars & Sense 285, 293, 296
Doolittle School 32
Dorsey, Tommy 78
Douglass, Frederick 9, 215
Douglas, Kirk 137
Douglas National Bank 16, 39
Douglas Park 127, 128
Douglas, Paul 250
Douglass School 214
Dreamland 39
DuSable High Jinks of 1939 81
DuSable High School 28, 70, 76, 83, 86, 105, 111, 165, 185, 188, 190
DuSable Hotel 114
DuSable House 2, 3
DuSable, Jean Baptiste Pointe 70, 73,
DuSable Lounge 114
Draft Board 96
Dream Books 35
Dreamland Cafe 78
Drexel National Bank 160
"Dunk the Darkie in the Water"-Riverview 27
DuBois, W.E.B. 42, 48, 68, 219
Dunbar High School 144
Dunbar, Paul Lawrence 247
Duster, Alfreda (see also Alfreda Barnett) 15, 18, 211-215
Duster, Ben (children) 213
Duster, Charles 213
Duster, Donald 213
Duster, Troy 213
Dyett, Walter 73, 81
East Peoria, Illinois 3
Eastman, Francis 9
Ebony 73, 296, 297
Ebony Jr. 73
Edelen, John 139
Edenborn, Pennsylvania 63
Edgewater, Alabama 64
Edgewater Beach Hotel 212
Edgewater Mine 63, 65
Edward, Lucille (cousin) 54

Eighth Illinois National Guard 16
Eighth Regiment Armory 43
Eisenhower, Dwight D. 117
Eldridge, Roy 78, 80, 110
El Grotto Club 114
Elks Rendevous 112
Ellington, Duke 32, 70, 77, 78, 80, 81, 96, 110, 121
Ely, Kermit 147
Emanuel, Fannie 219
Embry, Ruth 25
Englewood, California 274
Englewood Evening Junior College 121
Englewood High School 229
Englewood "L" 94
Entertainer Club 39
Equitable Holding Company 233
Equitable Life Insurance Co. 233
ERA (Equal Rights Amendment) 282
Ernst, Ernest (Dr.) 122
Evans, Lovelyn 13, 18, 216, 220
Evans, Mary 186
Executive Club of Chicago 180
Everleigh Club 38
Evers, Medgar 166
Exchange National Bank 160
Factory Employment Agency 85
Fair Employment Practice Commission 89
Fairbanks, Douglas "The Three Musketeers" 32
Fairfax, Julia 147
Fambro, Tony 70
Farmer, James 247
Farren School 190
Fashion Fair & Ultra Sheen 73
Faulkner, William 137
Federal Bureau of Investigation 231
Federal Arts Project 83
Federal Claims Court 141
Federal Deposit Insurance Corporation 33
Federal Housing Administration 126, 149, 154, 157, 158, 159
Fine, Joseph 279
First National Bank 258
Fitzgerald, Ella 113
Fletcher, Arthur 280
Florida A. & M. University 224
Flory, Ishmael 147
Flower Technical High School 213
Floyd "Guitar Blues" 114
FNMA (See Federal National Mortgage Assoc.) 158, 171
Foran, Thomas 279
Ford, Gerald 180
Forman, James 168, 169
Fort Custer Michigan 97, 99, 103
Fort Dearborn 3

Fort Gibson Mississippi 237
Fort Henry G. 134
Fort Knox, Kentucky 242
Fort Sheridan 278
Foster, A. L. 52
Four Step Brothers 78
Foxx, Redd 78, 81
Franklin Park 251,
Free Negro Property Owners in Chicago 1860 . . . . 6, 7
Freedom Fund Dinner 144, 151
Freeman, Oscar 13, 18
Freeman, Story (Rev) 147
Friars Point, Mississippi 237
Fugitive Slave Law of 1850 . . . . 9, 10
Fuqua, Carl 148
Fuqua, Charles (Rev.) 151
F. W. Woolworth 146
Galloway, Horace 127
Garfield Hotel 36
Garvey, Marcus 34, 37, 43, 72, 219, 222, 223, 248, 287
George Bizet's Opera 112
George Williams College 146
Gershwin, George 81
"Giver Dam" Jones 36
Gold Coast 212, 288
Goodman, Benny 78, 80
G.O.P. Convention (1960, Chicago) 148
Gottlieb, Harry 161
Governor's State University 197, 199
Grand Terrace 78, 79
Grandma Strickland Simms Recipes 54, 56, 57, 60
Grandma Winnie Simms Bible Verses 53, 54
Graves, John 219
Gray, Harry W. 73
Gray, Sadie Mae 214
Green, Mrs. (teacher at Doolittle) 32
"Green Pastures" 12, 15
Green, Riley 204
Green, Theodore 147
Greene County, North Carolina 9
German Siegfried 114
Great Chicago Fire 1871 10
Grier, George (Dr.) 146
Grinnell, Mary Anna 18, 26
Grove Bathhouse & Hotel 36
Groundbreaking-Lake Grove Village-1970 177
Guardians 262
Guice, Garland 222
Gunther, Emil 86
"Gypsy Witch" 36
Hale County, Alabama 198
Haley, George 156
Half Century Magazine 16, 39

Haliburton, Lawrence (Attorney) 134
Hall, Cleveland (Dr.) 207
Hamer, Fannie L. 168
Hamilton, "Kiddo" 94, 95
Hammond (1st Sgt.) 98, 99, 101
Hampton, Fred 166, 280, 281
Hampton, Lionel 80, 81, 120
Hansberry, Carl 232
Hansberry, Lorraine 232
Hanson, O. C. 9
Harding, George F. 204
Harding Restaurants 186
Hardwick, Mose 2, 3
Hardwick, Moselynne E. (also see Moselynne Travis) 124
Harlem 111
Harlem Airport 89
Harlem's Appollo Theatre 112
Harps, William 138
Harris, Adolphus 205
Harris, George S. 150, 170
Harrison, Richard B. 12, 15, 20, 213
Harvard University 141
Hastie, William (Judge) 231
Haven Elementary School 17
Hawkins, Erskine 110
Hawkins, Rachael 146
Hawkins (Judge) Scottsboro Trial 49
Hayes, Charles 147
Hayes, Roland 219
Henderson, Ernie 219
Henderson, Fletcher 80
Hernandez, Juano 137
Herrick, Mary 79, 105
Hi Jinks (1936)
Hill, Normal 148
Hill, Richard C. 124
Hilton Hotel 120
Hines, Earl "Fatha" 40, 96
Hinton, Milton 80
Holder Court 278
Holly Springs, Mississippi 215
Holland, Theodore 219
Holman, L. D. (Dr.) 147
Holy Angels Parish-Chicago 32, 271
Home Finance Agency 154
Homested Act of 1970 .... 99, 167
Hooks, Benjamin 282
Hoover, Herbert (President 1930) 47, 52
Hoover Hobos 47
Hopkins, Claude 110
Hopson, James W. 104
Horne, Lena 78
Housing Act of 1949 153

Housing Proclamation 154
Houston, Charlie 282
Howalton Day School 224
Howard, Donald (Mr. & Mrs.) 131
Howard, University 216, 229, 230
Howard Theatre, Philadelphia 109, 110, 111
Howell, Brenetta 147, 222
Hub Clothing Store 257
HUD - See Housing & Urban Development
Hudland, Maude 213
Hughes, Langston 111, 113
Hughes, Robert 156
Hughes, William 127
Hull House 2, 15
Humphrey, Hubert H. 160, 162
Hunt, Jarvis 218
Hunter, Frank 28, 60, 63
Hunter, Oakley 171
Huntsville, Alabama 48
Hyde Park/Kenwood 208
Hyde Park High School 229
Hyde Park Area 128
Illinois Black Panthers 291
Illinois Central Station 97
Illinois Federal Savings & Loan Assoc. 236 237
Illinois Institute of Technology 88, 180
Independence Bank 170, 194
International Amphitheatre 148
International Ladies Garment Workers Union 158
International Labor Defense (ILD) 50
Interreligious Foundation for Community Organizations (IFCO) 167
Jack Johnson's Cafe de Champion 40
Jackson County 49
Jackson, Jesse (Rev.) 170, 177, 277, 280, 283, 284, 285
Jackson Park Hospital 279
Jacobs, J. Goodsel 139
Jamal, Ahmad 121
James, Harry 80, 150
James, Lincoln A. 147
Japanese Internment 93, 94
Jeffries, Jim 37
"Jelly Martin" 97
Jelly Roll Morton 29
Jenkins, Claude 97
Jenkins, Miss 238
Jensen Pavilion 52
Jet 73
Jim Crow 16, 60, 61, 87, 96, 103, 110, 124, 137, 138, 140, 144, 145, 146
Johnson, Albert 139
Johnson, Arthur 37
Johnson, Bennett 148
Johnny Brown Tire Co. 197, 199, 200
Johnson, George 194

Johnson, Jack 34, 37, 38, 42, 43, 79
Johnson, James Weldon 113
Johnson, Jesse Jr. 156
Johnson, John H. 73, 76
Johnson, Lyndon Baines 153, 180
Johnson "Mushmouth" 39
Johnson Products 200, 219
Johnson Publishing Co. 73
Joliet, Illinois 38
Jones Commercial High School 10
Jones, Eddie 36
Jones, George 36
Jones, John 1, 5, 6, 7, 9, 10, 11, 218
Jones, John G. 1
Jones, Lola 89
Jones, Mark 124
Jones, Mildred Bryant 70
Jones, Teennan 36
Jones, Theodore A. 147
Jones, William (also see Jones Commercial High School) 10
Joplin, Scott 29
Jordan, Marion 161
Jordan, Vernon 280, 281
Julian Black Realty Co. 150
Kansas (friend) 105, 106, 107, 108
Kansas City, Missouri 48, 156
Kansas City Royals Baseball Team 274
Kelly, Illy 36
Kelly, Ross 36
Kelly, Walter 36
Kennedy, John F. 153, 154, 159, 165, 166, 170
Kennedy, Robert 155, 170
Kent College of Law 180
Kenwood-Oakland Community Organization 263, 363
Keppard, Freddy 40
Kerner, Otto 162
Keyhole Lounge 97
Key, Ulysses 130
Kierney, Al 219
Kimbrough, Robert L. (Dr.) 124, 147
King, Dr. Martin L. 137, 143 144, 148, 149, 151, 152, 166, 167, 198,
                                 208, 251, 252, 253, 279, 283
King Oliver 40
King, Paul 221-227
Kinzie House 2
Kirk, Andy 109, 110,
Kitchenettes 206
Knoxville, Tennessee 186
KOCO (Kenwood Oakland Community Organization) 254
Krupa, Gene 80, 81, 110
Ku Klux Klan 25, 38,126, 225 288
Labor Board 238, 239
Lafantant, Jewel (attorney) 228-235

Lake Charles, Louisiana 193
Lake Geneva, Wisconsin 257
Lake Grove Village 1970 177
Lake Michigan (Chicago) 26, 28, 35
Lake Shore Drive 216, 117
Landrum, Robert N. 157
Lang, James T. 65
Las Vegas, Nevada 78
Latham, Charlie 49
Lattimore, Carl 231
Laurenti, Louis 146
Lawson, Louise 236, 242
Leak, A.R. 147
Leavenworth, Kansas 38
Lee, Baron 110
Lee, Bernard 149
Lee, Bill 260
Leighton, George M. (Judge) 130
Leonard, Thomas 123
Lewis, Pop 36
Lexington, Kentucky 61
Liberty Baptist Church 147, 148
Library Theatre 111
Lilydale Area 35, 204
Lime, Jean La 3
Lincoln, Abraham 52
Lincoln Park 13, 45
Lincoln, Robert Todd XIX
Little Rock, Arkansas 144
Local 208 Musicians Union 61
Lodge, Henry Cabot 234
Lorman, Mississippi 238
Louis, Joe 36, 68, 80, 114, 150
Louis, Marva 115, 116
Love, Ruth (Supt. Chicago Public Schools) 189, 190
Lowe's Theatre 110
Lucas, Robert 243, 255
Lucas, Scott 110
Lunceford, Jimmie 32, 77, 110
Lyceum Theatre 28
Lynch, James 156
Macon, Georgia 16
Malcolm X 166, 248, 263, 294
Mandel Brothers Dept. Store .... XVII, 19
Mann Act-1919 "White Slave Traffic" 37
Mann, James Robert 38
March on Washington 148
Markham, Illinois 165
Marine Corps 94, 244
Marowitz, Abraham Lincoln (Judge) 266
Marshall Field Foundation 208
Marshall, Prentice (Judge) 266
Marshall, Thurgood (U.S. Supreme Court Justice) 144, 282
Martin, "Big Jim" 36

Martin, Ruby 73
Maudin, Bill 166
Mays, Willie 199
M.B.A. School of Mortgage 161
Mead, Ripley 139
Mead, Ripley Sr. 256-258
Memphis, Tennessee 9, 237
Merchandise Mart 246
Messina, James (pfc) 109
Metcalfe, Ralph 176
Metropolitan Theatre 71, 96
Mexico City, Mexico 36
Midland Savings & Loan Assoc. 129
Mid-Manhattan Area 112
Mid-Nite Club 78
Midstate Homes, Inc. 170
Milam, J.W. 137
Mill Run Theatre 298
Millinder, Lucky 110
Miller Brothers 113
Miller, Jessie 48
Miller, Joseph 13, 217
Miller Buena Park Warehouse & Moving Co. 13, 217
Mills, Art 113
Mills Brothers 77, 113
Ming, Bob 293
Miss Alcorn 238
Mitchell, Abby 219
Mitchell, Parrin (U.S. Congressman) 176
Model T Ford 29
Mollison, Irving 141, 232
Money, Mississippi 137
Monroe, Louisiana 16
McCauley, Tom 193
McCormick Place 243
McCormick, Vivian 124
McDougall, Curtis (Dr) 146
McDowell, Mary 2
McGee, Robert 132
McGhee, Henry (1st Black Postmaster in Chicago) 250
McGray, Bessie 124
McKay, Claude 113
McKissick, Eddie 36
McKissick, George 36
McKey & Pogue 258
McMillen, Henrietta L. 122
McNeal, Theodore 126
McRoberts, Kentucky 60, 61, 63
Monte Carlo Wheel 36
Montgomery, Alabama 137
Montgomery Improvement Association 285
Montgomery Ward Catalogue 16
Moody's 195

Moore, Willie (Buck Sgt.) 98
Morehouse College 72
Morgan Park 35
Morgan Park Neighborhood 90
Morgan Park Savings & Loan Assoc. 240
Morris, Ed 203
Morris Eat Shop 73
Morris Perfect Eat Shop 74
Morrison Hotel 144
Mortgage Bankers of America 159, 161
Morton, Jelly Roll 40
Mose "Funky" 90
Moser Evening School 146
Moser, Paul 140
Motley, Constance Baker 282
Mozart Sonata 32
Muller (Architect) 217
Mundy, Jimmy 80
Murphy, Velma 149
Murray, Charles Jr. 28, 29, 173
Murray, Charles (Mrs.) 29
Murray, Charles, Sr. 28
Murray, Charlie 97
Murray's Pomade 28
Musicians Protective Union Local 208 74
Nance, Ray 80
Nash, Diane 149
NAACP (National Assoc. for the Advancement of Colored People)
2, 25, 50, 130, 131, 143, 144, 145, 146, 147, 148, 149, 150, 151, 152, 233, 295
National Assoc. of Real Estate Brokers 157, 159, 166
National Bar Association 230, 231, 234
National Basketball Association 273
National Black Economic Development Conference 168
National Guard 130, 131, 164, 167, 250
National Housing Policy Act of 1949 153
National Negro Business League 136
National Negro Museum & Historical Foundation 120
National Youth Administration 185
"Native Son" (see Richard Wright)
Navy Pier University of Illinois Campus 146
NBA All Star Team 273
NBC Orchestra 81
Near South Side 129
Nelson, Donald 89
Negro American Labor Council 89
Negro History Week 120
Negro Property Owners in Chicago-1870 8
New Deal Westside Improvement Program 112
Newhouse, Richard 263
New Orleans Jazzmen 39, 40
New Orleans, Louisiana 223
New Orleans Storeyville 39
New York Central Railroad 113

New York's Cotton Club 79
New York Life Insurance Co. 195
New York's Savoy Ballroom 112
New York State's Commission Against Discrimination 136
New York's Zanzibar Cabaret 112
Niagara Movement 2
Nicholas Brothers 78
Nicholson, Odas 147
Nick & Angel's Hamburger Grill 70, 71
Nixon, Richard M. 153, 158
Norman, James 105
Morris, Clarence 52
Noon, Jimmy 116
North Africa 109
North Shore 128
Northerly, Roxanne 278
Northrup, Herbert R. 64
Northwestern Railroad 255
Northwestern University Medill School of Journalism 146
Northwestern University 119, 180
Notre Dame 86
NRA (National Recovery Act) 82
Oakland, California 138
Oak Park 222
Oakwood Cemetery 146
Oakwood Junior College 48
Oakland/Kenwood area 123
Oakland Square Theatre 32
Oberlin College 229, 230
Odell, S.B. 138
Officers Candidate School 193
Offensive Images 26
Ohio Company 168
Ogilvie, Richard 234
Oliver, King 79
Open Development Corporation 254
Operation Breadbasket 170, 277, 283
Operation PUSH 270, 277, 280, 283
Osceola, Arkansas 16
Overton, Anthony 16, 39, 294, 295
Overton-Hygienic Products Co. 16
Oxford, Mississippi 137
Pace, Harry Herbert (also see Supreme Life Insurance Company) 16
Packingtown (Stockyards) 90
Paint Rock, Alabama 49
Palmer House 252,
Palmer's Skin Whitener 72
Panama Cafe Nite Club 78
Paradise Cafe 80
Park Manor Area 126
Parks, Rosa 137
Parkway Ballroom 136, 139, 140, 145
Parson, James B. (Judge) 276

Patriarchs & Prophets 52, 53
Payne, Aaron (Atty.) 150
Pearl Harbor 91, 92, 93, 94, 104
Pelt, Owen D. (Rev) 147, 148
Pennsy Mines 65
Peola Class System 72
Pershing Ballroom 121
Pershing Hotel 121
Peterson (Major) 99
Pettigrew, E. P. (Rev) 147
Pickford Theatre 28
Pitts, Victoria 121
P. King Produce 224
Pla-mor Ballroom 120
Plantation Club 39
Plotnicks Arcadia 78
Poitier, Sidney 137
Police Department Intelligence Division 280
Policy Games (also see Dream Book) 36
Polk Street Freight Station 254
Pollard, Fritz 222
Post Exchange, U.S. Army 109
Post Librarian, U.S. Army 187
Potawatomi Indian 3
Powell, Austin 81, 121
Prairie Shores 278
Presbyterian School 186
Presidential Task Force on Urban Renewal 176
Price, Victoria 49, 52
Primm, Thomas H. (Bishop) 177
Provident Hospital 203
Pullack, Walter (Atty) 51
Pullman, George Mortimer XVII
Pullman Porters 25, 35, 83, 257
Pullman Strike 210
Pushkin, Alexander 74
Quality Laundry 37
Quality Wet Wash Laundry 86
Quarles, Anthony 139
Quartermaster Corp., U.S. Army 244
Quartermaster School for Administration 111
Quinn Chapel 219
Quinn, Joe 86
Quinn, Mary 86
Raby, Al 151, 251
Racial Violence, Cicero 129
Radio Station WJPC 73
Railroad Chapel 2
Rainbow Beach 149
Randall, Willie 52
Randolph, A. Phillip 87, 88, 89, 145, 148, 230, 231, 253
Ransom, John "Stormy Monday" 95
Ransom's Reverdy (Rev) 2

Rawls, Louis (Rev.) 148
Ray, James Earl 166
Real Estate Brokers 125, 127
Reciprocity Law 193
Reconstruction Era 279
Reconstruction Finance Corp. 206
Red Ball Express 245
Red Cross 107
Red Moon Lounge 97
Regal Theatre 69, 77, 112
Regulatory System 194
Reitzes, Dietrich (Dr.) 146
Restrictive Covenants 124, 153, 204, 232
Reynolds, A. L. (Dr.) 177
Rialto Theatre 114
Rigsby, Thomas 25, 73
Riley Green Brown Realty 15, 202
Riverview Amusement Park 27
Robbins, Illinois 35
Robbins, Millard 156
Robert Mine Operation 65
Robert Taylor Homes 81, 186, 261
Robert Todd Lincoln's Pullman Co. 19
Robeson, Paul 48, 112, 219
Robinson, Bill Bojangles 69, 78
Robinson, Eugene 126
Robinson, J. W. 156
Robinson, Jackie 11, 123
Robinson, Mae 128
Robinson, Renault 259, 272
Robinson, William 147
Rockefeller Foundation 254
Rockefeller, Nelson 140, 148, 175, 180
Rockne, Knute 86
Rogers, William P. 137
Romney, George 163
Roosevelt, Franklin D. 7, 93, 94, 114
Roosevelt Univesity 119, 123, 126
Rose, Billy 112
Rose, John 98
Rose, Slim 69, 70, 71, 72, 73
Rosenwald Building 17, 126
Rosieburg, West Virginia 244
Royal Circle of Friends 213
Royal Garden 39
Rustin Bayard 145
Sacred Heart School 192
Saldukus, August 129
Solomon Brothers 195
Samuels, William 75
Sanford, Fred 81
Savage, Augustus (U.S. Congressman) 124, 147
Savage, Eunice 124

Savoy Ballroom 81
Sax, Jerome M. 159, 160
SBA (Small Business Association) 199, 201, 223, 225
Schreiber, Belle 38
Scott, Clark 129, 130, 131
Scott Joplin 29
Scott, Maurice 129, 130, 131
Scott, Maurice, Jr. 130
Scottsboro Boys 49, 50, 51, 52
Seaway Bank 171, 194
Selma, Alabama 198
Sengali, Leonard 254
Sengstacke, John 251
Seventh Day Adventists 48, 52, 53
Shaltuck, Henry Lee 141
Shapiro, Samuel 164
Sharon, Pennsylvania 105
Shaw, Artie 28
Sherman House 120
Shiloh Seventh Day Adventist Church 53
Shubert Theatre 112
Shuttlesworth, Fred 152
Simmons, Joe 97
Simms, Winnie Strickland (grandma) 52, 53, 54, 55, 56, 57, 62
Simpson, Cassinod 78
Simpson, Elmer 29
Singleton, Zutty 80
Sivart Mortgage Corp. 129, 136, 149, 157, 158, 159
Sloan (Maj.) 110
Small's Paradise Carabet 112, 113
Smith, Bessie 96
Smith, Bishop 37
Smith, Major H. Clark 80
Smith, Malcolm B. 70
Smith, Mamie 96
Smith's Trio 112
Smith, Whitney 122
Sneed, Ray, Jr. 111
Social Security Act 1935 60
Social Settlement House Support Use 2
South Contract Buyers League 128
South Loop (Dearborn Park) 11
South Shore 126
South Side 137, 140, 141, 170
South Water Market 224
Southeast Commission 208, 209
Southern Christian Leadership Conference (SCLC) 166, 258
Southern Law School 281
Sparling, Edward 119
Spraggans, Edward 132
Strayhorn, Earl 186
St. Ignatius 226
St. Lukes Hospital 27

St. Marks Church 213
St. Simon Island, Georgia 16
State House Insurance Committee 144
State Street Cable Car XIII
Stevens Hotel 120
Stevenson, Adlai 131
Stewart, Ellis (See Supreme Life Ins. Co.) 16
Stone Temple Baptist Church 148, 151
Stoner's Restaurant 238
Storeyville 39
Story, Elliott (uncle) 63, 64, 65, 66
Stradford Hotel 230
Stradford, John 229
Strayhorn, Earl (Judge) 186
Strickland, Claudie (aunt) 26, 47
Strickland, Della (aunt) 60, 161, 162
Strickland, Joe (cousin) 55, 60
Strickland, Glenn (uncle) 47
Strickland, Joseph 53, 55
Stroll, The 37
Strong, Curtis 147
Strong, Savannah 81
Students Non-Violent Coordinating committee (SNCC) 168
Stuckey, Sterling 147
Suall, Joan 148
Sunset Cafe 39
Supreme Court Desegregation Decision 1954 136
Supreme Life Ins. Co. 16, 170
Summerower, James 139
Sutton, Bessie 81
Swift & Company 90
Sykes, Nelson 93
Tabernacle Baptist Church 148
Tallachatchie River, Mississippi 137
Tate, Emmett 96
Tate, Erskine 79, 94, 95, 96,
Tate, Evelyn 96
Tatum, Art 78
Tatum, Charles 160
Taylor, Graham (Rev.) 2
Tenant Evictions "Reds" 48
Texas, Austin 156
Theus, Reggie 273, 276
Thomas, John W.E. (Atty.) 11
Thompson, Bill 258
Thompson, Lovie 219
Three Deuces 78
Three Witches 36
Till, Emmett Louis 137
Tipton, Missouri 16
Todd, Thomas N. 292
Towns, Clarence 124
Travis, Charlie (uncle) 50

Travis, Dempsey J.

early childhood 27-33
first interracial experiences.................... 27, 28, 32
music debut 29-32
first jobs 29, 33
initial education.. 32
introduction to black history........................... 35-44
life with Grandma... 52-63
Seventh Day Adventist 48
cousin Ralph 47-52
Willard School... 48
Cook County Hospital 59
Jim Crow.. 60-61
first Southern experience - maternal family................. 59-66
newspaper job 60
DuSable High 69-81
new Wendell Phillips High 70, 74
Jack Travis Orchestra.................................. 75-80
classy night spots 78-79
first champion fight 79, 80
job hunting.. 83-91
first factory job 85
March on Washington Movement 87
Armour Employment Office.................................. 90
Pearl Harbor 93-94
Erskin Tate 95
the draft board 96
Fort Custer in Michigan 97-100
Army race riots 104-106
Veteran General Hospital in Butler, Pa. 108
Camp Lee, Virginia....................................... 110
Aberdeen Proving Grounds, Maryland 111
Major Sloan 111
New York's Harlem 111-113
Indian Town Gap, Pa..
Roosevelt University 119
sweet pickle department at Armour & Company 120
Wilson Junior College 121
remedial reading 122-123
marriage to Moselynne Hardwick........................... 126
State Theater.. 127
first real estate commission 127
Dr. Allen L. Wright 127
contract selling.....................................128-129
Sivart Mortgage Corporation 129
Cicero...129-131
Trumbull Park..131-132
Billings Hospital 135
NAACP Life Membership.................................... 131
I met George S. Harris 138
Dearborn Real Estate Board Presidency 138
National Association of Real Estate Brokers 138
Jim Crow Insurance 140

Negro Politics 141
Dr. Martin Luther King, Jr. 144
President of NAACP 144
telegram from Martin Luther King, Jr.
and A. Philip Randolph 144-145
"A Blueprint for Democracy in Housing" 146
March for Freedom Now 148
United Mortgage Bankers of America, Inc. 154-160
International Ladies Garment Workers Union 158
Sivart Mortgage approval as mortgagee 160
Drexel National Bank 160
Central National Bank 160
Chicago Mortgage Bankers 160
President Lyndon Baines Johnson 161
Mortgage Bankers of America 161
Harry Gottlieb 161
Northwestern University 161
President John F. Kennedy 165
Mayor Richard J. Daley 167
The 1970 Homestead Act 167-168
James Forman 168
Black Manifesto 168
Contract Buyers League 169-171
Moselynne E. Travis 175
Nelson Rockefeller 175
Rev. Jessie Jackson 170
Chicago Tribune 172
President Jimmy Carter 178
President Ronald Reagan 180
Roy Wilkins 181
Travis, Glenn (uncle) 47
Travis Ins. Agency 135, 136
Travis, Joseph (uncle) 14, 41, 44, 50, 91
Travis, Louis (father) 1, 11, 14, 19, 20, 30, 42, 43, 44, 49, 59, 60, 62,, 84, 95,
112, 173
Travis, Mittie (mother) 20, 31, 42, 43, 62, 96, 199
Travis, Moselynne (wife) 126, 166, 128, 175
Travis, Otis (uncle) 1937, 41, 43, 44, 50, 80, 90, 91
Travis Realty Co. 136, 149
Truman, Harry 16, 117, 136
Trumbull Park 124, 132, 133
Tucker, Robert 140
Turner, Milton 97
Twelfth Street Station 60
Uncle Tom's Cabin 28
Underground Railroad 229
United Mine Workers Union 64
United Mortgage Bankers of America 156, 157, 158, 159, 161
United Nations Service Center 105
United Negro College Fund 306
United Packing House Workers Union 120
U. S. Factors House 3
U.S. Post Office 255

U.S.S. Arizona 92
University of Chicago Hospital 135
University of Chicago Settlement House 2
University of Chicago 209, 213, 237
University of Nevada, LAS Vegas 273
Universal Homes 170
Vendome Theatre 96
Veterans Administration 123, 154, 157
Veterans General Hospital 110, 107, 108
Vice Lords 222
Victory in Europe (V.E.) 117
Victory Life Insturance 16, 39
Vienna Bathhouse 36
Vienna Hotel 36
Village of the Deserted Homeless 35
Vincennes Hotel 36
Vine, Gene 39, 69, 70, 11, 72, 74
Volunteer Home Mortgage Credit Program(1954) 157
Waldorf Astoria Hotel 153
Wall Street Journal 52
Walker, C. J. 294, 295
Walker, Donald 293, 299
Walker, George 239
Walker, Josephine 147
Walnut Theatre 112
Wang, C. H. 160
Waner, John 177
Warm Spings, Georgia 114
War Stabilization Board 237
Warwick Hall 70
Washington, Bernadine(also see Winsomettes) 144
Washington, Booker, T. 42, 44, 48
Washington, Harold (U.S. Congressman) 124, 134
Washington Park 48, 49, 50
Washington Park Race Track 15
Waters, Ethel 96
Wayne (friend) 28
Weaver, Robert C. 154, 155, 159
Weinstein, Jacob (Rabbi) 147
Weisner Act 209
Welcome Wagon 129
Wells, Ida B. 14, 15
Wendell Phillips Evening School 70, 73, 131
Wendell Phillips High School 80, 88
Western Citizens Newspaper 19
Western Herald Newspaper 19
Western Union 60
West Point Baptist Church 29
West Side (Madison & Western) Riot 1968 164
West Side 167
West Side Builders 222, 223
West Suburban Board of Real Estate 280
Wharton School of Finance & Commerce 64

Wheeler, Lloyd G. 10
Whiteman, Paul 78
White, Charles 142
White City Roller Rink 120
White, Walter 50, 131
Wilkins, Roy 131, 143, 147, 148
Willard Elementary School 41, 48, 96
Williams, A. W. 239, 240
Williams, Bert 139
Williams, Eugene 26
Williams, Frank 93
Williams, Freddie 52
Williams, Kale 147
Williams, R. A. 203, 213, 218
Williamson, Q. V. 138, 156, 166
Willis, Benjamin 244, 247
Willis Wagons 244, 247, 248
Willoughby, Abner 147
Wilson & Co. 85, 90
Wilson, Flip 78
Wilson, James Q 141
Wilson Junior College 121, 123, 125, 245, 246
Wilson, Kenneth 174
Wilson, Quinn 80, 86
Wilson, Woodrow 145
Winsomets NAACP Fund Raising Affair 144, 150
Wonder Bar 97
Woodard, Oneida Daniels 13
Woodlawn 260
Wooley, Celia Parke 15
Women's Army Corps Service (WACS) 187
World War I 16, 110
World War II 102, 103, 104
Wright, Allen L. (M.D.) 127, 128
Wright, Alyce 128
Wright, James 147
Wright, Ralph 147
Wright, Richard 247
Wright, Roy 49
Wright, Willie 134
Yates, Richard 9
Young, John 74
YMCA 2
YWCA 2